# econoguide '97

# Walt Disney World, Universal Studios Florida, Epcot,

## and other major Central Florida attractions

**Corey Sandler**

## CONTEMPORARY BOOKS

A TRIBUNE COMPANY

**Library of Congress Cataloging-in-Publication Data**

Sandler, Corey, 1950– .
    Econoguide '97—Walt Disney world, Universal Studios Florida,
  Epcot, and other major central Florida attractions / Corey Sandler.
        p.  cm.
      ISBN 0-8092-3318-5
        1. Florida—Guidebooks.   2. Walt Disney World (Fla.)—Guidebooks.
    3. Universal Studios Florida (Orlando, Fla. : Amusement park)—
  Guidebooks.   4. EPCOT Center (Fla.)—Guidebooks.   I. Title.
      F309.3.S253   1996
      791'.06'875924—dc20                                              96-31411
                                                                         CIP

*To Willie and Tessa*
*May their lives always be a magic theme park*

Cover design by Kim Bartko
Econoguide is a trademark of Word Association, Inc.

Published by Contemporary Books, Inc.
Two Prudential Plaza, Chicago, Illinois 60601-6790
Manufactured in the United States of America
International Standard Book Number: 0-8092-3318-5
10   9   8   7   6   5   4   3   2   1

# Contents

Stefan's Banquet Hall. **Tomorrowland:** Cosmic Ray's Starlight Café / Plaza Pavilion / Auntie Gravity's Galactic Goodies

Television / The Monster Sound Show / Indiana Jones Stunt
Spectacular! / Star Tours / The Voyage of the Little Mermaid / Beauty
and the Beast Stage Show / Hunchback of Notre Dame / The Magic of
Disney Animation / Honey, I Shrunk the Kids Movie Set Adventure /
Jim Henson's Muppet*Vision 3D 4D / Backstage Studio Tour / Inside
the Magic: Special Effects and Production Tour / Toy Story Parade /
Sorcery in the Skies

# Acknowledgments

Dozens of hard-working and creative people helped move my words from the keyboard to the place where you read this book now.

Among the many to thank are editor Linda Gray and publisher Christine Albritton of Contemporary Books for working with me as we expand the *Econoguide* series and Dan Bial for his capable agentry. Thanks, too, to Eugene Brissie, our original champion, and to Bill Gladstone of Waterside Productions.

Dawn Barker of Contemporary Books gave the text a professional polish, and Kathy Willhoite managed the editorial and production processes with professionalism and good humor.

Thanks to the capable production staff including: Kim Bartko, Monica Baziuk, Dana Draxten, Gigi Grajdura, Pamela Juárez, Todd Petersen, Audrey Sails, and Terry Stone.

Our appreciation extends to Universal Studios Florida, Sea World Orlando, and Busch Gardens Tampa for their assistance. Among those who have gone out of their way to help us are Kena Williams Christian, Tricia Baker, Michael Goldstein, Edie Emerald, Shawna Allen, Melissa Tomasso, and MORE MORE MORE MORE . . .

Thanks to the hotels, restaurants, and attractions who offered discount coupons to our readers. Special thanks go to Janice Keefe who worked long and hard in the Word Association offices to collect and process the discount coupons. Thanks, too, to Dan Keefe, the official *Econoguide* golf pro.

And finally, thanks to you for buying this book. We all hope you find it of value; please let us know how we can improve the book in future editions. (Please enclose a stamped envelope if you'd like a reply; no phone calls, please.)

Corey Sandler
Econoguide Travel Books
P.O. Box 2779
Nantucket, MA 02584

# Introduction to the 1997 Edition

Welcome to the 1997 edition of the *Econoguide—Walt Disney World, Universal Studios Florida, Epcot, and Other Major Central Florida Attractions.*

We're huge fans of Orlando. We don't know of many other places with so much to do, so many interesting places to visit . . . and so many ways to spend your hard-earned dollars.

Our goal in the Econoguide series is to help you get the most for your money and make the best use of your time.

We've gone back once again and walked every mile of every park and attraction and looked everywhere for changes and new features.

At Walt Disney World, you'll learn about the ExtraTERRORestrial Alien Encounter at the Magic Kingdom, the Hollywood Tower of Terror at Disney-MGM Studios, and the thrilling GM Test Track at Epcot. You'll also glimpse the future with details of Disney's newest park, the Disney Animal Kingdom.

At Universal Studios, we've got the latest on the explosive new Terminator 2 3-D attraction, and you'll learn about Universal's Islands of Adventure and the E-Zone, new parks that will more than double the size of Universal Studios Orlando.

We'll take you on tours of Sea World's new Key West and Wild Arctic attractions. At Busch Gardens Tampa, we've got the inside details on the spectacular Montu roller coaster. And we'll tell you about the latest and greatest at the Kennedy Space Center.

## The Econoguide to the
## Best of Orlando and Central Florida

| | | |
|---|---|---|
| Magic Kingdom | Epcot | Disney-MGM Studios |
| Universal Studios | Busch Gardens | Sea World |
| Kennedy Space Center | Gatorland | Blizzard Beach |
| Wet 'n Wild | Green Meadows Farm | |
| | (for young children) | |

And, of course, we've got a new selection of money-saving coupons. Pardon us for saying so, but we think buying this book is a no-brainer: you'll save many times the cover price by using just a few of the coupons, including ticket discounts at Universal Studios, Sea World, Busch Gardens, Adventure Island, and Cypress Gardens, to name a few. You'll also save money at restaurants and hotels.

## About Walt Disney World and Orlando

Walt Disney World is a magical kingdom of fantastic delights for children of all ages; we recommend it highly.

We also love Universal Studios Florida, Sea World, and dozens of other excellent attractions and recreational opportunities in the Orlando and Central Florida region.

But let's get one other thing straight: Walt Disney World is a gigantic vacuum cleaner aimed at your wallet.

Looking for a vacation spot? Disney has got the number one tourist draw in the nation.

Need a place to stay? They've got tens of thousands of rooms at more than two dozen resorts inside the boundaries of the park with several major new properties opening each year.

Hungry? No problem—nearly every type of restaurant you can imagine can be found somewhere in Walt Disney World: French, Italian, Chinese, Japanese, Mexican, Moroccan, Norwegian, British, fine food of every description, and all sorts of American fast food.

And once you're back in your room, if you get the midnight munchies, Walt's crew will be glad to bring a Disney pizza to your door.

The bottom line is this: Disney has almost everything . . . and wants it all.

Walt Disney World started as an extension of Disneyland in California, an amusement park originally conceived for youngsters. But nearly every corporate move since then has been aimed at expanding its appeal to adults.

When the Disney Company saw how outside water parks were siphoning some dollars from the pipeline, it built River Country. When the competitors tried to fight back, along came the spectacular Typhoon Lagoon and the even-more-spectacular Blizzard Beach.

Were you planning to visit Sea World? Why leave Walt Disney World when you can go to The Living Seas at Epcot? Love the animals at Busch Gardens Tampa, or the alligators at Gatorland? By the end of the century, Disney will have its own animal theme park.

Is the lure of the movie magic of Universal Studios strong? Disney says, "Don't bother: you can keep your dollars in the park at Disney-MGM Studios."

We all know what the kids want. But does Dad's idea of a vacation consist of a week of golfing? Or does Mom dream of seven days on the tennis courts? Walt Disney World has it all in one place.

Like miniature golf? There are plenty of independent courses all around

Kissimmee; now Disney wants it all with the Fantasia Garden Miniature Golf area.

Does Church Street Station sound like nighttime fun for the adults? That's why Disney built Pleasure Island on its own property inside the park.

You don't even have to leave Walt Disney World to go to a movie, get a haircut, have the family car tuned, or visit a travel agency to extend your stay.

Now, don't get me wrong: Walt Disney World may be the best-designed, best-run and most overall satisfying tourist attraction on this planet. But you also have the right to spend your time and money as carefully as possible. That's what this book is all about.

And we don't spare Universal Studios, Sea World, Busch Gardens, and other non-Disney attractions from our search for ways to save your money and enhance your visit, either.

## Not Too Cute

After visits that have totaled up to months at Walt Disney World, Disneyland, Euro Disneyland, and Tokyo Disneyland, I've come up with my All-Purpose Disney Attraction Classification Guide. I've decided that Disney attractions can be divided into "Disney Cute," "Disney Smart," and "Disney Wow."

Disney Cute is Mickey Mouse, Aladdin, It's a Small World, Tiki Birds, Snow White, Cinderella, and Dumbo. That's where they set the hook with young children and their parents.

Disney Smart is Epcot's Future World, Epcot's World Showcase, Epcot's Innoventions, the Hall of Presidents, the Carousel of Progress, and the Special Effects and Production Tour. Here's where Disney magic helps us learn.

Disney Wow is Space Mountain, Twilight Zone Tower of Terror, Star Tours, The Great Movie Ride, Thunder Mountain Railroad, and Splash Mountain. These are the things that make us say, "Ooh."

One of the reasons for Disney's success is that they have learned to mix Cute, Smart, and Wow. It's the reason children come back as adolescents and then as parents; it's the reason adults can have a good time accompanying their youngsters.

Add to this Disney's impressive devotion to expanding its attraction to adults with things like water parks, golf courses, tennis courts, nightclubs, and spectacularly sybaritic hotels, and it's only just begun: Sports Center Disney, including The Walt Disney World Speedway, the Spring Training home of the Atlanta Braves, and even a possible Olympics bid. And in 1996, the Disney Institute opened. Call those "Disney for Adults," and they will be the reason Disney will continue to be a lure for us all once we are too jaded for Cute, too educated for Smart, and (alas) too old for Wow.

## About Independence

That other book about Walt Disney World, the one with "The Official Guide" stamped on its cover, is an impressive collection of material. But, in our humble opinion, it suffers from a fatal closeness to its subject: it is prepared with the Walt Disney Company (and published by a Disney company). I suspect that explains why it finds very little that is anything less than wonderful within the boundaries of Walt Disney World, and why it almost ignores the world outside.

In that official book, there is hardly a mention of Universal Studios, Sea World, or Busch Gardens, for example. This is not because they are unworthy of mention, or that visitors to Walt Disney World don't visit those attractions and others. The reason for their absence is the fact that the Walt Disney Co. does not profit from them.

So, let us state again our independence: the author and publisher of this book have no connection with Walt Disney World, Universal Studios, Sea World, Busch Gardens, or any of the other attractions written about here. Similarly, there is no financial interest in any of the discount coupons published within the book.

Our profit comes from you, the readers of this book, and it is you we hope to serve as best we can.

## About the Author

Corey Sandler is a former newsman and editor for the Associated Press, Gannett Newspapers, IDG, and Ziff-Davis Publishing. He has written more than 90 books on travel, video game, and computer topics; his titles have been translated into French, Spanish, German, Italian, Portuguese, Polish, and Chinese. When he's not traveling, he lives with his wife and two children on Nantucket island, 30 miles off the coast of Massachusetts.

Look for these other *Econoguide* titles, also from Contemporary Books: *Econoguide '97—Las Vegas, Reno, Laughlin, Lake Tahoe*; *Econoguide '97— Disneyland, Universal Studios Hollywood, and Other Major Southern California Attractions*; and *Econoguide '97—Washington D.C., Williamsburg, Busch Gardens, Richmond, and Other Area Attractions*.

# I
# From Your World to Disney World

## Chapter 1
## A Central Florida Vacation Calendar

Here are two hypothetical days spent at Walt Disney World:

**July 4.** It wasn't exactly the flight you wanted. However, you're grateful for the privilege of forking over $840 for a coach seat in the jammed cabin of the jet. All of the rooms inside the park—at $240 per night—are sold out, but you were lucky enough to pay just $100 for a very ordinary hotel room that is a 20-minute bumper-to-bumper drive from the parking lots.

According to the tram driver, you are parked in the same county as the Magic Kingdom, although you're not really sure. When you get to the ticket booths, there's a 30-minute wait just to get on the monorail to the entrance.

Once inside, you sprint to Tomorrowland to find that the line for the ExtraTERRORestrial Alien Encounter includes what seems like the entire population of Boston. And you'd better plan on showing up for lunch at 10:45 and dinner at 4:30 if you hope to find a table at the lowliest overpriced burger stop. But there are always the cooling thrills at Blizzard Beach, right? True, but the line for Florida's only chairlift stretches back to Philadelphia.

**March 20.** It seems like it's just your family and a crew of flight attendants, stretched out at 30,000 feet. Even nicer, you were able to grab a deep-discount excursion fare ticket for $298. Your hotel room cost $29.95 (you could have rented one within the park for $69), and the road to the park is empty.

The monorail stands empty and waiting for you at the transportation center. Your leisurely walk to Space Mountain puts you into a 10-minute queue; later in the day you drop into a rocket car without breaking stride.

Take your pick of restaurants, and feel free to take a break in the afternoon and run over to Typhoon Lagoon; temperatures often reach 80 degrees, and the lagoon is like the beach on a semi-private tropical island.

**Do we have to point out which trip is likely to be more enjoyable?**

### Our Guiding Rule

The basic *Econoguide* strategy to getting the most out of your trip is this: *Go when most people don't; stay home when everyone else is standing in line.*

Specifically, we suggest you try to come to Florida when school is in session and in the weeks between holidays: between Labor Day and Thanksgiving, between Thanksgiving and Christmas, between New Year's Day and Presidents' Week, between Presidents' Week and Spring Break/Easter, between Easter and Memorial Day.

We're not just talking about the crowds at Walt Disney World, Universal Studios, Sea World, and elsewhere in Central Florida. We're also talking about the availability of discount airline tickets, off-season motel rates, and restaurant specials.

You'll find lower prices when business is needed, not when the "No Vacancy" lamp is lit. The best deals can be found in low-season or what travel agents call the shoulder-season, midway between the slowest and busiest times.

This doesn't mean you can't have a good time if your schedule (or your children's) requires you to visit at high-season. We'll show you ways to save money and time any time of the year.

## A Central Florida Vacation Calendar

KEY:   🕴 = Semi-private        🕴 🕴 = Moderate crowds

🕴 🕴 🕴 = Heavy crowds   🕴 🕴 🕴 🕴 = Elbow-to-elbow

**January** *New Year's Day*   🕴 🕴 🕴

*Second week through end of month*   🕴

*Disney World Indy 200 Weekend*   🕴 🕴 🕴
*(Semi-private. Warmer than most anywhere else.*
*Room rates at low-season level.)*

New Year's Day and a few days afterward are the crowded aftermath of the Christmas rush. But when the kids go back to school and most of the adults return to work after the Christmas–New Year's holiday, attendance drops off sharply. The second week of January through the first week of February is usually the second least crowded period of the year, with attendance averaging about 25,000 visitors per day at Walt Disney World. Watch out, though, for the late-January weekend when the new Disney World Indy 200 is held; the race draws as many as 50,000 visitors and many of them spill over to the parks after the race. The parks close early and do not offer nighttime parades or fireworks, but you'll be able to walk right onto most major rides and attractions; room rates are at their lowest level.

**February** *First ten days*   🕴 🕴
*(Moderate crowds. Warm but not hot.*
*Room rates at shoulder-season level.)*

Early February is a period of average attendance, reaching 30,000 to 35,000 visitors daily. The parks generally close early except for weekends, and there are no nighttime parades or fireworks.

## February *Presidents' week holiday period* 🚶 🚶 🚶

*(Heavy crowds for holiday week. Room rates at high-season level.)*

Presidents' Week (celebrated in many school districts in and around the period from February 12 to February 22) is a time of fairly heavy attendance, up to about 45,000 visitors daily. Watch out for Race Week in Daytona, too. The parks are open late, with nightly parades and fireworks.

## Late February 🚶 🚶

## March *Entire month* 🚶 🚶

*(Back to moderate attendance. Thermometer nudges into the 80s. Room rates at shoulder-season level.)*

Attendance falls off to moderate from the end of February through the first week of April, averaging about 35,000 visitors. There are days in early March when you will have the parks to yourself, but at other times you will join thousands of college kids on early Spring Break or baseball fans drawn south for Spring Training. Nevertheless, this is not a bad time to come to Florida— with luck you will run into 80-degree water park weather. The parks generally close early and there are no nighttime parades or fireworks in the first half of the month; during Spring Break the parks are open later.

## April *Second and third weeks* 🚶 🚶 🚶

*(The Easter Parade can get pretty thick. Consistent 80-degree weather. Room rates at high-season.)*

The second and third weeks of April are among the most crowded times of the year, with Easter visitors and Spring Break students clogging the turnstiles at rates of up to 60,000 per day. The parks are open late, with nighttime parades and fireworks.

## April *First and fourth week* 🚶 🚶

*(A lovely time, with moderate attendance and room rates at shoulder- or creeping into high-season rates.)*

Sneak in before or after the Spring Break rush. The parks generally close early, and there are no nighttime parades or fireworks.

## May *Entire month* 🚶 🚶

*(Moderate attendance, swimming weather, and shoulder-season rates.)*

Another relatively quiet period, from the end of April through the first week of June. Expect average attendance of 30,000 to 35,000 per day. The parks generally close early, and there are no nighttime parades or fireworks.

## June to August *The crazy days of summer* 🚶 🚶 🚶

*(Lots and lots of company. Hot sun and high-season rates.)*

Just after Memorial Day the throngs of people come. And stay. Crowds of about 60,000 per day can be expected from the first week of June through the third week of August. Room rates are at high-season for the entire summer. Temperatures average in the 90s; and you can expect a few heavy downpours or steady rains. Parks are open late, with nighttime parades and fireworks scheduled.

And just to make things even more crowded, sometimes it seems as if half of Brazil comes north for warm weather in August.

### September to Mid-November *The post-summer doldrums* 👤

*(Theme park heaven: no lines, no crowds, low, low rates. Temperatures still high.)*

Where have all the tourists gone? On the day after Labor Day, the turnstiles slow to a crawl, averaging about 20,000 visitors per day. Room rates reach bottom, too. The weather is quite good, although the occasional tropical storm or hurricane can dampen a few days here and there. The parks generally close at 6 P.M. or 7 P.M., but the lack of lines should allow you to see everything you want. There are some late hours on weekends, with parades or fireworks.

One special warning: the Walt Disney World/Oldsmobile Golf Classic, a stop on the PGA Tour, is scheduled in October of each year. As many as 100,000 participants and 200,000 spectators may descend on the park at this time, and hotel accommodations may be a bit difficult to obtain for the several days of the tournament. The park may be unusually crowded for this time of the year because of family members of golf fans.

### November Thanksgiving *Thanks for what?* 👤 👤 👤

*(Merchants give thanks for the huge crowds at Thanksgiving. Rates at high-season level.)*

The one-week period around Thanksgiving brings a brief return to "No Vacancy" at motels and in attraction lines. Average attendance is about 55,000 visitors. The parks generally close early, except for the holiday week and weekends surrounding it.

### December *First through third weeks* 👤

*(Mickey can get lonely at times like these, and hotels will almost pay you to come and stay.)*

This is it: the secret season. From after Thanksgiving until the day Christmas vacation starts is the quietest time of the year for a visit. Attendance levels average 15,000 to 20,000 per day, and lines are rare. Room rates are rock-bottom, too. The parks generally close early, and there are no nighttime parades or fireworks, except for weekends.

### December *Christmas Holiday* 👤 👤 👤 👤

*(Your sisters and cousins and aunts will all be in line, in front of you. You may need a loan for the super-high-season room rates.)*

The Christmas–New Year's holiday is the most crowded, least time-efficient time to visit Central Florida. You'll be shoulder to shoulder with an average of 75,000 to 80,000 other visitors each day at Walt Disney World, with large crowds and long lines at Universal Studios, Sea World, and other area attractions. Parks are open late, with nighttime parades and fireworks.

The crowds can become so large that some of the parks actually close the gates by mid-morning. Don't feel too bad if you're shut out. It could be worse: you could be inside. In line.

You cannot count on temperatures warm enough for swimming, either. Room rates are at their highest levels, too. It's a festive, happy time, but frankly, we'd rather be alone or close to it. If you must go, be sure to arrive at the park early and follow the Power Trip plan for your best chance.

## The Best Day to Go to the Park

When Mommy, Daddy, Willie, and Tessa arrive in Orlando on Sunday (the most common arrival date) for a week's visit (the most common length of vacation) the first place they will go is the Magic Kingdom on Monday. Epcot comes next, then the Disney-MGM Studios. The remainder of the week is usually given over to other area parks and attractions.

So, we feel the best plan for your visit is to adopt what we call a Contrarian View. In other words, go against the common logic that says, "We came here for the Magic Kingdom and that's where we'll go first."

**SPECIAL EVENTS**
**Late January–Early February.** Chinese New Year at Epcot.
**Late January.** Disney World Indy 200.
**Mid-February.** Pleasure Island Mardi Gras.
**Mid-March.** St. Patrick's Day Celebration at Pleasure Island.
**Walt Disney World Easter Parade.** Magic Kingdom.
**Spring (Mid-April through early June).** Epcot International Flower & Garden Festival.
**Memorial Day Weekend.** Special late-night entertainment and late hours at all parks.

## AVERAGE RAINFALL AND TEMPERATURE FOR CENTRAL FLORIDA

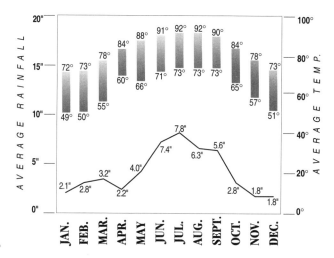

|  | GO | DON'T GO |
|---|---|---|
| Magic Kingdom | Sunday | Monday |
|  | Thursday | Tuesday |
|  | Friday | Wednesday |
|  |  | Saturday |
| Epcot | Sunday | Tuesday |
|  | Monday | Wednesday |
|  | Thursday | Saturday |
|  | Friday |  |
| Disney-MGM Studios | Sunday | Tuesday |
|  | Monday | Wednesday |
|  | Friday | Thursday |
|  | Saturday |  |
| Universal Studios and other area attractions | Sunday | Wednesday |
|  | Monday | Thursday |
|  | Tuesday | Saturday |
|  | Friday |  |

Herewith is one schedule you might want to consider if you are visiting Central Florida during one of the busy times of the year. It starts, you might note, with arrival on Saturday, which is a bit against the tide; if you get to Orlando early enough you may be able to visit a water park or other attraction (other than the Magic Kingdom) that night.

By the way, it should be obvious that seven days is not enough time to come close to sampling all that Orlando and Central Florida has to offer; if time and money is no object, we'd suggest a two-week visit with about half of the time devoted to Disney World and the other days for Universal Studios, Sea World, Busch Gardens, and all of the other attractions of the area.

## The Econoguide Contrarian Schedule

**SATURDAY**
Arrive in Orlando. Visit water parks, smaller attractions, dinner theaters, Pleasure Island, or Church Street Station

**SUNDAY**
Magic Kingdom, Disney-MGM Studios, or Universal Studios

**MONDAY**
Universal Studios or Disney-MGM Studios

**TUESDAY**
Sea World, beach, golf, water parks, or other attractions

**WEDNESDAY**
Busch Gardens, Space Center, Cypress Gardens, or Splendid China

**THURSDAY**
Epcot Center

**FRIDAY**
Magic Kingdom

**SATURDAY**
A second chance at the park of your choice (avoid Magic Kingdom)

# FLORIDA HIGHWAYS

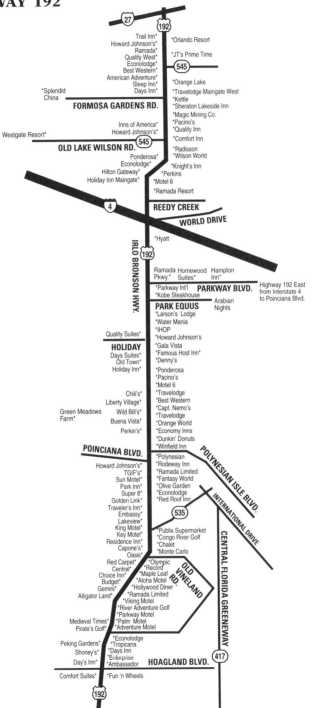

**27** **192**

Trail Inn*
Howard Johnson's*
Ramada*
Quality West*
Econolodge*
Best Western*
American Adventure*
Sleep Inn*
Days Inn*

*Orlando Resort

*JT's Prime Time

**545**

*Orange Lake
*Travelodge Maingate West
*Kettle
*Sheraton Lakeside Inn
*Magic Mining Co.
*Pacino's
*Quality Inn
*Comfort Inn

*Splendid China

## FORMOSA GARDENS RD.

Inns of America*
Howard Johnson's*

Westgate Resort*

**545**

*Radisson
*Wilson World

## OLD LAKE WILSON RD.

Ponderosa*
Econolodge*
Hilton Gateway*
Holiday Inn Maingate*

*Knight's Inn
*Perkins
*Motel 6
*Ramada Resort

**4**

## REEDY CREEK
## WORLD DRIVE

*Hyatt

**192**

Ramada   Homewood   Hampton
Pkwy.*    Suites*        Inn*

Highway 192 East
from Interstate 4
to Poinciana Blvd.

*Parkway Int'l
*Kobe Steakhouse

## PARKWAY BLVD.

Arabian
Nights

## PARK EQUUS
*Larson's Lodge
*Water Mania
*IHOP

Quality Suites*

*Howard Johnson's
*Gala Vista

## HOLIDAY

*Famous Host Inn*

Days Suites*
Old Town*
Holiday Inn*

*Denny's
*Ponderosa
*Pacino's
*Motel 6

Chili's*
Liberty Village*
Wild Bill's*
Buena Vista*

*Travelodge
*Best Western
*Capt. Nemo's
*Travelodge
*Orange World

Green Meadows
Farm*

Perkin's*

*Economy Inns
*Dunkin' Donuts
*Winfield Inn

## POINCIANA BLVD.

Howard Johnson's*
TGIF's*
Sun Motel*
Park Inn*
Super 8*
Golden Link*
Traveler's Inn*
Embassy*
Lakeview*
King Motel*
Key Motel*
Residence Inn*
Capone's*
Oasis*

*Polynesian
*Rodeway Inn
*Ramada Limited
*Fantasy World
*Olive Garden
*Econolodge
*Red Roof Inn

## POLYNESIAN ISLE BLVD.

## INTERNATIONAL DRIVE

**535**

*Publix Supermarket
*Congo River Golf
*Chalet
*Monte Carlo

Red Carpet*
Central*
Choice Inn*
Budget*
Gemini*
Alligator Land*

*Olympic
*Record
*Maple Leaf
*Aloha Motel
*Hollywood Diner
*Ramada Limited
*Viking Motel

## OLD VINELAND RD.

## CENTRAL FLORIDA GREENEWAY

*River Adventure Golf
*Parkway Motel
*Palm Motel
*Adventure Motel

Medieval Times*
Pirate's Golf*

Peking Gardens*
Shoney's*

Day's Inn*

*Econolodge
*Tropicana
*Days Inn
*Enterprise
*Ambassador

## HOAGLAND BLVD.

**417**

Comfort Suites*

*Fun 'n Wheels

**192**

# Chapter 2
# Planes, Trains, Monorails, and Automobiles

I'm flying to Orlando on a new jumbo jet. The ticket I handed in at the counter in Boston cost $309 for a round-trip.

The businessman across the aisle will suffer through the same mystery meal, watch the same crummy movie, and arrive at Orlando International Airport at the same millisecond I do—and pay $804 for his ticket.

Somewhere else on this plane there is a couple who were happily bumped off a previous flight because of overbooking and are discussing where to use the two free round-trip tickets they received in compensation.

Up front in first class, where the food is ever so slightly better, a family of four is traveling on free tickets earned through Mom's frequent flyer plan.

Me, I've got that cut-rate ticket and I'm due for a 5 percent rebate on airfare, hotel, and car rental arranged through my travel agent.

And on my trip back home, I will get on the flight I really wanted to take instead of the less-convenient reservation I was forced to sign up for when I bought that cut-rate ticket.

## Orlando International Airport

Orlando's airport has grown from a backwater Florida strip to one of the busiest—and most efficiently operated—terminals in the country. Located about 20 minutes west of Walt Disney World and other Orlando and Kissimmee attractions, it is served by several major highways as well as bus and limousine service.

There are three main clusters of gates at the airport; each cluster is connected to the single ticketing and baggage claim area by an automated monorail; you won't be the first to observe that your first ride at Orlando is at the airport.

Here are the gate assignments as they existed in early 1996; be sure to check with your airline on arrival for any changes:

**Checking in again.**
Having a boarding pass
issued by a travel agent
is not the same as
checking in at the
airport; you'll still need
to show your ticket at
the counter so that the
agent knows you're
there.

**Gates 1–29**

| | |
|---|---|
| Air Jamaica | (800) 523-5585 |
| American | (800) 247-8726 |
| American Trans Air | (800) 225-2995 |
| Bahamasair | (800) 222-4262 |
| Continental | (800) 525-0280 |
| LTU | (800) 888-0200 |
| Lacsa | (800) 225-2272 |
| TWA | (800) 221-2000 |

**Gates 30–59**

| | |
|---|---|
| All Nippon Airways | (800) 235-9262 |
| Kiwi | (800) 538-5494 |
| Northwest | (800) 225-2525 |
| United | (800) 241-6522 |
| US Air | (800) 428-4322 |
| Valujet | (800) 825-8538 |

**Gates 60–99**

| | |
|---|---|
| Aero Costa Rica | (800) 237-6274 |
| America West | (800) 235-9292 |
| British Airways | (800) 247-9297 |
| ComAir | (800) 354-9822 |
| Delta | (800) 221-1212 |
| TransBrasil | (800) 872-3153 |
| Virgin Atlantic | (800) 862-8621 |

In 1996, Orlando International Airport added helicopter service from the roof of the main terminal to downtown Orlando (tickets from about $50 to $75), and embarked on a major renovation of the international arrivals concourse. Also underway is construction of a fourth runway and a new international terminal with 24 gates.

When the current round of expansion is finished, the airport will be able to handle 75 million passengers a year.

## Alice in Airlineland

In today's strange world of air travel, there is a lot of room for maneuvering for the dollarwise and clever traveler. You can pay an inflated full price, you can take advantage of the lowest fares, or you can play the ultimate game and parlay tickets into free travel. In this chapter, we'll show you how to do each.

There are three golden rules to saving hundreds of dollars on travel: be flexible, be flexible, and be flexible.

• Be flexible about when you choose to travel. Go to Orlando during the off-season or low-season when airfares, hotel rooms, and other attractions offer substantial discounts. Try to avoid school vacations and the summer unless you enjoy a lot of company on line.

• Be flexible about the day of the week you travel. In many cases, you can save hundreds of dollars by changing your departure date one or two days in either direction. Ask your travel agent or airline reservationist for current fare rules and restrictions.

The days of lightest air travel are generally midweek, Saturday afternoons, and Sunday mornings. The busiest days are Sunday evenings, Monday mornings, and Friday afternoons and evenings.

In general, you will receive the lowest possible fare if you include a Saturday in your trip, buying what is called an excursion fare. Airlines use this as a way to exclude business travelers from the cheapest fares, assuming that business people will want to be home by Friday night.

> **Double indemnity.** Your homeowner's or renter's insurance policy may include coverage for theft of your possessions while you travel, making it unnecessary to purchase a special policy. Check with your insurance agent.

• Be flexible on the hour of your departure. There is generally lower demand—and therefore lower prices—for flights that leave in the middle of the day or very late at night.

• Be flexible on the route you will take, or your willingness to put up with a change of plane or stopover. Once again, you are putting the law of supply and demand in your favor. A direct flight from Boston to Orlando for a family of four may cost hundreds more than a flight from Boston that includes a change of planes in Raleigh-Durham or Atlanta before proceeding to Florida.

• Don't overlook the possibility of flying out of a different airport, either. For example, metropolitan New Yorkers can find domestic flights from La Guardia, Newark, or White Plains. Suburbanites of Boston might want to consider flights from Worcester or Providence as possibly cheaper alternatives to Logan Airport. From the Los Angeles area there is LAX, Orange County, Burbank, and San Diego.

• Plan way ahead of time and purchase the most deeply discounted advance tickets, which usually are noncancelable. Most carriers limit the number of discount tickets on any particular flight; although there may be plenty of seats left on the day you want to travel, they may be offered at higher rates.

• In a significant change over the past few years, most airlines have modified "nonrefundable" fares to become "noncancelable." What this means is that if your plans change or you are forced to cancel your trip, your tickets retain their value and can be applied against another trip, usually for a fee of about $35 or $50 per ticket.

• Conversely, you can take a big chance and wait for the last possible moment, keeping in contact with charter tour operators and accepting a bargain price on a "leftover" seat and hotel reservation. You may also find that some airlines will reduce the prices on leftover seats within a few weeks of departure date; don't be afraid to check regularly with the airline, or ask your travel agent to do it for you. In fact, some travel agencies have automated computer programs that keep a constant electronic eagle eye on available seats and fares.

• Take advantage of special discount programs like senior citizens' clubs, military discounts, or offerings from organizations to which you may belong. If you are in the over-60 category, you may not even have to belong to a group like AARP; simply ask the airline reservationist if there is a discount available.

You may have to prove your age when you pick up your ticket or boarding pass.

## Air Wars

Airlines are forever weeping and gnashing their teeth about huge losses due to cutthroat competition. And then they regularly turn around and drop their prices radically with major sales.

We won't waste time worrying about the bottom line of the airlines; it's our own wallets we want to keep full. Therefore, the savvy traveler keeps an eye out for airline fare wars all the time. Read the ads in daily newspapers and keep an ear open to news broadcasts that often cover the outbreak of price drops. If you have a good relationship with a travel agent, you can ask to be notified of any fare sales.

The most common times for airfare wars are in the weeks leading up to the quietest seasons for carriers, including the period between Labor Day and Thanksgiving and again in the winter with the exception of Christmas, New Year's, and Presidents' Day holiday periods.

There are three important strategies to employ here:

• If you can, hold off on vacation travel plans as long as you can in hopes of snaring a discount fare. Don't wait too long, though—the deepest standard discounts are for tickets purchased at least 21 days before the date of travel. And remember that the chances for a fare sale for Memorial Day weekend or Thanksgiving are very slim; tickets may be hard to obtain at any price.

• Consider grabbing a discount fare ticket even if your travel dates are not firm. In most cases (be sure to check with the airline) you will be able to adjust dates for a small penalty; the final price of the ticket should still be less than a regular fare.

• Ask for a refund on previously purchased tickets if fares go down for the period of your travel. The airline may refund the difference, or you may be able to reticket your itinerary at the new fare, paying a $35 to $50 penalty for cashing in the old tickets. Be persistent—if the difference in fare is significant, it may be worthwhile making a visit to the airport to meet with a supervisor at the ticket counter.

Another moneysaving strategy involves the use of discount coupons distributed directly by the airlines, or through third parties such as supermarkets, catalog companies, and direct marketers. A typical coupon offers $50 or $100 off full fare or certain types of discount fare. It has been our experience that these coupons are often less valuable than they seem—they are certainly better than paying full fare, but often result in a price that is higher than readily available discounts. Read the fine print carefully and be sure to ask reservationists if the price they quote you with the coupon is higher than another fare you qualify for.

### Convention Fares

If you are traveling to a convention that happens to take place in Orlando, you may be able to get in on a discount negotiated by the group with a particular airline.

In fact, you may not have to have any affiliation at all with a convention group in order to take advantage of special rates, if offered. All the airline will ask is the name or number of the discount plan for the convention; the reservationist is almost certainly not going to ask to see your union card or funny hat.

Check with conventions and visitors bureaus at your destination to see if any large groups are traveling when you plan to fly. Is this sneaky and underhanded? Yes. But we think it is sneaky and underhanded for an airline to charge hundreds of dollars more for the seat to the left and right of the one we're sitting in.

> **Finding a bucket shop.** Look for ads for ticket brokers and bucket shops in places like the classified ads in *USA Today*, the "Mart" section of the *Wall Street Journal* or in specialty magazines like *Frequent Flyer*.

• Consider doing business with a discounter, known in the industry as consolidators or, less flatteringly, as "bucket shops." Look for their ads in the classified sections of many Sunday newspaper travel sections. These companies buy the airlines' slow-to-sell tickets in volume and resell them to consumers at rock-bottom prices. Be sure to study and understand the restrictions; if they fit your needs and wants, this is a good way to fly.

• A bit more in the shadows are ticket brokers who specialize in the resale of frequent flyer coupons and other free or almost-free tickets. Although most airlines attempt to prohibit the resale or transfer of free tickets from the original "owner" to a second or third party, the fact is that very rarely are they successful in preventing such reuse. Are you willing to take a small financial risk with the chances of saving hundreds or even thousands of dollars on a long trip? If you are, make sure that the tickets you receive are listed in your name.

We're not going to make a recommendation about using such brokers, but we will note that many flyers use them with success. If you join them, be sure to read and understand the terms of your contract with the broker, and pay for your ticket with a credit card, if possible.

## Playing the Ticket Game

In my opinion, the airlines deserve all the headaches we travelers can give them because of the illogical and costly pricing schemes they throw at us— things like a fare of $350 to fly 90 miles between two cities where they hold a monopoly, and $198 bargain fares to travel 3,000 miles across the nation. Or even more annoying are round-trip fares of $300 if you leave on a Thursday and return on a Monday, and $1,200 if you leave on a Monday and return on the next Thursday.

But a creative traveler can find ways to work around most of these roadblocks. Here are a few strategies:

**Nested tickets.** This scheme generally works in either of two situations— where regular fares are more than twice as high as excursion fares that include a Saturday night stayover, or in situations where you plan to fly between two locations twice within less than a year.

Let's say you want to fly from Boston to Orlando. Here's how a nested purchase works: Buy two sets of tickets in your name, one from Boston to Orlando and back to Boston with the return date for when you want to come back from your *second* trip, and the other ticket from Orlando to Boston and back to Orlando, this time making the first leg of the ticket for the date you want to come back from the first trip, and the second leg of the trip the date you want to depart for the second trip.

If this sounds complicated, that's because it is. But it is perfectly legal, and any capable travel agent should be able to help you construct the nested pair of tickets. It will be up to you to keep your tickets straight when you travel.

**Split Tickets.** Fare wars sometimes result in super-cheap fares through a connecting city. For example, an airline seeking to boost traffic through a hub in Dallas might set up a situation in which a pair of round-trip tickets from Chicago to Dallas, and then from Dallas to Orlando work out to be considerably less expensive than a single nonstop from Chicago to Orlando and back.

Once again, this is perfectly legal and a place where a good travel agent should be able to help you. The possible fly in the ointment involves missed connections; be sure to book a schedule that allows enough time between flights and offers backups.

**Hidden City Fares.** Here's an area that is a bit chancy and may not be worthwhile unless there is a lot of money to be saved. In certain competitive situations, an airline might offer a long distance fare with a stopover en route that is cheaper than a direct ticket to the stopover city. This sort of fare is rarely available to a popular destination like Orlando, but we present it here for your other travel.

Confused? Here's an example: You might find a flight from Atlanta to Las Vegas with a stopover in Dallas priced at $300, while a ticket from Atlanta to Dallas is set at $400. If Dallas is your goal, all you have to do is get off the plane when it lands there.

The problem with this scheme is that airlines have learned how to use their computers to track this sort of practice, and some will cancel a return ticket if they find a passenger has deplaned somewhere other than the agreed-upon destination. That's no problem at all if your trip is one-way, or if the special fare is less than half of the regular fare—in that case, just buy two cheap round-trip fares and throw away the tickets you don't use.

Once again, a good travel agent should be able to help you here, although some may be squeamish about violating airline regulations. You might have to construct this sneaky itinerary yourself.

### A Loophole Closes a Bit

The biggest change to hit the airline industry in 1995 had nothing to do with fancy new jetliners, improved service, or (heaven forbid) a decent meal at 30,000 feet: it was the near-universal end to transferable tickets.

It used to be that for any domestic airline flight, all you needed to get on board the plane was your ticket. Just like showing your ticket at the theater, all that mattered was that you had an admission pass.

Travelers were often able to resell or give away unneeded "nested" ticket pairs, sell off promotional free tickets, or sell tickets issued under a frequent flyer program.

But in the fall of 1995, the federal government called a security alert at the nation's airports because of perceived threats from the Middle East and elsewhere. As part of a package that included elimination of some parking spaces directly in front of terminals, increased scrutiny of carry-on and checked baggage, and other measures, airline check-in agents began asking for a photo ID for each ticketholder and comparing that name against the ticket. The airlines took to this practice with particular relish, and news reports said that some of the major carriers found they were earning a significant increase in profits by blocking the use of tickets issued under another name.

Although the security alert was reduced later in the year (subject to reinstatement), many airlines have continued to ask for identification.

## Standing Up for Standing By

One of the little-known secrets of air travel on most airlines and most types of tickets is the fact that travelers with valid tickets are allowed to stand by for flights other than the ones for which they have reservations; if there are empty seats on the flight, standby ticketholders are permitted to board.

Some airlines are very liberal in their acceptance of standbys within a few days of the reserved flight, while others will charge a small fee (usually $35 to $50) for changes in itinerary. And some airline personnel are stricter about the regulation than others.

Here's what I do know: if I cannot get the exact flight I want for a trip, I make the closest acceptable reservations available after that flight and then show up early at the airport and head for the check-in counter for the flight I really want to take. Unless you are seeking to travel

**Second chance.** Tour cancelations are rare. Most tour operators, if forced to cancel, will offer another package or other incentives as a goodwill gesture. If a charter flight or charter tour is canceled, the tour operator must refund your money within 14 days.

**Lug-it-yourself.** If you are using a scheduled airline to connect with a charter flight, or the other way around, your baggage will not be automatically transferred. You must make the transfer yourself.

Charter and tour flights operate independently of other flights. If you are on a trip that combines scheduled and nonscheduled flights, or two unrelated charter flights, you may end up losing your money and flight because of delays.

It may make sense to avoid such combinations for that reason, or to leave extra hours or even days between connections. Some tour operators offer travel delay insurance that pays for accommodations or alternative travel arrangements necessitated by certain types of delays.

**Don't wait to drop a card.** Keep in touch with your travel agent or tour operator. In many cases they can anticipate major changes before departure time and will let you know. And many operators will try hard to keep you from demanding a refund if you find a major change unacceptable. They may offer a discount or upgrade on a substitute trip or adjust the price of the changed tour.

during an impossibly overbooked holiday period or arrive on a bad weather day when flights have been canceled, your chances of successfully standing by for a flight are usually pretty good.

One trick is to call the airline the day before the flight and check on the availability of seats for the flight you want to try for. Some reservation clerks are very forthcoming with information; many times I have been told something like, "There are 70 seats open on that flight."

Be careful with standby maneuvers if your itinerary requires a change of plane en route; you'll need to check availability of seats on all of the legs of your journey.

And a final note: be especially careful about standing by for the very last flight of the night. If you somehow are unable to get on that flight, you're stuck for the night.

My personal strategy usually involves making a reservation for that last flight and standing by for one or more earlier flights on the same day.

## About Travel Agencies

Here's my advice about travel agents, in a nutshell: get a good one, or go it alone.

A good travel agent is someone who remembers who he or she works for: You.

Of course, there is a built-in conflict of interest here, since the agent is in most cases paid by someone else. Agents receive a commission on airline tickets, hotel reservations, car rentals, and many other services they sell you. The more they sell (or the higher the price) the more they earn.

I would recommend you start the planning for any trip by calling the airlines and a few hotels and finding the best package you can put together for yourself. Then call your travel agent and ask them to do better.

If your agent contributes knowledge or experience, comes up with dollar-saving alternatives to your own package, or offers some other kind of convenience, then go ahead and book through the agency. If, as I often find, you know a lot more about your destination and are willing to spend a lot more time to save money than will the agent, do it yourself.

There is one special type of travel agency worth considering. A number of large agencies offer rebates of part of their commissions to travelers. Some of these companies cater only to frequent flyers who will bring in a lot of business; other rebate agencies offer only limited services to clients.

I use an agency that sends me a check after each trip equal to 5 percent of all reservations booked through them. I have never set foot in their offices, and I conduct all of my business over the phone; tickets arrive by mail or by overnight courier when necessary.

You can find discount travel agencies through many major credit card companies (Citibank and American Express among them) or through associations and clubs. Some warehouse shopping clubs have rebate travel agencies.

And if you establish a regular relationship with your local travel agency and bring them enough business to make them glad to see you walk through their door, don't be afraid to ask them for a discount equal to a few percentage points.

## Your Consumer Rights

The era of deregulation of airlines has been a mixed blessing for the industry and the consumer. After a period of wild competition based mostly on price, we now are left with fewer but larger airlines and a dizzying array of confusing rules.

The U.S. Department of Transportation and its Federal Aviation Administration still regulate safety issues, overbooking policies, baggage limits, and no-smoking rules. Almost everything else is between you and the airline.

Policies on fares, cancelations, reconfirmation, check-in requirements, and compensation for lost or damaged baggage or for delays all vary by airline. Your rights are limited and defined by the terms of the contract you make with an airline when you buy your ticket. You may find the contract included with the ticket you purchase, or the airlines may "incorporate terms by reference" to a separate document which you will have to request to see.

Whether you are buying your ticket through a travel agent or dealing directly with the airline, here are some important questions to ask:

• Is the price guaranteed, or can it change from the time of the reservation until you actually purchase the ticket?

• Can the price change between the time you buy the ticket and the date of departure?

• Is there a penalty for cancelation of the ticket?

• Can the reservation be changed without penalty, or for a reasonable fee?

**The best policy.** Consider buying trip cancelation insurance from a travel agency, tour operator, or directly from an insurance company (ask your insurance agent for advice). The policies are intended to reimburse you for any lost deposits or prepayments if you must cancel a trip because you or certain specified members of your family become ill. Read the policy carefully to understand the circumstances under which the company will pay.

Take care not to purchase more coverage than you need; if your tour package costs $5,000 but you would lose only $1,000 in the event of a cancelation, then the amount of insurance required is just $1,000. Some policies will cover you for health and accident benefits while on vacation, excluding any pre-existing conditions.

And be sure you understand your contract with your airline; you may be able to reschedule a flight or even receive a refund after payment of a service charge; some airlines will give full refunds or free rescheduling if you can prove a medical reason for the change.

**Fast food.** One advantage to bringing a car to the park is the chance to save a bit of money and get a more relaxed, better meal by ducking out of the park at lunch and visiting a decent buffet or menu restaurant; come back to the park for some evening rides and the fireworks. (Be sure to get your hand stamped when you leave the park *and* hold on to your ticket stub—both are needed for readmission on the same day. Your parking receipt is also valid for reentry to any of the parking lots.)

Be sure you understand the sort of service you are buying.

• Is this a non-stop flight, a direct flight (an itinerary where your plane will make one or more stops en route to its destination), or does the itinerary require you to change planes one or more times?

• What seat has been issued? Do you really want the center seat in a three-seat row, between two strangers?

And you might also want to ask your travel agent the following:

• Is there anything I should know about the financial health of the airline offering me this ticket?

• Are you aware of any significant threats of work stoppages or legal actions that could ruin my trip?

## Overbooking

Overbooking is a polite industry term that refers to the legal business practice of selling more than an airline can deliver. It all stems, alas, from the rudeness of many travelers who neglect to cancel flight reservations that will not be used. Airlines study the patterns on various flights and city pairs and apply a formula that allows them to sell more tickets than there are seats on the plane in the expectation that a certain percentage will not show up at the airport.

But what happens if all passengers holding a reservation do show up? Obviously, the result will be more passengers than seats, and some will have to be left behind.

The involuntary bump list will begin with the names of passengers who are late to check in. Airlines must ask for volunteers before bumping any passengers who have followed the rules on check-in.

Now, assuming that no one is willing to give up his or her seat just for the fun of it, the airline will offer some sort of compensation—either a free ticket or cash, or both. It is up to the passenger and the airline to negotiate an acceptable deal.

The U.S. Department of Transportation's consumer protection regulations set some minimum levels of compensation for passengers who are bumped from a flight due to overbooking.

If a passenger is bumped involuntarily, the airline must provide a ticket on its next available flight. Unfortunately, there is no guarantee that there will be a seat on that plane, or that it will arrive at your destination at a convenient time.

If a passenger is bumped involuntarily and is booked on a flight which arrives within one hour of the original arrival time, no compensation need be paid; if the airline gets the bumpee to his or her destination more than one hour but less than two hours after the scheduled arrival, the traveler is entitled to receive an amount equal to the one-way fare of the oversold flight, up to $200; if the delay is more than two hours, the bumpee will receive an amount equal to twice the one-way fare of the original flight, up to $400.

It is not considered "bumping" if a flight is canceled because of weather, equipment problems, or the lack of a flight crew. You are also not eligible for compensation if the airline substitutes a smaller aircraft for operational or safety reasons, or if the flight involves an aircraft with 60 seats or less.

## How to Get Bumped

Why in the world would you want to be bumped? Well, perhaps you'd like to look at missing your plane as an opportunity to earn a little money for your time instead of an annoyance. Is a two-hour delay worth $100 an hour to you? A voucher for $800 for a family of four to wait a few hours on the way home will pay for a week's hotel plus a heck of a meal at the airport.

If you're not in a tremendous rush to get to Florida—or to get back home— you might want to volunteer to be bumped. We wouldn't recommend doing this on the busiest travel days of the year, or if you are booked on the last flight of the day, unless you are also looking forward to a free night in an air-port motel.

## Tour Packages and Charter Flights

Tour packages and flights sold by tour operators or travel agents may look similar, but the consumer may end up with significantly different rights.

It all depends whether the package uses a scheduled or nonscheduled flight. A scheduled flight is one that is listed in the Official Airline Guide and available to the general public through a travel agent or from the airline. This doesn't mean that a scheduled flight will necessarily be on a major carrier or that you will be flying on a 747 jumbo jet; it could just as easily be the propeller-driven pride of Hayseed Airlines. In any case, though, a scheduled flight does have to meet stringent federal government certification requirements.

In the event of delays, cancelations, or other problems with a scheduled flight, your recourse is with the airline.

A nonscheduled flight is also known as a charter flight. The term *charter* is sometimes also applied to a package that includes a nonscheduled flight, hotel accommodations, ground transportation, and other elements.

Charter flights are generally a creation of a tour operator who will purchase all of the seats on a specific flight to a specific destination or who will rent an airplane and crew from an air carrier.

Charter flights and charter tours are regulated by the federal government, but your rights as a consumer are much more limited than those afforded to scheduled flight customers.

### Written Contracts

You wouldn't buy a hamburger without knowing the price and specifications

**Extra miles.** Don't let it force you to pay too much for a rental car, but all things being equal, use a rental agency that awards frequent flyer mileage in a program you use.

(two all-beef patties on a sesame seed bun, etc.) Why, then, would you spend thousands of dollars on a tour and not understand the contract that underlies the transaction?

When you purchase a charter flight or a tour package, you should review and sign a contract that spells out your rights. This contract is sometimes referred to as the "Operator Participant Contract" or the "Terms and Conditions." Look for this contract in the booklet or brochure that describes the packages; ask for it if one is not offered. The proper procedure for a travel agent or tour operator to follow requires that they wait until the customer has read and signed the contract before any money is accepted.

Remember that the contract is designed mostly to benefit the tour operator, and each contract may be different from others you may have agreed to in the past. The basic rule here is: if you don't understand it, don't sign it.

Depending on your relative bargaining strength with the provider, you may be able to amend the contract so that it is more in your favor; be sure to obtain a countersignature from an authorized party if you make a change in the document, and keep a signed copy for yourself.

## How to Book a Package or Charter Flight

If possible, use a travel agent—preferably one you know and trust from prior experience. In general, the tour operator pays the travel agent's commission. Some tour packages, however, are available only from the operator who organized the tour; in certain cases, you may be able to negotiate a better price by dealing directly with the operator, although you are giving up one layer of protection for your rights.

Pay for your ticket with a credit card; this is a cardinal rule for almost any situation in which you are prepaying for a service or product.

Realize that charter airlines don't have large fleets of planes available to substitute in the event of a mechanical problem or an extensive weather delay. They may or may not be able to arrange for a substitute piece of equipment from another carrier.

If you are still willing to try a charter after all of these warnings, make one more check of the bottom line before you sign the contract. First of all, is the air travel significantly less expensive than the lowest nonrefundable fare from a scheduled carrier? (Remember that you are, in effect, buying a nonrefundable fare with most charter flight contracts.)

Have you included taxes, service charges, baggage transfer fees, or other charges the tour operator may put into the contract?

Are the savings significantly more than the 10 percent the charter operator may boost the price without your permission? Do any savings come at a cost of time? Put a value on your time.

Finally, don't buy a complete package until you have compared it to the a la carte cost of such a trip. Call the hotels offered by the tour operator, or similar ones in the same area, and ask them a simple question: "What is your best price for a room?" Be sure to mention any discount programs that are applicable, including AAA or other organizations. Do the same for car rental agencies, and place a call to Disneyland and any other attractions you plan to visit to get current prices.

And, of course, don't overlook the discount coupons for hotels, motels, restaurants, and attractions that are included in this book—that's why they're there.

## Kids in Mid-Air

If you are flying with children, discuss with your airline or travel agent any special needs you might have. These might include a request for a bulkhead seat to give children a little extra room for fidgeting (although you will lose the storage space underneath the seat in front of you) or special meals (most airlines offer a child's meal of a hot dog or hamburger on request, which may be more appealing to a youngster than standard airline fare).

Be sure to pack a special bag for young children and carry it on board the plane. Extra diapers in the baggage compartment won't help you at all in an emergency at 25,000 feet. Include formula, food, and snacks as well as a few toys and books to occupy young ones.

Changes in altitude at takeoff and landing may cause some children discomfort in their ears. Try to teach them to clear their ears with an exaggerated yawn. Bubble gum or candy, or a bottle for babies, can help, too.

## Drive?, He Said

Everyone's conception of the perfect vacation is different, but for me, I draw a distinction between getting there and being there. I want the getting part to be as quick and simple as possible, and the being there part to be as long as I can manage and afford. Therefore, I fly to most any destination more than a few hundred miles from my home. The cost of driving, hotels, meals en route, and general physical and mental wear and tear rarely equals a deeply discounted excursion fare.

If you do drive, though, you can save a few dollars by using the services of the AAA or another major automobile club. Spend a bit of time and money before you head out to make certain your vehicle is in traveling shape: a tune-up and fully inflated, fully inspected tires will certainly save gas, money, and headaches.

If you plan to travel by bus or train, be aware that the national carriers generally have the same sort of peak and off-peak pricing as the airlines. The cheapest time to buy tickets is when the fewest people want them.

## Renting a Car

If you are planning to stay at a hotel within Walt Disney World you may be able to do without renting a car, although you will not be able to get to attractions and restaurants outside of the Disney boundaries without calling a cab or car service. If you are staying at a hotel outside of Walt Disney World, you

| Mileage to Orlando from America and Canada: | | Mileage from Orlando to Elsewhere in Florida: | |
| --- | --- | --- | --- |
| Albany, N.Y. | 1,236 | Bok Tower | 55 |
| Atlanta | 460 | Cape Kennedy | 56 |
| Baltimore | 920 | Clearwater | 106 |
| Boston | 1,350 | Cocoa Beach | 46 |
| Buffalo | 1,210 | Daytona Beach | 54 |
| Chicago | 1,200 | Ft. Lauderdale | 209 |
| Cleveland | 1,100 | Ft. Myers | 153 |
| Dallas | 1,130 | Gainesville | 109 |
| Disneyland (Calif.) | 2,511 | Jacksonville | 134 |
| Indianapolis | 990 | Key West | 371 |
| Las Vegas | 2,349 | Miami | 228 |
| Minneapolis | 1,550 | Ocala | 72 |
| Montreal | 1,460 | Okeechobee | 102 |
| Nashville | 695 | Pensacola | 428 |
| New York | 1,100 | Sarasota | 127 |
| Ottawa | 1,443 | St. Augustine | 98 |
| Philadelphia | 1,020 | St. Petersburg | 105 |
| Pittsburgh | 1,020 | Tallahassee | 242 |
| Richmond | 761 | TampaT | 85 |
| Syracuse | 1,221 | Tarpon Springs | 109 |
| Toronto | 2,302 | W. Palm Beach | 166 |
| Washington, D.C. | 857 | Winter Haven | 51 |

may be able to use a shuttle bus to the parks, but again, you will find yourself with limited options.

We therefore recommend renting a car. The good news is that Orlando is perhaps the most competitive rental market in the country. You may be able to rent a small car for about $100 per week, or a luxury car for twice that amount.

Car rental companies will try—with varying levels of pressure—to convince you to purchase special insurance coverage. They'll tell you it's "only" $7 or $9 per day. What a deal! That works out to about $2,500 or $3,330 per year for a set of rental wheels. The coverage is intended primarily to protect the rental company, not you.

Check with your insurance agent before you travel to determine how well your personal automobile policy will cover a rental car and its contents. We strongly recommend you use a credit card that offers rental car insurance; such insurance usually covers the deductible below your personal policy. The extra auto insurance by itself is usually worth an upgrade to a "gold card" or other extra-service credit card.

The only sticky area comes for those visitors with a driver's license but no car, and therefore no insurance. Again, consult your credit card company and your insurance agent to see what kind of coverage you have, or need.

Your travel agent may be of assistance in finding the best rates; you can make a few phone calls by yourself, too. Rental rates generally follow the same low-shoulder-high-season structure. We have obtained rates as low as $59 a week for a tiny subcompact (a convertible, no less) in low-season.

Although it is theoretically possible to rent a car without a credit card, you will find it to be a rather inconvenient process. If they cannot hold your credit card account hostage, most agencies will require a large cash deposit—perhaps as much as several thousand dollars—before they will give you the keys.

Be aware that the least expensive car rental agencies usually do not have their stations at the airport itself. You will have to wait for a shuttle bus to take you from the terminal to their lot, and you must return the car to the outlying area at the end of your trip. This may add about 20 to 30 minutes to your arrival and departure schedule.

Pay attention, too, when the rental agent explains the gas tank policy. The most common plan says that you must return the car with a full tank; if the agency must refill the tank, you will be billed a service charge plus what is usually a very high per-gallon rate.

Other optional plans include one where the rental agency sells you a full tank when you first drive away and takes no note of how much gas remains when you return the car. Unless you somehow manage to return the car with the engine running on fumes, you are in effect making a gift to the agency with every gallon you bring back.

We prefer the first option, making a point to refill the tank on the way to the airport on getaway day.

## Busing Yourself Around

Public transportation is a fine idea, saving money and the environment . . . but in our experience, the more they are needed, the less convenient they are. Such is the case with "I-Ride" and "Lynx" bus services. The I-Ride is a fleet of 15 buses that cruise International Drive every five or ten minutes from Sea World to American Way from 7 A.M. to midnight. If you're staying right on International Drive and your destination is on the road, the bus will serve

---

**Interstate 4 Exits in Kissimmee/Orlando Area**

| | |
|---|---|
| 25A | US 192 East. Motel strip toward downtown Kissimmee. Water Mania, Old Town, Medieval Times. |
| 25B | US 192 West. Main gate of Walt Disney World. Motel strip, Splendid China. |
| 26A/B | Epcot Center, Disney-MGM Studios, Typhoon Lagoon, Epcot Resorts, Disney Village, Pleasure Island. |
| 27 | SR 535 to Kissimmee and Lake Buena Vista. Hotel Plaza Resorts, Disney Village Resorts, Fort Wilderness, River Country. |
| 27A | Sea World. Central Florida Parkway Eastbound (toward Orlando) only. |
| 28 | 528 East (Beeline) to Sea World, Orlando International Airport and Kennedy Space Center. (Toll road.) |
| 29 | SR 482 (Sand Lake Road) to Orlando, Orlando International Airport, and International Drive. |
| 30A/B | Highway 435 (Kirkman Road). Universal Studios. |
| 31 | Florida Turnpike south to Miami or north to Wildwood. |
| 33A | Hwy. 441, 17-92 (South Orange Blossom Trail). |
| 38 | Anderson Street, Orlando. Church Street Station. |

you well; connections between any other points in Orlando and Kissimmee are too slow and involved for most vacationers.

I-Ride fare is a reasonable 75 cents for adults; children ride free. For information, (407) 855-7972.

## Accident and Sickness Insurance

The idea of falling ill or suffering an injury while hundreds or thousands of miles away from home and your family doctor can be a terrifying thought.

But before you sign on the bottom line for an Accident and Sickness insurance policy, be sure to consult with your own insurance agent or your company's personnel office to see how far your personal medical insurance policy will reach. Does the policy cover vacation trips and exclude business travel? Are all international locations excluded? Can you purchase a "rider" or extension to your personal policy to cover travel?

The only reason to purchase an Accident and Sickness policy is to fill in any gaps in the coverage you already have. If you don't have health insurance of any kind, a travel policy is certainly valuable, but you might want to consider whether you should spend the money on a year-round policy instead of taking a vacation in the first place.

Also be aware that nearly every kind of health insurance has an exclusionary period for preexisting conditions. If you are sick before you set out on a trip, you may find the policy will not pay for treating the problem.

# Chapter 3
# Sleeping and Eating for Less

## Negotiating for a Room

Notice the title of this section: it's *not* called "buying" a room. The fact of the matter is that hotel rooms, like almost everything else, are subject to negotiation and change.

Here is how to pay the highest possible price for a hotel room: walk up to the front desk without a reservation and say, "I'd like a room." Unless the "No Vacancy" sign is lit, you may be charged the "rack rate," which is the published maximum nightly charge.

Here are a few ways to pay the lowest possible price:

1. Before you head for your vacation, spend an hour on the phone and call directly to a half dozen hotels that seem to be in the price range you'd like to spend. (We recommend membership in AAA, and use of their annual tour books as starting points for your research.)

Start by asking for the room rate. Then ask them for their *best* rate. Does that sound like an unnecessary second request? Trust us, it's not: we can't begin to count the number of times the rates have dropped substantially when we ask again.

*[True story: I once called the reservation desk of a major hotel chain and asked for the rates for a night at a Chicago location. "That will be $149 per night," I was told. "Ouch," I said. "Oh, would you like to spend less?" the reservationist answered. I admitted that I would, and she punched a few keys on her keyboard. "They have a special promotion going on. How about $109 per night?" she asked.*

*Not bad for a city hotel, I reasoned, but still I hadn't asked the big question. "What is your best rate?" I asked. "Oh, our best rate? That would be $79," said the agent.*

*But, wait: "Okay, I'll take it. I'm a triple A member, by the way." Another pause. "That's fine, Mr. Sandler. The nightly room rate will be $71.10. Have a nice day."]*

When you feel you've negotiated the best deal you can obtain over the phone, make a reservation at the hotel of your choice. Be sure to go over the

**Here's my card.**
Membership in AAA brings some important benefits for the traveler, although you may not be able to apply the club's usual 10 percent discount on top of whatever hotel rate you negotiate. (It doesn't hurt to ask, though.) Be sure to request a tour book and Florida and Orlando maps from AAA, even if you plan to fly to Florida; they are much better than the maps given by car rental agencies.

**Weekly, not weakly.**
Are you planning to stay for a full week? Ask for the weekly rate. If the room clerk says there is no such rate, ask to speak to the manager: he or she may be willing to shave a few dollars per day off the rate for a long-term stay.

dates and prices one more time, and obtain the name of the person you spoke with and a confirmation number if available.

2. But wait: when you show up at your hotel on the first night, stop and look at the marquee outside and see if the hotel is advertising a discount rate. Most of the hotels in the Walt Disney World area adjust their prices based on attendance levels at the park. It is not uncommon to see prices change by $10 or more over the course of a day.

Here's where you need to be bold. Walk up to the desk as if you *did not* have a reservation, and ask the clerk: "What is your best room rate for tonight?" If the rate they quote you is less than the rate in your reservation, you are now properly armed to ask for a reduction in your room rate.

Similarly, if the room rate advertised out front on the marquee drops during your stay, don't be shy about asking that your charges be reduced. Just be sure to ask for the reduction *before* you spend another night at the old rate, and obtain the name of the clerk who promises a change. If the hotel tries a lame excuse, like "That's only for new check-ins," you can offer to check out and then check back in again. That will usually work; you can always check out and go to the hotel across the road that will usually match the rates of its competitor.

3. And here is the way to make the most informed choice, in the low-season only. Come down without a reservation, and then cruise one of the motel strips like I-192 (Irlo Bronson Highway) or International Drive. Check the outdoor marquees for discount prices and make notes. Find a phone booth and make a few phone calls to the ones you found attractive. Once again be sure to ask for the best price. The later in the day you search for a room, the more likely you are to find a hotel ready to make a deal.

## Dialing for Dollars

As we cited in our "True Story," you must be aggressive in representing your checkbook in negotiations with a reservation agent. Sometimes, you will also need to be persistent.

A few years back, *Condé Nast Traveler* magazine conducted a survey of hotel rates and found wide discrepancies between the prices quoted by central toll-free services, by a clerk called directly at a particular hotel, and by a travel agent. The survey was indecisive: no one source consistently yielded the lowest prices.

The magazine's recommendation: use the services of a travel agent you trust, and request that the agent verify the lowest rate with a direct call. The agent can check the computer first and then compare that rate against the hotel's offer.

## Where Should You Stay?

Except for the busiest days of the year—Christmas through New Year's and the Fourth of July among them—you're not going to have *any* trouble locating a place to stay in the Orlando-Kissimmee area. In fact, the biggest problem facing most visitors is choosing among the various places.

In this chapter, we'll offer a tour of the main hotel areas in and around Walt Disney World.

How should you choose a place to stay? We'd suggest you start by deciding on a price range you'd be willing to pay. Few would argue with the statement that some of the most exciting and most convenient hotels are to be found within the Walt Disney World park boundaries, but this comes at a not insignificant premium.

**Wrong numbers.** Be sure you understand the telephone billing policy at the motel. Some establishments allow free local calls, while others charge as much as 75 cents for such calls. (We're especially unhappy with service charges for 800 numbers.) Be sure to examine your bill carefully at checkout and make sure it is correct. We strongly suggest you obtain a telephone credit card and use it when you travel; nearly all motels tack high service charges on long distance calls and there is no reason to pay it.

Following are some ranges for low-season rooms; high-season rates can be as much as double:

**$25 to $60 per night. East and West of I-4 on I-192.** (The further east or west you go—up to about eight miles from I-4—the lower the prices.) **South Orange Blossom Trail** area. **Downtown Orlando** budget motels.

**$50 to $100 per night. Walt Disney World** budget hotels. **International Drive** budget motels. **I-192 resort hotels.** (Some lower.) **Apopka-Vineland Road** area. **Orlando International Airport. Downtown Orlando.**

**$100 to $300 per night. Walt Disney World** premium hotels. **Lake Buena Vista, International Drive** first-class hotels.

As you can see, the room rates are pretty self-selecting for location and, to a large extent, the quality of the room. Next you can make decisions on extras including special recreational facilities.

## Hotels Within Walt Disney World

Within Walt Disney World are five clusters of hotels and resorts. Reservations can be made through travel agencies or through the Disney central travel desk at (407) 934-7639.

**Disney World Resorts Price Ranges**
**Budget**
Disney's All-Star Sports and Music Resorts
$69 to $88 per night

**Safety first.** The small safes available in some hotels can be valuable to the traveler; be sure to inquire whether there is a service charge for their use. We've been in hotels that apply the charge regardless of whether we used the safe or not; look over your bill at check-out and object to any charges that are not proper. In any case, we'd suggest that any objects that are so valuable that you feel it necessary to lock them up should probably be left home.

**Secret stock of rooms.** Delta Airlines is the "official airline" of Walt Disney World and, as a result, has quite a few rooms at park hotels allotted to it. You may be able to save a small amount on rooms within Walt Disney World, or at least get into otherwise sold-out hotels by purchasing an air-room package from Delta.

**Moderate**

Disney's Caribbean Beach Resort
  $99 to $149 per night
Disney's Dixie Landings Resort
  $99 to $149 per night
Disney's Port Orleans Resort
  $99 to $149 per night

**Deluxe**

Disney's Contemporary Resort
  $200 to $333 per night
Disney's Wilderness Lodge
  $161 to $250 per night
Disney's Polynesian Resort
  $200 to $333 per night
Disney's BoardWalk Inn
  $233 to $349 per night
Disney's Yacht and Beach Club Resorts
  $233 to $349 per night
Disney's Grand Floridian Beach Resort
  $277 to $389 per night
Villas at Disney Institute
  Bungalows from $194 to $244 per night
  2 BR Treehouses from $372 to $433
Dolphin and Swan Resorts
  $270 to $389 per night

**Housekeeping Villas**

Disney's Old Key West Resort
  Rooms from $200 to $250 per night
  2 BR suites from $389 to $439 per night
Disney's Fort Wilderness Homes
  $183 to $244 per night
Disney's BoardWalk Villas
  Studios from $217 to $261 per night
  1 BR from $300 to $355 per night

Disney hotels have two to four "seasons" for room prices. Super Value rates are generally in effect in January and September. Value rates are offered in early February, post-Easter to early June, the end of August, and from October 1 through mid-December. Regular rates are generally in effect from mid-February through mid-April, and from mid-June through mid-August. The highest Holiday rates are charged from mid-December through New Year's Eve.

## Magic Kingdom Resort Area

**Disney's Wilderness Lodge.** 728 rooms in a rustic lodge patterned after the famous "Old Faithful Inn" located at Yellowstone National Park. The structure, opened in 1994, includes massive log columns, totem poles, and stone fireplaces—just the sort of thing you'd expect in Central Florida, right? But wait: there's also a 12-story geyser, a waterfall, and a rocky swimming pool that begins in the lobby as a hot spring and works its way outside. The resort, located between the Contemporary Resort and Fort Wilderness, offers a view of the Electrical Water Pageant, with launch service to the parks.

Eateries include **Artist Point**, a moderate-to-expensive gourmet eatery that celebrates the flavors of the Pacific Northwest with items including maple-glazed king salmon, elk sausage, and rainbow trout; and the **Whispering Canyon Cafe**, which features all-you-can-eat buffets for breakfast and lunch and a campfire cookout each evening. Call (407) 939-3463.

**Quick tickets.** Guests in hotels within Walt Disney World can purchase tickets—at regular prices—at guest services desks within their hotels, saving a few minutes of waiting at the park.

Transportation to the Magic Kingdom includes boat service from the hotel dock, and buses to Epcot, Disney-MGM Studios, and elsewhere in Walt Disney World. The direct phone is (407) 824-3200.

**Disney Contemporary Resort.** Is it a hotel with a monorail running through the middle, or a monorail station with a hotel surrounding it? Either way, it's a most unusual setting and just a mouse trot from the main gate of Walt Disney World. It's a great place to view the nightly Electrical Water Pageant in season, especially if your rooms face the lagoon. The resort includes 1,052 rooms, a health club, marina, and pool. Note that not all of the rooms are in the A-shaped main building with the monorail station but may be located in the more ordinary annex buildings along the lake. There are suites on the hotel's 14th floor that include private concierge and special services.

The **Concourse Steak House** has trellised ceilings that allow peeks through to the 90-foot-high atrium lobby. Breakfast, lunch, and dinner are offered from 7 A.M. through 10 P.M., with dinner entrees from about $15. Specialties include charbroiled steak, oven-roasted chicken, and seafood.

The **Contemporary Café's** breakfast buffet ($10.95 for adults, and $7.95 for children from 3 to 11) includes a French toast and fruit bar; the dinner buffet ($13.95 for adults, $7.95 for juniors from 7 to 11, and $4.95 for children from 3 to 6) features prime rib, shrimp, and international specialties. Breakfast is served from 8 to 11 A.M.; dinner from 5:30 to 9:30 P.M.

High above it all, on the 15th floor, is Disney's newest gourmet eatery. The **California Grill** has offerings ranging from sushi and lemon grass soup to spicy braised lamb shank with Thai red curried lentils, and pan-seared yellowfin tuna with black beans. The expensive restaurant, open from 5:30 to 10 P.M., is centered around a "Stage Kitchen" where specialties are prepared.

Guests can rent Water Sprites from the hotel's marina, or they can hire a waterskiing boat with driver and skis. The **Mouseketeer Clubhouse** is open from 4:30 P.M. to midnight for children from 3 to 9 years old with a four-hour maximum; rates are about $4 per hour for the first child and $2 per hour for each additional youngster. Two different movies (Disney titles, of course) are shown each night in the theater at the **Fiesta Fun Center**, which is also the home of a large collection of video arcade machines.

Transportation to the parks is by monorail, water taxi, and bus. You can

**Babysitter club.** Guests at hotels at Walt Disney World can hire an in-room babysitter by consulting with Guest Services or the In-Room KinderCare Learning Center.

**Clearing the air.** If you don't indulge, ask for a nonsmoking room at check-in. With luck, the air will be somewhat cleaner and furniture somewhat fresher.

also catch a water taxi to Discovery Island. Room rates ranged from $210 to $280 in 1996; off-season rates were about $20 less. Direct phone: (407) 824-1000.

**Disney's Grand Floridian Beach Resort.** An opulent resort along the shores of Seven Seas Lagoon with its own monorail station, it is a mixture of Victorian elegance and modernity in white and coral trim—in typical Disney fashion, it is much prettier than the real thing probably ever was. The hotel drew its design from some of the grand old hotels of Palm Beach at the turn of the century, including the Royal Poinciana.

The spectacular five-story Grand Lobby is topped by stained glass skylights and lit in the evening by grand chandeliers. A Big Band entertains nightly. Some of the rooms include quirky dormers and turrets as well as balconies with close-up views of the Magic Kingdom.

Special rooms include 15 honeymoon suites and other suites with as many as three bedrooms.

The prime restaurant is **Victoria and Albert's**, with just 65 seats and a most refined atmosphere. The prices, too, are refined: the prix-fixe menu, which usually includes meat, fish, and poultry offerings, is priced at about $80 per person before orders from the extensive and expensive wine list. Some samples: salmon sautéed in olive oil with olives, capers, and tomato; roasted rack of lamb with Madeira almond sauce; and Bailey's Irish Cream soufflé. The restaurant is one of the few in Walt Disney World that requires men to wear jackets. Seatings are at 6 and 9 P.M. You'll be attended by a butler and maid in Victorian dress.

**Flagler's** offers, apropos of nothing we can think of, Italian fare and singing waiters and waitresses for dinner, with entrees including grilled Florida swordfish over steamed portobello mushrooms and saffron sauce, half moon cheese ravioli with tomato and meat sauce, and grilled beef tenderloin with green peppercorns and Barolo wine sauce. Entrees begin at about $20 and climb sharply from there. Reservations are suggested.

**1900 Park Fare** offers buffet breakfasts and dinners in an attractive room that features carrousel horses, a hundred-year-old band organ, and Disney characters. The breakfast buffet is priced at $14.95 for adults and $9.95 for children; at dinner the adult price is $18.50.

The showplace seafood and steak eatery is **Narcoossee's**, with diners surrounding an open kitchen in a building that is built out into Seven Seas Lagoon. Open for lunch and dinner, entrees start at about $15 and climb sharply. Some samples: Key West conch fritters and grilled grouper.

Afternoon tea is served at the **Garden View Lounge.**

The resort includes 901 rooms, a health club, tennis courts, a marina with Water Sprites and sailboats, a white sand beach on Seven Seas Lagoon, and a huge pool. The **Mouseketeer Club** for children from 3 to 9 years old is open from 4:30 P.M. to midnight with a four-hour maximum. Call (407) 824-2433 for reservations.

Transportation to the parks is by monorail, water taxi, and bus. The parking lot is across the road. The direct phone is (407) 824-3000.

**Disney's Polynesian Resort.** A Disneyfied version of Hawaiian Island architecture and landscaping, including palm-lined walkways (torchlit at night) and tropical gardens, two exotic swimming pools (including one with a slide built into a volcano), and a station on the monorail. Oh, and did we mention the indoor waterfall in the lobby? Dancers perform at the nightly Polynesian Revue dinner show; there are four other restaurants in the complex. The resort includes 855 rooms in two- and three-story island-style longhouses, plus a marina, pools, and a kid's club. You can rent Water Sprites, sailboats, and other watercraft at the marina.

Every room has a patio, with most offering a view of the lagoon or one of the swimming pools. Special suites that include King Kamehameha concierge services are on the lagoon side of several of the longhouses.

Restaurants include the **Papeete Bay Verandah** in the Great Ceremonial House, which features breakfast buffets Mondays through Saturdays, a brunch buffet on Sundays (about $14.95 for adults and $7.95 for children), and formal dinners each night, with international entrees from about $10 to $25. The view from the verandah extends across Seven Seas Lagoon to a spectacular view of the park and is especially impressive at night.

The **'Ohana Feast**, served nightly from 5 to 10 P.M., includes firegrilled meats, fowl, and shrimp, and stir-fried vegetables and noodles.

The **Tangaroa Terrace** near the Oahu longhouse offers a breakfast buffet priced at about $8.95 for adults and $5.95 for children, plus menu items. A specialty is Belgian waffles in the shape of mouse (Mickey, who else?) ears. At dinner, offerings include a seafood stir-fry, Polynesian pork ribs, and teriyaki chicken.

Kids have their own club at **Neverland**, for children from 3 to 12. Open from 5 P.M. to midnight, there is a three-hour minimum at $8 per hour; there's even a special buffet for the kids. Call for reservations at (407) 824-2170.

Transportation to the parks is by monorail, water taxi, and bus. You can also see the nightly Electrical Water Pageant from the resort. The direct phone is (407) 824-2000.

**Fort Wilderness Resort and Campground.** Park your camper, pitch a tent, or rent one of Disney's Fleetwood Trailer Homes, complete with air-conditioning, television, telephone, kitchen, and daily housekeeping service. All of the 784 campsites at the secluded 780-acre site include electrical hookups, water, and a charcoal grill; most have sanitary hook-ups. The sites are intended for tent or trailer campers up to 65 feet. Comfort stations, a trading post, and shower and laundry facilities are nearby.

Pay attention to the campsite number you are assigned; a knowledgeable visitor (like all of the readers of this book) may be able to improve on the location. Low numbers from 100 to 599 are near the beach and Pioneer Hall. The high numbers, from 1500, are quiet and remote.

Inside one of the 408 wilderness homes, you'll probably have a hard time remembering you are within the woods; the homes include a living room, small kitchen, and bathroom.

The resort includes a petting farm, horseback riding, fishing, canoeing, and biking. There are two heated swimming pools and a large beach on Bay Lake. Nearby are Disney's two newest golf courses, Osprey Ridge, and Eagle Pines. Also close by is **River Country** and **Discovery Island.** There's a nightly campfire gathering near the **Meadow Trading Post** including free sing-alongs with Chip and Dale and Disney movies. Fort Wilderness is also a good place to watch the nightly Electrical Water Pageant.

In the center of the resort is **Pioneer Hall**, which includes the **Hoop-Dee-Doo Musical Revue**, an all-you-can-eat Wild West dinner show.

**Crockett's Tavern** is open for dinner only from 5 to 10 P.M. nightly and until 10:30 P.M. on Fridays and Saturdays, featuring buffalo burgers, steaks, and fish, with entrees priced from about $5 to $15. A folk singer entertains nightly.

The **Trail's End Buffeteria**, which features a dramatic high-beamed ceiling, offers meals all day, from 7:30 A.M. to 9:30 P.M. Specialties include country dishes, homemade bread, and desserts and a Saturday night Italian buffet. Every night after the last dinner is served at 9 P.M., the Buffeteria becomes a popular pizza joint, open until 11 P.M., midnight on weekends. Entrees for lunch and dinner range from about $5 to $15.

You can purchase groceries at the **Crossroads of Lake Buena Vista** shopping center just outside of the Walt Disney World park or bring them with you in your own vehicle.

Transportation to the parks is by bus, tram, and water taxi.

Campsite rates range from about $38 to $60 per night. A limited number of tents are available for rent if you don't want to bring your own equipment. The direct phone number is (407) 824-2900.

**Shades of Green on Walt Disney Resort—U.S. Armed Forces Recreation Center.** The former Disney Inn, situated between two PGA tour golf courses (probably the only ones in the world with sand traps shaped like Mickey Mouse), this 288-room rustic resort is offered to vacationing servicemen and women from all branches of the armed forces as well as civilian employees of the Department of Defense and certain other present and former employees and spouses of military branches; reservations are made through the central accommodations office.

## Epcot and Disney-MGM Resort Area

**Disney's Yacht and Beach Club Resorts.** A pair of attractive resorts nearby to Epcot Center and the Disney-MGM Studios Theme Park and set around their own lake. The Yacht Club is the more formal of the two, made to appear like a New England grand hotel with its own small lighthouse. Both hotels share **Stormalong Bay**, a fantasy lagoon filled with pools and water activities including water slides, bubble jets, and a whirlpool. A fleet of boats is available for rent, too.

The Yacht Club includes 635 rooms and the Beach Club an additional 580; it also has a health club, tennis courts, marina, beach, pool, and the **Sandcastle Club** for kids from 3 to 12, open from 4:30 P.M. to midnight with a charge of about $4 per hour for the first child and $2 per hour for additional kids.

Food at the Beach Club includes a nightly indoor New England–style clambake with clams, mussels, chicken, chowders, and more at the **Cape May Café**, served buffet style for about $16.95 per adult and $8.95 for children; lobster is available for an extra charge. There's also a breakfast buffet for $12.95 and $7.95.

**Ariel's** features mesquite-grilled seafood in a room where the fish eye the diners from a huge aquarium; specialties include stuffed lobster with entrees starting at about $18.

At the Yacht Club, there's the **Yachtsman Steakhouse**, where you can dine on Chateaubriand, steak, fish, or poultry, priced from about $17. The **Yacht Club Galley** features a buffet breakfast and menu items all day.

Down by the beach shared by both clubs is **Hurricane Hanna's Grill**, for burgers and dogs, and the **Beaches and Cream Soda Shop**, a Disneyfied old-fashioned ice cream fountain.

The resorts are within walking or quick tram distance of the International Gateway entrance to Epcot Center; you can also catch a water taxi to the Disney-MGM Studios or a bus to the Magic Kingdom. Room rates ranged from $230 to $295 in 1995; off-season rates were about $20 less. The direct phone number is (407) 934-8000.

**Walt Disney World Dolphin** and **Walt Disney World Swan.** Why not have a gigantic triangular hotel with a huge dolphin's head on top, or a rounded building graced by a pair of tremendous swans? This is Walt Disney World, after all. Two of the most distinctive hotels of the park face each other across a large grotto pool with a waterfall and whirlpools.

The Dolphin, operated by Sheraton, includes **Harry's Safari Bar & Grille** offering seafood and beef, **Sum Chow's** gourmet Oriental restaurant, **Juan & Only's Cantina** for Mexican specialties including a fajita bar and offering a Sunday brunch, the **Coral Cafe** buffet, the **Tubbi Checkers Buffeteria**, and the **Cabana Bar and Grill**.

Next door at the Swan (operated by Westin Hotels and Resorts) you will find the pricey Italian eatery **Palio**, as well as the **Garden Grove Cafe** in a greenhouse, and **Kimono's**, an Oriental lounge and sushi bar.

The resorts include a health club, tennis courts, marina, beach, and pools. **Camp Swan** at the Swan is open from 4 P.M. to midnight for children from 3 to 12, at $5 per hour for the first child and $3 per hour for an additional child; dinner is available for an extra charge through room service. **Camp Dolphin** across the way has one program for kids from 3 to 5 and another for youngsters from 6 to 12, with hourly rates of $6.50 per child. There's also a children's dinner club for $26.50. Parents can also purchase a $40 lifetime membership for Camp Dolphin, which reduces the hourly rates by approximately half.

Epcot is within walking distance or a short tram ride to the International Gateway entrance of Epcot near the France Pavilion. Water taxis run to Disney-MGM Studios. Buses head to the Magic Kingdom and other parts of Walt Disney World.

The Dolphin offers 1,509 rooms, with 1996 prices starting at $255 to $365 and suites priced from $525 to $2,400; the Swan has 758 rooms, with 1996 prices starting at $275 to $350 and suites priced from $350 to $1,650. That's per night, folks. The direct phone is (407) 934-3000.

**Disney's Caribbean Beach Resort.** One of the best bargains within the park, the sprawling 2,112-room resort spreads across five "villages" named after Caribbean islands (Aruba, Barbados, Jamaica, Martinique, and Trinidad). Each colorful village has its own pool and beach, with rooms in two-story buildings.

In addition, the five communities are linked to **Old Port Royale**, which lies along **Barefoot Bay.** Within the port is a food court with a wide range of fast food choices including **Wok Shop** (for basic Chinese fare), **Cinnamon Bay Bakery, Montego's Deli, Port Royale Hamburger Shop, Bridgetown Broiler** (grilled chicken and fajitas), and **Royale Pizza & Pasta Shop**; outside is a large swimming pool that includes a fort with water slides and water cannon. The **Captain's Tavern** includes blackened scallops, paella, ribeye steak, chicken, and fish dishes.

Guests can also rent a bike or boat at the marina, and there is a lovely 1.5-mile walking or jogging path around the lake at the resort. And there is **Parrot Cay**, a children's playground on a small island.

Transportation to the parks is by bus. The direct phone number is (407) 934-3400.

## Disney's All-Star Resorts

**Disney's All-Star Sports and Music Resorts.** The newest and some of the most fanciful resort areas within the park are intended as Disney's "economy" zone; the hotels are spiffed-up motels with comparatively small rooms.

The 246-acre site is just southwest of the Disney-MGM Studios and near the new **Blizzard Beach** water park.

The 1,920-room **All-Star Sports Resort** focuses on five sports themes: football, baseball, basketball, tennis, and surfing. All around are unusual sports scenes, including palm trees arranged to look like a basketball team at tip-off, an interior courtyard that resembles a football field, a quiet pool in the shape of a baseball infield, and wild sports icons. There are large video game arcades at both resorts.

At the **Surf's Up** building, bold colors glisten on 38-foot-tall surfboards and nearly a thousand colorful fish appear to be swimming along a wavy balcony; two giant shark fins encircle a free-form pool surrounded by swaying palms. At the **Hoops Hotel,** huge pennants from favorite college teams cover the roof line, and five-foot basketballs hang from the railings. The baseball-theme **Home Run Hotel** features stadium lights, scoreboards, and an outfield fence. Footballs and helmets big enough for Godzilla welcome guests to the **Touch-down Hotel.** And stairwells shaped like cans of tennis balls decorate the **Center Court** hotel.

The central check-in is at **Stadium Hall,** which features red, white, and blue seats, caged basketball court lighting, and red lockers. At the **End Zone** food court, giant sports figures perch atop brightly colored dining booths.

The scheme carries over to the guest rooms, too, which offer sports bedspreads, megaphone light fixtures, and bold artwork.

The 1,920-room **All-Star Music Resort** features country, rock, Broadway, calypso, and jazz themes.

Check-in for the music-theme hotel is in **Melody Hall,** where you'll also find the **Intermission** food court.

Transportation is by bus. The direct phone for All-Star Sports is (407) 939-5000; for All-Star Music, dial (407) 939-6000.

**Disney's BoardWalk Resort.** Way back before there was such a thing as a Disney theme park (yes, kids, there was such a time) our forebears ventured to the beach to grand "boardwalk" resorts including famed Coney Island in New York, and others along the Jersey Shore. It's a place of striped awnings and balconies like those of oceanfront inns of the 1920s on the Jersey Shore.

Flash forward to 1996 with the opening of Disney's new BoardWalk Resort, which re-creates some of the old-time fun with 378 hotel rooms and 532 Vacation Club timeshare units in a 45-acre area along Crescent Lake near Epcot, across the water from Disney's Yacht and Beach Club Resorts with views of Crescent Lake or gardens. Guests can walk along the boardwalk to Epcot, take a boat to the Disney-MGM Studios or a bus to the Magic Kingdom and other destinations within Walt Disney World.

Among the guest rooms are 14 two-story **Garden Suites,** luxury accommodations made to look like New England homes with white picket fences and gardens. The foremost place to stay is the 2,000-square-foot **Steeplechase Suite** at the **Innkeeper's Club.**

The resort features entertainment facilities including the **ESPN World** sports bar, **Jellyroll's Dueling Piano Bar,** and the **Big River Grille & Brewing Works,** Disney's first brew pub. **The Atlantic Dance Club** is a "big band" lounge. Also at the resort is **Spoodles,** featuring Mediterranean cuisine from France, Italy, and Greece, and the **Flying Fish Café,** offering seafood and steaks.

The original concept for this resort seemed to imply that Disney would add a rock-em, roll-em wooden coaster; as built, the coaster is a water slide that enters into the Luna Park swimming pool, including a 200-foot roller-coaster water slide and water-spouting elephants.

Outside the **BoardWalk Inn,** one of the vacation resorts, is a fully operational miniature carrousel dating from the 1920s from famed carrousel-maker Marcus Illions.

**Disney's Coronado Springs Resort.** The fall of 1997 will see the dawn of what is billed as the first moderately priced convention hotel in Walt Disney World, an attractive 1,900-room spread styled after the American Southwest.

Located on 136 acres on the west side of World Drive, near Blizzard Beach and the Disney-MGM Studios Theme Park, the resort's haciendas lie in the shade of palm trees, nearby to a white sand beach and four themed pools. Other facilities include a health shop, dining court, and restaurants.

The resort features a 95,000-square-foot convention center, and a 60,214-square-foot ballroom, the largest hotel ballroom in the Southeast.

## Disney Village Resort Area

**Disney's Port Orleans Resort.** A re-creation of the French Quarter of New Orleans, packed with G-rated Disney detail. The resort's swimming pool is located at **Doubloon Lagoon** and includes a sea-serpent water slide (down his tongue and into the water).

Restaurants at **Port Orleans Square** include some of the more unusual offerings in the park. At the **Sassagoula Floatworks & Food Factory**, check out the **King Creole Broiler**, with Creole specialties; **Basin Street Burgers and Chicken; Preservation Pizza Company**, and **Jacques Beignet's Bakery**, featuring New Orleans beignets, fried dough fritters.

The **Bonfamilles Café** offers steaks, seafood, and other dishes with a creole flair served in an attractive courtyard setting with dinner entrees priced from about $5 to $20; breakfast is also served.

The resort includes 1,008 rooms in seven three-story buildings, a marina, and a pool. Transportation to the parks is by water taxi and bus. The direct phone is (407) 934-5000.

**Disney's Dixie Landings Resort.** A bit of the old South, this is another in Disney's more affordable new resorts. The huge 2,048-room resort, divided into "parishes," includes a marina and five pools; the buildings are styled after plantation mansions and low bayou homes. The Mansion rooms are a bit more formal, evoking memories of grand staircases and columns; the Bayou rooms in tin-roofed structures look like they would fit in well with the swamp.

Boats and bicycles are available for rent at Dixie Levee.

A food court is offered at a central marketplace called **Colonel's Cotton Mill** and includes the **Acadian Pizza 'n Pasta, Bleu Bayou Burgers and Chicken, Cajun Broiler, Riverside Market and Deli**, and the **Southern Trace Bakery**.

**Boatwright's Dining Hall** offers a Cajun and American menu in a reproduction of a shipbuilding shed. Specialties include gumbos, roasted chicken, and prime rib with dinner entrees from about $5 to $20; breakfast is also served.

Transportation to the parks is by water taxi and bus. The direct phone is (407) 934-6000.

**Disney's Village Resort.** A collection of light and open townhouses, "treehouses," and multi-level villas in the woods near the Disney-MGM Studios Theme Park and Epcot Center.

For some families, renting one of these villa rooms may be less expensive or more convenient than taking two small hotel rooms. Most of the smaller one-bedroom Club Suites include refrigerators, and one- and two-bedroom Vacation Villas include fully equipped kitchens.

> **Kiss me, you bull.** Kissimmee has been among Florida's premier cattle raising areas, best known for its Brahma cattle way before the mice arrived.

Nearby are the **Lake Buena Vista Golf Course**, five lighted pools, tennis courts, and a marina. The resort includes 585 units and a health club. Villas range from one- and two-bedroom villas to the fancier Fairway and Treehouse Villas. You can also rent one of four Grand Vista Suites, fully furnished homes originally intended as model homes for a residential or timesharing resort.

A special attraction for some is the fact that some of the best bass fishing in Walt Disney World is right outside the door of many of the villas in one of the canals.

The resort is across the lagoon from Pleasure Island and next to the Disney Village Marketplace shops and restaurants. Groceries for the villas are available at the **Gourmet Pantry** within the resort, or you can take a short drive outside the park to the Crossroads of Lake Buena Vista shopping center (outside the park, it is nevertheless on Disney property . . . don't want to let any of those dollars leak out of the company's hands, do we?).

The restaurant at the resort is the **Lake Buena Vista Club**, a family eatery in the clubhouse on Club Lake Drive. Open all day, specialties include Key West Caesar Salad, burgers, and chicken priced from about $7 to $20 at dinner. On Sunday, a special brunch, priced at $10.95 for adults and $8.95 for children, features eggs Benedict, roast beef, and more.

Transportation to the parks is by bus. The direct phone is (407) 827-1100.

**Disney's Vacation Club Resort.** One of the newest resorts at Walt Disney World, units range from studios that sleep four to one-, two-, and three-bedroom units and Grand Villas with beds for as many as 12. Disney built the Vacation Club as a timesharing resort and hopes to eventually sell all of the units to repeat visitors to Walt Disney World. The homes are on the **Lake Buena Vista Golf Course**.

I could write a book about real estate—until I do, here's my best advice about buying a timeshare at Walt Disney World or anywhere else: don't do it on an impulse. Talk to your accountant or a financial advisor or someone else who is not in the business of selling you something other than advice.

In any case, you don't have to buy a timeshare to stay at the resort; unsold rooms, or rooms turned back to Disney for resale by owners, are available for rent. The direct phone for rentals is (407) 827-7700.

The restaurant at the club is **Olivia's**, which specializes in Key West specialties from conch fritters to key lime pie, with entrees priced from about $5 to $20.

**House calls.** House Med, an in-room health care service, can dispatch a medical technician to your hotel room between 8 A.M. and 11 P.M.; the technician can consult with a physician to obtain certain pre-scription medicines if necessary. Call 648-9234 for assistance.

You can also find many walk-in medical clinics listed in the Orlando or Kissimmee phone book.

## Disney Hotel Plaza

| | |
|---|---|
| Hotel Royal Plaza | $77 to $163 |
| Travelodge Hotel | $81 to $163 |
| Courtyard by Marriott | $99 to $179 |
| Grosvenor Resort | $117 to $183 |
| Buena Vista Palace | $143 to $322 |
| Doubletree Guest Suites Resort | $130 to $225 |
| The Hilton Resort | $196 to $261 per night |

Seven hotels built and operated by major (non-Disney) hotel companies are clustered near the Disney Village Marketplace and Pleasure Island. Guests can drive or use Disney buses to get to the park. These are high-quality but very standard hotels, without the fanciful touch of Disney-owned properties.

**Buena Vista Palace.** A 27-story lakeside tower with views of Epcot and nine restaurants and a **Recreation Island** with three pools. The resort includes more than 1,028 rooms and suites, a health club, tennis courts, and pools. Restaurants include the top-of-the-tower haute cuisine **Arthur's 27** and **Arthur's Wine Cellar in the Sky.** There's also the less-formal **Outback** restaurant with seafood and steaks. **Summer Kid Stuff** is a recreational pro-gram for children from 5 to 17. Phone (407) 827-2727 or (800) 327-2990.

**Courtyard by Marriott.** A family-oriented hotel with a 14-story central atrium and 323 rooms. Until early 1995, this was the Howard Johnson Resort Hotel, until it was converted lock, stock, and towels to a Marriott. Phone (407) 828-8888 or (800) 223-9930.

**Grosvenor Resort.** A lakeside tower with 628 rooms that includes a large recreation facility including tennis and handball courts, a children's play-ground, and heated swimming pools. **Baskerville's**, a British-theme restau-rant, is modeled after Sherlock Holmes' 221B Baker Street home in London; next door is **Moriarty's**, a pub named after the great detective's arch neme-sis. Phone (407) 828-4444 or (800) 624-4109.

**Doubletree Guest Suites Resort.** Each one- or two-bedroom suite includes a microwave, refrigerator, and small wet bar and the 229-room hotel offers a pool and tennis courts. The restaurant is the **Parrot Patch**. This hotel had previously been the Guest Quarters Suite Resort. Phone (407) 934-1000 or (800) 424-2900.

**Hotel Royal Plaza.** This 396-room hotel includes four restaurants and lounges with nightly entertainment, a pool, and recreation center and tennis courts. The **Plaza Diner** is a 24-hour family eatery. Phone (407) 828-2828 or (800) 248-7890.

**The Hilton.** A large resort and conference center directly across from the Disney Village Marketplace. It includes nine restaurants and lounges including the **American Vineyards, County Fair,** and a **Benihana** Japanese steakhouse. Also featured is an outdoor spa. The Vacation Station Kid's Hotel caters to kids from 4 to 12 years old, charged at $5 per hour for the first child and $1 per hour for additional family members. Phone (407) 827-4000 or (800) 782-4414.

**Travelodge Hotel.** A lakeside hotel with a Caribbean flavor and a rooftop nightclub called **Toppers** that offers a spectacular view of Walt Disney World. The **Traders** restaurant offers breakfast and dinner, and the **Parakeet Café** has pizza and snacks. Phone (407) 828-2424 or (800) 348-3765.

## Why Stay at a Hotel Within Walt Disney World?

The hotels within Walt Disney World are among the most attractive, most imaginative places to stay at any major tourist area we know of. They offer all sorts of extras not available outside of the park, and quite a few conveniences.

> **I-192 is a many-named splendor.** I-192 bears several different names in its traverse from I-27 west of the park to and through downtown Kissimmee. For much of its length near the park, it is called Irlo Bronson Memorial Highway. (Bronson was a prominent local politician and developer.) Near Kissimmee, it is called Vine Street; past Kissimmee toward St. Cloud, it is called 13th Street. Some segments are also called Space Coast Highway. *You can call it 192 anywhere and people will know what you mean.*

However, all of this comes at a price. The lowest rates at Walt Disney-owned or -operated hotels, or those operated by major chains on the park property, generally start at around $100 per night in low-season, which is the high end of most off-site hotels. It is up to you to decide what value to place on the extras that come with your higher room rates; you should also consider the possibility of obtaining similar special treatment outside the park. (We heard of one family that booked perfectly nice rooms a few miles outside of the park and used the money they saved to engage limousine service to and from the park.)

Insider advantages to guests who stay at Walt Disney World Resorts include:

Complimentary use of the Walt Disney World transportation system, including monorail, bus, ferryboat, and launch transportation to the parks, avoiding crowded parking lots.

Advance reservations for dining, Disney Dinner Shows, and Disney Character Breakfasts. Guests can make reservations as soon as they receive confirmation of hotel reservations.

Preferred access to tee times on all five championship golf courses. Also available are horseback riding, swimming, tennis, health clubs, and other facilities.

## All You Can Eat, à la Disney?

You decide if it's the ultimate convenience or a new wrinkle in dollar vacuuming: guests at Disney resorts using a limited number of Disney plans (including the basic Classic Plan) have the option to purchase **Disney's**

**Food 'n Fun Card** as an add-on to their vacations. The card allows breakfast and dinner at more than 60 selected restaurants in the park or the Walt Disney World resort, including tax and gratuity, but excluding alcohol. The card (and a similar **Disney's Dining Club** package for Swan, Dolphin, and Hotel Plaza guests) offers some free time on selected watercraft and horseback riding. Prices in 1996 were $58 per day for adults and $21 for children, ages 3 to 9.

No two visitors are the same, or eat the same, but here's our analysis: you can buy a decent breakfast anywhere for $5 to $10, and a fine dinner for $20 to $40. We don't see much of a deal there, except if you plan to make heavy use of boats or horses every day. If you miss out on a single meal, or pick up a pizza instead of a clambake one night, or if you don't make heavy use of recreational facilities, we think you're probably better off going a la carte.

## Hotels Outside the Park
### I-192/Irlo Bronson Memorial Highway/ Vine Street Kissimmee

Katella Avenue, which fronts on the main entrance to Disneyland in California, turned out to be one of Walt Disney's worst nightmares. When Disneyland was first built, it was surrounded by lush green orange groves. But with the success of the park, the environs became an unending stretch of unattractive strip motels, gift shops, miniature golf courses, and fast food restaurants.

When Disney began secretly buying up tens of thousands of acres of central Florida swamp and cypress groves in the 1960s, it was with the intention of shielding his new park deep within a green barrier. There was to be no Katella Avenue at Walt Disney World.

And, in fact, Disney was successful. The Magic Kingdom, Epcot Center, Disney-MGM Studios Theme Park, and all of the other attractions within the park seem to exist in a world unto themselves. There are, of course, tens of thousands of hotel rooms within the park as well as places to eat for all guests and day visitors, but the sheer size of the park swallows them up and hides them from sight of each other.

But, of course, the Walt Disney Company cannot own *every* square mile of Florida, even though they probably would if they could. There are two main places where Disney meets the real world: at Apopka-Vineland Road (S.R. 535) and at I-192. And then there is the rest of the Orlando-Kissimmee area.

Most of the hotels and attractions on I-192 can be found between I-4 and I-441 (Main Street/South Orange Blossom Trail) in Kissimmee. I-4 at I-192 actually lies within the southern end of the huge Walt Disney World property. The undeveloped Disney land here was set aside by Disney as a nature preserve, and not incidentally serves as a buffer to keep development away from the main entrance to the park.

West of I-4, toward I-27, is the less popular side of I-192, although a number of newer hotels have been built in the area. Room rates at low-season range from as low as $29 at I-27 to about $75 per night closer to the park. Hotels in this area often include the label "Main Gate" or "West Gate" in their name, and include: **Ramada Resort Main Gate, Holiday Inn Main Gate West, Hilton Inn Gateway, Econolodge Hawaiian Main Gate, Quality Inn Main Gate West, Motel 6 Main Gate West, Knights Inn Main Gate, Wilson World Main Gate, Radisson Inn Main Gate, Comfort Inn Main Gate, Howard Johnson's, Days Inn West Gate, Best Western West Gate, Econolodge West Gate, Quality Inn Main Gate, Sheraton Lakeside Inn, Travelodge Main Gate West,** and **Ramada West Gate.**

The busier side of I-192 runs about 10 miles from I-4 east to Main Street in Kissimmee. The area closest to I-4 is often called "Main Gate East." Near I-4 you will find attractions including Arabian Nights, Old Town, Fort Liberty, and Water Mania. Between the intersection of S.R. 535 and Kissimmee are Medieval Times, Fun 'n Wheels, and the Kissimmee Municipal Airport. A few miles past South Orange Blossom Trail and just short of the intersection with the Florida Turnpike is the Osceola County Stadium, the Spring Training home of the Houston Astros.

> **The real Old Town.** Orlando was established as a campground for soldiers during the Seminole Indian War of 1835 to 1842 and then continued as a trading post. The war resulted in the removal of most Native Americans in Florida to reservations in Oklahoma.
>
> The Orlando Metropolitan Area was the seventh-fastest growing area in the country, according to the 1990 Census. Its population grew 53 percent between 1980 and 1990, to 1,072,748. The city itself includes 54 lakes.

## Lake Buena Vista, Apopka-Vineland Road, Crossroads, World Center

The "back door" to Walt Disney World can be found off S.R. 535: Apopka-Vineland Road. Here Hotel Plaza Boulevard leads into the Disney Hotel Plaza area, Disney Village, and Pleasure Island. Further along the road are the entranceways to the Magic Kingdom, Epcot, Disney-MGM Studios, and the other attractions within the park.

Some of the property in this area is actually owned and controlled by the Walt Disney Company, although it is not technically within the park. Many of the area hotels offer free transportation to Walt Disney World, and some may be on the route for transportation companies that pick up passengers at Orlando International Airport; inquire when you call for information.

**Comfort Inn.** A 640-room motel with rates as low as $39 in the off-season and about $69 at peak times. Phone (407) 239-7300 or (800) 999-7300.

**Doubletree Club.** A budget chain offering 167 rooms, a pool, and a modest restaurant with a breakfast buffet. Rates start at about $69 in low-season and reach to about double that level in peak times. Phone (407) 239-8500 or (800) 228-2846.

**Embassy Suites.** An all-suite hotel in Lake Buena Vista, with bedroom, living room, dining, and kitchen areas, refrigerator, and microwave. Room rates range from $145 to $250. Phone (407) 239-1144 or (800) 257-8483.

**Holiday Inn Sunspree–Lake Buena Vista.** A family resort just outside the Disney Village Marketplace area on S.R. 535. All of the 507 rooms include a refrigerator and microwave. There's also a free activity program for children from 2 to 12 from 5 P.M. to 10 P.M. Restaurants include **Maxine's**, with breakfast and dinner buffets. Room rates started at about $80 up to about twice that in 1996. Phone (407) 239-4500 or (800) 366-6299.

**Howard Johnson Park Square Inn.** At Vista Centre. A family-oriented resort with 308 rooms; suites include a refrigerator and microwave. **The Courtyard Cafe** offers a breakfast buffet and dinner from a menu. Room rates range from about $65 to $105, and suites range from $80 to $130 in low-season. Phone (407) 239-6900 or (800) 635-8684.

**Hyatt Regency Grand Cypress.** Near the Disney Village Hotel Plaza. A 750-room tower plus 146 villas in and around 45 holes of golf, 12 tennis courts, and a huge pool with waterfalls and a 45-foot water slide. Room rates range in price from about $160 to $420; villas range from about $225 to more than $1,200 per night. Phone the Hyatt Regency Grand Cypress at (407) 239-1234 or (800) 233-1234 or the Villas of Grand Cypress at (407) 239-4700 or (800) 835-7377.

**Orlando World Center.** Off S.R. 535 in Orlando. The huge hotel, part of the Marriott chain, was once one of the largest in the state. It sits on some 200 landscaped acres and includes 1,503 rooms and suites, an 18-hole golf course, several large pools, and tennis courts. There are five restaurants, including **Mikado's**, a Japanese steakhouse. There's a children's "lounge" for ages 5 to 12, open from 4 P.M. to midnight. The Orlando World Center is often used for large conventions, offering Disney and other entertainment for spouses and children while business goes on within its meeting rooms. Room rates start at about $125 per night and go on up to the near stratosphere (okay, about $2,000) for suites. Phone (407) 239-4200 or (800) 228-9290.

**Radisson Inn.** At the Vista Centre. Offering 200 rooms and a pool with waterslide. Rooms start at about $69 in low-season and reach to double that level in high-season. Phone (407) 239-8400 or (800) 333-3333.

Other area hotels on S.R. 535 include the **Hawthorne Suites, Days Inn Resort, Compri, Park Square Inn** and **Blue Tree Resort.**

## International Drive (From Sea World to Universal Studios)

The next major stop on our tour is the International Drive area, a five-mile uninterrupted stretch of every national hotel and restaurant chain you've ever heard of, and some you probably haven't. This road serves no purpose other than for the tourist; it's a convenient midway location for the visitor looking to explore in all directions. Room rates run from about $50 to $100 in low-season at motels; a few fancy hotels have rooms at about double those prices.

One end of International Drive begins south of the Beeline Expressway at the entrance to Sea World. From there, it wanders more or less northerly to pass by the Orange County Convention and Civic Center, the Mercado shopping area, across Sand Lake Road (S.R. 482), in front of Wet 'n Wild and then heads east across Kirkman Road near the main entrance to Universal Studios Florida.

International Drive is, then, just minutes from Sea World, Universal Studios, Wet 'n Wild, and half a dozen other smaller attractions. There are restaurants of all descriptions on the road, as well. The road is about a 15-minute drive south to Walt Disney World or north to Orlando.

Hotels south of the Beeline near Sea World include the **Stouffer Resort** on Sea Harbor Drive and **Lexington Hotel Suites, Wynfield Inn**, and **Sheraton World** on Westwood Boulevard.

North of the Beeline, International Drive includes several internationally named hotel circles. Off Hawaiian Court, look for **Days Inn, Rodeway Inn**, and **Red Roof Inn.** On the other side of International Drive, across from the Civic Center, are the **Peabody Orlando** and the **Heritage Inn**, two of the fancier hotels on the road. Next to the Civic Center is a **Clarion Hotel.** A huge new hostelry, the **Omni Rosen Convention Hotel** opened next to the Convention Center in 1996.

Off Samoan Court is the **Quality Inn Plaza.**

In the stretch that includes Austrian Court and Jamaican Court, extending to Sand Lake Road, you will find **Park Suites International Drive, Gold Star Inn, Summerfield Suites Hotel, Courtyard by Marriott, Radisson Inn, Fairfield Inn, Ramada Inn Plaza, Embassy Suites, Inns of America, Howard Johnson's**, and **Marriott.**

North of Sand Lake, hotels include **Quality Inn, The Enclave Resorts, Ramada Hotel North, Days Inn, Lakefront Inn**, and **Holiday Inn.** At this point, you will be across the road from Wet 'n Wild. Area hotels include **International Inn, Rodeway Inn, Las Palmas, Continental Plaza**, and **Knight's Inn.**

Just before Kirkman Road, look for American Way on the left side, home to **Super 8 Motel, International Gateway Inn, Orlando Sunshine Resort, Comfort Inn**, and **Quality Resort.**

Enough already? Almost. To get to Universal Studios, you'll need to turn left onto Kirkman Road. Several newer motels can be found along Kirkman, including **Days Inn, Howard Johnson's Florida Center, Twin Towers**, and **Delta Court of Flags.** And there are also hotels on nearby Turkey Lake Road, including a **Comfort Suites** and **Sonesta Villa Resort.**

Along the way, we have skipped over the hotel that may be the queen of International Drive, the elegant and somewhat unusual **Peabody Orlando.** The first-class hotel, with rooms that range from about $180 to $240, and suites that climb to $1,300, includes concierge services, an Olympic swimming pool, health club, and extensive meeting and convention facilities. (There are special rates for seniors and special promotions through the year.) Restaurants include the gourmet eatery **Dux**, a Northern Italian trattoria called **Capriccio**, and the **B-Line Diner**, which is reminiscent of a 1954 burger and milk shake diner. But, we have skipped over the most unusual feature of the Peabody; while Disney has its mouse, Sea World has its whale, and Universal Studios has its shark, the Peabody has its trained ducks. Every day at 11 A.M.,

**Bunkhouse logic.** The far distant reaches of I-192 and the backroads outside the obvious tourist areas are the homes of the lowest rung on the ladder—I have seen rates as low as $19.99 for the night. Be sure to read the fine print; some prices are for single guests only, with an additional $5 or $10 for a second person. Several hotels advertise a low price and then add a "service charge" to the nightly bill.

And don't be afraid to ask to see the room you are being offered *before* you sign the register. If the room is dirty or otherwise unacceptable, you can walk away; if they refuse to show you a room when you ask, run away.

five somewhat trained mallards march down a red carpet to the lobby fountain, accompanied by the official duck master and marching to the tune of John Philip Sousa's "King Cotton" march. At 5 P.M., the procession goes the other way and the ducks return to their Royal Duck Palace. The show is free and open to visitors as well as guests. The hotel's shuttle to the theme parks, by the way, is called the Double Ducker.

## Orlando International Airport Area

The airport is located about 30 minutes away from Walt Disney World. If your plane arrives late, or if you are preparing for an early morning departure, you might want to consider staying near the airport. Room rates for "name" hotels are higher than those in the tourist areas of Kissimmee; expect to pay $60 to $125 per night in low-season and from $70 to $150 per night in high-season.

The closest hotel to your airline's arrival gate doesn't even require you to leave the airport. The **Hyatt Airport** hotel is within the main airport building; you might want to consider one night's stay there if your plane arrives very late or leaves very early.

Other hotels close to the airport can be found along Semoran Boulevard (S.R. 436), which leads into Frontage Road and McCoy Road, two service roads that run parallel to the Beeline Expressway (Route 528).

On Semoran Boulevard, look for **Park Suite Airport, Holiday Inn Airport**, and **Radisson Airport**. Frontage Road hotels include **Courtyard by Marriott Airport, Sheraton Airport**, and **The Renaissance Hotel, Orlando Airport** (formerly the Penta Hotel Airport). On McCoy Road, you'll find **Econolodge Orlando Airport** and **Days Inn Airport**.

Less than a mile north of the airport on Semoran Boulevard is an office park and hotel complex that includes the **Holiday Inn–Orlando International Airport** on T. G. Lee Boulevard and **Guest Quarters Suite Orlando** and **Orlando Airport Marriott** on Augusta National Drive.

Moving west from the airport you are heading for the South Orange Blossom Trail area.

## South Orange Blossom Trail/ Sand Lake Road/Florida Mall Area

Near the intersection of the Beeline Expressway and the combined Route 17-92 and 441—which is better known as the South Orange Blossom Trail—you will find a collection of more than a dozen brand-name motels. The further north you travel, toward Orlando, the more likely you are to find lower-priced locally owned motels. (You'll also find some "adult" bookstores and strip joints.)

We are not in any way recommending this area as an attractive place. Rumor has it that there once was grass in the neighborhood. This is strictly a place to sleep, with the exception of the intersection of South Orange Blossom Trail with Sand Lake Road (S.R. 482). Here you will find the Florida Mall, with shopping, movie theaters, and chain restaurants. Sand Lake connects to the east with McCoy Road and runs directly into the airport.

Nightly rates in this area range from about $40 to $100 in off-season and $50 to $150 per night in high-season. Some of the national chain hotels on South Orange Blossom Trail between the Beeline and Sand Lake Road include **Days Inn Midtown, Comfort Inn, Holiday Inn–Central Park, La Quinta Motor Inn–Florida Mall, Quality Inn Executive Suites, Ramada Inn South, La Quinta Inn, Sheraton Plaza Hotel, Howard Johnson's Airport,** and **Travelodge.**

## A Guide to Area Motels

Economy: $25 to $45 low-season; $45 to $65 high-season
Moderate: $45 to $75 low-season; $65 to $90 high-season
High: $75 to $125 low-season; $100 to $200 high-season
Luxury: $125 to $200 low-season; $200 to $400 high-season

### Kissimmee (1 to 10 miles from Disney)

**A-1 Motel.** 4030 West U.S. Highway 192. (407) 847-9270. Pool. Economy.

**Adventure Motel.** 4599 West Irlo Bronson Highway. (407) 396-0808. Pool. Economy.

**Ambassador Motel.** 4107 West Vine Street. (407) 847-7171. Pool. Economy.

**Best Western–Maingate.** 8600 West Irlo Bronson Highway. (407) 396-0100. Pool. Moderate.

**Budget Inn.** 307 East Vine Street. (407) 847-8010. Economy.

**Budget Inn–West.** 4686 West Irlo Bronson Highway. (407) 396-2322. Moderate.

**Casa Rosa Inn.** 4600 West U.S. Highway 192. (800) 874-1589, (407) 396-2020. Pool. Economy.

**Central Motel.** 4698 West Irlo Bronson Highway. (407) 396-2333. Pool. Economy.

**Chateau Motel II.** 3518 West Vine Street. (407) 847-3477. Economy.

**Choice Suites.** 4694 West Irlo Bronson Highway. (800) 432-0695, (407) 396-1780. Suites. Moderate.

**Comfort Inn–Maingate.** 7571 West Irlo Bronson Highway. (800) 223-1628, (407) 396-7500. Pool. Moderate.

**Comfort Suites–Kissimmee.** 4018 West Vine Street. (800) 222-2222, (407) 870-2000. Suites. Pool. Moderate.

**Comfort Suites Hotel.** 4018 West Vine Street. (407) 870-2000. Suites. Pool. Moderate.

**Continental Motel.** 4650 West Irlo Bronson Highway. (800) 344-1030, (407) 396-1030. Pool. Economy.

**Crown Motel.** 3834 West U.S. Highway 192. (407) 933-4666. Pool. Economy.

**Days Inn East of The Magic Kingdom.** 5840 West Irlo Bronson Highway. (800) 327-9126, (407) 396-7900. Pool. Moderate.

**Days Inn–North Kissimmee.** 4125 West Irlo Bronson Highway. (800) 874-5557, (407) 933-5732. Pool. Moderate.

**Days Inn–South Kissimmee.** 4104 West Vine Street. (800) 874-5557, (407) 846-4714. Pool. Moderate.

**Days Inn–West.** 7980 West Irlo Bronson Highway. (800) 327-9173, (407) 396-1000. Pool. Moderate.

**Days Suites East of Magic Kingdom.** 5820 West Irlo Bronson Highway. (800) 327-9126, (407) 396-7900. Suites. Pool. Moderate.

**Econolodge Maingate Central.** 4985 West Irlo Bronson Highway. (800) 228-2027, (407) 396-4343. Pool. Economy.

**Econolodge Maingate Hawaiian Resort.** 7514 West Irlo Bronson Highway. (800) 365-6935, (407) 396-2000. Pool. Moderate.

**Economy Inns of America–Kissimmee.** 5367 West Irlo Bronson Highway. (800) 826-0778, (407) 396-4020. Pool. Economy.

**Enterprise Motel.** 4121 West Irlo Bronson Highway. (800) 833-2655, (407) 933-1383. Pool. Economy.

**Four Winds Motel.** 4596 West Irlo Bronson Highway. (800) 826-5830, (407) 396-4011. Pool. Economy.

**Gemini Motel.** 4624 West U.S. Highway 192. (800) 336-6621, (407) 396-2151. Pool. Economy.

**Golden Link Motel.** 4914 West Irlo Bronson Highway. (800) 654-3957, (407) 396-0555. Pool. On Lake Cecile. Economy.

**Hampton Inn–Maingate.** 3104 Parkway Drive. (800) 426-7866, (407) 396-8484. Pool. Moderate.

**HoJo Inn–Maingate.** 6051 West Irlo Bronson Highway. (800) 288-4678, (407) 396-1748. Pools. Economy.

**Holiday Inn Maingate East.** 5678 West Irlo Bronson Highway. (800) 366-5437. Pool. Moderate.

**Holiday Inn Maingate.** 7300 West Irlo Bronson Highway. (407) 396-7300. Resort. Pool. High.

**Holiday Inn Maingate West.** 7601 Black Lake Road. (800) 365-6935, (407) 396-1100. Pool. Moderate.

**Holiday Villas.** 3187 Vine Street. (800) 344-3959, (407) 870-9655. Suites. Pools. High.

**Homewood Suites Maingate at the Parkway.** 3100 Parkway Boulevard. (800) 255-4543, (407) 396-2229. Suites. Pool. High.

**Howard Johnson–Fountain Park Plaza Hotel.** 5150 West Irlo Bronson Highway. (800) 327-9179, (407) 396-1111. Lakeside. Pool. Moderate.

**Howard Johnson–Maingate West Hotel.** 7600 West Irlo Bronson Highway. (800) 654-2000, (407) 396-2500. Pools. Moderate.

**Hyatt Orlando.** 6375 West Irlo Bronson Highway. (800) 233-1234, (407) 396-1234. Resort. Pools. High.

**Inns of America.** 2945 Entry Point Boulevard. (800) 826-0778, (407) 396-7743. Pool. Economy.

**Key Motel.** 4810 West Irlo Bronson Highway. (407) 396-6200. Lakefront. Pool. Economy.

**Knight's Inn.** 4669 West Irlo Bronson Highway. (800) 523-8729, (407) 396-2890. Pool. Economy.

**Knight's Inn–Maingate.** 7475 West Irlo Bronson Highway. (407) 396-4200. Economy.

**Knight's Inn–Orlando Maingate East.** 2880 Poinciana Boulevard. (407) 396-8186. Pool. Economy.

**Lakeview Motel.** 4840 West Irlo Bronson Highway. (407) 396-8282. Lakeside. Pool. Economy.

**Lambert Inn.** 410 West Vine Street. (407) 846-2015. Pool. Economy.

**Larson's Lodge–Main Gate.** 6075 West Irlo Bronson Highway. (800) 327-9074, (407) 396-6100. Pool. Moderate.

**Magic Tree Resort.** 2795 North Old Lake Wilson Road. (407) 396-2300. Suites. Pool. Moderate.

**Maple Leaf Motel.** 4647 West U.S. Highway 192. (800) 333-5477, (407) 396-0300. Pool. Economy.

**Motel 6–Eastgate.** 5731 West Irlo Bronson Highway. (407) 396-6333. Pool. Economy.

**Motel 6–West.** 7455 West Irlo Bronson Highway. (407) 396-6422. Pool. Economy.

**Oasis Inn.** 4736 West Irlo Bronson Highway. (800) 998-4748, (407) 396-0400. Pool. Economy.

**Olympic Inn.** 4669 West Irlo Bronson Highway. (800) 523-8729, (407) 396-1890. Pool. Economy.

**Orlando/Kissimmee Gateway Hilton Inn.** 7470 West Irlo Bronson Highway. (800) 327-9170, (407) 396-4400. Pool. Moderate.

**Palm Motel.** 4519 West Irlo Bronson Highway. (800) 231-6362, (407) 396-0744. Pool. Economy.

**Park Inn International Cedar Lakeside.** 4960 West Irlo Bronson Highway. (800) 327-0072, (407) 396-1376. Pool. Economy.

**Quality Inn–Lake Cecile.** 4944 West Irlo Bronson Highway. (800) 228-4427, (407) 396-4455. Lakeside. Pool. Moderate.

**Quality Inn–Maingate.** 7675 West Irlo Bronson Highway. (800) 638-7829, (407) 239-4503. Pool. Moderate.

**Quality Inn–Maingate West.** 8660 West Irlo Bronson Highway. (800) 327-9129, (407) 396-4500. Pools. Moderate.

**Quality Suites Maingate East.** 5876 West Irlo Bronson Highway. (800) 848-4148, (407) 396-8040. Suites. Pool. Moderate.

**Radisson Inn Maingate.** 7501 West Irlo Bronson Highway. (800) 333-3333, (407) 396-1400. Resort. Pool. Moderate.

**Ramada Inn.** 4559 West Irlo Bronson Highway. (800) 544-5712, (407) 396-1212. Pool. Economy.

**Ramada Inn–Orlando Westgate.** U.S. Highway 192 at U.S. Highway 27. (800) 322-2575, (813) 424-2621. Pool. Moderate.

**Ramada Limited.** 5055 West Irlo Bronson Highway. (800) 446-5669, (407) 396-2212. Pool. Moderate.

**Ramada Resort Maingate.** 2950 Reedy Creek Boulevard. (800) 365-6935, (407) 396-4466. Pool. Moderate.

**Ramada Resort Maingate at the Parkway.** 2900 Parkway Boulevard. (800) 634-4774, (407) 396-7000. Resort. Pools. Moderate.

**Record Motel.** 4651 West U.S. Highway 192. (800) 874-4555, (407) 396-8400. Pool. Economy.

**Residence Inn By Marriott on Lake Cecile.** 4786 West Irlo Bronson Highway. (800) 468-3027, (407) 396-2056. Lakeside. Suites. Pool. High.

**Rodeway Inn–Eastgate.** 5245 West Irlo Bronson Highway. (800) 228-2000, (407) 396-7700. Pool. Moderate.

**Sevilla Inn.** 4640 West Irlo Bronson Highway. (800) 367-1363, (407) 396-4135. Economy.

**Sheraton Inn Lakeside.** 7769 West Irlo Bronson Highway. (800) 848-0801, (407) 396-2222. Resort. Pool. Moderate.

**Sol Orlando Village Resort Hotel.** 4787 West Irlo Bronson Highway. (800) 292-9765. Suites. Pool. High.

**Sun Motel.** 5020 West Space Coast Parkway. (407) 396-2673. Pool. Economy.

**Thrifty Inn.** 1620 West Vine Street. (407) 847-7224. Pool. Economy.

**Traveler's Inn.** 4900 West Irlo Bronson Highway. (800) 643-8657, (407) 396-1668. Lakeside. Pool. Economy.

**Travelodge Hotel Maingate East.** 5711 West Irlo Bronson Highway. (800) 827-1128, (407) 396-4222. Resort. Pool. Moderate.

**Travelodge–Kissimmee Flags.** 2407 West Irlo Bronson Highway. (407) 933-2400. Pool. Economy.

**Travelodge Maingate West.** 7785 West Irlo Bronson Highway. (800) 634-5525, (407) 396-1828. Pool. Moderate.

**Travelodge Suites–East Gate Orange.** 5399 West Irlo Bronson Highway. (407) 396-7666. Moderate.

**Wilson World Hotel Maingate.** 7491 West Irlo Bronson Highway. (800) 669-6753, (407) 396-6000. Pool. Moderate.

## Kissimmee (10 to 15 miles from Disney)

**Best Western–Kissimmee.** 2261 East Irlo Bronson Highway. (800) 547-3278, (407) 846-2221. Pools. Economy.

**Broadway Inn.** 201 Simpson Road. (407) 846-1530. Pool. Economy.

**Choice Inn–Turnpike East.** 2050 East Irlo Bronson Highway. (407) 846-4545. Pool. Moderate.

**Colonial Motor Lodge.** 1815 West Vine Street. (800) 325-4348, (407) 847-6121. Pools. Moderate.

**Days Inn Downtown.** 4104 West Irlo Bronson Highway. (800) 647-0010, (407) 846-4714. Pool. Moderate.

**Days Inn–Kissimmee/Turnpike Exit 244.** 2095 East Irlo Bronson Highway. (800) 325-2525, (407) 846-7136. Pool. Moderate.

**East Gate Motel.** 900 East Vine Street. (407) 846-4600. Pool. Economy.

**Friendly Village Inn.** 2550 East Irlo Bronson Highway. (407) 846-6661. Pool. Moderate.

**Gator Motel.** 4580 West U.S. Highway 192. (407) 396-0127. Pool. Economy.

**Hasten Inn.** 2385 North Orange Blossom Trail. (407) 847-2583. Pool. Economy.

**Howard Johnson–Kissimmee Lodge.** 2323 U.S. Highway 192 East. (800) 654-2000, (407) 846-4900. Pool. Moderate.

**Kissimmee Inn.** 512 West Irlo Bronson Highway. (407) 847-8905. Economy.

**Riviera Motel.** 2248 East Irlo Bronson Highway. (407) 847-9494. Moderate.

## Lake Buena Vista (1 to 10 Miles from Disney)

**Days Inn Lake Buena Vista Village.** 12490 Apopka-Vineland Road. (800) 521-3297, (407) 239-4646. Pool. Moderate.

**Embassy Suites Resort Lake Buena Vista.** 8100 Lake Avenue. Suites. (407) 239-1144. Pool. High to Luxury.

**Holiday Inn Sunspree Resort Lake Buena Vista.** 13351 State Road 535. (800) 366-6299, (407) 239-4500. Pool. Moderate.

**Howard Johnson Park Square Inn and Suites.** 8501 Palm Parkway. (800) 635-8684, (407) 239-6900. Pool. Moderate.

**Hyatt Regency Grand Cypress.** One Grand Cypress Boulevard. (800) 233-1234, (407) 825-1234. Resort. Pools. Luxury.

**Marriott's Orlando World Center.** One World Center Drive. (407) 239-4200. Resort. Pool. High.

**Radisson Inn Lake Buena Vista.** 8686 Palm Parkway. (407) 239-8400. Pool. High.

**Residence Inn By Marriott Lake Buena Vista.** 8800 Meadow Creek Drive. (800) 331-3131. Suites. Pool. High.

**The Villas of Grand Cypress.** One North Jacaranda. (800) 835-7377, (407) 239-4700. Suites. Pools. Luxury.

**Vistana Resort.** 8800 Vistana Centre Drive. (800) 877-8787, (407) 239-3376. Suites. Pool. Luxury.

**Wyndham Garden Hotel Lake Buena Vista.** 8688 Palm Parkway. (800) 996-3426, (407) 239-8500. Pool. Moderate.

## International Drive and Convention Center Area (10 miles from Disney, 1 to 5 miles from Sea World and Universal Studios)

**Arnold Palmer's Bay Hill Club.** 9000 Bay Hill Boulevard, Orlando. (800) 523-5999, (407) 876-2429. Marina. Pool. Luxury.

**Best Western Buena Vista Suites.** 14450 International Drive. (800) 537-7737, (407) 239-8588. Suites. Pool. High.

**Best Western Plaza International.** 8738 International Drive, Orlando. (800) 654-7160, (407) 345-8195. Pool. High.

**The Castle Hotel–Holiday Inn.** 8620 Republic Drive, Orlando. (800) 952-2785. Pool. High.

**Clarion Plaza Hotel Orlando.** 9700 International Drive, Orlando. (800) 627-8258, (407) 352-9700. Pool. Moderate.

**Comfort Suites Orlando.** 9350 Turkey Lake Road. (800) 277-8483. Suites. Pool. Moderate.

**Courtyard By Marriott International Drive.** 8600 Austrian Court, Orlando. (800) 321-2211, (407) 351-2244. Suites. Pool. Moderate.

**Crystal Tree Inn–Super 8.** 5900 American Way, Orlando. (407) 352-8383. Pool. Economy.

**Days Inn Civic Center/Sea World.** 9990 International Drive, Orlando. (800) 224-5055, (407) 352-8700. Pool. Moderate.

**Days Inn East of Universal Studios.** 5827 Caravan Court. (800) 327-2111, (407) 351-3800. Pool. Moderate.

**Days Inn International Drive.** 7200 International Drive. (800) 224-5057, (407) 351-1200. Pool. Moderate.

**Days Inn Lakeside.** 7335 Sand Lake Road. (800) 777-3297, (407) 351-1900. Lakeside. Pool. Moderate.

**Delta Orlando Resort.** 5715 Major Boulevard. (800) 634-4763, (407) 351-3340. Pools. Moderate.

**Embassy Suites Orlando Plaza International.** 8250 Jamaican Court. (800) 327-9797, (407) 345-8250. Suites. Pool. High.

**Embassy Suites Orlando South.** 8978 International Drive. (800) 433-7275, (407) 352-1400. Suites. Pool. High.

**Enclave Suites at Orlando.** 6165 Carrier Drive. (800) 457-0077, (407) 351-1155. Suites. Pool. Moderate.

**Fairfield Inn by Marriott.** 8342 Jamaican Court. (800) 228-2800, (407) 363-1944. Pool. Moderate.

**The Floridian Hotel of Orlando.** 7299 Republic Drive. (800) 445-7299, (407) 351-5009. Pool. High.

**Gateway Inn.** 7050 Kirkman Road. (800) 327-3808, (407) 351-2000. Pool. Moderate.

**Hampton Inn at Universal Studios.** 5621 Windhover Drive. (800) 231-8395, (407) 351-6716. Pool. Moderate.

**Hampton Inn South of Universal Studios.** 7110 South Kirkman Road. (800) 763-1100, (407) 345-1112. Pool. Moderate.

**Hawaiian Super 8.** 9956 Hawaiian Court. (800) 826-4847, (407) 351-5100. Pool. Moderate.

**Hawthorn Suites Hotel.** 6435 Westwood Boulevard. (800) 527-1133, (407) 351-6600. Suites. Pool. High.

**Heritage Inn Orlando.** 9861 International Drive. (800) 447-1890, (407) 352-0008. Pool. Moderate.

**Holiday Inn Express International Drive.** 6323 International Drive. (800) 365-6935, (407) 351-4430. Pool. Moderate.

**Holiday Inn International Drive Resort.** 6515 International Drive. (800) 286-2747, (407) 351-3500. Resort. Pool. Moderate.

**Holiday Inn Universal Studios.** 5905 Kirkman Road. (800) 327-1364, (407) 351-3333. Pool. Moderate.

**Howard Johnson Lodge International Drive North.** 6603 International Drive. (800) 722-2900, (407) 351-2900. Pool. Economy.

**Howard Johnson Universal Tower.** 5905 International Drive. (800) 327-1366, (407) 351-2100. Pool. Moderate.

**Inns of America.** 8222 Jamaican Court. (800) 826-0778, (407) 345-1172. Pool. Economy.

**La Quinta International Drive.** 8300 Jamaican Court. (800) 531-5900, (407) 351-1660. Pool. Moderate.

**Las Palmas Hotel.** 6233 International Drive. (800) 327-2114, (407) 351-3900. Pool. Moderate.

**MIC Lakefront Inn.** 6500 International Drive. (407) 345-5340. Lakeside. Pool. Moderate.

**Orlando Marriott.** 8001 International Drive. (407) 351-2420. Resort. Pool. High.

**Parc Corniche Condominium Suite Hotel.** 6300 Parc Corniche Drive. (800) 446-2721, (407) 239-7100. Suites. Pool. High.

**The Peabody Hotel Orlando.** 9801 International Drive. (800) 732-2639, (407) 352-4000. Pool. Luxury.

**Quality Inn Plaza International.** 9000 International Drive. (800) 999-8585, (407) 345-8585. Pools. Economy.

**Quality Suites International Drive Area.** 7400 Canada Avenue. (800) 228-2027, (407) 363-0332. Suites. Pool. Moderate.

**Radisson Barcelo Hotel.** 8444 International Drive. (800) 304-8000, (407) 345-0505. Pool. Moderate.

**Radisson Twin Towers Hotel.** 5780 Major Boulevard. (800) 843-8693, (407) 351-1000. Pool. Moderate.

**Ramada Hotel Resort Florida Center.** 7400 International Drive. (800) 327-1363, (407) 351-4600. Pool. Moderate.

**Ramada Suites at Tango Bay.** 6800 Villa de Costa Drive. (407) 239-0707. Suites. Pools. High.

**Residence Inn By Marriott Orlando Attraction Center.** 7975 Canada Avenue. (800) 227-3978, (407) 345-0117. Suites. Pool. High.

**Sheraton World Resort.** 10100 International Drive. (800) 327-0363, (407) 352-1100. Resort. Pool. Moderate.

**Stouffer Orlando Resort.** 6677 Sea Harbor Drive. (800) 327-6677, (407) 351-5555. Resort. Pool. Luxury.

**Summerfield Suites Hotel.** 8751 Suiteside Drive. (800) 833-4353, (407) 238-0777. Suites. Pool. High.

**Travelodge Orlando Flags.** 585 International Drive. (800) 722-7462, (407) 351-4410. Pool. Economy.

**Wellesley Inn Orlando.** 5635 Windhover Drive. (800) 444-8888, (407) 345-0026. Pool. Moderate.

**Westgate Lakes.** 10000 Turkey Lake Road. (800) 424-0708, (407) 345-0000. Lakeside. Suite. Pool. High.

**Wynfield Inn Westwood.** 6263 Westwood Boulevard. (800) 346-1551, (407) 345-8000. Pool. Moderate.

## Orlando International Airport and Southeast Orlando (10 to 20 miles from Disney)

**Budget Lodge.** 3300 South Orange Blossom Trail, Orlando. (800) 352-4667, (407) 422-4521. Pool. Moderate.

**Budgetel Inn.** 2051 Consulate Drive, Orlando. (800) 428-3438, (407) 240-0500. Pool. Moderate.

**Choice Inn.** 4201 South Orange Blossom Trail, Orlando. (800) 422-9446, (407) 849-6110. Pool. Economy.

**Comfort Inn Orlando.** 8421 South Orange Blossom Trail, Orlando. (800) 327-9742, (407) 855-6060. Pool. Moderate.

**Days Inn/Lodge–Florida Mall.** 1851 West Landstreet Road. (800) 331-3954, (407) 859-7700. Pool. Economy.

**Gold Key Inn.** 7100 South Orange Blossom Trail. (407) 855-0055. Pool. Moderate.

**Guest Quarters Suite Hotel Airport.** 7550 Augusta National Drive. (407) 240-5555. Suites. Pool. Moderate.

**Holiday Inn Central Park.** 7900 South Orange Blossom Trail. (407) 859-7900. Pool. Moderate.

**Holiday Inn Orlando International Airport.** 5750 T. G. Lee Boulevard. (407) 851-6400. Pool. Moderate.

**Howard Johnson Hotel.** 8700 South Orange Blossom Trail. (800) 327-7460, (407) 851-2330. Pool. Moderate.

**Howard Johnson Plaza Hotel Orlando Airport.** 3835 McCoy Road. (407) 859-2711. Pool. Moderate.

**Hyatt Regency Orlando International Airport.** Main Terminal. (800) 233-1234, (407) 825-1234. Pool. High.

**Orlando Airport Marriott.** 7499 August National Drive. (800) 766-6752, (407) 851-9000. Resort. Pool. High.

**Quality Inn & Suites.** 4855 South Orange Blossom Trail. (800) 444-3001, (407) 851-3000. Suites. Pool. Moderate.

**Radisson Hotel Orlando Airport.** 5555 Hazeltine National Drive. (800) 333-3333, (407) 856-0100. Pool. Moderate.

**Renaissance Hotel Orlando.** 5445 Forbes Place. (800) 762-6222, (407) 240-1000. Pool. Moderate.

**Rodeway Inn Airport/Florida Mall.** 8601 South Orange Blossom Trail. (407) 859-4100. Pool. Moderate.

**Sheraton Plaza Hotel at the Florida Mall.** 1500 Sand Lake Road. (800) 231-7883, (407) 859-1500. Pool. High.

**Travelodge Orlando Central Park.** 7101 South Orange Blossom Trail. (800) 578-7878, (407) 851-4300. Pool. Economy.

## West Orlando, Downtown Orlando, East Orlando (10 to 20 miles from Disney)

**Best Western Orlando West.** 2014 West Colonial Drive. (800) 645-6386, (407) 841-8600. Moderate.

**Buckets Bermuda Bay Hideaway.** 1825 North Mills Avenue. (800) 929-2428, (407) 896-4111. Lakeside. Pool. High.

**Colonial Plaza Inn.** 2801 East Colonial Drive. (800) 321-2323, (407) 894-2741. Pool. Moderate.

**Holiday Inn at the Orlando Arena.** 304 West Colonial Drive. (800) 523-3405, (407) 843-8700. Pool. Moderate.

**Holiday Inn Express–Midtown.** 3330 West Colonial Drive. (407) 299-6710. Pool. Economy.

**Omni Orlando Hotel at Centroplex.** 400 West Livingston Street. (407) 843-6664. Pool. Moderate.

**Radisson Plaza Hotel Orlando.** 60 South Ivanhoe Boulevard. (800) 333-3333, (407) 425-4455. Pool. High.

**Ramada Orlando Central.** 3200 West Colonial Drive. (800) 828-5270. Pools. Moderate.

## Altamonte Springs, Winter Park (25 to 30 miles from Disney)

**Days Inn/Lodge of Orlando.** 450 Douglas Avenue. (800) 327-2221, (407) 862-7111. Pools. Economy.

**Days Inn–Orlando North/Altamonte.** 235 South Wymore Road. Near Orlando Sports Arena. (800) 325-2525, (407) 862-2800. Pool. Economy.

**Fairfield Inn Winter Park.** 951 Wymore Road. (800) 228-2800, (407) 539-1955. Pool. Economy.

**Hampton Inn Orlando–Altamonte Springs.** 151 North Douglas Avenue. (800) 848-1436, (407) 869-9000. Pool. Moderate.

**Hilton Hotel and Towers–Altamonte Springs.** 350 South Northlake Boulevard. (800) 247-1985, (407) 830-1985. Pool. High.

**Holiday Inn Orlando–Altamonte Springs.** 230 West Highway 436. (800) 242-6862, (407) 862-4455. Pool. Moderate.

**Holiday Inn Orlando–Winter Park.** 626 Lee Road. (407) 645-5600. Pool. Moderate.

**Langford Resort Hotel.** 300 East New England Avenue, Winter Park. (407) 644-3400. Pool. Moderate.

**LaQuinta Inn.** 150 South Westmonte Drive. (800) 531-5900, (407) 788-1411. Suites. Pool. Moderate.

**Orlando North Hilton.** 350 South North Lake Boulevard, Altamonte Springs. (800) 445-8667, (407) 830-1985. Pool. High.

**Sheraton Orlando North Hotel.** 600 North Lake Destiny Drive. (800) 628-6660, (407) 660-9000. Pool. High.

**Sundance Inn.** 205 West Highway 436. (800) 327-5560, (407) 862-8200. Pool. Economy.

## Apopka (25 to 35 miles from Disney)

**Budget Inn.** 429 East Main Street. (407) 886-2092. Pool. Economy.

**Crosby's Motor Inn.** 1440 West Orange Blossom Trail. (407) 886-3220. Pool. Moderate.

**HoJo Inn.** 1317 South Orange Blossom Trail. (407) 886-1010. Moderate.

**Knight's Inn–Apopka.** 228 West Main Street. (800) 553-2666, (407) 880-3800. Pool. Economy.

## Clermont (10 to 30 miles from Disney)

**Citrus Sun Family Resort.** 20384 U.S. Highway 27 at Florida Turnpike. (904) 429-4111. Pool. Moderate.

**Flagship Inn.** 20349 U.S. Highway 27. (904) 429-2163. Pools. Economy.

**Holiday Inn Express–Clermont.** 20329 North U.S. Highway 27. (407) 429-3660. Moderate.

**Orlando Vacation Resort.** 1403 U.S. Highway 27 South. (800) 874-9064, (904) 394-6171. Continental. Pool. Moderate.

**Vacation Village.** South U.S. Highway 27. (800) 962-9969, (904) 394-4091. Lake cottages. Pool. Moderate.

## Davenport (10 miles from Disney)

**Best Western–Ted Williams Inn.** Interstate 4 at U.S. Highway 27. (813) 424-2511. Pool. Moderate.

**Budget Inn–Davenport.** 3800 U.S. Highway 27 North. (813) 424-2444. Pool. Economy.

**Comfort Inn–Maingate South.** 5510 U.S. Highway 27 North. (800) 255-4386, (813) 424-2811. Pool. Moderate.

**Days Inn–South of the Magic Kingdom.** 2425 Frontage Road, U.S. Highway 27. (800) 424-4999, (813) 424-2596. Pool. Economy.

**Howard Johnson–South of Disney.** Interstate 4 at U.S. Highway 27. (800) 654-2000, (813) 424-2311. Pool. Moderate.

**Motel 6.** Interstate 4 at U.S. Highway 27 North. (813) 424-2521. Pool. Economy.

**Red Carpet Inn.** 10736 U.S. Highway 27. (800) 251-1962, (813) 424-2450. Pool. Moderate.

## Fern Park (30 miles to Disney)

**Comfort Inn–Fern Park.** 8245 South U.S. Highway 17-92. (800) 221-2222, (407) 339-3333. Pool. Moderate.

**Holiday Inn Express–Fern Park.** 7400 South U.S. Highway 17-92. (800) 446-6900, (407) 339-4408. Pool. Economy.

# Campgrounds and RV Parks

**Disney's Fort Wilderness Resort.** Lake Buena Vista. (407) 934-7639. Within Walt Disney World in 740 acres of woods.

**Fort Summit Camping Resort.** I-4 and U.S. 27, Baseball City. (800) 424-1880, (813) 424-1880. 300 sites. Shuttle to Disney. Pool.

**Kissimmee/Orlando KOA.** 4771 West Irlo Bronson Highway, Kissimmee. (800) 331-1453, (407) 396-2400. Shuttle.

**Tropical Palms Resort.** 2650 Holiday Trail, Kissimmee. (800) 647-2567.

**Yogi Bear's Jellystone Camp Resort.** 9200 Turkey Lake Road, Orlando. (800) 776-9644, (407) 351-4394.

## Eating for Less

As a tourist magnet, the Orlando area offers just about every type of restaurant from fancy to ordinary, from American to European to Asian. (The largest single collection of foreign restaurants can be found within the World Showcase pavilions of Epcot Center.) But the emphasis seems to be on "family" restaurants. If there is a single major franchise fast-food restaurant in America that is not represented in the Orlando area, we don't know about it.

The biggest collections of fast-food restaurants can be found on I-192 (Irlo Bronson Highway) and International Drive. If you're really into deep-fried grease, you can probably find seven different McDonald's or Burger Kings or Pizza Huts, one for every night of a week's stay.

Somewhat unique to the South are the "all-you-can-eat" buffets which usually offer breakfasts in the range of $2 to $5, lunches from $4 to $8, and dinners from $6 to $12. Chains include Ponderosa Steak House, Sizzler, Shoney's, and Gilligan's.

# WALT DISNEY WORLD RESORT

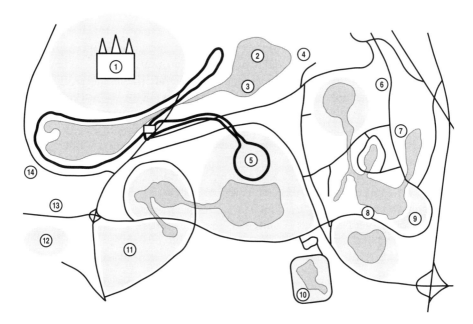

1. Magic Kingdom
2. Discovery Island
3. River Country
4. Osprey Ridge Golf Course
5. Epcot
6. Eagle Pines Golf Course
7. Lake Buena Vista Golf Course
8. Pleasure Island
9. Disney Village Marketplace
10. Typhoon Lagoon
11. Disney-MGM Studios
12. Blizzard Beach
13. Palm Golf Course
14. Magnolia Golf Course

# Chapter 4

# Walt Disney World: You've Got to Have a Ticket

As if you don't already face enough decisions—dates, airlines, hotels, and more—there is also the matter of those little pieces of cardboard called admission tickets. Actually, they are not all that little: a family of four visiting Walt Disney World for five days could easily spend (are you ready for this?) nearly $700 for daily tickets. Add in a day at Universal Studios and a day at Sea World, and the cost is approaching $1,000.

But, like everything else we write about in this *Econoguide*, there are various ways to analyze the available options. The very best thing you can do is to sit down with a piece of paper and make a plan *before* you leave for Florida. Don't wait until you are standing at the ticket counter with a hundred people eyeing your back, your children tugging at your sleeves, and tears in your eyes to decide on your ticket strategy.

Instead, fit your plans to one of the available ticket packages. And don't overlook the money-saving strategies we discuss here—or the discount coupons for Universal Studios, Sea World, and other attractions you'll find in the back of this book.

**Home delivery.** Tickets can be purchased by mail by sending a check, made payable to the Walt Disney World Company, to Box 10030, Lake Buena Vista, FL 32830-0030. Mark the envelope "Attention: Ticket Mail Order," and include an additional $2 for the privilege. Allow as much as six weeks for processing. We'd advise calling Walt Disney World first to check if ticket prices have changed: (407) 824-4321.

You can purchase tickets by phone using credit cards by calling the same number.

And, you can also purchase tickets at Disney Stores in many malls around the country.

## First the Bad News

Remember what we said about Walt Disney World being a gigantic vacuum aimed at your wallet? Well, the great sucking sound begins at the ticket counter.

**Walt Disney World
1996 Prices**
(Prices include tax and
are subject to change.)
**1-DAY/
1-PARK-ONLY TICKET**
Adult     $40.81
Child     $32.86
(Ages 3 to 9.)
**4-DAY
PARK-HOPPER PASS**
Adult     $152.64
Child     $121.90
   Four days of
admissions to the Magic
Kingdom, Epcot, and
Disney-MGM Studios
with park-hopping
privileges. No
expiration date.
**4-DAY VALUE PASS**
Adult     $136.74
Child     $109.18
   Four separate
admissions to the Magic
Kingdom, Epcot, and
Disney-MGM Studios.
No expiration date.
**5-DAY WORLD-
HOPPER PASS**
Adult     $207.76
Child     $166.42
   Personal pass allowing
park-hopping for five
days; no expiration date.
Also allows unlimited
admission for seven
consecutive days to
Pleasure Island, Typhoon
Lagoon, River Country,
Blizzard Beach, and
Discovery Island.

If one of the Disney ticket plans matches your schedule exactly, you're in luck and you'll save some money. But if the plans are not exactly what you need, you *could* end up wasting money instead of saving.

All ticket prices and limitations listed here were in effect in mid-1996 and are subject to change. In recent years, Disney has adjusted prices in early spring; the "adjustments" have almost always been upward.

As in the past, tickets have no expiration date; if you have leftover days on a pass, you can take it with you and use it the next time you visit the park. And since park ticket prices seem to be on an inexorable march upward, you may end up with a small return on your investment when you return in later seasons.

In recent years, though, Disney has made it difficult to use one money-saving trick. The tickets have always been "non-transferable," but Disney had no way to enforce that rule. It used to be that you could give your unused tickets to a friend or other family member, or sell your unused entrance passes to one of the many "gray market" ticket booths in the vicinity of the park. The gray marketeers would buy and sell extra tickets at a discount.

In 1994, Disney began imprinting a computer-generated picture of the ticketholder onto the multi-day "Hopper" passes, ending the loophole. Why would Disney do this? There's only one reason we can think of: money. Some percentage of unused multi-day tickets will be lost or simply never used, and that represents pure profit for Disney.

And as if all this wasn't complicated enough, in 1996 Walt Disney World began a changeover to the electronic age with the issuance of magnetically encoded cards for entry to the parks. Electronic turnstiles have been installed at park entrances; put your card into the reader on the front and then grab it when the gate opens. Disney plans a high-tech hand-recognition device or other scheme to pair the card to its rightful owner.

Old tickets with unexpired admission will still be honored.

You may still be able to resell certain types of tickets, like the Value Pass, and the gray marketeers may be able to obtain discount tickets from other sources including tour packagers. Be sure to read the fine print on the tickets at the time you make a purchase.

One gray marketeer even offered to purchase my partially used World-Hopper pass with my picture on it. The offer was not a very good one: $10 per day for a pass worth about $38 per day. I suspect they would resell the ticket to some visitor willing to take a chance that the ticket taker would not check the picture very closely.

And though Disney does not advertise this, Guest Relations at Magic Kingdom, Epcot, or Disney-MGM Studios will allow you to update a World Hopper ticket on a return visit. It works like this: let's say you visit the Magic Kingdom in 1996 and use three of your five day passes to one of the major theme parks and visit Pleasure Island and the water parks several days during your week's stay. After a week has passed, your admission privileges to Pleasure Island and the water parks have expired but the theme park tickets are valid forever. Six months or a year or whenever you return to Walt Disney World, visit Guest Relations with your tickets and ask to update the passes. You will receive credit for the unused theme park days against a new World Hopper ticket.

**Walt Disney World 1996 Prices**
**ANNUAL PASSPORT**

| | |
|---|---|
| Adult | $250.16 |
| Renewal | $227.90 |
| Child | $217.30 |
| Renewal | $195.04 |

Includes 12 months of unlimited admission to Disney-MGM Studios, Epcot, and the Magic Kingdom during regular operating hours, free parking, and reduced prices on special events such as the Night of Joy, and Mickey's Very Merry Christmas Party, plus discounts to selected resorts and restaurants. Annual passports can be upgraded to include use of River Country, Discovery Island, Pleasure Island, and Typhoon Lagoon. Contact Guest Relations for prices.

There is a small caveat here: the credit you will receive will be based on the value of the day passes at the time you bought the original ticket. If day tickets have gone up in price, you will have to make up the difference in price.

## Walt Disney World Ticket Plans

**One-Day/One-Park Ticket.** Good in one park only. You will be allowed to exit and return to the park on the same day—be sure to have your hand stamped—but cannot go to another park or ride the monorail or bus system to another park.

**Four-Day Park-Hopper Pass.** Good in all three parks for any four days. You can go from one park to another on the same day—be sure to have your hand stamped. The four passes do not have to be used consecutively, and they are valid forever. Includes unlimited use of Walt Disney World transportation system.

**Four-Day Value Pass.** This ticket offers a slight reduction in cost at the price of a bit of flexibility: it offers one day at Magic Kingdom, one day at Epcot, one day at Disney-MGM Studios, and a fourth day at your choice of one park; you cannot go from one park to another on the same day.

**Five-Day World-Hopper Pass.** Good in all three parks for any five days.

**Walt Disney World
1996 Prices
PREMIUM ANNUAL
PASSPORT**

| | |
|---|---|
| Adult | $348.74 |
| Renewal | $315.88 |
| Child | $306.34 |
| Renewal | $278.78 |

Includes 12 months of unlimited admission to Disney-MGM Studios, Epcot, the Magic Kingdom, Pleasure Island, Typhoon Lagoon, River Country, Discovery Island, and Blizzard Beach during regular operating hours, free parking, and reduced prices on special events such as the Night of Joy, and Mickey's Very Merry Christmas Party, plus discounts to selected resorts and restaurants. Holders can also use a special advance reservation system for restaurants.

You can go from one park to another on the same day—be sure to have your hand stamped. The five passes do not have to be used consecutively and are valid forever. Also valid for admission to Typhoon Lagoon, River Country, Discovery Island, and Pleasure Island for seven days from the first use of the pass. Also includes unlimited use of Walt Disney World transportation system.

**Annual Passport.** Valid for unlimited admission to all three parks during regular operating hours, for one year from the issue date. The annual pass is priced at about the equivalence of six day passes. The pass also includes free parking and special advance reservation privileges for restaurants and shows.

You can "add on" annual access to other parks for additional charges. For example, adding a year's worth of admissions to Pleasure Island to an Annual Pass will cost about $28.

**Premium Annual Passport.** The gold ticket at Walt Disney World, this pass adds Pleasure Island and all of the water parks for a year's time; also included is free parking and some special privileges for reservations.

**Resort Guest Special Tickets.** Guests at Disney-owned or -operated hotels within the park can purchase special **Length of Stay** passes based on hotel reservations, and good from the moment you arrive until midnight of the day you check out. These plans, priced slightly lower than those offered to visitors, include various combinations of access to theme parks and other attractions; the plans change over the course of the year, depending on current marketing efforts. They don't always make economic sense: be sure to compare the package price to individual tickets or other packages that might better fit your plans. And be sure to compare any pass for a lengthy stay against the cost of an Annual Passport.

## An Econoguide to Disney Tickets

Which of the three types of tickets should you buy? There is no one answer because no two families follow the same schedule on a trip to Central Florida.

Obviously, if your plans call for a full week's stay and you plan to visit every corner of the park—from the Magic Kingdom to Epcot to MGM Studios to Pleasure Island at night, and Blizzard Beach, Typhoon Lagoon, River Country, and Discovery Island on hot afternoons, then the Five-Day World Hopper Pass makes the most sense. You can visit multiple parks on the same day with a multi-day pass; with the five-day pass you can also make unlimited, repeat visits to the water parks and Pleasure Island.

If you are in town for a weekend and plan only a two-day visit, you'll probably want to buy just single admission tickets.

Now, here's a more complex decision: suppose you plan to visit Disney theme parks for four days and also want to go to Blizzard Beach, Typhoon Lagoon, Pleasure Island, Discovery Island, or River Country or all of them during your stay. It *may* make more sense to buy a five-day pass. Add up the value of admission to the secondary parks you will visit and subtract them from the cost of the pass. Then you'll have to decide what to do with the unused ticket.

What do you do if your child graduates to adult ticket status while you still have days left on your non-expiring multi-day ticket? Go to Guest Services where you can apply the value of the ticket against a new adult ticket. Or, tell your 11-year-old to look like a 9-year-old at the ticket turnstile.

And then, here's another interesting plan. We call it the Annual Pass 11-month Year: Suppose you know that a yearly visit to Walt Disney World is in the cards for the next several years. Here's a way to save hundreds of dollars over a one-year period: purchase an Annual Pass and then schedule two trips within 365 days. For example, visit Orlando once in April of 1996 for Spring Break, and then come back just short of a year later for Presidents' Week in February of 1997.

How much money could you save with an 11-month year? Let's say you visit Walt Disney World for five days at the theme parks, buying a Five-Day World-Hopper Pass. At 1996 prices, this visit would cost $748.36 for a family of two adults and two children. Come back again in 1997, and you'll pay at least $748.36 more for another set of passes: total ticket cost is about $1,496.72 for the two visits.

Now consider annual passes, good for one year from the date of first use. Passes for two adults and two children at 1996 rates would cost $907.36.

**PLEASURE ISLAND**
$17.97 after 7 P.M.; includes admission to all clubs and performances. Children under the age of 18 must be accompanied by a parent and will not be allowed in some of the clubs.

Annual Passport: $43.41; Annual Passport renewal: $36.94.

**BLIZZARD BEACH ONE-DAY TICKET**
Adult     $25.39
Child     $19.03

**BLIZZARD BEACH ANNUAL PASSPORT**
Adult     $90.05
Child     $72.03

**TYPHOON LAGOON ONE-DAY TICKET**
Adult     $25.39
Child     $19.03

**TYPHOON LAGOON ONE-DAY TICKET**
(After 4 P.M. in Summer)
Adult     Check at booth
Child     Check at booth

**TYPHOON LAGOON ANNUAL PASSPORT**
Adult     $90.05
Child     $72.03

**RIVER COUNTRY ONE-DAY TICKET**
Adult     $15.64
Child     $12.19

**RIVER COUNTRY ONE-DAY TICKET**
(After 3 P.M. in Summer)
Adult     Check at booth
Child     Check at booth

**RIVER COUNTRY ANNUAL PASSPORT**
Adult     $58.56
Child     $58.56

Your potential savings under this example: $589.36. In fact, the savings can be even higher if you include the value of free parking, included in the price of the Annual Passes.

## Buying Discount Tickets

Yes, you can get Disney tickets for wholesale. But it takes a bit of doing. There are two routes to discounts: an unofficial, unauthorized path and an official path.

First the **official** ways:

1. Book an all-inclusive hotel and park admission package from the Walt Disney Company. Packages include the top-of-the-line "World Adventure," "Grand Plan," and "Admiral Plan" packages, which offer rooms, tickets, use of recreational facilities, and breakfast, lunch, and dinner every day at the hotel or within the parks. Other plans that include some or all meals are "Family Vacation Fun," "Festival Magic," "Resort Romance," and "Camping Adventure."

Be sure to figure the true value of the package. Ask for the regular room rate, and then add in the value—to you—of recreation and meals to determine if there is a real discount.

2. Book a hotel and admission package from one of the hotels outside of the park. Again, find out the regular hotel charge to determine if your admission tickets are being offered at a discount.

3. Use an admission pass discount such as the **Magic Kingdom Club,** described later.

4. Look for very occasional promotions by the Walt Disney Company through some of the official tourist agencies in the Orlando area. One place to check is the Orlando/Orange County Convention & Visitors Bureau, which operates an office at 8445 International Drive. Write to the bureau at P.O. Box 690355, Orlando, FL 32869.

5. Buy tickets through AAA or other travel associations or through credit card companies that may offer slightly discounted tickets.

**OTHER TICKETS AND PRICING**
Adult    Child
(10+)    (3 to 9)
**Guided Tour** (with appropriate theme park admission—available at Magic Kingdom and Epcot Center only)
$5.00    $3.50
**Transportation** (included in multi-day tickets and Annual Passes)
$2.50    $2.50
**Day Guest Parking**
Autos                    $5.00 per day (free to guests at WDW hotels)
Camper/Trailer           $6.00 per day
Shuttle/Limousine        $7.00 per day
Bus                      $10.00 per day
**Kennel**
Day                      $6.00
Overnight                $11.00 (available to resort guests only)

## Unofficially Yours

Now, a few unofficial ways.

1. Buy your tickets from one of the official tourist and convention offices. They may have discount tickets directly from Walt Disney World, or they may have some tickets that have come through the gray market such as extra supplies from hotel packages.

2. Buy your tickets from one of the ticket brokers along tourist roads described above. You'll likely be offered passes at 10 to 20 percent off the list price. Their sources include hotel packages as well as any tickets they may have bought from visitors. Be sure to examine the tickets carefully to make sure they are valid. We'd advise against trying to use one of the "picture" tickets that is not yours; but you may find some older and still valid tickets without the photos. The safest way to pay for anything is with a credit card, next safest is with a personal check, and least safe is with cash.

**A mark, a yen, a buck, or a pound.** Ticket booths at Walt Disney World accept American Express, MasterCard, Visa, traveler's checks, personal checks with ID, cash, pennies, children . . . just kidding about the kids.

Lines at the ticket booths are usually within reasonable limits within half an hour before and after opening time; lines will build at mid-morning to as much as 15 minutes. You can save some time by purchasing tickets at all Disney-owned or -operated hotels and many large area resorts.

## Joining the Club

Think of the Magic Kingdom Club and the Magic Years Club as the Mickey Mouse Club for adults and seniors.

The **Magic Kingdom Club Gold Card** offers a small discount on admission tickets to Disneyland, Walt Disney World, Disneyland Paris, and Tokyo Disneyland. There are also discounts to Walt Disney World attractions including Pleasure Island, River Country, Typhoon Lagoon, Blizzard Beach, and Discovery Island. There are also some discounts from regular prices at the more expensive restaurants in the Magic Kingdom, Epcot, and Disney-MGM Studios resorts.

Other benefits include discounts on selected Disney Resort hotels, at The Disney Store, at Disney Village Marketplace and Pleasure Island shops, and special rates with National Car Rental.

In 1996, a two-year membership sold for $65 for a family. It all sounds very good—and it might be—for a family that is serious about all things Disney. We'd estimate the card makes sense if you spend $500 or more over a two-year period on flights, rooms, and meals that are covered by the card. Note that you may end up spending more money on a Disney room than you would outside one of the parks.

To join the Magic Kingdom Club, call (800) 413-4763.

As with any "deal," be sure to compare prices you could obtain by yourself. For example, the airfare discount generally applies to full ticket price, and excursion fares may be cheaper; the hotel discounts may still be more costly than a direct booking at a lower-priced hotel, even another Disney property.

## Tickets for Other Attractions

**A golden goose is dead.** In 1993, the Walt Disney Company discontinued another of the little insider secrets, the discounts on tickets, accommodations, and other perks it used to offer to all 800,000 or so of the stockholders in the company. All it took was as little as one share, and according to Disney as many as 30 percent of the company's new record owners in 1992 bought only one share.

In its place, shareholders can now purchase a Magic Kingdom Club Gold Card at a $10 discount, which is much less of a deal.

**When it rains . . .** you will get wet. Most of the Magic Kingdom, Epcot, and Disney-MGM Studios are out in the open, which can be a bit of a problem in one of Florida's patented sudden downpours. However, rain rarely lasts all day and there are lots of canopied walkways and shops to duck in. Most of the major shops magically sprout stacks of thin plastic ponchos on wet days.

The other attractions in the Orlando area are much more willing to strike a deal. You can usually purchase slightly discounted tickets for Universal Studios, Sea World, many dinner theaters, and other entertainment from brokers in hotels and on tourist strips. Shop around before you buy, and examine the tickets carefully.

And be sure to check out the many discount coupons from attractions that you will find in the back of this book.

## Free Tickets!

Two Disney Tickets for $5! Free Universal Studios Passes!

Impossible? Not at all.

Completely free? Well . . .

You can't help but notice the come-ons as you travel in the prime tourist areas of Irlo Bronson Highway (Highway 192) in Kissimmee and International Drive in Orlando. And in many hotels, you'll be assaulted in the lobby.

We've already discussed the discount ticket deals, available from brokers who have tickets available for a few dollars off the list price for dinner theaters and some of the theme parks other than at Walt Disney World. (You can also use the discount coupons in the back of this book for Universal Studios, Sea World, Busch Gardens, Splendid China, Cypress Gardens, and a host of other attractions.)

No, here we are talking about those seemingly impossible offers of free or near-free tickets. Here's the deep secret behind them: they are come-ons for one of the dozens of timesharing or similar real estate schemes in and around the theme parks.

The pitch works something like this: "All you've got to do is go to this wonderful resort, eat a free breakfast, and listen to our two-hour presentation about our timesharing/interval ownership/vacation club. Even if you don't buy, we'll give you two free tickets to Walt Disney World. There's no pressure."

Well, it's all true, except for the "no pressure" part.

You'll start by filling out a simple form at the ticket counter. There are usually a few qualifying questions to see if you have sufficient income to make a timesharing purchase—the threshold is usually pretty low, around $30,000 per year in annual income. And then you'll likely be asked to make a "deposit" of about $20 to hold your place at the presentation. The deposit will be returned along with your "free" tickets. (There are two reasons for the deposit: the deposit is the commission earned by the ticket broker for delivering you to the sales group, as well as an inducement to make sure you show up for your appointment.)

I've sat through a few of the presentations and have earned my free tickets and the return of my deposit, just as promised. I've also had to fight off some pretty insistent sales pitches. Sometimes the two or nearly three hours of my time have been worth the $75 value of a pair of tickets; sometimes I've felt like it would be worth $100 to pay the sales people to let me escape before the time was up.

The typical pitch tries to compare the amount of money you have spent on your hotel room to the annual cost of a mortgage for a timeshare. The operations typically sell a specific week, or period of weeks. The rate ranges from about $10,000 to $25,000; there are also additional charges for maintenance, owner's groups, and other expenses.

Some of the operations are more upright than others. Some of the major hotel operations including Marriott and Hilton have built some spectacular buildings in and around Orlando, and their pitches are very polished. Some smaller companies may offer properties and sales pitches that may be less polished. Either way, expect all sorts of pressure: buy today for a special offer; buy today so that I won't waste my time; buy today or you're crazy.

Should you consider buying a timeshare? Most hard-nosed financial experts consider them to be less-than-wonderful investments. They talk about the fact that you may be locked into a location or time period that may not always work with your changing lifestyle. They worry about unexpected expenses—if the elevator fails or the swimming pool leaks or other major expenses occur, the bill will come to the homeowners. And finally, there is not a very good history of increasing monetary value for timeshare purchases.

One way to check on the value of timeshares is to go to the resale market. There are several agencies in and around Orlando that specialize

**Mickey'll take Manhattan.** The Magic Kingdom opened on October 1, 1971. Walt Disney World includes 28,000 acres or some 43 square miles of land, making it about the size of San Francisco or twice the size of Manhattan.

The Magic Kingdom takes up about 107 acres; its parking lot is even bigger, at 125 acres. (By way of comparison, Disneyland occupies just 80 acres in California.)

Here are a few more measurements of the elements of Walt Disney World: Epcot Center, 300 acres including a 40-acre lake; Disney-MGM Studios Theme Park, 154 acres; Ft. Wilderness, 600 acres; Dixie Landings/ Port Orleans, 325 acres; Disney Wilderness Preserve, 8,500 acres.

And the new Disney's Animal Kingdom will occupy 500 acres when it opens in a few years.

in unloading timeshares from private parties. If there is a big disparity between buying from the developer and buying from a reseller, or if the reseller has an unexpectedly large inventory of shares for sale, you should be very suspicious.

In any case, make sure you consult your accountant or attorney before signing anything.

# Chapter 5

# Disney World (and Universal Studios) with Children

Doesn't the title of this section sound ridiculously obvious? Well, yes and no: the fact is that for many kids a visit to Walt Disney World is the biggest thing that has ever happened to them—and although it almost always will be the most wonderful vacation they've ever had, there are also special concerns for youngsters and their parents.

Here are 10 suggestions to make a trip with young children go well.

1. Involve the children in the planning. Obtain maps and brochures and study them at the dinner table; read sections of this book together. Work together on a schedule for the places you want to go on each day.

2. Draw up the "rules" for the visit and make sure each child understands them and agrees with them. The basic rule in our family is that our young children always have to be within an arm's length of mom or dad.

3. Study and understand the height and age minimums for some of the more active rides at the parks. Don't build up expectations of your 41-inch-tall child for a ride that requires you to be 42 inches in height. (Did we hear someone say something about lift pads in shoes? Just remember that the rules are there to protect children from injury.)

4. Come to a family agreement on financial matters. Few parents can afford to buy everything a child demands; even if you could, you probably wouldn't want to. Consider giving your children a special allowance they can spend at the park; encourage them to wait a day or two into the trip so that they don't hit bottom before they find the souvenir they really want to take home.

5. When you arrive at the park—and as you move through various areas—always pick a place to meet if you become separated. Landmarks include Cinderella's Castle or the carrousel in the Magic Kingdom, Spaceship Earth in Epcot, the Chinese Theater in Disney-MGM Studios, and the Back to the Future steam locomotive or the Gak fountain at Universal Studios. You should also have a backup plan—instruct your children to find a uniformed park attendant if they are lost and plan on checking with attendants yourself if you have misplaced a child.

You might want to attach a name tag to youngsters (available at Guest Services in the parks if you don't have your own) or put a piece of paper with your name and hotel in your child's pockets. Some parents even issue their kids walkie-talkie radios and keep one in their own pockets!

6. For much of the year, the sun in Central Florida is quite strong. Keep your kids (and yourself) under hats and behind sunscreens, especially at midday. You may want to bring bottles of water for the entire family—it's a lot cheaper than soda at the snack bars, and better, too.

7. You are not supposed to bring food into the park. There are picnic tables just outside the gates, and you can leave lunch in your car and come out for a break—this is easier at Epcot or Disney-MGM Studios because of the proximity of the parking lot to the park. Then again, we've never seen a paying guest being searched for hidden sandwiches inside the park.

8. A good strategy with youngsters, especially if you are staying inside the park or nearby, is to arrive early and then leave at lunchtime for a quick nap or a swim; return at dusk to enjoy the evening at the park. You'll miss the hottest and most crowded part of the day and probably enjoy yourself much more. Be sure to have your hands stamped when you leave the park and hold onto your tickets (including your parking pass) if you intend to return.

9. Although you can bring your own stroller into the park, it is also easy to rent one for the day at the park. Park the stroller near the *exit* to the attraction so that it is waiting when you come out. Don't leave any valuables with the stroller. If you move from one Disney park to another during a single day, show your receipt at the new park to obtain a stroller when you arrive.

10. Most restrooms (male and female) include changing tables. You can also purchase diapers and even formula at Baby Services or City Hall in the Magic Kingdom, at Baby Services or Earth Station in Epcot, or at Guest Services in Disney-MGM Studios. There are also places set aside for nursing mothers.

## Dad, I Promise . . .

One of the best things about going to Walt Disney World with kids is that a resourceful parent should be able to milk the trip for at least three weeks of "If you don't behave right now, I'm not taking you to Florida" threats.

My even-more-resourceful preteen son Willie went even further and came up with his own contract. Call it:

### The Ten Commandments of Walt Disney World for Kids

I. Thou shalt not leave thy parents' sight.

II. Thou shalt not go on twister rides after a meal.

III. Thou shalt not complain about the lines.

IV. Thou shalt not fight with thy sister or brother.

V. Thou shalt not ask to buy something at the shops
that costs more than the admission ticket.

VI. Thou shall enjoy any of the boring things
that Mom and Dad want to see.

VII. Thou shall stand still so Dad can take at least one picture.

VIII. Thou shalt not pester the characters to talk.
IX. Thou shalt not sing, "It's a Small World After All"
more than 16 times in a row.
X. Thou shall go on at least one educational ride even if it has a long line.

## A Kid's Eye View of the Best of Walt Disney World

What are the best attractions for youngsters (3 to 10 years old)? Well, you know your particular child's interests and fears better than anyone else, but here are some of the more common favorites and a few warnings.

### Magic Kingdom

Dumbo, the Flying Elephant
Cinderella's Golden Carrousel
It's a Small World
Jungle Cruise
Pirates of the Caribbean*
Peter Pan's Flight
Mad Tea Party**
Mickey's Toontown Fair
Country Bear Jamboree
Tom Sawyer's Island
Grand Prix Raceway***
Tropical Serenade (Tiki Birds)
Splash Mountain***

### Epcot

Journey Into Imagination
Food Rocks (The Land)*
Universe of Energy*
Wonders of Life****
The Living Seas
River of Time (Mexico)

### Disney-MGM Studios

Jim Henson's Muppet*Vision 3D 4D*
Honey, I Shrunk the Kids Movie Set Adventure
Voyage of the Little Mermaid*
The Great Movie Ride*
Beauty and the Beast Show
Teenage Mutant Ninja Turtles Show

### Universal Studios Florida

Animal Actors Stage
Fievel's Playground
The Funtastic World of Hanna-Barbera**
E.T. Adventure

Earthquake—The Big One*/****
Ghostbusters*
Jaws*/****
Dynamite Nights Stunt Spectacular*
Wild, Wild, Wild West Stunt Show*
Back to the Future****
Notes:
*Loud noises and special effects (pirates, skeletons, beasts) may startle unprepared children.
**Can make some children dizzy.
***Adult must accompany small children.
****DISNEY-MGM STUDIOS: Body Wars, Cranium Command may be too intense for very young. EPCOT: Parental guidance advised for "The Making of Me." UNIVERSAL STUDIOS: Back to the Future is too intense for some children; use your judgment based on your knowledge of your own child. Jaws and Earthquake have some wild effects but most children find them fun. MAGIC KINGDOM: Splash Mountain is charming, but it does include one drop over a waterfall; it's not as scary as it looks, but some children may not be ready.

### Special Programs for Young Children

**KinderCare** offers a "learning while playing" program for children from one year old through 12 on weekends from 6 A.M. to 8 P.M. Call (407) 827-5437.

The **Neverland Club** at Disney's Polynesian Resort hotel offers a Peter Pan–theme evening of activities, every night from 5 P.M. to midnight. It includes a buffet dinner and live entertainment, for children from 3 to 12. Call (407) 824-2170 for reservations.

At the **Mouseketeer Clubhouse** at Disney's Grand Floridian Beach Resort Hotel and at Disney's Contemporary Resort, there are videos and games. The maximum stay is four hours during the period from 4:30 P.M. to midnight; no meals are served, but snacks are available. Call (407) 824-1000 for the Contemporary or (407) 824-2985 for the Floridian.

The **Sandcastle Club** includes computers, videos, and games at Disney's Yacht and Beach Club Resorts. Meals can be ordered from Room Service. Call (407) 934-8000, extension 6290 for reservations.

### Babysitting

Guests at resorts within Walt Disney World can hire in-room babysitters from KinderCare Learning Centers, at (407) 827-5444. The service may also be able to provide sitters for guests at major hotels outside of the park.

An interesting option for parents with children from ages 2 through 10 is **Kids Time**, which operates a supervised play area with toys, sports, video games, and art activities seven days a week from early morning through late evening. Snacks and meals are available. Kids Time is located in the West Colonial Oaks Shopping Center at 7230 West Colonial Drive, near Universal Studios and International Drive. Call (407) 298-5437 for information.

# II
# WALT DISNEY WORLD

## Introduction

So, you want to go to Disney World. Great! Which Walt Disney World do you have in mind?

• The world of Mickey and Minnie and Alice and Dumbo and the Enchanted Tiki Birds?[1]

• The only place on the planet where China touches Norway and where you can drive among the dinosaurs?[2]

• The home of R2D2, Humphrey Bogart, the Alien, Kermit the Frog, and an elevator guaranteed to fail hundreds of times a day?[3]

• The stately adult pleasure dome of Merriweather A. Pleasure, where you can boogey (almost) all night?[4]

• Florida's only ski resort?[5]

• The terrifying plunge of Humunga Kowabunga or the splashdown at Whoop 'n Holler Hollow?[6]

• The campfire sing-along at the trading post?[7]

• The home of Moe, Larry, Curly, and hundreds of other trained and untrained parrots, peacocks, and tortoises?[8]

• A place with five championship-level golf courses, including two stops on the PGA Tour?[9]

• The home port of the largest private flotilla in the world, bigger than many navies?[10]

---

[1]The Magic Kingdom
[2]Epcot Center
[3]Disney-MGM Studios
[4]Pleasure Island
[5]Blizzard Beach
[6]Typhoon Lagoon and River Country
[7]Fort Wilderness
[8]Discovery Island
[9]Disney Inn, Bonnet Lakes, and Lake Buena Vista
[10]The Walt Disney World marinas

**Pets.** Never leave your cat, dog, mouse, or other pet in your car; heat can build up tremendously in a parked vehicle and animals can die. If you must bring a pet with you on your trip, be sure to bring proof of vaccination and use one of the Pet Care Kennels outside the Transportation and Ticket Center at the Magic Kingdom, or outside the gates of Epcot Center or the Disney-MGM Studios. Animals can be boarded here for the day only.

**Front seat drivers.** There is one row of seats in the front cab with the driver of the monorail. Ask one of the attendants to place you there for an interesting and different perspective; you may have to let a train pass by if there are many people waiting in line.

**Fixing your flivver.** If your car needs emergency mechanical repairs, it doesn't necessarily mean a lost day at the park. The Disney Car Care Center, located just to the left of the main parking tollbooth, has a garage that is open Monday through Friday.

Oh, *that* Disney World.

Let's define an important term here at the start:

**Walt Disney World** is the huge entertainment complex that includes within it the **Magic Kingdom, Epcot Center,** and the **Disney-MGM Studios Theme Park** as well as **Pleasure Island, Blizzard Beach, Typhoon Lagoon, River Country, Discovery Island,** the six Disney golf courses, **Disney Village,** and the hundreds of Disney-operated and Disney-licensed hotels and restaurants within the property lines of the World.

Our goal in this, the largest section of the book, is twofold: first, to break down the huge World into smaller and more understandable pieces and, second, to put them back together again in a way that shows how to get the most out of it.

There are seven chapters in this section:

• The Magic Kingdom
• Epcot Center
• Disney-MGM Studios
• Disney Water Parks
• Nightlife and Disney Shopping
• Walt Disney World Seminars
• Inside the World of Disney, an exploration of the international and future of things Disney.

Later on in the book, we'll return to Walt Disney World to discuss dinner theaters, sports, recreation, and educational opportunities.

We'll begin each of the first three chapters with our list of "must-see" attractions and the exclusive "Power Trip" tour. We hope you'll take the time to read the chapters before you go and once again when you're in Florida.

## Getting to the Park

The idea behind the Walt Disney World transportation system was a good one: getting to the Magic Kingdom *should* be a magical experience. When you leave your car you *should* be in an entirely different world.

"We'll have visitors park way on the other side of a large lagoon and then let them take an exciting monorail ride or a soothing ferryboat to the main gate," the planners said. "By the time they're in the park, they'll completely forget about the outside world."

So far, so good, but let's consider how it works out some 30 years after the planners made their drawings.

First you park way out in East Overshoe, practically the next county. Then you must walk to the central aisle of the parking lot and wait for a gigantic snake-like tram to take you to the Transportation and Ticket Center (TTC). You'll have to show your ticket to the attendant there and then choose between a monorail or a ferryboat ride around or across the Seven Seas Lagoon to the main gates.

Total time from parking to your first step onto Main Street is about 30 minutes at the start of the day and as much as an hour at peak periods from about 10 A.M. to noon when there are long lines at the monorail or ferryboat.

At the end of the day, you'll have to reverse the process. And you *did* remember where you parked your car, right?

For most visitors to the Magic Kingdom staying outside of the park, there's no easy way around the process, except to follow one of our general rules: arrive early. (The situation is very different at Epcot Center and Disney-MGM Studios, where you can park and walk or take a single short tram ride to the gates.)

## From Within Walt Disney World

One of the advantages of staying at a hotel within Walt Disney World is the availability of Disney's own bus, monorail, and boat fleet. Disney operates more than 125 buses over 125 miles of paved roads in the park. And the 750 watercraft of Walt Disney World qualify as the fifth largest navy in the world.

The buses go directly to the entrance of the Magic Kingdom, Epcot, and MGM Studios. Similarly, the boat services from some Disney hotels go directly to the Magic Kingdom or to the back door International Gateway entrance to Epcot. Visitors staying at a Disney hotel with a monorail stop have direct service only to the Magic

**Commuting from Epcot.** If your plan for the day calls for a start at the Magic Kingdom and ends with a special dinner at Epcot, you might try this strategy: arrive early at Epcot and park there. Ride the monorail to the transfer point at the Transportation and Ticket Center and pick up the monorail to the Magic Kingdom. Then reverse that route in the afternoon and you will be able to stay as late as you want at Epcot and pick up your car there. The alternate plan works, too, on nights when the Magic Kingdom is open later than Epcot; park at the Magic Kingdom, and ride the monorail to Epcot to begin your day.

**Back of the bus.** Can you park at a Disney hotel lot and ride a monorail, boat, or bus directly to one of the parks? The answer is yes . . . and no. In theory, you must have a guest ID card to ride one of the internal modes of transport. However, cards are rarely asked for, and Disney encourages guests at Walt Disney World to sample the restaurants and shops at its hotels. Disney also quietly sells a daily transportation ticket for $2.50.

**Everything you always wanted to know about the monorails.** Well, almost everything.

The current models have eight 113-horsepower motors in the various cars of the train; the train cannot be split up into smaller units. The monorails run on 600-volt DC power drawn from Disney's own power plant north of the Contemporary Resort and across the road from the monorail maintenance shop.

There is a total of 13.6 miles of rail, including spur lines and maintenance areas. More than half, 7.6 miles, is the Epcot "beam"; the Lagoon beam to hotels and the Exterior beam to the Magic Kingdom are each about 2.6 miles in length.

When World Showcase at Epcot was built, it included buried footers for pylons to extend the monorail to the Disney-MGM Studios park and hotels in the Epcot area, but construction of that line seems increasingly unlikely as time goes on because of growing expense and the complexity brought by new development in the area. One possibility calls for construction of a light rail trolley to connect the outlying area, but for the foreseeable future plan on buses and private transportation.

Kingdom; you'll have to transfer at the TTC to an Epcot train or a Disney-MGM Studios bus if either is your destination.

The principal transportation system at the Magic Kingdom—and one of the most famous—is the Mark IV Monorail system, which links the Magic Kingdom and the TTC, and a second route that runs from the TTC to Epcot Center. A local version of the Magic Kingdom loop stops at several of the major hotels within the park.

## Five if by Monorail, Seven if by Ferry

Another component of the transportation system at the Magic Kingdom is decidedly low-tech: Disney's fleet of ferryboats that cross the lagoon from the TTC to the gates of the park. At most times, there are two boats in constant operation with a third available for peak periods.

The scaled-down versions of the famous Staten Island Ferries in New York are double-ended vessels, meaning they don't need to turn around at either end of their trip. You walk on at one end and walk off at the other. By the way, the ferries are free-floating; unlike the riverboat at the Magic Kingdom, there is no rail beneath the water.

The ferries are a very pleasant way to travel, especially on a pretty evening at the end of a long day.

Although the monorail may look speedy, in truth it is only about a minute or two faster than the ferryboat in getting from the TTC to the Magic Kingdom. And the two ferryboats can carry about three times as many passengers as one monorail train. So, if the line for the monorail is lengthy, go by sea.

# Chapter 6
# The Magic Kingdom

Once upon a mouse, back in 1928, Walter Elias Disney created a character who came to be known as Mickey Mouse for a short cartoon called "Steamboat Willie."

Everything else since then has been built upon the slender shoulders of the cute little rodent, along with his gal, Minnie, and buddies Donald, Daisy, Snow White, as well as a cast of thousands of other cartoon and movie favorites.

Disney's film studio began to grow rapidly; Walt set up a little park alongside his first movie studios to entertain visitors, exhibiting his collection of scale model trains among other things. When he moved into television in the early 1950s, Disney struck a deal with ABC Television to help fund the construction of the Disneyland park in California, which opened in a former orange grove in 1955. Although much has changed in the more than 40 years since Disneyland was first planned, the basic structure of that park, and all that have followed, is the same. Here's a how-de-doo: In 1995 Disney bought the entire ABC network.

**Closing time.** Closing time varies according to the season, and is sometimes adjusted from day to day based on attendance patterns; it can be as early as 6 P.M. or as late as midnight. Check at the park for details. The announced closing time is actually a relative thing, usually meaning the time when the last person is allowed to join a ride line. The parks themselves are cleared out about an hour or so after then, and the final bus or other transportation to parking lots or hotels leaves about 90 minutes after closing time.

Today, breathes there a man, woman, girl, boy, or mouse who has not dreamed of visiting the Magic Kingdom? The entertainment vision of Walt Disney—along with the incredible marketing skills of the company he left behind—has made Disney's parks and symbols probably the world's best-known popular icons. You can see Mickey Mouse T-shirts on the streets of Moscow, Epcot towels on the beaches of the Caribbean, Minnie dresses on the boulevards of Paris, and Roger Rabbit hats in the alleys of Tokyo.

# MAGIC KINGDOM MUST-SEES

**Space Mountain**
*(New Tomorrowland)*

**The ExtraTERRORestrial Alien Encounter**
*(New Tomorrowland)*

**The Timekeeper**
*(New Tomorrowland)*

**It's a Small World**
*(Fantasyland)*

**Mickey's House**
*(Mickey's Toontown Fair, adults excused)*

**The Haunted Mansion**
*(Liberty Square)*

**Pirates of the Caribbean**
*(Adventureland)*

**Jungle Cruise**
*(Adventureland)*

**Big Thunder Mountain Railroad**
*(Frontierland)*

**Splash Mountain**
*(Frontierland)*

In 1992, Disneyland Paris joined the three other parks—Disneyland, Walt Disney World, and Tokyo Disneyland—on the global map.

In Florida, by far the largest of all of the Disney parks, the empire sprawls across miles of land and includes three major theme parks and dozens of other attractions. However, it is still The Magic Kingdom—home of Fantasyland, Adventureland, Frontierland, and New Tomorrowland—that is what visitors think of when they first set out for Orlando.

In this section, we'll offer the Ultimate Unauthorized Tour of the Magic Kingdom, area by area. We'll tell you which rides are "must-sees" and which ones are not worth crossing the road for. We'll sample all of the restaurants of the park. And we'll pass along inside information that we trust will add to your fun.

## Power Trip #1

*Adults and Adventurous Kids:*
*Space Mountain/Alien Encounter Plan*
The ExtraTERRORestrial Alien Encounter ride joined the pantheon of big draws at the Magic Kingdom, and that guarantees long lines through the heart of the day at New Tomorrowland. Space Mountain next door continues as a crowd magnet.

To ride one or both, get to the park before opening and wait at the rope barrier at the right side of the top of Main Street, as close to New Tomorrowland as you can get. Join the gate-opening sprint to **Space Mountain** in New Tomorrowland for an eye-opening start to your day. When you're back on Earth, join the growing line for the new **Alien Encounter**. Or go first to Alien Encounter and then ride Space Mountain.

If there is not much of a waiting line, hop onto the **Skyway** for a lift to the far end of Fantasyland.

Walk to **Splash Mountain** and **Big Thunder Mountain Railroad** and ride both. By now, alas, the lines for major attractions are probably starting to grow.

Backtrack to the **Haunted Mansion** in Liberty Square for a howl. You have now completed five of the most exciting and most crowd-drawing attractions for older visitors. Take an early lunch and then walk across the top of Frontierland and into Adventureland to join the line for **Pirates of the Caribbean.**

At this point, we'd suggest changing direction and walking in a clockwise direction back toward New Tomorrowland; visit any other ride that appeals to you as you go. Visit the **Transportarium** to see the *The Timekeeper* movie. If you have the time, come back for a ride after dark on **Splash Mountain** or **Big Thunder Mountain Railroad.** Or, take another trip on **Space Mountain**; try the opposite set of tracks from the one you took the first time.

# Power Trip #2
*Adults and Adventurous Kids: Splash Mountain Plan*
Get to the park before opening and wait at the lefthand rope barrier at the top of Main Street near the Crystal Palace. Join the gate-opening sprint to **Splash Mountain** in Adventureland.

Or, here's an interesting alternate: enter the park before the opening, and go up to the Disney World Railroad immediately; there will be a train waiting there which will depart at the moment the park officially opens. Ride to the Splash Mountain exit and get off the train and into line; you should be able to beat most of the thundering horde racing across the park on foot.

When your feet are back on dry land, sprint over to **Big Thunder Mountain Railroad** for a tour.

Head across the park to Liberty Square and enter the **Haunted Mansion** for a howl. Continue into Fantasyland and, if there is not much of a waiting line, hop onto the **Skyway** for a lift to the far end of New Tomorrowland. Blast off on **Space Mountain.** If the lines are reasonable, visit the **Alien Encounter.**

We'd grab lunch now and work our way back across the park to the last remaining big draw, **Pirates of the Caribbean** in Adventureland.

For the rest of the day, visit any other ride that appeals to you as you go. If you have the time, come back for a ride after dark on both **Splash Mountain** and **Big Thunder Mountain Railroad**—it's a whole new experience after the sun goes down.

# Power Trip #3
*Children (and Parents Under Their Control)*
Head left from Main Street and enter Adventureland. Ride **Pirates of the Caribbean** and the **Jungle Cruise.** (You can also take the Disney World Railroad from the top of Main Street to the Adventureland stop.)

Depending on how adventurous your children are, you may want to go early to Splash Mountain, which is an utterly charming ride that also includes a few seconds' drop over a waterfall—it looks a lot more scary than it really is.

Walk into Frontierland and (depending on the ages and inclinations of the children) ride **Splash Mountain** and **Big Thunder Mountain Railroad.** Resist the temptation to take the raft to Tom Sawyer Island at this time.

**Lockers.** Store extra clothing and other items at one of the coin-operated lockers beneath the Main Street Railroad Station and at the Transportation and Ticket Center. The lockers demand 50 cents to lock once; you'll have to pay again if you open the box during the day and want to shut your stuff away again.

Enter Liberty Square. Ride **The Haunted Mansion** if your children don't mind a few hundred Disney spooks.

At Fantasyland, visit **It's a Small World** and (if absolutely necessary) ride **Dumbo, the Flying Elephant.** The lines for **Grand Prix Raceway** and **20,000 Leagues Under the Sea** (if it is reopened) will probably have built up to 30 or more minutes by now; we'd suggest skipping them on the Power Trip and coming back some other morning or evening.

Escape to New Tomorrowland, bypassing Mickey's Toontown Fair for the moment. Ride the **Astro Orbiter** and (if the children are up to it, and if the lines are of a reasonable length)
**Space Mountain.** Parental Guidance: we would recommend against taking young children into **Alien Encounter.**

Now you are free to reverse direction and explore the less-crowded rides. We recommend families next visit **Mickey's House** in Mickey's Toontown Fair, **Cinderella's Golden Carrousel** in Fantasyland, the raft ride to **Tom Sawyer Island** in Frontierland, and **The Hall of Presidents** in Liberty Square for children studying American history.

## The Opening Dash

The Magic Kingdom usually opens at 9 A.M., although it may open at 8 A.M. at extremely busy times of the year. Guests at Walt Disney Resorts are allowed an hour's head start to certain areas of the park on some days.

The first part of the park that officially opens is Main Street; you can visit some of the shops or grab a bite to eat before your day really begins. Visitors are stopped at gates at the top of Main Street—one to the left near the Crystal Palace, one in the center heading toward Cinderella Castle, and one to the right just short of New Tomorrowland.

The first rule of the Power Trip called for you to get to the park early; the second rule is to get yourself a good position in the line at one of the three gates. Go to the left if your first goal is Splash Mountain, Big Thunder Mountain, or another attraction in Adventureland or Frontierland. Line up at the rightmost gate if you want to go to Space Mountain, Alien Encounter, Grand Prix Raceway, or another New Tomorrowland ride. And head up the center to go to Fantasyland.

Just before the gates open for the masses, you'll hear a bit of music and an announcement that quotes Walt Disney's dedication of the park; then the speaker will conclude by asking visitors to walk slowly and carefully into the park; of course, the crowds will stampede wildly instead.

Whether you walk or run, if you are anywhere near the front of the waiting line when the gates open, you should be able to get onto any ride in the park with no more than a 15-minute wait, which is about as good as it gets.

A general rule for any part of Walt Disney World is to head immediately for the ride or rides you expect will have the longest lines and get them out of the way early. Then go on to as many other major attractions as you can before the lines become too long. Spend the afternoon visiting lesser attractions, and then go back to major draws at the end of the day as the crowds lessen and the parades and fireworks pull people out of line.

## Attractions at the Magic Kingdom

### Main Street, U.S.A.

Somewhere, someplace, at some time, there was an America like this. It's a place of small stores with friendly proprietors, where the streets are clean and the landscape neat, and where a scrap of paper never lingers on the ground.

At the start of your visit to the Magic Kingdom, think of Main Street, U.S.A. as an interesting place to walk through on the way to somewhere else. Come back later to browse, shop, or eat; if you are following our advice, you will have arrived early at the park with a specific destination in mind.

But when you do come back, marvel at the attention to detail of the storefronts and interior decorations of the shops. Most of the names on the second story windows are those of former and present Disney employees responsible for creation or maintenance of the park.

**Harmony Barber Shop.** Not quite a "Shave and a haircut, two bits," but that's the general idea. It's a real old-timey barbershop, and you can get your ears lowered for about $12.50 or a shave for about $8. A barbershop quartet entertains within and outside the shop from time to time.

Other barbershops—as well as beauty shops—can be found within Disney's Contemporary Resort and Disney's Polynesian Resort.

**Art gallery.** Disneyana Collectibles, between Walt Disney Story and Tony's Town Square Cafe, offers rare and not-so-rare memorabilia, including animation art. More animation is for sale at shops in the Disney-MGM Studios park and inside Pleasure Island.

Main Street is also the place to be if you are a serious parade fan; the entertainment moves toward the railroad station just inside the gates—that may be the best seat in the house to watch the parade. You can, though, also see the parades near Cinderella Castle and on the streets of Frontierland, both of which are nearer the major attractions of the park.

The famous Disney parades change every few years, and in high season there may be as many as three parades a day—an afternoon Disney character parade and two evening electrical events. Pick up an Entertainment Show Schedule at the ticket booth or at City Hall.

In 1996, the big daytime parade was **Mickey Mania**, a totally Mickey daytime parade with more than 100 singers, dancers, musicians, and Disney characters, and more ears than a Kansas cornfield. The parade begins in Frontierland near Splash Mountain and travels through Liberty Square, passing in front of Cinderella Castle and then down Main Street to the Fire Station.

**Disney phone numbers.** Walt Disney World Dining Reservations: (407) 939-3463 Disney Resort Hotel Reservations: (407) 934-7639 Golf Tee Times: (407) 824-2270 Pleasure Island: (407) 934-7781

**Meeting places.** Try not to select the front of Cinderella Castle as a meeting place for groups that go their own way within the park. This location can become quite crowded during the daily parades and other events. Instead, choose the back side of the castle near the carrousel or a landmark off the parade route.

The after-dark show was **SpectroMagic**, a traveling circus of spectacular lighting effects, artificial smoke and fog, strobes, and more than 600,000 twinkling lights. In high-season, the parade is presented nightly at 9 P.M. and again at 11 P.M.; at ordinary times you can expect weekend-only shows at 8 P.M.; in off-season, when the park closes before dark, the parade has the night off.

One place worth stopping before you begin your exploration is **City Hall** in Town Square. Step up to the counter to obtain entertainment and Disney Character schedules; maps in English, French, German, Spanish, or braille; written show descriptions for visitors with special needs; and other information. By the way, City Hall opens when the ticket gates open (up to half an hour or so before the rope is dropped at the top of Main Street), allowing you to make a quick stop there before you join the dash to Space Mountain or Splash Mountain or Dumbo or whatever's your immediate pleasure.

**Walt Disney Railroad.** A pleasant way to tour the park (our favorite way to end a day), these real steam engines take passengers on a 1½-mile, 15-minute circuit of the park.

Walt Disney was a railroad nut, even running a small-scale system in his own backyard. The four engines that are part of the Magic Kingdom's rolling stock were built in the United States but spent much of their working lives in Mexico's Yucatan peninsula hauling sugar cane. The wheels, side rods, and other major parts of the engines are original, although the boilers and cabs have been rebuilt. Originally constructed to burn coal or wood and later converted to oil, the steam engines are now powered by diesel fuel.

The "Lilly Belle," named for Disney's wife, was built in 1928, coincidentally the same year Mickey Mouse made his screen debut. Also on the tracks is the "Roy O. Disney," named for the boss's brother, the "Walter E. Disney," named for the man himself, and the less-often seen "Roger Broggie," christened after a long-time Disney employee and friend.

**Main Street Cinema:** *The Walt Disney Story.* What else would you expect to be playing in the moviehouse on Disney World's main drag but continuous Disney cartoons? Among the biggest treats are those that reach back to the dawn of Disney, like "Steamboat Willie," the first Mickey Mouse cartoon, which was shown at the Colony Theater in New York in 1928.

Also shown at the theater is an amusing little film called "Mickey's Big Break" that makes light fun of the Disney film tradition. The short movie stars funnymen Mel Brooks, Dom DeLuise, and Jonathan Winters in the supposed story of how Mickey became a movie star. Watch for Roy Disney (Walt Disney's nephew) portraying Walt and company chairman Michael Eisner who makes a visit to Mickey in the star's office; is that a Michael Eisner telephone on Mickey's desk?

**Penny Arcade.** Disney has brought together a marvelous collection of antique games and amusements, including penny hand-crank movies, an old Wurlitzer PianOrchastra mechanical orchestra from the 1920s, pinball and baseball games, and fortune-telling machines like the one from the motion picture *Big*. In the back of the arcade, where there is a side entrance next to the Crystal Palace, are some of the most impressive modern machines. The back room is a deafening place, pretty much out of character with the rest of the park. Game prices range from a bargain rate of 25 cents to 50 cents and even $1.

**Main Street Vehicles.** Old-fashioned cars, a horse-drawn trolley, and fire engines move slowly down Main Street to Cinderella Castle. (Following not far behind the horses are uniformed sanitation engineers with shovels.)

**Cinderella Castle.** The hallmark of the Magic Kingdom, it is, of course, every child's mind's-eye image of the way a castle really should be. It sits at the focal center of the park marking both the top of Main Street, U.S.A. and the entrance-way to Fantasyland.

Walt Disney World's castle is loosely based on Sleeping Beauty's castle as described in the fairy tale and the Disney movie that brought it to life. It is constructed of fiberglass over steel beams.

Way up top in the castle is a small apartment originally intended for Walt Disney and his family, but never used. As far as we are aware, it's not for rent, even on New Year's Eve when the nearest available room may be in Philadelphia.

You can, though, go halfway up the tower to **King Stefan's Banquet Hall** for a theme park theme meal. And be sure to check out the elaborate mosaics in the entranceway; they tell the familiar story of the girl with the glass slipper in Italian glass, real silver, and gold.

**Au revoir.** When SpectroMagic debuted at the Magic Kingdom, the Main Street Electrical Parade was shipped, lock, stock, and fuse boxes, to Paris for display at Disneyland Paris.

**Ones of a kind.** The following attractions are among those found only at the Magic Kingdom at Walt Disney World, and not at Disneyland:
Alien Encounter (Tomorrowland)
The Hall of Presidents (Liberty Square)
Carousel of Progress (Tomorrowland)
Mickey's Toontown Fair
SpectroMagic (Main Street)

**Tall tale.** Cinderella Castle is 189 feet tall—nine feet higher than Spaceship Earth in Epcot. (The castle at Disneyland in California, by the way, is called Sleeping Beauty Castle and is much smaller, with towers rising just 71 feet.)

## New Tomorrowland

When Tomorrowland was originally conceived, it was as a showcase of the

**Family matters.** The Coat of Arms above the castle on the north wall (facing Fantasyland) is that of the Disney family. Outside the entrance to King Stefan's Banquet Hall are plaques for other Disney executives. There's no word on whether Michael Eisner has commissioned a family portrait for the public portion of the park.

future. Ironically, the world of tomorrow at the Magic Kingdom eventually became the most dated and tired part of the park.

In 1995, the newly renamed New Tomorrowland was unveiled—the most complete remake of an original area at any Disney park.

The new world at Walt Disney World looks forward and backward at the same time: the setting is straight out of Buck Rogers' science fiction movies of the 1920s and 1930s. The concept was first tried out at Disneyland Paris.

Only in the world of Disney could a place begin way out in the future, fall way behind the times, and then be remade at a cost of millions so that it appears to be a 1930s view of the year 2000.

New Tomorrowland has been recast as an Interplanetary Convention Center. **Space Mountain** is now the headquarters for the Intergalactic Tracking Network. The scary new **Alien Encounter** is the setting for a trade fair for products that are a few hundred years away from your neighborhood Kmart. Overhead is the **Tomorrowland Transit Authority** and you'll be able to visit the **Metropolis Science Center** for an extraordinary experiment in time travel.

New Tomorrowland is once again a must stop on your visit to Walt Disney World. Only now the lines are going to be at least as long as anywhere in the park; head here early or at the end of the day to avoid the lines.

**WOW! Space Mountain.** Every Disney visitor with a bit of spunk—and his or her mom and dad—has got to visit New Tomorrowland at least once to catch a rocketship to Ryca 1.

Space Mountain is the big enchilada, the highmost high, the place where hundreds of Magic Kingdom visitors have dropped their eyeglasses, cameras, and hairpieces. It is also one of the most popular of all of the attractions at Walt Disney World (as is the similar—but not identical—ride at Disneyland; another version, called Discovery Mountain and based on Jules Verne's book, *From the Earth to the Moon,* is at Disneyland Paris).

Space Mountain is a masterpiece of Disney Imagineering, merging a relatively small and slow (top speed of about 28 mph) roller coaster with an outer space theme. The small cars zoom around indoors in near-total darkness, the only light coming from the projected images of stars and planets on the ceiling. The ride is a triumph of scene-setting, the amusement park equivalent of a big-budget movie's special effects.

The cars feel like they are moving much faster than they are because you have no point of reference in the dark. And no, the cars don't turn upside down.

As part of the retooling of New Tomorrowland, the indoor waiting areas for Space Mountain received a bit of a makeover. As you enter the building, you'll see a chart of the FX-1 Intergalactic Tracking Network, representing some of the launches and satellites of a future civilization. When you reach the loading area for the ride—the final queue that can give you 20 more minutes of exquisite teasing torture before you are loaded into your spaceship—check out the video monitors hung from the ceiling.

The televisions bring you continuous reports from PNN—the Planetary News Network. You'll hear from the Hubble Traffic scanner on traffic congestion on Route 4066 in the outer galaxy. Wendy Beryllium's weather report calls for 620 degrees on Mercury and a chilly negative 360 degrees on Neptune. The extended forecast for the planet Earth calls for partly cloudy skies, rising oceans, and a giant comet smashing into the planet sometime in the next hundred million years.

There's a report on the construction of the Mall of Mars. And if you hang on long enough, you will get to see an episode in the lifestyles of the rich and alien.

And be sure to catch the wild ads from Crazy Larry, the used spaceship dealer. What a deal: free floor mats with any intergalactic cruiser!

Overhead, a projector paints the pictures of huge rolling asteroids; you will not be the first to observe that they look like close-ups of chocolate chip cookies. Disney has never revealed its recipe.

Finally, you'll reach the busy launching pad packed with technicians and engineers loading spacecraft.

There are two tracks within the building and the ride is slightly different on each; the left side has more sharp turns, while the right side has more sharp dips. The waiting line splits into left and right queues as you enter the loading area.

Professional Space Mountain riders—and there are tens of thousands of them—will argue over which seat affords the best ride. The last row of seats seems to benefit from a "whip" effect as the cars make sharp turns; we prefer the very front row, where you don't have the back of someone else's head to mar the illusion of space travel and there is a terrific blast of onrushing air as you move on the track. At busy times, you probably will not be able to cajole an attendant into allowing you to select the seat of your choice; late at night or on the occasional slow day you might be in luck.

Do keep a hand on your personal belongings; wrap camera and purse straps around your feet and make sure that children are properly placed beneath the restraining bar. (Disney launch technicians will double-check the safety arrangements, too.)

And then it's over. The ride is about 2 minutes and 40 seconds in length, and nowhere near as fast or as wild as a major roller coaster like Kumba at Busch Gardens, but Space Mountain has that certain Disney touch that will keep you coming back again and again to wait in line for your next space voyage.

Now, speaking of waiting lines: they can easily extend to 90 minutes or more on a busy afternoon. The general rule to avoid long lines at the Magic Kingdom especially applies here. Get to the ride when the gates first open and

**Under foot.** Among the most amazing wonders of the Magic Kingdom is one that most visitors never see. Below your feet are nine acres of underground "utilidor" corridors hiding the sewers, water pipes, air conditioning, electrical cables, communications links, and garbage collection facilities. There is also an extensive system of tunnels allowing employees to come and go within the park virtually unseen; have you ever wondered why you have never seen Mickey walking to work, or seen a Mike Fink keelboat captain strolling through Tomorrowland?

Actually, the tunnels are the first level of the Magic Kingdom. Because of the high water table of much of Florida, the tunnels were put in place first and then covered over with dirt, much of it from the excavation of the lagoon.

About that trash: as you might expect in a Magic Kingdom, Disney does not use an ordinary garbage truck. Refuse is sucked to a central collection point through a huge network of pneumatic tubes.

you may be able to stroll right on board, or come back to the ride at the end of the day. Another somewhat quiet time is during the dinner hour, from about 6 to 7 P.M.

If both tracks are operating and the doors are open, a crowd backed up to the front door means a wait of about one hour; sometimes, though, attendants will build up the line outside while the inside queues clear out. This is often done at the end of the day to discourage huge crowds as closing hour approaches.

Children under three cannot ride Space Mountain, and those under seven must be accompanied by an adult; all riders must be at least 44 inches tall, and pregnant women and others with back or health problems are advised against riding.

Space Mountain, along with other major rides like Big Thunder Mountain Railroad and Splash Mountain, offers a "switch off" arrangement if not all of the people in your party want to ride the coaster, or if you are traveling with a child too young or too small to ride. Inform the attendant at the turnstile at the launching area that you want to switch off; one parent or adult can ride Space Mountain and change places with another at the exit so everyone can take a turn.

**WOW** **Alien Encounter: The ExtraTERRORestrial.** We've come a long, long way from Mickey Mouse to an up-close and personal meeting with the ExtraTERRORestrial. The attraction was the subject of some of the most intensive hype of any new project at the Magic Kingdom; visitors were promised they would be participants in a terrifying "sensory thriller." But when the show opened in January of 1995, it lasted only a few weeks before the powers that be ordered it shut down and reworked to make it scarier.

Alas, we found the encounter to be a lot more hype than horror. The show is not as technologically impressive as "Honey, I Shrunk the Audience" at Epcot nor as stomach-turning as the Twilight Zone Tower of Terror at the Disney-MGM Studios. It's worth a visit and it's still a Must-See, but we'd recommend against joining a lengthy line for the privilege.

As you stroll through New Tomorrowland, you'll see billboards from the

Tomorrowland Chamber of Commerce inviting you to visit the "Tomorrowland Interplanetary Convention Center" for an exhibit by X-S Tech, a mysterious company promoting a mysterious new technology. When you enter the convention center, you will see displays on some of their strange businesses, including Electro Robotics, Cryo Cybernetics, and more. There are also some clever billboards advertising such attractions as "Lunar Disneyland—The Happiest Place Off Earth" and an invitation to the "Tomorrowland Swap Meet" where the offerings include a collection of previously owned robots.

**Lost and found.** A family of four touring Walt Disney World for four days and not losing at least one backpack, two sets of sunglasses, and three hats is unlike any we know. On the day of a loss, check at City Hall in the Magic Kingdom or Guest Services at Epcot or the Disney-MGM Studios. After a day, items are taken to a central lost and found at the Transportation and Ticket Center.

Once you're in the preshow area you will meet L. C. Clench, the otherworldly spokesman for X-S Tech . . . there's something not quite right about this guy, er . . . alien. His slogan: "If something can't be done with X-S, it shouldn't be done at all."

When you enter into the display area, you'll meet the robotic host T.O.M. 2000 (Technobotic Oratorical Mechanism, Series 2000) who is there to demonstrate the X-S Series 1000 Teleportation System. He's going to show the use of teleportation using the aid of his cute little alien friend, Skippy. Hmm . . . teleportation, as in *The Fly*? You don't suppose there's a chance of something going wrong with the device, do you?

When you are escorted into the demonstration area and locked into your seat by an overhead harness (locked into your seat!), the members of the audience will be scanned for a suitable subject.

Of course, something goes wrong. A wild alien is loose among the audience . . . which is locked into its seats!

Much of the show consists of very loud sound effects, bright flashes, and a whole lot of screaming coming from all around you. It took a moment before we realized that most of the screaming was on the soundtrack.

Alien Encounter replaced the hopelessly outdated *Mission to Mars* show (so old, it was originally called *Voyage to the Moon*). There are two theaters, each seating 134 persons; visitors must be at least 48 inches tall.

**WOW** *The Timekeeper.* Jules Verne, H. G. Wells, and a few modern-day stars led us on a stunning multimedia exploration of time and space, presented in Circle-Vision 360 and including an appearance by English actor Jeremy Irons and wildman Robin Williams as the voice of Timekeeper.

The adventure begins with a preshow in which you are introduced to Timekeeper and his robotic assistant "9-Eyes," who has guess-how-many cameras. The amusing introduction includes a newsreel about the development and testing of 9-Eyes, including a test trip of Niagara Falls.

It seems that Timekeeper has perfected the long-sought-after art of time travel and is about to embark on a journey back in time to visit some of the great visionaries of all time, including Jules Verne and H. G. Wells. Many of Frenchman Verne's predictions, including space travel, subways, and submarines have come true; Englishman Wells was a great visionary but few of his dreams, including time travel and alien invasions, have (thus far) come true.

Timekeeper sets out on a voyage back in time to the Universal Scientific Exposition of Paris in 1900. There he meets Verne and Wells who are in the midst of an argument about their beliefs. Verne accuses Wells of being a hopeless dreamer and scoffs at his idea of time travel.

9-Eyes comes into the middle of it all when it is spotted by Verne, who grabs hold of the strange device and suddenly becomes dragged along on a fantastic voyage that includes the high-speed TGV train in modern France, downtown Parisian traffic, an undersea trip, and a stop at the madhouse of New York City ("home of 10 million dreams and one parking space").

After a few more spectacular visits, including a glimpse of the higher-tech future of the year 2189 in Paris (note that the Eiffel tower has a 300th anniversary banner on it, and watch for Jules Verne and H. G. Wells flying by in a time machine), the entourage is deposited back at the site of the science exposition of Paris.

The film may be a bit over the heads of young children—literally and figuratively, since there are no seats in the theater—but for all others *The Timekeeper* is sure to be an instant Disney classic.

The Transportarium is located in the former *American Journeys* theater. The show debuted at Le Visionarium at Disneyland Paris. In the European version of the film, French superstar Gérard Départdieu made a cameo appearance as an airport baggage handler in a sequence involving the Concorde at Orly Airport in Paris. And if you watch very carefully, it is apparent that most of the actors spoke French with English overdubbed later.

The theater is large and at most times of the day you should be able to get into the 20-minute show with no more than a 20-minute wait; if the line extends out the door, you may want to come back at another time in the day.

**Dreamflight.** Not very dreamy and not much of a flight, the ride combines some attractive sets and scenery with short snippets of spectacular film.

The purpose of the ride is to emphasize the thrill and history of flight, but this exhibit doesn't have a dream of surpassing any of the technology pavilions at Epcot. The best effect in the ride is a rather simple one: rotating light beams within a fog tunnel to simulate high speed and a feeling of takeoff through the clouds.

Still, it's a pleasant way to get off your feet for a while, and there is rarely a line for this five-minute ride, sponsored by Delta Air Lines.

**Tomorrowland Transit Authority.** The former **WEDway PeopleMover**, reworked a bit as part of the remake of New Tomorrowland. The new loading station is **Rockettower Plaza**. Trains of 20-passenger cars of the Tomorrowland Transit Authority Metroliner Blueline circle slowly above New Tomorrowland, taking a quick peek into a part of Space Mountain (a good way for the faint of heart to get some idea of what the excitement is about).

The PeopleMover is a pet project of the Magic Kingdom, demonstrating an unusual means of propulsion—the linear induction motor. The track and the car form a motor together, as magnetic pulses pull the car down a flat coil.

There is rarely a significant line for this 10-minute ride, which we still found to be about seven minutes too long. Still, it's a seat and a bit of a view.

**Astro Orbiter.** A basic amusement park ride with rotating rockets and an up/down lever, but in typical Disney fashion it seems like much more.

Nowhere near as threatening (to some) as Space Mountain, it nevertheless is not for people with fear of heights.

As part of the overall remake of New Tomorrowland, the ride was rebuilt and is now one of the most recognizable features of that section of the park, with the Jules Verne theme of rotating planets and moons. It is especially impressive at night. If you think about it, Astro Orbiter is a slightly faster and somewhat higher version of Dumbo, the Flying Elephant.

**Tomorrowland Arcade.** The fanciful power station for the world of the future, located at the exit from Space Mountain, also contains a fabulous video arcade. Disney designers again looked backward to the rounded, streamlined architecture of the art deco 1930s for their presentation of the future.

**Carousel of Progress.** The future ain't what it used to be. That was very evident as the Carousel of Progress grew further and further out of date in the 1980s. Its concept of the future had moved into the past.

This ride, originally presented at the 1964–65 World's Fair in New York, tells the story of the march of technology in American homes. It was interesting in 1964 and amusing in 1984, but hopelessly outdated in the 1990s; in 1994, Disney opened a retooled and updated version of the show featuring the voices of cartoon voice master Noel Blanc and raconteur Jean Shepherd.

The basic concept of the Carousel remains unchanged; the theater seats revolve around a stationary central core populated by Audio-Animatronic robots. The show takes about 22 minutes.

The wait for the ride, short as it is, includes television monitors on which you can see an old videotape of Walt Disney on his TV show introducing song-

**Left, right, up, down.** Check out the world of transportation at the right corner of the Space Mountain building near the Carousel of Progress. In one spot you can see the Disney steam train, the modern monorail, and the electric Tomorrowland Transit Authority cars. To your left is the aerial skyride and the earthbound Grand Prix Raceway. Above it all are the Astro Orbiters. And then think of the rocket ships on rails within the mountain.

**Robo-stars.** Disney claims that the Carousel of Progress has had more performances than any other stage show in the history of America; of course, it's not really a stage show since all of the actors have electric motors inside them.

writers Dick and Bob Sherman of the Walt Disney Studios; the trio—none of them singers—performs the original theme song for the show, "It's a Great Big Beautiful Tomorrow," which was written for the GE Pavilion at the 1964 New York World's Fair. The song was rescued from the vaults for the slightly updated version.

The first few scenes of the show are unchanged from the earlier version, with a new narration by Jean Shepherd and the return of the original theme song. The show starts at the turn of the century as electricity was first making its appearance in the home; the second scene takes place at the time of Lindbergh in the 1920s, and then we move on to the promising 1940s. (Many adults will be amused to see a working model of the vibrating belt exercise machines that were the rage into the early 1950s.)

The fourth stage setting takes us a few years beyond the current day. A young boy loans his grandmother his virtual reality game, which she takes over. When grandma calls out her score of 550, the voice-actuated oven burns the turkey.

Even with the small amount of updating, it is still worth noting that the Carousel is an all-white middle-class world, and one in which dad is still pretty much the indisputable king of the castle.

The best seat is down front in the center of the auditorium. Note the eyes on the various robot dogs in each scene.

By the way, longtime fans of Jean Shepherd, one of the great cynics of our time as well as a great storyteller, may be a bit disconcerted to hear him end the show by saying "Have a great big beautiful today."

**Skyway.** Entrance to the aerial tramway that runs to Fantasyland. Passengers must exit at Fantasyland, although it is a simple matter to go down the stairs and back up again to return to New Tomorrowland if you desire. For most of the day, lines for the five-minute ride are rarely longer than a few minutes; however, when a parade or show lets out, a sudden influx of visitors can cause buildups of half an hour or more; at those times we'd suggest walking instead. The trip is especially dramatic in the evening.

**Grand Prix Raceway.** Every kid we know dreams of getting behind the wheel of Daddy's car; most adults we know dream of taking a spin around a Grand Prix racecourse. Perhaps that's why this attraction, which doesn't have much to do with New Tomorrowland that we can think of, is such a popular destination. Adults, alas, will probably find the trip rather boring; children will often beg for another go around the course.

There are four parallel tracks of about a half-mile each, and the little race cars have real gasoline engines that will propel them forward at up to a zippy seven mph. The steering gear works, too, allowing the driver to move the car left and right down the course, although there is a center rail that will keep the car from completely leaving the track.

Children must be at least 52 inches tall to ride in one of the cars alone; otherwise their feet won't reach the gas pedal. Mom or Dad, though, can sit alongside and press the pedal while junior happily steers.

Waiting lines can reach to nearly an hour on the most crowded days; visit the track early or late to make the best use of your time. A circuit takes about four minutes.

**His, hers, and its.** The little signs over the restrooms in Tomorrowland depict male and female robots.

**Merchants of Venus.** Outfit yourself for intergalactic travel with unusual clothing and souvenirs. An unusual feature of the shop is the robotic T-shirt painting machine that creates customized outfits. And be sure to check out the color hologram outside the store, facing the Astro Orbiters.

## Fantasyland

This is the stuff of young dreams: Dumbo, Peter Pan, Alice in Wonderland, Snow White, and the toy riot of It's a Small World. Fantasyland is a bright and cheerful place, decorated in splashes of color and sprinkled with snippets of song. Over it all is Cinderella Castle (described already in the section about Main Street, U.S.A.).

**Dumbo, the Flying Elephant.** Disney has taken a very ordinary amusement park ride and made it something special, at least for little visitors. Riders sit within fiberglass flying elephants that can move up and down as they circle around a mirrored ball and a statue of Timothy Mouse, the little guy who becomes Dumbo's manager in the classic Disney animated movie.

The ride received a makeover in 1994, with a new Renaissance Fair design and 16 new Dumbos (up from 10) circling a golden crown with a set of gears and huge pinwheels that looks like a kid's drawing of a machine. This ride has always held a tremendous draw for young children, with lines of up to an hour for the 90-second ride. The new design should cut those lines by almost half, but still, if your kids insist on an elephant-back ride, head for Dumbo early or late in the day. One of the rites of passage for youngsters, we suspect, is the day they announce they're willing to skip the lines for Dumbo in favor of a second pass at Space Mountain.

**Cinderella's Golden Carrousel.** One of the few mostly "real" things in this world of fantasy, the carrousel dates back to 1917 and was used by generations of kids in New Jersey. Many of the horses are hand-carved originals, although the herd has been augmented with some fiberglass replicas and the overhead canopy has been Disneyfied with images from the company's films. No two of the horses are identical. The musical organ, which plays selections from Disney hit movies, is an Italian original.

The lines for the two-minute ride ebb and flow; we'd suggest you wait for the times when you can walk right on board.

**WOW It's a Small World.** Every little girl's wildest dream: a world of beautiful dancing dolls from all over the world. There is nothing to get your heart beating here, but even the most cynical—including little boys and adults— will probably find something to smile about in this upbeat boat ride. We especially enjoy the Audio-Animatronic cancan dancers.

This 11-minute ride was originally designed for the 1964–65 World's Fair

**It's a dangerous world, after all.** In August of 1994, riders on Small World pitched in to rescue a five-year-old girl who fell into the water. According to witnesses, a mother had lifted her daughter into the air before the boat arrived at the exit, and the girl fell between the boat and the wall.

A number of passengers stepped into the shallow artificial river and lifted the boat off the girl; she reportedly suffered a broken arm and ribs and other injuries.

Disney would not comment on the accident to reporters except to claim it was the first such incident on the ride. Some of the rescuers were rewarded with lifetime passes to Walt Disney World.

**Disney Dollars.** Here's your chance to make an interest-free loan to the company. "Disney Dollars," available at all of the parks, are sold without any discount. They are valid anywhere within the Disney properties and nowhere else. Do we sound unimpressed?

in New York, but unlike the Carousel of Progress, the Small World ride has timeless appeal. The sound system was updated and improved in 1995.

The boats are large and the lines move pretty quickly (if two queues are being formed, the line to the left moves a bit faster), but we'd advise coming to this attraction early or late in the day. Children who like this ride will probably also enjoy the Rivers of Time ride at the Mexican pavilion of Epcot.

**Peter Pan's Flight.** A mellow excursion into some of the scenes from Disney's version of the story of the little boy who doesn't want to grow up. Riders sit in a small pirate ship that suspends them a foot or so off the floor. Everyone's favorite scene is the overhead view of London by night, which does a pretty good job of simulating Peter's flight. Strictly for kids.

At Disneyland Paris, a jazzed-up version of this ride is one of the more popular attractions; not so at the Magic Kingdom, although lines can still reach to 45 minutes or more on busy days.

**Mad Tea Party.** A Disney version of a rather common amusement park ride in which circular cars move around a track and also spin around on platforms. If it sounds dizzying, that's because it is: the very young and others with sensitive stomachs or ears might prefer the carrousel across the way. However, the riders have some control over how fast the cups spin; grab hold of the wheel in the center of the cup and don't let go for the least movement.

The ride is covered over with a tent-like structure, taking the cups and most of the waiting line out of the elements. The ride has been designed like a scene from Disney's classic 1951 film, *Alice in Wonderland*. Our favorite part is the drunken mouse who pops out of the teapot in the center.

The ride itself is only about 90 seconds long; the wait can be much more than that. We'd recommend hopping on board only if lines are short.

**20,000 Leagues Under the Sea.** We love the idea of a submarine ride, but if that's what you are looking for this is not a very fine example. Maybe that's why the ride was shut down in early 1995 with vague promises of a renovation, refurbishment, or reworking. It was expected to reopen for the Summer of 1996.

The original ride included a fleet of 61-foot-long subs and a large lagoon filled with fish, giant clams, coral, icebergs, caves, and more—all of it fake. Oh, did we neglect to mention the lost city of Atlantis and the polar ice cap?

The attraction was loosely based on the Jules Verne book of the same name, and in particular the 1954 Disney movie. And despite repeated warnings from those in the know, it was a very popular attraction.

Passengers clambered down ladders into the narrow confines of the sub and sat alongside underwater windows; some riders found the loading and unloading very difficult. The 8½-minute ride moved rather slowly and loading was even slower; long lines built up by midday and did not disappear until late.

**Mr. Toad's Wild Ride.** Not all that wild, but a rather entertaining ride based on one of Disney's more obscure films, *The Adventures of Ichabod and Mr. Toad,* which was in turn loosely based on the book *The Wind in the Willows.*

You will ride in an antique car on the road to Nowhere in Particular, crashing through fireplaces, into a chicken coop, and on a railroad track headed straight for an oncoming locomotive. It's light enough fare for most children, although the very young might become a bit scared by the Day-Glo devils and the somewhat loud sound effects. There are two sets of tracks in the building, both the same length but following with slightly different views of the road. The tracks come together in a few places, but serious fans of Toad Hollow will want to visit both ends of the line.

Adults will find this two-minute ride among the more ordinary at the Magic Kingdom; we'd recommend against joining a midday line unless a youngster is in charge.

**Snow White's Adventures.** The sign over the door originally read "Snow White's Scary Adventures," a tipoff to the fact that this ride emphasized the grimmer parts of the Brothers Grimm fairy tale, as presented in Disney's 1938 animated movie. The ride couldn't hold a fading candle to the spooks in the Haunted Mansion across the way in Liberty Square, but there were a lot more skeletons and witches than very young children might have expected.

The Magic Kingdom version of the ride was different from the versions at Disneyland, Tokyo Disneyland, and Disneyland Paris in its emphasis on the dark side and, according to Disney insiders, was the source of many complaints at the Florida park from parents of young children.

But now, a kinder, gentler Snow White: the revised version removes some of the darker elements of the ride at Walt Disney World, making it more like its California and overseas cousins.

Parents be warned: it's still a bit scary at the start with some ghoulish ghouls and wicked witches, but happier at the end. The new version uses about half of the old "sets," but now Snow White herself appears for the first time in Florida. In fact, she's there in five scenes: at the wishing well in the courtyard of the castle, in the scary forest, at the dwarf's cottage, with the Prince

**Child under tow.** On a crowded day, it is possible to lose sight of your children from time to time. Discuss with them beforehand a place to meet if you get separated; you can also obtain name tags to place on your children at City Hall or the Baby Center next to the Crystal Palace. Disney employees are well trained on how to deal with a lost child; track one down for assistance.

The Baby Center is specially designed to assist in nursing or changing infants; most other rest rooms throughout the parks have some accommodation for these needs. The Baby Center also offers for sale emergency rations of formula, replacement pacifiers, bottles, and diapers. Strollers are available for rent beneath the railroad overpass at the entrance to the Magic Kingdom.

when he kisses her to break the Witch's spell, and (of course) riding off with the Prince to live happily ever after.

The revision of the show was accompanied by a 50 percent increase in capacity for the vehicles; cars now carry six passengers instead of four.

**The Legend of The Lion King.** A sophisticated live actor and puppet show with special effects, music, and animation based on Disney's *Lion King* cartoon feature. Presented in the Fantasyland Theater (the former Magic Journeys location), the show puts the audience into the shadow of huge puppets on a 125-foot-wide stage.

The eight-minute standing preshow opens with a (small) live actor dressed as Rafiki, introducing the story of *The Lion King* and including the "Circle of Life" song from the movie.

Once you enter the theater itself, you will be asked to move all the way across the row to the far side of the auditorium. If you want to try to claim the best view in the middle, hold back until about 25 people have entered a row.

The puppets—some of which require as many as four puppeteers beneath the stage to operate—speak and sing with the recorded voices of some of the humans who gave words to the film characters, including Jeremy Irons as Scar, James Earl Jones as Mufasa, Whoopi Goldberg as Shenzi, and Cheech Marin as Banzai. The theater uses fantastic lighting effects, wind machines, and curtains of water as part of its effects. Jets of steam erupt from the floor, and lightning crashes from above. Mountains and grasslands rise from below.

Some young children may find the sound a bit loud, but the familiar story of *The Lion King* will entrance all.

Lines for the 28-minute show will build during the middle of the day; come early or late or during a parade. If the waiting line extends outside from under the canopy you will not make it into the next show, which means your waiting line will be at least an hour.

**Skyway.** The Fantasyland entrance to the aerial tramway, which returns to New Tomorrowland; it's a great way to get a glimpse of the north end of the park. Passengers must exit at New Tomorrowland, although it is a simple matter to go down the stairs and back up again to return to Fantasyland if you desire. The trip is especially dramatic in the evening; time your voyage properly and catch an aerial view of the nightly parade.

## Mickey's Toontown Fair

Walt Disney World, Disneyland, and the entire Disney empire were in fact built from the ears of the most famous rodent of all, but until 1989 Mickey didn't have a place of his own. That year, Disney honored the mouse's 60th (!) birthday with the first new area at Walt Disney World since its opening. Mickey's Starland became one of the most popular areas of the park for the youngest visitors. In the spring of 1996, as part of the 25th Anniversary celebration at Walt Disney World, Starland received a major makeover, reopening as Mickey's Toontown Fair.

New elements include:

• **The Barnstormer.** A kid-size roller coaster with kid-size thrills. Riders sit in cars that look like old biplanes. The tracks include a wide turn that flies through a barn where kids are waiting their turn to ride. Similar to Gadget's Go-Coaster at Mickey's Toontown at Disneyland, it is about twice as long.

• A house of her own for Minnie, next door to Mickey's, making it a mousely neighborhood; across the way is **Goofy's Wiseacre Farm**.

• **Mickey's House** was spruced up as the entrance to a new place to meet the mouse.

• Donald's boat, *The Miss Daisy*, which has seen better days and sprouts leaks from all over. Disney Imagineers have created a dry lake to surround the boat—here's your chance to walk on pseudo-water. Alas, Grandma Duck's Petting Farm was removed to make room.

**WOW** **Mickey's House.** If you have kids, or ever were one, then there's not a whole lot of doubt about this: you've got to visit Mickey Mouse's house.

**World's fair fare.** Disney was involved in four major pavilions at the 1964–65 New York World's Fair, including Pepsi's "It's a Small World—A Salute to UNICEF" ride, General Electric's "Carousel of Progress," the Illinois pavilion's "Great Moments with Mr. Lincoln," and Ford's "Magic Skyway" ride.

The first three World's Fair exhibits were later recycled for use at Disney parks: "It's a Small World" was moved to Disneyland and became the model for very similar and popular rides at Walt Disney World, Tokyo Disneyland, and Disneyland Paris. The GE "Carousel" was moved to Walt Disney World; it was updated a bit in 1994 but remains essentially unchanged. And "Great Moments with Mr. Lincoln" was Disney's first big success with Audio-Animatronics and was moved to Disneyland's Main Street.

There are no outerspace roller coasters or multimillion dollar water slides at Mickey's Toontown Fair; instead we have the sort of giddy happiness that has sustained the mouse's popularity for all of these years. Disney also uses the area to present and promote some of its newer cartoon stars, including Goof Troop, Dark Wing Duck, Rescue Rangers, Tale Spin, and DuckTales.

You'll explore Mickey's house from corner to corner—he has some great remembrances scattered about, including souvenirs of his greatest films, songs, and TV shows. From the house you'll head into the **Magical TV World** for a rollicking live stage presentation starring the Mick and some of his favorite cohorts including the ultimate cheapskate, Scrooge McDuck, the world's worst pilot, Launchpad McQuack, and the silliest rescuers we know, Chip and Dale.

The show will obviously appeal most to youngsters up to about the awkward teens; adults will find it a pleasant 15-minute diversion.

From the show, it's on to the **Mickey Mouse Club Funland** tent, packed with a bunch of neat and silly buttons to push and games to play. Parents be warned: the tent is a busy place and it is easy to misplace an overexcited child.

Ah, but the best is yet to come for those in the know. After the show, move through the tent, head outside and to the right. There—thrill of thrills—you can enter into **Mickey's Dressing Room** for a semi-private photograph and autograph session.

Note that Mickey's dressing room is small, and only a few people are let in at one time; to avoid wasting a lot of time in line, we suggest you either head immediately for his door after the show or go to the petting farm and wait for the shortest lines between shows.

Outside the theater is a walk of fame for Disney characters with a hand print and paw print. Check out Pluto's paw and bone prints and Goofy's gigantic feet.

**Duck County Courthouse.** It's basically a big gift shop, with some play activities that may distract youngsters while the clerks (dressed in Mickey Mouse Club cheerleader outfits) take your spare cash. Check out the carnival mirrors, and the cutout sets where you can pose your kids within comic book covers or scenes from the cartoons. A blue-screen video area lets you put yourself into a cartoon.

And be sure to grab a gander at the statue of Cornelius Coot at Cornelius Coot Commons outside of the courthouse. Coot, of course, was the founder of Duckburg.

**Walt Disney World Railroad.** The vintage railroad that circles the Magic Kingdom has a station here at the back of the Toontown Fair. The next stop is Main Street, and the third stop is in Frontierland.

## Liberty Square

A peaceful laid-back corner of America, home of the presidents (robotically assisted), a festive riverboat (which runs on underwater tracks), and a haunted mansion (which is too creepy to pass by without a tour). The square is also home to a massive live oak tree festooned with 13 lanterns—one for each of the 13 original colonies—like the Liberty Trees used as political statements in pre-Revolutionary times.

**WOW** **The Haunted Mansion.** Scare yourself silly in this masterpiece of an attraction with some of the most sophisticated special effects at Walt Disney World.

The experience begins in the graveyard waiting line; before you let the tombstones make you feel too creepy, stop and read some of the inscriptions. They're a howl!

The attendants, dressed as morticians, are among the best actors in the park, almost always staying in character. They will tell you to "fill in the dead space" in the line. When the elevator at the start of the ride fills up they may announce "No more bodies." They play their roles well—we've tried our best over the years to make them crack a smile, without any success.

Once you are admitted to the mansion itself, you will be ushered into a strange room with an interesting visual trick—is the ceiling going up or the floor going down? Either way, the portraits on the wall are a real scream. (Don't read this if you don't want to know. Okay, you have been warned: at Walt Disney World, the ceiling moves up and the floor stays where it is; at Disneyland, the floor moves down and the walls are stationary. The stretching room was put into place in California as a way to get visitors to the loading level which is on the other side of the railroad tracks. When the Florida house was built, there was no need to go down a level, but Imagineers wanted to keep the same illusion even if it was accomplished in a different way.)

The experience is accompanied throughout by a decidedly strange soundtrack that is among the more literate writing found at Walt Disney World—that is, if you are able to hear it in the rather fuzzy sound system.

Here's part of the introduction from the stretching room:

> When hinges creak in doorless chambers and strange and frightening sounds echo through the halls, whenever candlelights flicker where the air is deathly still, that is the time when ghosts are present, practicing their terror with ghoulish delight.
>
> Your cadaverous pallor betrays an aura of foreboding, almost as though you sense a disquieting metamorphosis. Is this haunted room actually stretching? Or is it your imagination? And consider this dismaying observation: this chamber has no windows, and no doors.
>
> Which offers you this chilling challenge: to find a way out! Of course, there's always my way.

**Tomb with a view.** Our favorite Haunted Mansion tombstones include: "Dear departed brother Dave. He chased a bear into a cave"; "Here rests Wathel R. Bender. He rode to glory on a fender"; and "Here lies good old Fred. A great big rock fell on his head." And there is, "Rest in peace cousin Huet. We all know you didn't do it."

More favorites, from the cemetery at the exit of the ride: Bluebeard's tomb reads, "Here lyeth his loving wives. Seven winsome wives, some fat some thin. Six of them were faithful, but the seventh did him in." Other pun-full names on the wall include Paul Tergyst, Clare Voince, Metta Fisiks, and Manny Festation.

Many of the names are drawn from the Imagineers who designed the original ride.

You'll enter onto a moving set of chairs and settle in for a tour through a house that is in the control of the largest collection of spooks this side of the CIA.

Says your Ghost Host: "We find it delightfully unlivable here in this ghostly retreat. Every room has wall-to-wall creeps and hot and cold running chills."

We've ridden the ride many times and see something different each time. Among the best effects are the dancing ghouls at the dinner party, the mov-

**Car talk.** One of the announcements you may hear if the Haunted Mansion ride stops to load a passenger in a wheelchair is: "Please remain seated in your doom buggy."

ing door knockers, and the face within the crystal ball.

This ride is probably the single best combination of Disney Audio-Animatronics, moviemaking, and scene setting at the Magic Kingdom. There are all sorts of delightful details on the ride, enough to make it worth several rides if you have the time. Here are a few you might want to look for: the needlepoint that reads "Tomb Sweet Tomb"; the legs sticking out from under the banquet table in the ghostly wedding reception; the skull-shaped notes rising out of the top of the organ at the reception.

You'll meet Madame Leota, a disembodied guide who will help you attempt to make contact with the spirits within the mansion.

> *Rap on a table, it's time to respond, send us a message from somewhere beyond. Goblins and ghoulies from last Halloween, awaken the spirits with your tambourine. Wizards and witches wherever you dwell, give us a hint by ringing a bell.*

The best special effect of the ride is the wedding party scene, where guests move from mortal coil to diaphanous spirit and back. After the party, you'll meet the famous Grim Grinning Ghosts, captured within luminous globes. Through dozens of rides at the Magic Kingdom, Disneyland, and Disneyland Paris we were completely unable to figure out what they were saying until recently. Here's part of their song:

> *When the crypt doors creak and the tombstones quake, spooks come out for a swinging wake. Happy haunts materialize and begin to vocalize; grim grinning ghosts come out to socialize.*
>
> *Now don't close your eyes and don't try to hide, or a silly spook may sit by your side. Shrouded in a daft disguise, they pretend to terrorize; grim grinning ghosts come out to socialize.*

As the ride comes to an end, Madam Leota will urge you to hurry back. Make final arrangements now; be sure to bring your death certificate.

Over the past year, Disney has been subtly increasing the realism of the ride, perhaps in reaction to the overall explicitness of our society. The skeletons are just a bit more real, the ghosts are just a bit more ghoulish. Most noticeable is a new ending, where your vehicle will travel through a graveyard full of ghostly trees, among the tombs.

Some very young children may become a bit scared, although most kids of all ages can see the humor among the horrors. And speaking of humor, stop to read the inscriptions on the tombs at the exit.

Lines for this show vary greatly; the best times to visit are early or late in the day. Try not to join the crowds streaming toward the mansion's door each time the Hall of Presidents lets out or the riverboat arrives. The ride lasts about nine minutes, including a two-minute preshow.

The original Haunted Mansion was at Disneyland in California. Because it

was to be built near the New Orleans area of
Frontierland, the idea was to make it look like an
early 1800s Southern mansion; however, it actu-
ally ended up looking more like an old home in
Baltimore. Walt Disney himself vetoed one
design that made the house appear to be derelict
(Disney's first falling-down house would come
some 30 years later with the construction of the
Twilight Zone Tower of Terror at Walt Disney
World).

**No rabbit ears
allowed.** One scene in
the historical drawings
shows television
coverage of an early
presidential campaign.
The cameras carry the
call letters of "WED-TV"
as in Walter Elias
Disney TV.

The original plans also called for a walk-
through tour, with groups of about 40 visitors escorted through the house by
a butler or maid who would tell the story. The first story line was quite different, too, and not at all sugarcoated: it told of a wealthy sea merchant who
built a fabulous mansion for his new bride, but then killed her in a rage after
she learned he was really a bloody pirate. Her ghost came back to haunt him
and tormented him so much that he finally hung himself from the rafters,
giving the mansion two unhappy spirits.

About all that is left of the gruesome story is the brief glimpse of a hanging body above the stretching room, the weathervane in the shape of a sail-
ing ship on the top of the cupola of the mansion, and some of the paintings
with a seafaring theme.

**The Hall of Presidents.** A living history lesson featuring some of Disney's
best Audio-Animatronic robots. The show is derived from the hit Illinois
pavilion at the 1964–65 New York World's Fair, which startled fairgoers when
a seated Abe Lincoln wearily came to life to address the audience. In the Magic
Kingdom version of the show, all 42 American presidents are represented on
stage.

The only two speaking parts in the Hall of Presidents are Lincoln and
Bill Clinton. In 1994, President Clinton became the first sitting president to
have a speaking role in the pageant, with a speech recorded in the Oval Office
in which he pays tribute to America as "a symbol of freedom and an inspi-
ration to people around the world." Clinton's speech includes the theme that
"there is nothing wrong with America that cannot be cured by what is right
with America."

As Clinton speaks, watch the small gestures and movements of the other
presidents. Abe Lincoln sneaks a peek at his notes every once in a while; some
of the others appear to make little comments to each other or fidget a bit.

The shows at the Hall of Presidents start on the hour and on the half hour.
The first part of the show involves a series of detailed paintings projected on
the large center screen; then the curtains pull back to reveal the assembled
presidents.

The first part of the show features a new narration by poet Maya Angelou,
who thrilled the audience at Clinton's inauguration with a poem. Angelou,
one of our great minds and great voices, is also one of the few women and

African-Americans given individual recognition in the park. Her presentation includes a brief but relatively frank discussion of slavery.

The flag-waving show and a spectacular film that precedes the robotics may have particular appeal to school children studying American history. Others may enjoy the technical artistry of the robots, and some may enjoy studying the details of the costumes on each of the chief executives.

The show takes about 22 minutes; the 700-seat auditorium quickly eats up waiting lines and the maximum wait should be no more than two shows, or about 40 minutes.

By the way, there is a show at the American pavilion at Epcot, the American Experience, that is somewhat similar but considerably flashier, concentrating on other great figures from the history of our nation.

**Liberty Square Riverboat.** One of the most nearly real of all of the exhibits at the Magic Kingdom, the *Richard F. Irvine* is a true steam-powered side-wheeler. Built at Walt Disney World for the ride, it circles the half-mile Rivers of America attached to an underwater rail. The ride itself is no great shakes, but it is a pleasant reprieve on a hot day. The Mike Fink Keelboats and Davy Crockett's Explorer Canoes make the same circle and see the same simulated Old West sights.

The ride takes about 20 minutes; lines rarely extend beyond a full boat load, so your waiting time should be 16 minutes or less.

**Mike Fink Keelboats.** Small riverboats that follow the same circuit as the Riverboat, a bit faster and a bit more personal with your own guide. Mike Fink, by the way, was a riverboat captain of legend who had an adventure with Davy Crockett. The small boats here, the *Bertha Mae* and the *Gullywhumper,* take about 10 minutes for a circuit. Because of the small capacity of the boats, we'd advise you avoid joining a long line if there is one; we'd also suggest against duplicating a trip on the keelboats and one on the riverboat. The keelboats run only during the day, and may not run during the off-season.

## Adventureland

Ahoy, mateys: welcome to a most unusual corner of Central Florida, where you will find a Caribbean island, an African veldt, a South Pacific bird tree, and more. Adventureland includes some of the most dramatic landscaping touches in the Magic Kingdom and the most popular band of pirates since Penzance.

**WOW Pirates of the Caribbean.** Yo, ho, ho . . . one of Disney's very best. After an approach through a dank dungeon waiting area, you'll settle into a broad-beamed boat for a cruise into the middle of a pirate raid on a Caribbean island town.

Before you enter the queue, check out the parrot hung above the entrance; he's wearing an eye patch!

We especially like the moonlit battle scene as your boat passes beneath the guns of two warring ships; cannonballs will land all around you in the cool water. Pay attention, too, to the jail scene where a group of pirates tries to entice a mangy dog to bring them the key. The ride includes a wondrous collection of Audio-Animatronic humans and animals, including robotic chickens and pigs.

Some young children may be scared by the simulated cannon fire and the skulls and bones that are fairly liberally strewn about in some of the caves of Pirates of the Caribbean. And some adults may find bones of their own to pick—things like the depiction of women as objects for sale at auction. However, the ride just might offer an opportunity to discuss such unhappy elements of history with youngsters.

The ride begins with a little bit of a watery drop; your boat is dropping below the Disney World Railroad tracks overhead to the ride area which (like Splash Mountain and Space Mountain) actually lies mostly outside the boundaries of the park.

In any case, Pirates of the Caribbean is a masterpiece of Disney artistry. You don't want to miss this one!

Lines can become quite long at midday; head for this popular trip when the park first opens or in late afternoon. As you enter the queue, keep to your left to save a few minutes in line. The waiting area is mostly under cover, which makes it a good place to be in the rain or on a very hot day. The ride itself takes about seven minutes.

**Swiss Family Treehouse.** This is one of those "no accounting for taste" attractions—you'll either love it or hate it, probably depending upon how deeply the story of the *Swiss Family Robinson* is engraved upon your memory. Actually, this attraction is a remembrance of the 1960 Disney movie version of the classic novel *Swiss Family Robinson*, written by Johann David Wyss and completed by his son Johann Rudolf Wyss in 1813.

The treehouse winds up and across a Disney simulation of a banyan tree (constructed of sculpted concrete and steel). There are a lot of stairs to climb and a few ropewalk bridges; on a busy day, your view may be mostly the backside of the tourist in front of you. It takes five to ten minutes to walk up, through, and down the tree; incredibly, there can sometimes be lengthy lines for the privilege; if there's a line and you're determined to climb this tree, come back late in the day.

**WOW** **Jungle Cruise.** Another Disney classic, this is an escorted boat tour through a simulated wild kingdom that somehow stretches from the African veldt to the Amazon rain forest to the Nile valley and the jungles of southeast Asia.

You'll see some of Disney's most famous special effects, like the automated hippos who lurk just below the water's top and the cavorting elephants who will spray water from their trunks. The shores are lined with robotic zebras, lions, and giraffes. The best part of the ride is the hokey but still entertaining patter of the tour guides in pith helmets. ("Be sure to tell all your friends about Jungle Cruise," our guide told us. "It cuts down the lines." He also apologized for some of the worst one-liners: "I'd tell funnier jokes, but they have to be Disney-approved.")

Amateur gardeners may be thrilled by the amazing collection of plants, flowers, and trees—most of them real—that Disney groundskeepers manage

**One-upsmanship.** Big Thunder Mountain Railroad at Disneyland Paris has a much sharper drop than its older American cousin.

to keep alive. One of the tricks is a network of gas heaters that warms the occasionally chilly air of Florida in the winter.

The ride is just short of ten minutes; the line to get on board, alas, can sometimes wind around and around the corral for more than an hour. Go early or late on busy days.

Sources say that Jungle Cruise is due for an update and expansion; one possibility is that some of the Audio-Animatronic figures from the former World of Motion ride at Epcot will move to the Magic Kingdom.

**Tropical Serenade.** The home of the **Enchanted Tiki Birds**, a collection of more than 200 wisecracking, wing-flapping, automated winged creatures, along with a collection of singing flowers, totem poles, and statues. Your hosts are José, Michael, Pierre, and Fritz.

Tropical Serenade is among the strangest of all of the attractions at the Magic Kingdom, and you've got to be in exactly the right frame of mind to enjoy the show. The birds were among Disney's first attempts at Audio-Animatronics, representing the state of the art as it existed around 1963 when a very similar show was introduced at Disneyland.

We know some young children who have been absolutely enchanted by the birds; the very young and the very cynical need not apply.

There is rarely much of a line to get into the 16-minute show; for us, the very best thing about this show is that it takes place in a dry, air-conditioned theater. Adults might want to bring a Walkman. Rumors are flying (sorry) about a new show for the tired old birds sometime soon.

## Frontierland

Almost anything goes in this wild western corner of the Magic Kingdom, home of Davy Crockett, Tom Sawyer, a bunch of vacationing bears, a runaway mining train, and the park's newest, wettest, and wildest big splash.

**WOW** **Big Thunder Mountain Railroad.** One of the best rides at the park, it is at the same time much more than and much less than it appears.

Big Thunder is a Disneyfied roller coaster, one of only three "thrill" rides in the Magic Kingdom (along with Space Mountain and Splash Mountain). As roller coasters go, it is fairly tame, with about a half mile of track and a three-and-one-half-minute ride with a few short drops and some interesting twists and turns. But in the Disney tradition, it is the setting and the attention to detail that make this one of the most popular places to be.

You will ride in a runaway mining train up through a quaking tunnel, across a flooding village, and back down around and through a 197-foot-high artificial mountain.

The mountain is bedecked with real mining antiques from former mines out West. As you enter the waiting line, you'll see part of a "stamping mill" made by the Joshua Hendy Works in San Francisco, possibly made for one of the mines of the Comstock in Nevada. Stamping mills were used to crush large pieces of rock into smaller pieces to allow the removal of ore.

Look, too, at the Audio-Animatronic animals, birds, and an old coot of a miner in a bathtub as you zoom by. The telegraph office lists the manager's name as Morris Code; get it?

Construction of the ride, completed in 1981, cost $17 million, which equals the entire price tag for Disneyland when it opened in 1955.

Picking the right time to visit the railroad can make a real difference at this very popular attraction; waits of more than an hour are common at midday in peak season. The shortest lines can be found early in the day or just before dinnertime. Coaster fans say the best ride (meaning the wildest) can be had with a seat in the last row of seats; we also like the very front of any coaster ride since it gives you a view of the perils ahead, over the top of the engine in front.

The line outside, near the rafts to Tom Sawyer Island, is only a small portion of the waiting area. There is a large upper corral and a winding path down through the mining station to the railroad. The ride takes on a very different feeling at night, and true fans should experience it then as well as during the day.

Children under seven must be accompanied by an adult; no one under 42 inches is allowed to ride. Warn young children about the loud noises they will hear as their railway car is pulled up the first lift on the ride.

Big Thunder Mountain Railroad at night is like another ride altogether. Like Space Mountain, the fun is increased because the darkness hides the track ahead of you.

**WOW** **Splash Mountain.** Disney's "highest, scariest, wildest, and wettest" attraction is a wild ride to contemplate; you may have a long time to contemplate it as you wait your turn on a busy day.

Splash Mountain includes three lifts and four drops, with the biggest plunging about 50 feet at a 45-degree angle and a top speed of about 40 miles per hour—Disney claims it's the steepest flume ride in the world. The big drop, visible to the crowds along the Rivers of America in Frontierland, will make it appear as if the log car has fallen into a pond.

Some of the best special effects take place within the mountain, with a story based on Disney's classic *Song of the South* cartoon, made in 1946. The ride follows Brer Rabbit as he tries to outwit Brer Fox and Brer Bear on a wild journey to the Laughin' Place.

**How wet do you like it?** Splash Mountain is a watery place, and the log cars make a huge wave as they land at the bottom of the big drop, but the fact is that you won't get very wet on the ride. The two wettest places seem to be the very first row of seats and the last—the wave flies over the car. The front row has the best view of the drop; the last row has the most suspense.

**No charge.** Splash Mountain, because it is one of the high places in the park and because of the watery path, is occasionally forced to close when a lightning storm is in the area. **Extra charge.** When you get off Splash Mountain, you'll be greeted by a wall of video monitors that have color pictures of each log car as it goes down the big drop. You can buy a large print (it includes everyone in your car, strangers and all) for $9.95 for the first copy and $8 for a second print.

**Inside Splash Mountain.** Disney engineers carefully control the amount of water in the flumes. Too much water will cause too much turbulence and splashing; too little can cause a loaded boat to bottom out. On the big drop, about one-quarter of the water is diverted around the boat to control the speed of the drop.

In any case, there's an emergency braking system at the bottom of the big drop; the brake is turned on when an infrared beam deter-mines that two boats are too close together for safety. Pressurized air inflates a set of air bags that lift the underside of the moving boat and push it against rubber strips in a safety channel on the side of the boat, bringing it to a halt.

By the way, the big splash at the bottom of the drop is not caused by the boat—it's an artificial splash produced by water cannons.

**Department of redundancy department.** There is a fire sprinkler system in the ceiling of the water tunnels within Splash Mountain.

The entrance to Splash Mountain is beneath the reconstructed Frontierland railroad station. (As you approach on the train, you will be able to see a small portion of Splash Mountain—it's the Zip-a-Dee Lady paddlewheeler that is at the end of the ride, *after* the big drop.)

Be aware that Disney has hidden the waiting lines within an open inner courtyard not visible from the entrance, and then a long and winding queue within the building itself; be sure to ask the cast member at the measuring pole (44 inches for youngsters) about the length of the line. We'd suggest you come back another time—very early or late if the line is unreasonably long. As usual at many of the attractions, you often will save a few minutes by picking the left-side line over the right. The capacity for the ride is about 2,400 passengers per hour, with 50 log boats in use at a time.

Once you enter the Splash Mountain building itself, there are a few interesting exhibits includ-ing a series of Brer Fox story needlepoints ("Some critters ain't never gonna learn" and "You can't run away from trouble. Ain't no place that far" among them). Check out the animated shadows on the wall in some of the dark areas.

The interior waiting line for Splash Mountain is not the place for claustrophobics. It is dark in places and tight—closer than the waiting queue for Pirates of the Caribbean. Actually, once the Splash Mountain ride is underway, you'll proba-bly think of Pirates of the Caribbean with a bit of It's a Small World mixed in.

You'll start by loading into your "log"; you may find the seats slightly wet. The logs will climb up into the mountain—you'll see the bot-tom of the big drop, and first-time riders will cer-tainly be expecting a sudden sharp drop over the precipice they've seen from the ground. And, just to build up the tension, there are a few small teasing drops.

But instead of the great fall, your log will move gently through a beautiful, tuneful, and peaceful water world filled with some 68 Ani-matronic characters and lots of delightful details. At the end of the first room there's a drop—but again it's not the big one.

Midway through the ride you'll pass through an opening to the outside and you'll be treated to one of the better views of the park—Thunder Mountain to your left, Cinderella Castle straight ahead, and Space Mountain and the distant Contemporary Resort behind it. (This peek is reminiscent of another Disney classic—the Matterhorn at Disneyland in California.) You'll also likely see a crowd of people staring up at you from below—actually, they're looking beyond you to the big drop over your shoulder.

All of a sudden you're back in the mountain and it's dark. Is this the big drop? Actually, no; you enter into another large room, this time illuminated with black light. Check out the bees circling around the bee hive. There's lots of water now, with splashing fountains and little squirts of water overhead. And there are now some signs of warning: "Enter at your own risk," "Danger," "Go Back, Beware, Watch Out."

But instead of going down, you'll go up one more sharp climb. Why do you suppose there are a pair of vultures hanging over the top of the hill? Listen to what they say: "Everybody's got a laughing place, maybe this is yours."

This is it, folks. The big one, the spectacular waterfall you've seen from the walkway below. You're over . . . and down in about four seconds.

There is one final surprise at the very end, yet another pretty inside room with a "Welcome Home Brer Rabbit" party.

Splash Mountain is actually one of the longer rides at the Magic Kingdom at nearly 11 minutes, and despite the brevity of the final drop it does give you a lot more for your waiting time than Thunder Mountain or Space Mountain. If you can convince the kids (or the adults) to look past the short drop, they are sure to love the rest of the ride which is pure Disney. And try the ride in the day and the night; the view of the park from near the top is worth the wait.

There are Splash Mountains at Disneyland and at Tokyo Disneyland; in California, guests sit one behind another while the Japanese and Florida versions load side-by-side.

**WOW!** **Tom Sawyer Island.** Another essential, at least for the youngsters, is the raft ride over to this little island in the middle of the Rivers of America. Based vaguely upon Mark Twain's classic book, you'll find dark caves, waterwheels, a barrel bridge, and a rope bridge to bounce on; at the far end of the island is a little bridge to Fort Sam Clemens, where kids can scramble around the parapets and fire air guns at passing sidewheelers.

The little snack bar at the fort sells, along with beverages, a most unusual fast food: whole sour pickles. There's also an interesting little gazebo out on the water called Aunt Polly's Landing, selling picnic basket fare: things like peanut butter and jelly sandwiches, cold fried chicken and apple pie.

Parents will appreciate the space to let their children burn off a bit of energy after standing in lines all day; be advised, though, that it is fairly easy to misplace a youngster in one of the simulated caves or on a trail. Discuss with your children a meeting place in case you become separated.

Lines for the raft rarely require more than 10 minutes waiting. The island closes at dusk.

**Country Bear Jamboree.** A doggedly cute show starring some 20 robotic bears of various sizes, shapes, and personalities, full of corny jokes and strained puns. Where else but at a Disney park could you possibly expect to see a trio of bears named Bubbles, Bunny, and Beulah singing a bowdlerized Beach Boys hit, "Wish They All Could Be California Bears"? (The soundtrack is changed annually for a Christmas Hoedown.)

For our money, we find this 15-minute attraction just barely (sorry) easier to take than the Enchanted Tiki Birds; youngsters and fans of Disney Audio-Animatronics will probably want to argue strongly in its favor. And the Hoedown is a very popular show, despite our opinion. The best time to visit is early, late, or during one of the parades. The best seats are at the very front or back of the hall.

**Frontierland Shootin' Arcade.** A durn-fancy shooting gallery, sort of a live video game and not like any other shooting gallery you have seen at a county fair. Players aim huge buffalo rifles at a Disney replica of an 1850s frontier town. The rifles fire infrared beams at targets on tombstones, clouds, banks, jails, and other objects; direct hits make the targets spin, explode, or otherwise surprise. Some of the signs on the objects tell a story: "Old Tom Hubbard died with a frown, but a grave can't keep a good man down." If you hit the skeleton of a steer, his horns will spin around.

To use the rifles you must pay an additional charge for a specific number of "bullets."

**Diamond Horseshoe Saloon Revue.** Disney's squeaky-clean version of a Western dance hall revue is a lot of fun for young and old, although it can be a bit of a hassle to work into a tight schedule.

The show itself is about 30 minutes in length; you'll need to arrive 30 to 45 minutes before showtime to make your way to your seat and place orders for drinks or sandwiches (strictly optional, although it may be difficult to prevent kids from badgering you for something at the table). Sandwiches go for about $6, and ice cream and brownies sell for about $2 to $3. In early 1996, the show operated on a space-available basis, ending years of "reservation-only" seating; of course, that is subject to change.

## Eating Your Way Through the Magic Kingdom

There are three types of restaurants at the Magic Kingdom: overpriced and bad, overpriced and barely acceptable, and overpriced and almost good. Well, okay, there are a few meals that are overpriced and good.

In any case, we'd recommend that you not consider meals to be an important part of your experience at the Magic Kingdom; save your time and money for one of the somewhat better Epcot Center or Disney-MGM Studios restaurants or for an evening outside of the Disney borders.

You do, though, have to eat. Disney has a rule against bringing your own sandwiches or other food into the park. In dozens of visits to Walt Disney World, though, we have never seen an attendant search a backpack or shoulder bag for tuna fish on rye, and you certainly can pack a baby's formula and a few candy bars for the kids.

If you don't pack your own, it is possible to pick and choose among the offerings at the park. Disney does offer a few nonstandard and more healthful offerings, like pasta salads, turkey hamburgers, and smoked turkey legs at some of its stands. Nevertheless, each year guests at Walt Disney World eat more than 7 million hamburgers, 5 million hot dogs, 5 million pounds of french fries, 265,000 pounds of popcorn, and 46 million Cokes.

**KEY:**

🍽 = Fast food

🍸 = Pub

🏛 = Full-service restaurant

We include general price ranges in our listings and mention specific prices for some items. Pricing on food and menus is subject to change. All food establishments within Disney World offer soft drinks at prices of about $2. (Did I hear someone say, "Why, I'll just throw a few cans of soda in a backpack."? Thought so.) By the way, in 1996 we found a hidden relative bargain near the main parking lot—a $1 soda can dispenser at the Ticket and Transportation Center near the bus loading area.

## Main Street, U.S.A.

🍽 **Main Street Wagons.** Located throughout the Main Street area. Espresso, cappuccino, soft drinks. Hot dogs and baked goods. Fresh fruit and vegetables and fruit drinks priced from about $1 to $3. A few umbrella-shaded tables are available on East Center Street beside the Main Street Market house.

🍽 **Main Street Bake Shop.** On Main Street near the Plaza Ice Cream Parlor. Unusual baked goods and beverages, $2 to $4. Cookies about $1. Watch cookies being made from scratch through the large window fronting on Main Street. There is a small seating area inside the pleasant, floral decorated shop, but most customers take their goodies to go, either to sit at one of the nearby umbrella tables or to carry with them as they move deeper into the park.

Very crowded at opening time, this shop is popular for breakfast sweets and coffee. Check out the oversized iced and glazed donuts and sweet rolls. A separate cookies and pastries line is available to the right of the entrance if that is all you want.

🍽 **Plaza Ice Cream Parlor.** Near Main Street Bake Shop, across from Refreshment Corner. Lines can be long in this pleasant, old-fashioned ice cream shop, but they move rather quickly. About $2 to $3 for most items.

🍽 **Casey's Corner.** At the top end of Main Street. Hot dogs, soda, soft drinks, and coffee. Attractive red and white umbrella tables on a sunny patio. A good place for a quick snack or a drink and a rest. Don't encourage the birds to beg for food; they'll try anyway.

🏛 **The Crystal Palace.** At the top of Main Street, toward Adventureland. Breakfast, lunch, and dinner buffets; the eatery was redone in early 1996.

The building is a replica of the Crystal Palace, built for the first International Exhibition in New York in 1851. The atmosphere is bright and airy with floral designs in a Victorian gazebo setting and a Dixieland jazz group often entertains diners.

**Tony's Town Square Restaurant.** Just inside the entrance gate to the right, next to Disneyana Collectibles and near The Walt Disney Story. Italian food, steaks, seafood, hamburgers, and salads, $15 to $21; appetizers, $3 to $8. Breakfast, lunch, and dinner from 8:30 A.M.; closing time depends on park hours. Reservations recommended; check in at the restaurant lobby.

The restaurant is modeled after the cafe in Disney's classic *Lady and the Tramp* movie. Seating for about 200. Entrees, priced from about $15 to $25, include sirloin steak with lobster and pasta, seafood linguine, and a seafood grill. Specialties include Joe's fettuccine, lasagna primavera, and Lady and the Tramp waffles.

**The Plaza Restaurant.** At the top of Main Street toward New Tomorrowland. Gourmet hamburgers, soups, sandwiches, and salads. Lunch and dinner. Open from 11 A.M. Entrees, $7 to $9.

This pleasant 19th-century-style dining room offers table service inside and bright yellow and white umbrella tables outside. Specialties include sandwiches, burgers, and generous sundaes.

## Adventureland

**Sunshine Tree Terrace.** At the north end of Adventureland, behind the Enchanted Tiki Birds' Tropical Serenade, this is worth a quick stop for a drink or light snack. Offerings include citrus drinks, frozen yogurt, shakes, and desserts, $2 to $3. A few umbrella tables give you a place to rest while you snack.

**The Oasis.** In the center of Adventureland. Soft drinks and snacks. A thatch-roofed shack with bamboo seating.

**Aloha Isle.** Pineapple and fruit drinks, $1.75. Try fresh pineapple spears for about $1 or raspberry/vanilla swirl for $1.75; a variety of tall fruit drinks.

## Frontierland

**Pecos Bill Cafe.** Just past the Country Bear Vacation Hoedown. Burgers, chicken barbecue, salads, and hot dogs, $5 to $7. Western saloon atmosphere in the side-by-side restaurants that share a common menu. Look carefully at the animals mounted on the wall; they're talking and singing robots.

The chicken and bean salad or a barbecue chicken sandwich is a good burger alternative, but if hamburger fits your fancy, try the Pecos Bill Trail Bacon Cheeseburger Basket. A large fixings bar offers a range of toppings including pickles, relishes, tomatoes, and more.

**Turkey Leg Wagon.** One of the strangest sights you are likely to see in Frontierland are visitors walking along the pathway absently chewing on what looks like the leg of a large dog. Actually, they're smoked turkey legs available from a stand directly across from the Country Bear Vacation Hoedown for about $4. Just follow the smell to the end of the line. As you carry along one of these interesting treats, watch out for sea gulls; they'll sometimes fly right at the turkey leg trying to take a bite out of it!

## Liberty Square

🍴 **Columbia Harbour House.** On Liberty Square across from Ichabod's Landing. Battered shrimp and chicken, cold sandwiches, pasta salads, salads. Lunch and dinner, $3 to $7. Children's menu includes a chicken sandwich or hot dog for about $4.

Seafood dining in seafaring atmosphere. Multiple small rooms break up the dining area. The dark, cool decor provides a comfortable respite from the sun. Larger tables seat six to eight. A few, small, semi-private dining rooms accommodate groups.

For an unusual appetizer or full meal, try the clam chowder served inside a large, round loaf of dark bread. When the chowder is gone, you can eat the bowl. A fruit plate is about $5.25. Sandwiches include smoked ham and cheese, tuna salad, and smoked turkey. Apple cobbler or chocolate and banana cream pies for dessert are about $3. A children's menu called the "Little Mariner's Meal" includes an entree, cookies, and a child's beverage for $2.49.

🍴 **Sleepy Hollow.** On Liberty Square near the Hall of Presidents.

Healthy fare in an early American decor. Notice the interesting wooden ceiling and plate rail displaying antique bottles, plates, and vases. The attractive blue and white tile floor enhances the atmosphere. Round tables and some picnic-style benched tables, some open and some covered. A pleasant outdoor-indoor dining area is under the brick-walled arbor.

Specialties include vegetarian sandwiches, vegetarian chili, feta salad, and tabbouleh; picky youngsters can order peanut butter and jam.

🍴 **Liberty Square Wagon.** On the walkway between Columbia Harbour House and the Hall of Presidents. Baked potatoes with toppings and beverages, $2 to $3. There's also a fresh fruit and pickle stand nearby.

In an area where sandwiches and other fast foods average about $5, the potato wagon is a popular alternative for a filling, low-cost lunch or snack. Fresh-baked white and sweet potatoes with a variety of toppings, about $2.50.

🍴 **Fruit and Vegetable Wagon.** Usually on the square behind the Columbia Harbour House and the Liberty Square Wagon. Various fruits and vegetables from a "farmer's market" wagon.

Attractively presented fruits and vegetables for alternative snacks and additions to meals. The selection includes apples, peaches, grapes, star fruit, and even pickles, squash, and potatoes.

🏠 **Liberty Tree Tavern.** Next to Diamond Horseshoe Jamboree and open for lunch (11:30 A.M. to 4 P.M.) and dinner (from 4:30 P.M.). Sandwiches, beef, chicken, seafood, salads, $7 to $16. Reservations recommended; request a seating time at the door.

Sit-down dining in a colonial atmosphere with a lot of interesting details including maple bench seats, fireplaces, and simulated peg flooring. A variety of sandwiches is available from $7 to $10. Seafood and other entrees from about $9.50 to $13.50. Luncheon specialties include New England Pot Roast, roast turkey dinner, and sautéed-shrimp pasta.

At dinner time, the Libery Tree features a Disney characters family-style dinner for $19.50 for adults and $9.95 for children nine and under. The meal includes salad, roast turkey, glazed ham, and marinated flank steak.

## Fantasyland

🍴 **Pinocchio Village Haus.** Next to It's a Small World under the Skyway. Turkey hamburgers, turkey hot dogs, chicken, salads, pasta. Lunch and dinner, $4.

A large dining hall in a Disneyfied Tudor style. Several small rooms, including a favored location overlooking the It's a Small World ride. Meals from about $5 to $6 with french fries or grapes and a regular beverage include choice of cheeseburgers (beef or turkey), a quarter pound turkey hot dog, or a grilled bratwurst. The eatery now includes a relish bar with pickles, tomatoes, onions, mushrooms, sauerkraut, barbecue sauce, cheese sauce, and more. The entrees are available a la carte, too.

Also available is a smoked turkey sub with provolone cheese, lettuce, and tomatoes for about $4.50.

As at many Disney fast food restaurants, the service lines move slowly at peak time. Come early or late to avoid wasting time.

🍴 **Lumière's Kitchen.** Across from 20,000 Leagues Under the Sea, near the Mad Tea Party ride. Sandwiches, children's meals, from about $3 to $5. Outdoor dining in front of a Tudor-style building. Open seasonally.

🍴 **Mrs. Potts' Cupboard.** Ice cream and soft drinks from about $2 to $3.

🍴 **Troubadour Tavern.** Next to Peter Pan's Flight and across from It's a Small World. Soft drinks and snacks, $1 to $2. Coffee and hot chocolate about $1, and a 20-ounce souvenir soft drink cup for about $2. Counter service; no seating.

🔺 **King Stefan's Banquet Hall.** Upstairs in Cinderella Castle. Prime rib, fish, chicken, beef, salads. Lunch ($5 to $15) and dinner ($21 to $25). Open from 11:30 A.M. to 3 P.M. for lunch; dinner begins at 4 P.M., with the closing time depending on park hours. Specialties include prime rib, grilled swordfish, and broiled chicken.

If you enter the castle from the Fantasyland side, the restaurant is on the outside left. Lines for lunch begin early because seating is limited. Among the more expensive restaurants in the Magic Kingdom, King Stefan's is a favorite of some children, especially little girls who dream of meeting Cinderella herself. Reservations are accepted at the door on the day you wish to dine; guests at Disney hotels can make telephone reservations up to two days ahead of time.

You enter the restaurant through a "great hall" entrance on the ground floor. This interesting room is complete with torch lanterns and swords on the wall. The slate floor and high, exposed-beam ceiling enhance the "castle" feeling of the restaurant. You'll move upstairs via an interesting, winding stairway or in an elevator.

The banquet hall is also the location for the **Once Upon a Time Character Breakfast** every morning; call 939-3463 for reservations. Admission is $14.95 for adults and $7.95 for children from ages 3 to 9.

## New Tomorrowland

**Cosmic Ray's Starlight Café.** Cosmic Ray's (get it?) is the largest fast food eatery in the Magic Kingdom, the former Tomorrowland Terrace. Decorated in brushed aluminum, purples, and blacks, there's a little stage at the back of the room for presentations. Food includes burgers, cheeseburgers, vegetarian burgers, chicken, and more; the catsup is dyed a ghastly purple, the mayonnaise is blue, and the mustard is a sharp yellow.

**Plaza Pavilion.** In the walkway between Main Street and New Tomorrowland. Pizza, sandwiches, salads, $3 to $5. Covered outdoor dining in a pleasant setting for about 650 people. There are three dining areas, one overlooking a portion of the central lagoon and offering an excellent view of Cinderella Castle. The area offers cool shade and ample seating away from the main service area and transient crowds.

Try the Italian hoagie at about $4.25 or the chicken Parmesan sandwich for a dollar more. Deep dish pizza is available by the slice for about $3.25 to $4.75. Fix up your ice cream with the brownie sundae ($2.75) or an ice cream float for about $2.30.

**Auntie Gravity's Galactic Goodies.** Across the broad plaza from Space Mountain at the base of the Astro Orbiter tower. Juice, snacks, frozen yogurt, $2 to $3. Mostly "natural" refreshments, such as an apple juice float made with yogurt at about $2.60. Offers a handful of outdoor tables and few within.

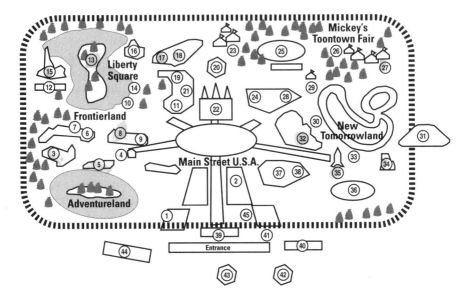

1. City Hall
2. First Aid
3. Pirates of the Caribbean
4. Swiss Family Treehouse
5. Jungle Cruise
6. Enchanted Tiki Birds
7. Country Bear Jamboree
8. Jungle Cruise
9. Diamond Horseshoe Saloon Revue
10. Liberty Square Riverboat
11. The Hall of Presidents
12. Splash Mountain
13. Tom Sawyer Island
14. Mike Fink Keelboats
15. Big Thunder Mountain Railroad
16. The Haunted Mansion
17. Skyway
18. It's a Small World
19. Peter Pan's Flight
20. Cinderella's Golden Carrousel
21. Fantasyland Theater: Lion King Adventure
22. Cinderella Castle
23. Dumbo, the Flying Elephant
24. Snow White's Adventures
25. 20,000 Leagues Under the Sea
26. Mickey's Hollywood Theater
27. Mickey's House
28. Mr. Toad's Wild Ride
29. Mad Tea Party
30. Grand Prix Raceway
31. Space Mountain
32. ExtraTERRORestrial Alien Encounter
33. Tomorrowland Transit Authority
34. Skyway
35. Astro Orbiter
36. Carousel of Progress
37. Transportarium
38. Dreamflight
39. Walt Disney World Railroad Main Street
40. Magic Kingdom Bus Transportation
41. Guest Relations
42. Ferry Boat to Parking
43. Launch to Discovery Island and Fort Wilderness
44. Monorail Station
45. Strollers

# Chapter 7
# Epcot Center

Walt Disney's original concept called for construction of a modern city from scratch: homes, offices, farms, and factories. It was intended as a showcase for new ideas and technologies from American industry and educational institutions.

Disney called his dream the Experimental Prototype Community of Tomorrow, which is the almost-forgotten name behind the Epcot acronym.

Disney lived long enough to set the broad outlines for Epcot, but the park as built was quite different from the prototype community he first planned. Instead, the second theme park at Walt Disney World is like a permanent World's Fair. Roughly half the park is given over to imaginative pavilions that explore the frontiers of science: communication, energy, human life, transportation, technology, creativity, agriculture, and the seas. And then spread around the World Showcase Lagoon are exhibits, films, and a handful of rides that share some of the cultures of the globe: from Canada, the United Kingdom, France, Morocco, Japan, America, Italy, Germany, China, Norway, and Mexico.

**Facts and figures.** Epcot, at 260 acres, is more than twice the size of the Magic Kingdom. The World Showcase Lagoon is about 40 acres in size; the promenade that circles it and leads to the national showcases is 1.2 miles in length. Initial construction costs were about $1.3 billion in 1982, one of the largest private construction jobs ever completed.

Although it is most likely the lure of Mickey and Minnie's Magic Kingdom that brings most visitors to Walt Disney World, many adults and quite a few children will tell you that the memory they bring home from Florida comes from Epcot: Figment at Journey Into Imagination, Alec Tronics at Innoventions, the troll at Norway, or the film view of the Great Wall at China.

Spend the time at Epcot and talk about the things you learn there; that may be the greatest legacy of Disney.

Epcot celebrates change, and the park itself is well along in a makeover that will bring a new generation of exhibits to the World Showcase. In 1997, look for the opening of the spectacular General Motors Test Track, a wild automobile-theme ride that is sure to be one of the major draws at Epcot, and a new show within the Universe of Energy pavilion.

The oddly misplaced Barbie show is gone, we're happy to report. Also shuttered is the Walt Disney Imagineering Laboratory, which offered a peek behind the curtain at an Aladdin virtual reality show in the making; Aladdin may reappear as an attraction elsewhere, perhaps at Disney-MGM Studios.

Disney could give lessons to the CIA on how to keep secrets, but enough information does leak out around the edges to give an indication of some of the future plans for Epcot.

Imagineers are said to be ready to blast off with a new show tentatively called "Journeys in Space" to replace the outdated Horizons pavilion.

Also waiting for the go-ahead is a mountain roller coaster, possibly behind the Japan pavilion in World Showcase. And the tantalizing possibility of an Indiana Jones ride—like the fantastic one at Disneyland—is also on the drawing board, with proposed locations including the Mexico pavilion or as part of a new Brazil pavilion.

Two other World Showcase buildings that we may see would represent Denmark and the African continent. Plans for a Russia and Switzerland pavilion are said to be on hold.

Finally, a new Illuminations show may be unveiled in 1996 or 1997, according to Disney sources.

Epcot includes an interesting range of special events. In recent years these events have included Holidays Around the World at Christmastime, featuring a candlelight processional, the Christmas Story presented at the America Gardens Stage with 400 voices and a 50-piece orchestra, and a "living" Christmas tree. The events were free to all ticketholders, but Epcot also made available a specially priced ticket that offered entrance to the park, reserved seating at the processional, free preferred parking, and special discounts on Epcot merchandise.

Many of the international pavilions have special celebrations on their national holidays. Chinese New Year is celebrated in February at China; Moroccan Throne Day is observed on March 3, and Italy holds a Carnivale Celebration at the opening of Lent.

In 1996, Disney was continuing with a split schedule for Epcot, with Future World open from 9 A.M. to 7 P.M., and the World Showcase open from 11 A.M. to 9 P.M. (Spaceship Earth and the Innoventions complex remain open through 9 P.M.) Operating hours are subject to change, and Epcot may return to its traditional full-park operation schedule in the busiest holiday and summer periods.

Epcot is unique among the three parks at Walt Disney World in that it has two entrances—the main door, which leads directly to the Spaceship Earth, and a second, less-used International Gateway at the World Showcase, between the pavilions of the United Kingdom and France. Trams or little ferry boats run between the International Gateway and the BoardWalk, Swan, Dolphin, Beach Club, and Yacht Club resorts.

# Power Trip

This plan is based on the split schedule that opens Future World two hours before the World Showcase.

The key to getting the most out of a visit to Epcot, as with every other attraction, is once again to adopt a Contrarian View of the park. Most visitors saunter into the park in mid-morning and join the crowds at the pavilions of Future World before beginning a slow—and crowded—circle of the World Showcase section in a clockwise direction. Another important bit of information is the fact that Spaceship Earth and the surrounding Innoventions usually open a bit before the rest of Epcot.

Get there early. If you're up for a thrill ride, this is the time to make tracks to the new GM Test Track (scheduled to open in the Spring of 1997). Bear to the left from the entrance and follow the signs. You may be able to go for a second ride in the early morning; it will probably be late in the day before lines drop back down to reasonable lengths.

While you're in the neighborhood, backtrack a bit to the Energy pavilion and see the new show there. If you're determined to see all the big draws before the lines build up, sprint across Future World to the Imagination pavilion and visit the "Honey, I Shrunk the Audience" show.

By this time, it should be near 11 A.M. and time to jump out ahead of the crowds. Move into the **World Showcase**.

The biggest crowds at the World Showcase can usually be found at the Norway, Mexico, and American pavilions. If you are at the head of the throng, go immediately to **Mexico** and then next door to **Norway** and then continue in a clockwise circle around the lagoon. If you find yourself behind the madding crowd, you might want to travel in the opposite direction, going counterclockwise and starting at **Canada**.

After you come out of the World Showcase,

**Springtime treat.** If you arrive at Epcot in March, April, or May, pay attention to the trees just at the base of the golf ball. The striking ornamental trees with blue trumpet-shaped flowers are jacaranda, native to northwestern Argentina.

**Tubular, dude.** The Spaceship Earth sphere is built from four structural parts. The outer shell is strictly for decorative purposes and is connected to an inner waterproof sphere by hundreds of small support columns. A column that runs up the center of the ball supports the internal ride, which circles around the column like a spiral staircase. And finally, a platform at the bottom of the sphere supports the inner structure and the ride itself.

tour the pavilions of **Future World**, this time moving in a clockwise direction—starting at Journey Into Imagination and heading toward the front of the park and Spaceship Earth. Double back at the golf ball and visit **Innoventions** and **Wonders of Life** to complete your tour.

With luck, you will complete the tour of Epcot at nightfall and can enjoy a leisurely dinner before coming out to the lagoon for a view of the spectacular **IllumiNations** show.

Here's a by-the-numbers Power Trip, pavilion-by-pavilion. 1: **GM Test Track** (when open); 2: **Universe of Energy**; 3: **Honey, I Shrunk the Audience**; 4: **Mexico**; 5: **Norway**; 6: **China**; 7: **Germany**; 8: **Italy**; 9: **The American Adventure**; 10: **Japan**; 11: **Morocco**; 12: **France**; 13: **United Kingdom**; 14: **Canada**; 15: **Journey Into Imagination**; 16: **The Land**; 17: **The Living Seas**; 18: **Spaceship Earth**; 19: **Innoventions**, and 20: **Wonders of Life**.

## Attractions at Future World

### Spaceship Earth

**WOW** **Spaceship Earth.** The huge geodesic sphere that is the symbol of Epcot—referred to by most visitors as the "golf ball"—is 180 feet (18 stories) high and 165 feet in diameter with 2.2 million cubic feet of space within. It weighs almost 16 million pounds including 1,750 tons of steel. Actually, the building is not a dome; it is a sphere.

As impressive as the shell is, the real excitement of Spaceship Earth can be found on the ride within, which is sponsored by communications giant AT&T. (Each of the major exhibits at Epcot's Future World is sponsored by a major American corporation, but the commercialism is relatively low-key.)

The original exhibit was designed by an interesting collaboration that included science fiction author Ray Bradbury, the Smithsonian Institution, and newsman Walter Cronkite. The ride was updated in 1995 with some new areas, a new narration by actor Jeremy Irons, and a new musical score. (The cloying "Tomorrow's Child" song is gone.) There's nothing here that will set your heart to pounding, but the lighting, video, and computer special effects are among the best at Walt Disney World.

You'll board "time machine" chairs for a trip through the sphere that will take you back through history from the age of the Cro-Magnon man some

30,000 years ago to the present, along the way passing through the great ancient civilizations of Egypt, Phoenicia, and Rome. The narration may be a bit beyond the comprehension of young children, but they'll still enjoy and learn from the sights.

**Who's counting?** The outside of the sphere is made up of some 11,000 triangular tiles, made of a composite of ethylene plastic bonded between two aluminum panels.

You'll note some of the truly important developments of our time, including the development of an alphabet and written language, the first books, the development of the printing press, and on to modern communications. You'll also see great cultural figures from Michelangelo (the painter, not the Ninja Turtle) at work in the Sistine Chapel to Howdy Doody and Ed Sullivan. At the very top of the ball is the most spectacular sight of all, a huge sky of stars and planets. Not all of the special effects of this ride are visual ones; Disney engineers created smell cannons that fill the air with odors including those of burning Rome.

**Hard ride.** As befits the unusual building, the time machines in this ride take an unusual route. You'll slowly spiral up, up, and up around the sides of the ball until you reach the starfield at top; then your chair will turn around for a steep, backward descent to the base. Some riders might find the trip down a bit uncomfortable.

The page from the Bible that Johannes Gutenberg is examining is an exact replica of a page from one of his early bibles. In the Egyptian scene, the hieroglyphics on the wall are reproductions of actual graphics; the words being dictated by the Pharaoh were taken from an actual letter sent by a pharaoh to one of his agents.

And then we move into the near future, where we see a young boy communicating in his room over the information superhighway. At the very top of the golf ball we move into a startlingly beautiful planetarium-like dome with Spaceship Earth and the stars all around it. Our chairs move into a view of a futuristic classroom embarking on a virtual field trip.

The dazzling new finale puts the audience in the heart of interactive global networks that tie all the peoples of the earth together. Fantastic special effects, animated sets, and laser beams that surround and encase the visitors will finish off the experience with a simulated trip into a microchip.

From there, it is on to the **Global Neighborhood** for hands-on demonstrations of new technologies in voice recognition, video telephony, and the information superhighway.

Because of its position at the front of the park, lines for this ride are usually longest at the start of the day, although early arrivals can still expect to be able to walk right on. If the line builds up, though, we'd suggest coming back in the afternoon or on your way out of the park at the end of the day.

**Early Value Meals.** Epcot sometimes offers discount early bird meals at many of its restaurants for diners who arrive between 4:30 and 6 P.M. Check at Earth Station when you arrive at Epcot to see if this unadvertised special deal is in effect when you visit.

## 🎆 Innoventions

Innoventions is a highly commercial version of a World's Fair or a major trade show like the Consumer Electronics Show. Although products will not be sold in exhibit areas, representatives will be on hand to explain and demonstrate. Guests may use interactive computer terminals to receive information by mail.

What Disney has done is truly an amazing thing: they have found a way to charge visitors nearly $40 each to enter a somewhat ordinary convention hall–like building and look at exhibits of commercial products. Even more amazing is the fact that Disney is able to charge major corporations millions of dollars for the right to build their own exhibits.

"Epcot visitors may never go to Mars," said Michael Eisner, chairman and CEO of The Walt Disney Company, "but they will use the machines, computer games, toys, phones, musical instruments, televisions, stoves, refrigerators, vacuum cleaners, and toilets which they will see, probably for the first time, in Innoventions."

Youngsters and fans of electronic gadgets will likely want to bear to the right of Spaceship Earth to **Innoventions West**, home of exhibits by companies including AT&T, IBM, **Sega of America**, Videonics, and others. On the left side of Spaceship Earth in **Innoventions East** are exhibits aimed mostly at adults, including displays from Apple, General Electric, Hammacher Schlemmer, Honeywell, General Motors, and others.

Eating establishments included within the Innoventions area are the **Electric Umbrella Restaurant**, **Pasta Piazza Ristorante**, and **Fountain View Espresso & Bakery**.

Parental Guidance: Innoventions is a tremendous lure for the video kid generation. I don't know about you, but I'm not very happy about the thought of spending thousands of dollars and traveling thousands of miles to Orlando to see my children head off to play video games for hours at a time. Other parents might be willing to trust their kids to stay in one place for a few hours while they head off to a leisurely dinner. In either case, be sure to have a plan of action with your children in the sprawling Innoventions building.

A hot new exhibit at Innoventions is the Virtual Reality Experience, presented by Enel, the Italian electric company that is the world's third-largest power utility. Small groups enter into a small room for a virtual visit to St. Peter's Basilica.

### Innoventions West

The resident expert at Innoventions is **Bill Nye the Science Guy**, host of a television show of the same name (not coincidentally produced by Disney's television division). Nye appears in a videotaped multimedia show explaining the basic principles of science that underlie many of the products on display at Innoventions.

**AT&T.** Voice and data-transfer technologies including a wrist telephone, recognition devices, video computer phones, on-line computer libraries, and a variety of new computer games.

***Discover* Magazine Awards for Technological Innovation.** A display of the current year's winning inventors and their inventions.

**Eclectronics.** A display of electronic devices assembled by Disney Imagineers, including a $500,000 stereo system, electronic keyboards with exotic special effects abilities, interactive video games, and Alec Tronic, the see-through Disney Audio-Animatronics rock 'n' roll performer. Alec sings a collection of rock hits, including a funny version of Joe Cocker's "Feelin' Alright" classic with the famous little hand motions of the real performer. He also imitates former President Richard Nixon's favored comment, "Let me make myself perfectly clear," which, of course, he is.

About that $50,000 stereo: you'll enter a closed room with sound baffles and listen as the system switches between a $1,500 consumer system and an ultimate audiophile setup. They are obviously not the same, but not all ears will value the difference at $48,500.

**IBM Corporation.** The Thinkplace presents the latest advances in information technologies, from electronic field trips to videoconferencing to thrilling special effects. Displays include The Face Factory where you can "morph" your visage on a huge video screen. You'll also be able to lay hands on several of IBM's latest personal computers.

**Lego Dacta.** Visitors will be able to operate elaborate models of equipment, buildings, and molecular structures which demonstrate principles of physics, engineering, architecture, biology, and other areas of science. That's right: Lego, as in Lego blocks.

**Sega of America.** Sonic the Hedgehog, almost as famous as Mickey Mouse, is the host to a demonstration area of more than 100 new video games. Also on display is Sega's Virtual Reality system, the AS-1 simulator space flight, and Virtua Racing multi-driver racing game. The video games are free; visitors have to pay a $4 charge to use the AS-1 and Virtua Racing games.

**Epcot ecology.** As a planned community, Epcot includes many interesting experiments in ecology.

The huge Disney development uses and disposes a tremendous amount of water, which is a particular problem in the wet Florida environment. Some of the effluent of the wastewater treatment plant is sprayed on the 145-acre Walt Disney World Tree Farm to make use of nutrients in the water. Another project involves the growth of water hyacinths in a pond fed by the wastewater plant; the plants help purify the water by absorbing nutrients and filtering solids through their roots. Grown plants are harvested and composted for use as fertilizer.

**The light fantastic.** Disney designers snuck a little extra bit of magic into the construction of the Innoventions building. Fiber optics embedded in the tiles of the walkways outside are computer controlled to dance along with the nightly IllumiNations show on the lagoon.

There may be a potential problem with the video games on busy days, by the way. I saw several instances where a youngster was parked in front of a game with no intentions of moving until the lights were turned out. According to Disney staffers, there is no rule requiring players to give up the controls after a particular time. In the case of my own son, I had to lean over a teenager and ask him repeatedly to step aside after half an hour with a single game. He finally left, muttering some distinctly un-Disney-like language.

**Videonics.** Guests will learn how to make better home videos and edit them into personal movies using the company's Thumbs-Up, Video Title-Maker and other products.

**Epcot Discovery Center.** Just outside the main entrance to Innoventions West, this is a resource center for teachers and anyone interested in education. The center includes an "Ask Epcot" information desk, on-line connection to major information services, and the Class-to-Class Pen Pal and Educator Idea Exchange. Also within the new area is **Field Trips**, a shop featuring educational software, games, and research material.

Visitors can register for a Class-to-Class Pen Pal Program, read current educational journals and magazines, and explore research materials to find ideas for classroom lessons. The Educator's Idea Exchange permits visitors to share information through a computer bulletin board system.

### Innoventions East

The **Magic House Tour** features new appliances, automatic plumbing facilities, and intelligent systems for computerized management of the home and business. Believe it or not, the early displays will include a self-cleaning rest room for business buildings that automatically washes walls, floors, and fixtures, and then turns a blow dryer on itself.

And check out one of the first consumer demonstrations of high-definition television (HDTV). Also on display are advanced versions of handheld computers, voice control modules to allow you to give orders to your car or home, and some highly advanced group video games.

**Apple Computer.** Try out computers for personal and business use, plus advanced technologies including an electronic still-picture camera.

**General Electric.** The wide-ranging operations of GE are represented here, from the National Broadcasting Company to jet engines to home appliances. Visitors will be able to sit next to an electronic image of Jay Leno and participate in a "Tonight Show" interview through the magic of blue-screen technology; be sure to bring your video camera.

**General Motors.** The display features the Impact prototype electric car. (Does anyone else out there think that "Impact" is a less than reassuring name for an automobile?) Also shown is Ultralite, a lightweight super-strong vehicle that had a bit part in the motion picture *Demolition Man*. New automobile navigation systems on display will provide a lost driver with an instant video map, sent by satellite. You'll also see demonstrations of heads up auto instrument panels that place images at the driver's eye level.

**Hammacher Schlemmer.** A display from the pages of the catalog of this specialist in unusual gadgets and devices, including a body-activated video control, a digital player piano, and an aroma steam personal sauna.

**Honeywell.** At Comfortville, see inside five homes where family and friends are enjoying "comfortable living at its best" using products for new and existing homes including temperature control, security, and energy-saving systems; electric windows; and the latest communications and entertainment products.

**Relativity.** All of Disneyland in California could fit within the lagoon at Epcot Center, or within the boundaries of the parking lot at the Magic Kingdom.

## Universe of Energy

**WOW Universe of Energy.** Forward to the past, and back to the future: after nearly a year of silence, the frighteningly lifelike dinosaurs of the Universe of Energy roared back to life in the fall of 1996 with a reworked and updated show.

The pavilion is based around a spectacular new film called "Ellen's Energy Crisis," starring comedian Ellen DeGeneres and featuring some exciting special effects. In the movie, Ellen dreams she is a contestant on the "Jeopardy" television game show. She's up against the reigning champion Dr. Judy Peterson, played by Jamie Lee Curtis. And the categories? They're all about energy, a subject that is clearly not Ellen's specialty.

Ellen has a secret weapon, though: her neighbor Bill Nye the Science Guy. She summons him for some hints, and he responds by taking Ellen—and all of the guests seated in the pavilion's famous moving grandstands—on a tour that travels back in time to the birth of the planet, and then on to a world tour of today's energy need and research.

The show is sure to be a major draw at Epcot and contribute to a lopsided draw to the west side of the park along with the new GM Test Track. Head there early, or come back late in the day to avoid lines that may stretch for eons.

## Wonders of Life

A world of its own. Under one geodesic domed roof you will find two of Epcot's best attractions, plus a healthful Fitness Fairground for children of all ages and a set of entertaining and informative films and presentations on subjects from exercise to reproduction.

You could easily spend a few hours here; it's an especially good place to escape bad weather.

**WOW Body Wars.** Strap on your seat belts and prepare for blast-off on a journey to inner space. Body Wars is a fantastic simulator ride that takes you on a repair expedition inside a human body—a training mission to remove a splinter from *within*. (Check out the pilot's cockpit for the Body Wars vehicle; we like the pink baby shoes hanging over the windshield.)

As usual in a sci-fi story like this, something goes wrong within the body and the medical craft begins to lose all power from its fuel cell. So, our pilot decides he must go to the brain and cross the blood-brain barrier and park next to a synapse in hopes that it will fire and recharge the cell.

The simulation cabin bounces and twists through the veins and arteries of

**Secret Mickey.** There is a hidden image of Mickey Mouse in the mural above the waiting area for Body Wars.

**How'd they do that?** The geodesic dome for the pavilion is 250 feet in diameter and 60 feet tall at the center; to construct it, engineers built a temporary tower crane in the center. Rings of triangles were then hoisted by cables attached to the tower and anchored to columns around the circumference. When the dome was up, the crane was dismantled and removed.

**Super helix.** The huge sculpture at the entrance to the Wonders of Life pavilion is a 75-foot-tall representation of a DNA molecule, the basic building block of life. A human built to the same scale would be several million miles tall.

the human body, ending up with an electrical bang.

Amazingly, for a vehicle that doesn't really go anywhere, this ride carries as many health warnings as a roller coaster. No pregnant women or persons with back or heart ailments are allowed aboard, and children under seven must be accompanied by an adult. Those less than three years of age cannot ride. If you're the type who gets queasy on an elevator—and you know who you are—you might want to pass this one by.

By the way, any serious sci-fi fan will recognize the Body Wars story as a spin-off of the classic science fiction movie, *Fantastic Voyage,* which featured Raquel Welch in a body suit.

**WOW** **Cranium Command.** One of the wildest and most offbeat shows anywhere in Walt Disney World, this is a combination Audio-Animatronics and film journey into one of the most unstable places on earth. Your screaming leader, General Knowledge, will inform you that you have been assigned to pilot the most erratic craft in the fleet—the mind of a 12-year-old boy.

This is a presentation that has something for everyone, from corny jokes and a food fight for the kids to smart one-liners and comic performances from well-known comedians including George Wendt (Norm from *Cheers*) as superintendent of the stomach, Bobcat Goldthwait in a typecast role as a hysterical adrenaline gland, and Charles Grodin as the smug, all-knowing Right Brain. All this to teach about the benefits of stress management!

It's a very clever show and rarely more than a 15- to 30-minute wait; don't pass it by.

**Fitness Fairgrounds.** The various exhibits in the center of the dome can occupy visitors for hours and are a great place to get out of the sun or rain. Our only warning about this place is that it is quite easy to misplace young children in the busy aisles.

**Goofy About Health.** You wouldn't ordinarily include our old friend Goofy on a list of contenders for the Olympic team, but this very entertaining film presentation teaches about the value of exercise and health habits as it entertains.

**AnaComical Players.** A lively and pun-filled tour of the human body, presented by a clever improvisational theater group. Are you really ready for "Flossed in Space"?

**The Making of Me.** Okay, parents: here's an opportunity to teach your children some of the facts of life in an entertaining 14-minute film starring comedian Martin Short. He begins with a visit to the birth of his mom and dad and follows them right through his own conception (lovemaking is described as a private moment between lovers, with just enough detail to guarantee your kids will come up with their own questions). There is spectacular footage of the beginnings of life and childbirth. Lines for this show—presented in a tiny theater—can begin to stretch to as much as an hour at the most crowded parts of the day; go early or late. Highly recommended.

**Coach's Corner.** Step up to the batting tee, the tennis net, or the fairway for a quick sports lesson. Your swing will be videotaped and you'll receive a quick taped comment from one of sport's greatest players. It's all in good fun, although some adults seem to take their moment of stardom *very* seriously.

**Wondercycles.** A very high-tech set of exercise bicycles that present videodisc images keyed to your pedaling speed. You can "visit" Disneyland, scoot in and among the floats in the Rose Bowl Parade in California, or enjoy a hilarious low-level pedal through Big Town, U.S.A., in which your cycle passes humans, dogs, cars, and furniture at rug rat level.

**Sensory Funhouse.** A set of interesting demonstrations of human senses, including sight, sound, and touch. It includes some unusual demonstrations including an area where you stick your hands through a black curtain so that you can't see what you are touching; like the old story of the blind men and the elephant, it's amusing to hear the descriptions visitors make of items that include a pair of ski goggles, a chess piece, a gyroscope, a toy train, and a toy dinosaur.

**Met Lifestyle Revue.** A computer will ask you all sorts of personal questions and then offer a personalized set of lifestyle suggestions.

The best way to tour Wonders of Life is to keep an eye on the waiting lines for Body Wars and Cranium Command and dive in when they seem reasonable. There is plenty to occupy visitors between trips to those attractions.

## Horizons

**Horizons.** One of our favorites, the Horizons pavilion reopened at the start of 1996, coinciding with the closure of the World of Motion. The ride, originally presented by General Electric, is an extension of the Magic Kingdom's Carousel of Progress theme that presents a vision of the future that includes the **Omega Centauri** space colony, the **Sea Castle** underwater city, and the robotic farm station **Mesa Verde**. In fact, we swear that it is the same dog and family from the Carousel, transported centuries into the future.

Rumors say Disney plans to close the pavilion again once the GM Test Track

**The vanishing star.** The King of Pop, also known as Michael Jackson, also known as "who?" used to star in a 3-D sci-fi dance movie called "Captain EO" in this theater. The Disney Company claims that the end of its relationship with Jackson has nothing to do with the Strange One's legal problems, and, in fact, the first *Honey* film had been in production for some time before Jackson's problems became public.

is up and running, with indefinite plans for a replacement attraction. If Horizons is still open when you visit, hop on board for a gentle World's Fair-like peek at the future.

The best part of this ride, one of the most spectacular moments in all of Epcot, comes when your ride car travels deep into a huge hemispherical screen; talk about a front row seat! (Large-size 70-mm film is run horizontally to allow for an extra-large projection frame.) You'll go to space, progress into a DNA molecule, swim with the fishes, and more.

The last segment of the ride allows the four passengers in your vehicle to "vote" on a destination for a quick exploration trip just for your car. Your three choices at the end of Horizons are space, desert, or under the sea.

## GM Test Track

**WOW GM Test Track.** Here's your chance to be your very own crash test dummy, on one of the most-anticipated new thrill rides at Walt Disney World, sure to be the greatest draw at Epcot for some time to come. The ride was scheduled to open in the spring of 1997, replacing the venerable but oh-so-safe World of Motion.

You'll climb into a version of one of GM's futuristic "concept" cars and visit a robot assembly factory and hot and cold temperature simulators before setting out on a little spin up and down and around corners, across Belgian Block, snow and ice, and then into a series of high-speed turns.

Tracks circle the exterior of the ride building and extend out into the back, narrowly avoiding head-on collisions with huge trucks and hurtling toward walls—not your basic Sunday drive in the park. The Disney design team includes veterans of the successful Indiana Jones and the Temple of the Forbidden Eye ride at Disneyland.

Until the ride opens, visitors will be able to grab a glimpse from the monorail or by climbing the steep embankment out front.

## Journey Into Imagination

**WOW Journey Into Imagination.** This attraction includes some of the most unusual special effects at Epcot and is a clear favorite among youngsters. The wonderment starts outside the doors: stop for a while at the fountains to the left of the entranceway and watch jets of water arc majestically from tube to tube.

The ride within introduces you to Dreamfinder and his pet purple dragon Figment (as in "of imagination"). They'll take you along on an expedition to collect colors, sounds, shapes, and stories with which to create new ideas. The opening segment of the ride puts your vehicle on the outside track of a large rotating room—there are several Dreamfinders and Figments in wedge-shaped stages that move with a group of viewers for a while. The ride is an interesting variation on the Carousel of Progress concept; in this case, both the cars and the turntable stage revolve together for a while before the cars move off on their own. If you look to your left as you complete the circle and start to move away, you will see cars hooking up with the turntable at the start of the ride.

The Magic Journeys segment of the 13-minute ride presents some of the highest resolution and most astounding 3-D images ever created. Disney technicians developed a 65-mm 3-D camera capable of shooting as many as 75 frames per second—three times the speed of a conventional camera—for use in creating slow-motion displays. The 3-D system consists of a pair of linked cameras—one that shoots through a partially silvered beam-splitter mirror and the other that shoots a right angle to the mirror. Some other images were entirely created on a computer, a glimpse at the future of 3-D imaging.

As noted, this ride is a treat for the kids; some adults find it a bit too sweet. Lines can build up to an hour or so by midday; visit early or late.

**WOW** **Image Works.** When the ride is over, don't pass up the chance to climb the stairs or ride the glass-tube elevator to the Image Works area upstairs. Here you'll find some of the most interesting hands-on experiences at Epcot.

You can conduct an **Electronic Philharmonic** by waving your hands through light beams. Youngsters can step into a special effects movie in **Dreamfinders School of Drama**, where computers merge foreground, background, and live-action video images. Banks of computers at **Making Faces** allow visitors to change their own appearance on video screens with fanciful ears, eyes, noses, and colors. At the **Rainbow Corridor**, visitors are assigned one of five colors by a computer and then tracked by infrared detectors as they walk or run through the tube. **Figment's Coloring Book** gives kids of all ages the opportunity to use the computer as a painting tool, adding colors to three-dimensional objects up on the ceiling.

In fact, for some younger children, Image Works is one of the high points

**What exactly is a figment?** The answer goes by awfully quickly in the song at the beginning of the ride, so pay attention here: the body of a lizard, the nose of a crocodile, the horns of a steer, two tiny wings, big yellow eyes, royal purple pigment, and a dash of childish delight.

**Count the Figments.** We counted 21 Figments in various places on the ride, including images in films and on monitors. Can you top our count? Send us a list.

**Where's the camera?** Actors at the Dreamfinders School of Drama use electronic magic that merges their images into a videotaped show. Can you spot the robotically controlled camera? It's hidden within the blue ball in the ceiling in the middle of the room. There are four different shows, by the way.

of Epcot, worth an hour or so of indoor exploration, especially valuable on a rainy or overly warm day.

By the way, you don't have to take the Journey Into Imagination ride to visit the Image Works. Just walk to the left of the waiting area for the ride and head for the stairs or elevator.

**WOW** **Honey, I Shrunk the Audience.** A spectacular 3-D thriller that takes off where the two shape-altering Disney films (*Honey, I Shrunk the Kids* and *Honey, I Blew Up the Baby*) left off. In this case, it's the audience that shrinks instead of the kids. This is a theatrical performance that is simply not to be missed.

It begins outside the theater with a preshow sponsored by Kodak and based on their "true colors" advertising theme, an attractive and somewhat inspiring collection of photographs on the general idea of imagination and an extension of the imagination exhibit upstairs.

Then we find ourselves as honored guests at the presentation of the "Inventor of the Year" award to Wayne Szalinski, played by actor Rick Moranis. Other members of the film cast also appear in the feature, and are joined by funnyman Eric Idle of Monty Python's Flying Circus.

And finally we are invited within to see a demonstration of some of Wayne's greatest new inventions including the Dimensional Duplicator and the No Mess Holographic Pet System. You'll go through the doors on the left side of the preshow auditorium into the theater. You'll be asked to move all the way across a row to fill up all the seats; if you want to try to grab one of the best seats hold back a bit until about 25 people have entered a row and then enter.

As far as what happens next, we don't want to spoil the fun or play a cat-and-mouse game with you; oops, disregard that last hint.

The wild conclusion of the show comes when one of the machines goes berserk and ends up shrinking the entire audience down to toy size. "Stay in your seats and we will blow you up as soon as possible," says Wayne.

The auditorium conspires with the 3-D images to complete the illusion with moving seats, spectacular lighting, special film effects, and unusual effects that will tickle your fancy and sprinkle you with laughter.

The large theater seats 575 guests and will eat up a full waiting line inside the building; if the line stretches out onto the plaza you can expect at least a 45-minute wait.

Lines will ebb and flow at the theater, reached from an entrance inside the doors of the Journey Into Imagination to the left of the loading area for the theme ride. Go early or late to avoid lengthy waits.

## The Land

Everyone has to eat, and The Land is a tasty collection of informative exhibits about food and our environment. The building, in part a gigantic greenhouse, also includes a popular food court restaurant.

**WOW** **Living with the Land.** A boat ride through the past and future of agriculture. In a 1994 remake, Disney Imagineers created a storm scene as an introduction to a tour that passes through a rain forest, desert, and plain—

traditional sources of food—and then into some amazing experiments with hydroponic farms, cultivated seafood farms of shrimp and fish, and a desert made to bloom with crops through high-tech irrigation.

**Wide world.** The Land is one of the largest attractions at Walt Disney World. It covers some six acres and is as big as the entire Tomorrowland area in the Magic Kingdom. Stop and take a look at the huge mosaic at the entrance: some 3,000 square feet in size, it is made of 150,000 separate pieces of marble, granite, slate, smalto (colored glass or enamel), Venetian glass, mirror, ceramic, pebbles, and gold in 131 colors.

The opening storm scene now includes some very nice special effects with lightning and a rain forest, and a cast of Audio-Animatronic creatures. Another significant change is that the opening segment of the ride is introduced by a woman, one of the few female voices in the park; once the boats enter into the farming areas the guide at the front of your boat will take over.

Among the advanced techniques you will see are "intercropping" of different plants to make the best use of soil and nutrients (coconut, cacao, and sweet potatoes in one example); growing plants vertically in hydroponic (soil-less) containers which makes them easier to feed and inspect for pests; and an experiment in growing plants in simulated lunar soil, based on analysis of the real thing brought back from the moon by American astronauts.

Plants you will see inside include bananas, papayas, ferns, rice, peanuts, pak choi, sugarcane, casaba, sweet potatoes, and some incredible varieties of squash. The simulated tropical and desert farms of The Land create vegetables for some of the restaurants in the pavilion.

One section of the farm includes a computer-controlled watering system that delivers individual amounts of moisture to plants as needed.

A fish farming "aquacell" grows crops of fish selected for their ability to thrive in a crowded environment. Fish under development on various trips have included sunshine bass, tilapia, catfish, pacu, sturgeon, and the strange-looking paddlefish, which is cultivated for its caviar. Some fish and vegetables you see here are served at some of the restaurants.

Among the most educational of all the exhibits at Epcot, Living with the Land is also a good place for a quick break. Preschoolers may be bored, but anyone else is sure to find something to learn. Lines build by midday to as much as an hour in length; come early or late.

On the walls by the waiting line are thoughts about nature from thinkers great and small. They include poet William Wordsworth's "Nature never did betray the heart that loved her" and "Take care of the Earth if you care for yourself," by the Kids for Saving the Earth Club in Valley, Washington. And there is 10-year-old Jessica Lee of Hong Kong: "The Earth is like my mother. You get punished if you make a mess. Why do you think this planet is called Mother Earth?"

**The Land Backstage Tour.** Serious gardeners and eaters will want to sign up to take this one-hour walking tour of The Land's greenhouses and labs,

**Real or artificial?**
Neil Sedaka, Cher,
Little Richard, and
Chubby Checker
actually performed
their own songs for the
"Food Rocks" show.
The other stars had
singing stand-ins.

concentrating on soil-free gardening, fish farming, plant biotechnology, and pest management. Sign up for the tour at the desk near the Green Thumb Emporium on the lower level. There are only a limited number of places on the tour. Tickets are $6 for adults and $4 for children ages 3 to 9.

**Food Rocks.** This revue gives new meaning to the term "vegetable." Only Disney would dare give us edible versions of our favorite rock 'n' roll stars. The Peach Boys (Beach Boys) sing about "good, good, good, good nutrition," Pita Gabriel (Peter Gabriel) wants to be your High Fiber, Chubby Cheddar (Chubby Checker) tells you "Come on baby, let's exercise," Neil Moussaka (Neil Sedaka) sings "Don't take my squash away from me; don't you leave me without broccoli. Eat your spinach. Yes, it's true, cause vegetables are good for you."

Cher-acudda (Cher) begs you to "Just keep him lean," and The Wrapper (Tone Lōc) discusses nutrient information labels. But wait, there's also Refrigerator Police (Sting) watching every little knish you eat, and The Get-the-Point Sisters (The Pointer Sisters).

At the end of the show, all of the stars come back and harmonize on the stage in the ultimate rock concert.

The Food Rocks Theater has a capacity of 250 for the 13-minute show and there should rarely be more than a 15-minute wait. This exhibit replaced the overly cute Kitchen Kabaret show.

Before you enter the theater, by the way, take a moment to read some of the interesting food facts in the waiting area. There I learned why cashews are never sold in the shell: they are related to poison ivy and their shells contain an irritating oil. I also found out that many famous French sauces including Mornay and Hollandaise were not named for the chefs that created them but instead for the nobleman who featured them at his table.

**WOW** **Circle of Life.** The animated stars of *The Lion King* reappear as the "actors" in an environmental spectacular.

Simba the lion, Timon the meerkat, and Pumbaa the warthog appear in 70-mm glory, along with actors in a fable that begins when King Simba finds that Timon and Pumbaa are planning a new subdivision in the jungle, the "Hakuna Matata Lakeside Village."

Simba warns his friends about the mistakes made by a creature who has from time to time forgotten how everything is connected in The Circle of Life. Those creatures, of course, are humans.

You'll learn about some of modern science's efforts to deal with thoughtful use of land in urban and rural settings around the world. The film includes scenes of polluted wildlife and an oil spill, an ironic antidote to the Exxon Pavilion across the way. There is some very spectacular photography that builds off *The Lion King* film. For example, the famous thundering herds of animals of the cartoon move into a film of the real thing.

The auditorium for the Circle of Life is a bit strange for Disney World; once you leave the waiting area, you'll go down a series of narrow stairways into the seating area. It may be a difficult climb for some. Those who climb all the way down will have to put up with a sometime overly loud sound track.

## The Living Seas

An ambitious but ultimately unsatisfying bust. There are a few interesting exhibits here, but if you or your children are truly interested in learning about the watery two-thirds of our planet, you would be much better off visiting Sea World or a big-city aquarium.

But, as long as you are in here, check out the exhibits and interactive areas including some of the antique diving equipment in the entrance and waiting area. When you enter the auditorium for a short film, lag back a bit and get a seat along the left side so that you will be first in line to enter the "hydrolators." The film is about 12 minutes and the ride about three minutes; allow a total of 30 to 45 minutes for the exhibit.

**Don't read this.** We don't want to spoil the illusion here. So, if you don't want to know an inside tip about the hydrolators, stop reading this sidebar right here. Okay? You've been warned. The hydrolators don't really dive down beneath the sea; the floor moves a few inches to simulate movement and bubbles move up the sides of elevator. Then you walk out the door on the other side of the wall. It's the same principle used in the Haunted Mansion and in more dramatic fashion in other simulator rides.

The movie does make one interesting point: humans have spent less time at the deepest points in the ocean than on the surface of the moon.

**Caribbean Coral Reef Ride.** The idea was great—take visitors on a tour within a huge saltwater aquarium filled with strange and wonderful marine life including sharks, stingrays, parrot fish, and more. But the trip takes just three minutes and the set-up to the ride—the trip deep down below the sea in elevator-like "hydrolators"—is hokey and there's no chance to stop and study. Check out the "Dept. of Pelagic Safety" certificate in the hydrolator.

**Sea Base Alpha.** A series of sometimes interesting exhibits about underwater technologies and sea life. Spend a few moments studying the wave tank to understand the physics of breakers at the beach. Youngsters will enjoy climbing into the diving suits, and adults can grab a good picture when they poke their heads into the breathing bubbles.

Dolphins at the exhibit are participants in a project that uses a large keyboard to communicate with humans; scientists believe the dolphins are responding to instructions given them by humans, and are able to communicate with their handlers using the same device.

One interesting new effort at the pavilion is the **Dolphin Exploration and Education Program (DEEP)**, which immerses a group of up to 16 visitors in three-hour up-close encounters with the dolphins; you'll be soaked for a $45 fee over and above your Epcot ticket. Call (407) 939-8687.

# Eating Your Way Through Epcot's Future World

## Innoventions

⟦🍴⟧ **Electric Umbrella.** A large fast-food eatery inside Innoventions East, offering burgers, chicken, and salads. An outdoor terrace is a good bet in temperate weather. The restaurant features an unusual electronic scoreboard for menus (easy to adjust offerings and prices). Items include a chicken sandwich with fajita seasoning for $6.59, hot dogs for $4.34, cheeseburgers for $4.34, and a meatless burger with fries for $5.24.

⟦🍴⟧ **Pasta Piazza Ristorante.** Pizza, pasta, and more, in the former Sunrise Terrace.

⟦🍴⟧ **Fountain View Espresso & Bakery.** Baked goods. Espresso, cappuccino, latté, cafe mocha, and other hot drinks ranging from about $1.50 to $2.50. Also available are coffees with Amaretto, Bailey's Irish Cream, Frangelico, or Sambucca for about $4.29, plus beer and wine. This is a good place—if you can get one of the relatively few seats—to sit and watch the fountain show.

## Wonders of Life

⟦🍴⟧ **Pure & Simple.** Within Wonders of Life, across from the AnaComical Players' stage. Waffles and fruit, salads, sandwiches, frozen yogurt, and sundaes. "Guilt-free goodies," $1.50 to $5.

Well named for its small offerings of frozen yogurt, shakes, muffins, and other healthful fare, presented in an attractive cafe-like setting. Seating is at colorful blue metal tables and chairs, like something out of the Jetsons.

Special offerings priced from about $3 to $5 include a beta carotene salad (assorted veggies with a cantaloupe–balsamic vinaigrette dressing), venison chili soup, Oriental chicken salad, and a submarine with turkey pastrami, turkey ham, turkey breast, turkey salami, low-fat mozzarella, lettuce, and tomato with tomato-basil vinaigrette served on a multigrain roll.

Sweets include nonfat yogurt sundaes, fruit cups, and a frozen fruit juice "smoothie."

## The Land

⟦🍴⟧ **Sunshine Season Food Fair.** Formerly called The Farmer's Market, this is an attractive food court located downstairs in The Land pavilion. Items range from about $1.25 to $7 for breakfast, lunch, or dinner.

Stands include the **Barbecue Store**, offering beef and chicken sandwiches ($4.50 to $5) or chicken and ribs ($6 to $7); the **Picnic Fare** with cheeses, sausages, and fruit; the **Bakery**, a fine place for bagels, rolls, muffins, luncheon breads, cakes, and cookies; the **Cheese Shoppe**, offering quiche, pasta, vegetable lasagna, and . . . cheese, and the **Potato Store**, selling baked potatoes with stuffing including cheese, bacon, and beef ($2 to $3.25). Dessert counters include the **Beverage House** ($1.25 to $2.50) and the **Ice Cream Stand** ($1.50 to $2.75). Also, select a double chocolate brownie, giant cookie, or apple pie. There is also a selection of regional beers. The Beverage House has added alcoholic drinks to its offerings, including beer, wine, piña coladas, and margaritas.

Note that all of the stands share the same kitchen and there is some duplication; the same excellent brownie, for example, is available at several counters (and in parts of the Magic Kingdom, as well).

For younger appetites, choose "Mickey's Children's Meal," with peanut butter and jelly sandwich, potato chips, cookie, and a surprise, for about $3.

**The Garden Grill.** Upstairs in The Land pavilion. One of the most attractive and interesting full-service restaurants in the Future World section of Epcot, the entire room revolves around a portion of the "Listen to the Land" boat tour down below. It is now given over to character dining "experiences" for breakfast, lunch, and dinner. Specialties include rotisserie chicken, hickory-smoked steak, and a variety of fresh vegetables including some from the gardens on site. Breakfast costs $14.95 for adults and $7.95 for children ages 3 to 11; lunch and dinner are priced at $16.95 for adults and $9.95 for children ages 3 to 11.

Parties holding confirmed reservation tickets will be permitted to bypass any lines and enter directly into The Land pavilion within 15 minutes of their reservation time.

Outside the entrance is a display of some of the fresh herbs and vegetables grown in the pavilion's greenhouses and served in the restaurant. You will see basil, chives, rosemary, parsley, thyme, and some beautiful cucumbers, peppers, beans, squashes, and eggplants.

> **Hold the grease.** One of the best things about eating at The Sunshine Season Food Fair in The Land is that everyone in your party can eat something different, shopping at the various stands and meeting at a table in the court. Just don't promise your kids a hot dog, a greasy burger, or fries when you arrive to eat; you'll have to get those elsewhere.

> **Fast food?** The speed of rotation of the Garden Grill is adjusted to about one revolution per meal. The lunchtime speed is slightly quicker (about 448 feet per hour); dinnertime slows the turntable down to about 422 feet per hour. Either way, you're not likely to suffer from jet lag.

## The Living Seas

**Coral Reef Restaurant.** In the lower level of The Living Seas exhibit, to the right of the main entrance. Fish, shellfish, beef, chicken, and salads. Lunch, $6 to $15; dinner, $19 and up. Children's lunch and dinner menu. Beer, mixed drinks, and a full wine list. Reservations are suggested; make them at the Earth Station on the day you wish to dine. Open for lunch from 11:30 A.M. to 2:45 P.M., and for dinner from 4:30 P.M. to the closing hour for the park.

This place gives a new meaning to the idea of a seafood restaurant. You see food, the food sees you. We kept seeing diners nervously eyeing the passing sharks in the coral reef behind the huge windows alongside the tables; we suspect they worried *they* were going to be the seafood.

**Glassy-eyed.** The best seats in the tank, er . . . restaurant called the Coral Reef are eight tables along the glass wall. Other tables are as much as 20 feet from the fish. However, the restaurant is arranged in three terraces that give all guests a relatively good view of the aquarium wall.

Anyhow, there is a fine selection of fish and shellfish; there are also some beef and chicken selections. Specialties include grilled filet of tuna wrapped in plantains, the Coral Reef Clambake with half a lobster and shrimp, maple-glazed salmon, and steak and chicken offerings.

New to the Coral Reef is the **Under the Sea Character Breakfast**, offered every morning and featuring Mickey Mouse in a diving suit and other favorite characters. Breakfast is priced at $14.95 for adults and $7.95 for children ages 3 to 9; make reservations at (407) 939-3463.

## Attractions at World Showcase

The rest of the World's Fair at Epcot is the World Showcase, a group of entertainment-education-tourism-trade exhibits from an unusual mix of countries. With the possible exception of the United Nations, nowhere else will you find Germany between Italy and China, or Mexico beside Norway.

And though other parts of the vast Disney empire may be individually more impressive, there are few vistas more spectacular than the viewing area at the six o'clock position on World Showcase Lagoon. Displayed in a circle before you are the pavilions of the select nations of the world; all around is lush vegetation (sometimes adapted to the vagaries of Central Florida weather) including tens of thousands of rose bushes and trees, Callery pears, Washingtonia fan palms, and camphor trees.

Most of the young staffers come from the country of the pavilion they work at, participating in the World Showcase Fellowship Program. During a one-year stay, the young people take part in a work-study curriculum.

Now, as at any World's Fair, it is important to draw an important distinction here: going to the Mexico pavilion is not the same as experiencing the ancient reality of Mexico. Seeing the spectacular movie at the Chinese exhibit does not mean you have been to Mongolia or Beijing. And taking the water ride at Norway does not qualify you to say that you have explored the Norwegian fjords.

Instead, the pavilions—some better than others—do an excellent job of whetting the appetite for travel and educating us all on how different and alike we all are. If you can get your kids excited about a visit to England or Canada or Italy, then a trip to Orlando may pay dividends all around; or, maybe it's your kids that have always wanted to go to Japan and they needed to convince you.

### World Showcase Tours

Here's your chance to take an insider's tour of Epcot's World Showcase.

**Gardens of the World.** A Disney horticulturist will escort a small group on a three-and-one-half-hour tour from the wilds of Mexico to the manicured beauty of France to the Canadian frontier. The guide will explore garden styles, plant selections, and horticulture practices. The tour is offered Tuesdays and Thursdays.

**Hidden Treasures of World Showcase.** A four-hour behind-the-scenes tour of the park concentrating on the art, architecture, costumes, and entertainment of each of the pavilions. Hidden Treasures East is offered Wednesdays, and Hidden Treasures West on Saturdays.

Each of the tours departs at 9:30 A.M. and costs $25 per person on top of an admission ticket for Epcot. Same day reservations can be made at the Tour Garden on the west side of the Main Entrance Plaza; advance reservations can be made by calling (407) 989-8687. Space is limited.

## Mexico

The pavilion is set within a striking pre-Colombian-style pyramid, festooned with giant serpent heads and sculptures of Toltec warriors and patterned after the Aztec Temple of Quetzalcoatl at Teotihuacán. Quetzalcoatl, the god of life, is represented by large serpent heads that can be seen along the entranceway.

The arid desert regions of Mexico are portrayed with the landscaping around the Cantina de San Angel; the moist tropics of the Yucatan jungle are echoed with the lush greenery around the Mayan temple.

Inside is a magical wonderland of a happy Mexican village. You'll enter into the colorful **Plaza de Los Amigos**, filled with carts selling handcrafted sombreros of varying sizes, toys, sandals, and other objects—sold at prices that are relative bargains within Walt Disney World. On a terrace near the "river," a mariachi band lets loose with its almost impossibly happy sound.

And down by the water, there's a charming Mexican cantina. The food is good, not great, but in our opinion the **San Angel Inn and Restaurant** is one of the most spectacular settings for dinner within the park, a magical indoor setting.

Take a few moments on your way into or out of the pavilion to look at the small but spectacular collection of ancient Mexican art.

**WOW El Rio del Tiempo.** A charming, happy journey to Mexico—sort of a south-of-the-border version of the Magic Kingdom's It's a Small World. This six-minute boat ride, though, is sure to appeal to children of all ages. There's a touch of Mexico's majestic past as a regional power, a greeting from a Mayan high priest, a humorous acknowledgment of the country's present day as a tourist mecca (enjoy the salespeople who scuttle from screen to screen to try to sell their wares), and a dazzling indoor fireworks salute as dozens of animated dolls dance around you. The indoor fireworks of El Rio del Tiempo (The River of Time) are produced with cool fiber optics.

The Mexican pavilion can become quite crowded at midday; we suggest a visit before 11 A.M. or after dinner.

## Norway

The Land of the Midnight Sun has constructed one of the more interesting exhibits at Epcot. You'll enter on cobblestone streets of a simulated ancient village; take special note of the wood-stave church modeled after one built in 1250 A.D. There's also an interesting—and very expensive—set of stores offering clothing, crafts, and toys. Children will love the Legos table in the gift shop; Legos are made by a company in neighboring Denmark.

The wooden building outside the main pavilion is a "stavkirke" or Stave Church, styled after the Gol Church of Hallingdal, which dates to about 1250; within is a display of Norse artifacts.

There are four distinct Norwegian architectural styles displayed in the pavilion. The Puffin's Roost and Kringla Bakeri are built in Setesdal style with grass roofs and thick log walls. The Fjoring shop uses the gables of Bergen style. The castle represents the Oslo-style 14th-century Akershus, which still stands guard in the harbor of Oslo. And the stucco and stone Informasjon building is built in Alesund style.

**WOW** **Maelstrom.** A dramatic and entertaining look at Norway from Viking times through modern days on a storm-tossed oil platform in the North Sea. You'll board Viking longboats like those used by Erik the Red 1,000 years ago and set sail into a world of fjords, forests, and the occasional troll. Some very young visitors may be momentarily scared by the "monsters"; all riders are likely to be thrilled by the indoor lightning storm in the North Sea.

You'll know you are in trouble near the end of the short four-minute ride when one of the trolls will get angry: "I cast a spell: back, back, over the falls." Sure enough, your boat will appear to travel over a cliff to land in the World Showcase Lagoon of Epcot, before reversing direction for a gentle plunge down a waterfall.

The Maelstrom ride can become quite crowded at midday; visit early or late.

Shops include **The Puffin's Roost**, featuring trolls, beautiful (but pricey) knit sweaters from Scandinavia, trolls, leather items, trolls, candy, and trolls.

**How high's the water?**
You probably didn't even notice it was there as you crossed it, but there is a small drawbridge between the Chinese pavilion and the Village Traders shop. Each day at about 5 P.M. the bridge lifts and some of the floating props for the IllumiNations parade are taken through onto the lake for the nightly show.

### China

One of the most successful of all of the Epcot pavilions at transporting the visitor to a foreign land. The building is a small-scale but beautifully replicated version of Beijing's Temple of Heaven. On busy days, look for dragon dancers and acrobats performing outside near the replica of the Zhao Yang Men (Gate of the Golden Sun).

**WOW** **Wonders of China: Land of Beauty, Land of Time.** Simply breathtaking and not to be missed. A Circle-Vision 360 tour of China guaranteed to open your eyes to the beauty and vastness of this still scarcely known nation. We've all seen pictures of the Great Wall, although never so spectacularly as presented here. And recently, we've been granted views of the fabulous Forbidden City of Beijing. But consider the thrill of being able to look back over your shoulder at the gate through which you came. But then, there is more: the incredible Shilin Stone Forest, the Gobi Desert, the Grand Canal, tropical palms, and snow-capped mountains.

In making the film, a Disney film crew had to carry the 600-pound camera up the 4,500 steps of the steep slopes of Huangshan Mountain in Annui Province for what ended up as just a few seconds on the screen.

By the way, if you are thrilled by the images of China presented in the film, you may want to make a visit to the Splendid China theme park in Kissimmee; read about it later in this book.

Lines for the 19-minute film build during the day, but rarely add up to more than about half an hour; come early or late to avoid them altogether. The only drawback to this presentation is the fact that the theater has no seats. There are rows of rails to lean upon—sitting on the rails is frowned upon—and small children and short adults may have a hard time seeing the screen without a lift. To make things worse, no strollers are allowed.

**House of Whispering Willows.** An impressive exhibit of ancient Chinese artifacts in the hallway as you leave the theater.

**Yong Feng Shangdian Shopping Gallery.** Just like it sounds, an indoor shopping mall of Chinese merchandise, including silk clothing, embroidered items, and crafts. A huge collection, it includes some of the more interesting foreign items at Epcot, including silk robes, wooden toys, jewelry, and prints. You can also have your name written in Chinese characters on a scroll, T-shirt, or sweatshirt at a booth outside.

**Twelve by twelve.** The Hall of Prayer for Good Harvests is a half-scale reproduction of the actual hall within the Temple of Heaven near Beijing. There are 12 outer columns supporting the roof, representing both the months of the year and the 12-year cycle of the Chinese calendar. Near the center of the room are four columns representing the four seasons; the columns support a square beam which stands for the Earth, and the assemblage is topped off by a round beam, representing heaven.

**Big thirst.** Germans are serious about their beer; if you ever had any doubts, check out the mugs available for sale at the **Weinkeller.** One of them is big enough for a couple of gallons of brew if you're prone to severe thirst.

## Germany

Wunderbar! A visit to a make-believe German village complete with a beer garden, teddy bear toy shop, wine cellar, and a pastry shop of your dreams. The high wall at the back of the showcase is based on the Eltz Castle on the Mosel River, and Stahleck Castle on the Rhine.

**Biergarten.** A lively full-service restaurant and beer garden, almost as loud and fun as a hall at the Oktoberfest in Munich—especially as the night goes on. Next door is the **Weinkeller,** which stocks several hundred varieties of German wines as well as a selection of beer mugs, wine glasses, and other drinking items.

**Der Bücherwurm.** A bookworm's delight, filled with books from and about Germany. The facade of the building is modeled after the Kaufhaus, a 16th-century merchants' hall in the Black Forest town of Freiburg.

**Der Teddybär.** You've been warned: this is a children-parent-grandparent

**Dragonslayer.**
The statue in the center of the square is of St. George and the dragon he slayed on a pilgrimage to the Middle East. St. George is the patron saint of soldiers, and statues in his honor are common in Bavaria.

trap full of fabulous toys, dolls, and various stuffed animals.

**Die Weihnachts Ecke.** It's Christmas every day in this shop full of ornaments, decorations, and gifts.

**Glas Und Porzellan.** An outlet of Goebel, a large glass and porcelain maker best known as the maker of Hummel figurines.

**Süssigkeiten.** We're uncertain whether to recommend you visit this shop on an empty or a full stomach. Let's put it this way: a full stomach will save you a lot of money. The cookies, candies, and pretzels are unlike anything you will find this side of Germany, and are worth a trip from anywhere.

**Volkskunst.** A wondrous crafts mart of carved dolls, cuckoo clocks, clothing, and more.

## Italy

Like China, the Italian pavilion is one of the more successful efforts in terms of giving the visitor a feeling of walking the streets of a foreign land. Take the time to study the various architectural styles. Out front is a 105-foot-tall campanile, or bell tower, a version of one of the landmarks of St. Mark's Square in Venice, and the replica of the square itself is beautifully constructed; all that is missing are the pigeons, which explains why this version of St. Mark's is so Disney-clean.

The detailed replica of the angel on top of the campanile in the re-created Venice is covered with real gold leaf. The marble stones for the buildings, though, have no marble in them: they are actually fiberglass that has been painted and treated.

At the top of one of the columns at the entrance to St. Mark's Square is a likeness of St. Theodore, an important military leader in early Venetian history. Topping the other column is the winged Lion of St. Mark's, the mythical guardian of the city of Venice. The stairway and portico alongside the Doge's Palace are drawn from Berona, while the town hall is reminiscent of the style of northern Italy.

Landscaping around the garden area includes bougainvillea, citrus plants including orange and lemon trees, and colorful blue, white, and pink hanging baskets.

Down at the edge of the World Showcase Lagoon is a gondola mooring. And around the square is a collection of delicious and attractive stores. Outside the square, look for the lively and irreverent performances of Il Commedia di Bologna.

**Delizie Italiane.** An open-air market with sweet delicacies of all description.

**La Cucina Italiana.** Gourmet foods and wines, and cooking accessories.

**Il Bel Cristallo.** Fine crystalware including Venetian glass and porcelain figurines.

## The American Adventure

**WOW** **The American Adventure.** In our early visits to Epcot, the United States pavilion was one we passed by as the day got long. It's located at the very "back" of the park, and besides, we're Americans, so why should we be interested in something called "The American Adventure"?

Boy, were we ever wrong! The exhibit here is the ultimate in Disney Audio-Animatronics, a rip-roaring, flag-waving show on a larger scale than almost anything else at Walt Disney World or anywhere else. The unlikely co-stars of the production are author Mark Twain and states-man and inventor Ben Franklin. Never mind that Twain wasn't born until 45 years after Franklin died; such things don't matter when figures from history are brought back as robots.

The walls of the main hall are adorned with an interesting group of quotes from an unusual collection of Americans, including:

**Wendell Willkie.** "Our way of living together in America is a strong but delicate fabric. It is made up of many threads. It has been woven over many centuries by the patience and sacrifice of countless liberty-loving men and women."

**Walt Disney.** "Our greatest natural resource is the minds of our children."

**Charles Lindbergh.** "I don't believe in taking foolish chances, but nothing can be accomplished without taking any chance at all."

**Ayn Rand.** "Throughout the centuries there were men who took first steps down new roads armed with nothing but their own vision."

**Herman Melville.** "Our blood is as the flood of the Amazon, made up of a thousand noble currents all pouring into one . . . we are not a nation so much as a world."

**No mistake.** The clock on the facade of the building uses a IIII instead of IV for the four o'clock hour; this is an accurate reproduction of Georgian architecture of the time.

**Grumpy and Dopey were absent that day.** In the auditorium of The American Adventure, the 12 statues flanking the stage are said to represent the "Spirits of America." On the right, from the back of the hall to the front, are Adventure, Self-Reliance, Knowledge, Pioneering, Heritage, and Freedom. On the left, from back to front, are Discovery, Compassion, Independence, Tomorrow, Innovation, and Individualism. The 44 flags in the Hall of Flags represent the banners that have flown over the colonial, revolutionary, and independent United States.

The 29-minute show starts with the Pilgrims landing at Plymouth Rock, moves on to scenes including the Boston Tea Party and General George Washington's winter at Valley Forge. There's an eclectic collection of well-known and lesser-known figures of American history and culture, including—to Disney's credit—women, Native Americans, and African-Americans. The audience will meet characters such as Teddy Roosevelt, Alexander Graham Bell, Susan B. Anthony, Charles Lindbergh, Frederick Douglass, Chief Joseph, and Martin Luther King, Jr. On the cultural side are representations of Lucille Ball, Muhammad Ali, Marilyn Monroe, John Wayne, and even Walt Disney himself. And don't overlook the imposing Georgian building itself and the various paintings and statues in the hallways.

Among the special effects employed in The American Adventure is multiplane cinematography, first developed by Disney technicians to add the illusion of depth to animated films including *Snow White and the Seven Dwarfs* and *Pinocchio*.

The buildings at the pavilion echo American public architecture from the late 1790s through 1830, including English Georgian, developed during the reign of King George III. Other examples are drawn from Williamsburg, Independence Hall, the Old State House in Boston, and Thomas Jefferson's Monticello home.

By the way, the 110,000 "bricks" on the exterior of the main building are made from fiberglass formed and colored to appear the correct age. The landscaping evokes a formal Philadelphia garden.

Lines at The American Adventure can build at midday but, except on the busiest days, are rarely larger than the seats in the large auditorium. The best seats are in the first few rows nearest the stage.

## Japan

**The Fantasy Dreammaker.** An entertainer/ artisan who works in candy, paper, and magic, re-creating ancient Japanese arts.

**Good luck charm.** The red Gate of Honor (Torii) at the entrance to the Japanese pavilion is a sign of good luck. The gates were originally intended as perches for roosters to welcome the daily arrival of the sun goddess. The one at the pavilion is modeled after one in Hiroshima Bay.

A typically understated but elegant Japanese setting, featuring a reproduction of an eighth-century pagoda from the Horyuji Temple, the oldest completely preserved temple complex in Japan. Each of the five levels of the Goju-no-to (five-story pagoda) symbolize one of the five basic elements: earth, water, fire, wind, and sky. Amateur gardeners will marvel at the detail in the rock gardens and ponds. Fish fanciers should check out the koi in the ponds. Rocks symbolize the long life of the earth; the water symbolizes the sea, a source of life.

Most of the plants and trees of the Japanese garden are native to the Southern U.S. but were selected because they were similar in appearance to those in Japan.

**Bijutsu-Kan Gallery.** A small museum of Japanese arts, culture, and craft. The exhibition is changed from time to time, making it worth a repeat peek if you've seen it before.

**Mitsukoshi Department Store.** The farthest west branch of a large Japanese department store, offering a selection of clothing, dolls, toys, and trinkets. The food section includes some unusual items such as fried sweet potatoes, shrimp flavored chips, and tomato crackers. Gardeners may want to bring home a grow-it-yourself bonsai kit.

## Morocco

Step through the Bab Boujoulad gate to a beautifully detailed replica of the Koutoubia Minaret in Marrakesh and a world of fezzes, saris, and belly dancers. Bab Boujoulad is the main gate to the ancient city of Fez, known as the Medina. It was founded in the year 786 by the Idrissids. In the Medina section of the pavilion is a reproduction of the Chella Minaret in the capital city of Rabat. There is also a reproduction of the Nejjarine Fountain in Fez.

**Festival Marrakesh.** The folklore, dances, and music of Morocco presented in the square outside the pavilion. Belly dancing and music and dance from the regions of Tangiers, Fez, Casablanca, the Andaluz, and Marrakesh are presented within the Restaurant Marrakesh.

Check out the very full Senegal date palm to the right of the pavilion. The intricate tilework of the Morocco pavilion is among the most authentic recreations of a foreign nation at Epcot; note that none of the tiles are perfect, for Muslims believe that only Allah is without flaw.

**Gallery of Arts and History.** A museum of arts, crafts, and culture, with a changing display. Nearby is a branch of the **Moroccan National Tourist Office** with information for visitors who would like to make a journey to the real thing.

Within the courtyard is a collection of fascinating shops, including **Casablanca Carpets** for handmade Berber and Rabat rugs; **Tangier Traders** for leather goods, woven belts, and fezzes; **Medina Arts** for crafts; and **Jewels of the Sahara,** selling silver, gold, beads, and precious and semiprecious jewel items. There's a sign at the shops inviting shoppers to "make an offer" for items they want to purchase; we'd suggest you start with a large discount from the list price and be happy with a small break.

### France

Vive la France. France lives in a small-scale reproduction of a section of the streets of Paris, complete with an elegant theater, shops, and a bakery and sweet shop of your dreams. There's even a one-tenth scale Eiffel Tower atop the pavilion. It's for appearance only, though—there

**Eiffel Tiny.** The one-tenth-scale replica of the Eiffel Tower was constructed using Gustave Eiffel's original blueprints.

is no top-level observation tower as there is in the real thing.

Take a few moments to look at the architectural styles, which include mansard roofs and ironwork harking from France's Belle Epoque (Beautiful Age) in the late 19th century. The park on the right side of the pavilion is stocked with Lombardy poplars, looking like the famous setting of Seurat's *Sunday Afternoon on the Island of La Grande Jatte.*

**Impressions de France.** Enter into the Palais du Cinema for a lovely 18-minute film that hits all of the highlights of France—from Paris to Versailles to Mont St. Michel to Cannes, and lots of lesser-known but equally beautiful settings, accompanied by lovely and familiar music including "Gaite Parisienne" by Jacques Offenbach, "Trois Gymnopedies" by Eric Satie, "Carnival of the Animals" by Camille Saint-Saëns, "Claire de Lune" by Claude Debussy, "Daphnis et Chloé" by Maurice Ravel, and other familiar French compositions. The large screens extend 200 degrees around the theater, which has the added

**Shadow kids.** If you'd like a souvenir silhouette of your children or yourself, you can usually find a group of artists parked outside the French pavilion.

**Ooh, la la.** The costumes of the pretty jeune filles at France's pavilion are modeled after dresses worn in Edouard Manet's famous nightclub painting, Le Bar aux Folies-Bergère.

**Disney reality.** Look for typical attention to detail in the construction of the buildings in the interesting streets of the United Kingdom. Never mind that the thatched roofs are made from plastic fibers (for fire protection) or the smoke stains applied by artists with paint brushes; you probably didn't notice that until we pointed it out.

**School ties.** The crests for four of the realm's most famous schools (Oxford, Cambridge, Eton, and Edinburgh) are displayed in the upstairs windows of The Queen's Table.

advantage of seats for all viewers. Lines build at midday; visit early or late on crowded days. Stop and take a look at the postshow area, which is modeled after Les Halles, the commercial marketplace of Paris.

**Plume et Palette.** One of the most high-tone of all shops in Epcot, with its entranceway modeled after one of the more famous decorative entranceways to the Paris Metro subway. The interior of the store and the showcases compete with the lovely gifts and artworks for sale here.

**La Signature.** Get a whiff of the perfumes and a peek at the clothing.

For the gourmand, there is **La Maison du Vin**, which, as its name suggests, is a Gallic House of Wines. You can also purchase tastes of finer bottles for about $2 to $4. And send your sweet tooth to **Galerie des Halles**, a bakery and candy store in a building that is modeled after the famous Les Halles market of Paris.

## United Kingdom

Merry Olde England (and the rest of the United Kingdom) is represented at Epcot by a selection of attractive shops and a first-class pub with a nice selection of British beers; it may be one of the few places in Florida where you can get a decent kidney pie.

The streetscape includes a thatched-roof cottage from the 1500s, a formal square with a Hyde Park–like bandstand, a London city square, and an exterior facade of the style of Hampton Court.

If you fancy you have a Green Thumb, or wish you did, be sure to check out the perfectly tended little English garden next to the Magic of Wales shop. The gardens include all sorts of roses from many parts of the former British Empire. By the way, the secret garden also is an excellent place to watch the IllumiNations show on the lagoon.

**The Toy Soldier.** Playthings for men and boys, women and girls of all ages. The shop's exterior is modeled after an ancient Scottish manor.

**Lords and Ladies.** More toys, of a slightly nobler fashion: chess sets, dart boards, beer mugs, stamps, coins, and more, inside a hall where the Knights of the Round Table would have felt at home.

**Pringle of Scotland.** Lay down your chips for beautiful knit sweaters and other articles of clothing.

**The Queen's Table.** Her highness may be the only one among us with the available cash to do some serious shopping here, but it's fun to poke (carefully) among the fabulous Royal Doulton china, figurines, and Toby mugs.

**The Magic of Wales.** A gift shop of small items and souvenirs from Wales; prices are the most reasonable among U.K. emporia.

**The Tea Caddy.** Here you'll find considerably more kinds of leaves in bags and cans than you're likely to find at the corner grocery.

## Canada

The vast range of experiences of Canada is reflected in the landmarks of the pavilion. At front is a native totem pole; out back is a scaled-down Canadian Rocky Mountain; and between is a scaled-down reproduction of the stone Château Laurier in Ottawa. The gardens of the Canada pavilion are based on the famed Butchart Gardens of Victoria, British Columbia, in western Canada.

**O Canada!** Another breathtaking Circle-Vision 360 movie that brings you up close and personal with bobcats, wolves, bears, and other creatures of the wild, with human glories like the Cathédral de Notre Dame, on the ski slopes of the Rockies, and onto the ice of a hockey game in a scene so real you'll wish you had a goalie's mask on. Did we mention getting caught in the middle of the rodeo ring in the Calgary Stampede or the breathtaking camera ride down the toboggan slide at Quebec City?

The waiting area for the film is a cave-like mountain lodge from the Canadian Rockies. Be advised that you'll have to stand to watch this extraordinary 18-minute movie.

**Northwest Mercantile.** A modern-day version of a frontier trading post. You'll trade dollars (credit cards accepted, too) for sheepskins, lumberjack shirts, maple syrup, and Indian artifacts and crafts.

**La Boutique des Provinces.** Canadian products from its French regions.

# Eating Your Way Through Epcot's World Showcase

## Mexico

KEY:

🍴 = Fast Food

🍸 = Pub

🏔 = Full-service restaurant

🍴 **Cantina de San Angel.** Tacos, salads, and burritos, $3.50 to $6.

This outdoor cantina is located opposite the Aztec pyramid, beside the lagoon. Get a quick Mexican fix at this attractive outdoor cafe: tortillas, tostadas, and sweet churros (fried dough dipped in powdered sugar and cinnamon).

Small, round, wooden tables seat four under colorful umbrellas during the day and under high, soft-light lanterns at night. Your meal is accompanied by Mexican music in a setting that includes native flowers on a tiled patio inside a stucco wall. The platos Mexicanos include

**Night light.** The outdoor Cantina de San Angel, outside of the Mexico pavilion along the lagoon, is an interesting place to view the nightly IllumiNations show over a cold beer or soft drink. Tables will fill up early.

corn or flour tortillas filled with chicken or beef, priced from about $4 to $6. Side dishes include refried beans or chips and salsa. Desserts, priced from about $2 to $3, include flan or churros. Drinks include frozen margaritas and Mexican beer.

**San Angel Inn.** Traditional Mexican dining. Lunch from $5 to $15. Dinner from $15. Children's menu. Reservations are suggested and necessary in busy season.

This restaurant is inside a simulated Aztec pyramid in the center of the Mexican exhibit, probably our favorite location for a restaurant at Epcot. Diners sit on a terrace overlooking the passing boats on the River of Time (El Rio del Tiempo), under a make-believe starlit sky. It feels about as real as any place north of Mexico City; in fact, the eatery is run by the same company that operates the well-known restaurant of the same name in Mexico City.

Live percussion music and a mariachi band add to the atmosphere and the enjoyment. Look beyond the River of Time to view pyramids, a volcano, and a campfire.

The food is above-average Mexican fare. Specialties include *carne asada Tampiquena, huachinango a la Veracruzana,* tacos, burritos, enchiladas, and much more.

On visits we have made, lunchtime offerings have included the interesting and traditional *mole poblano* (chicken and spices with a chocolate-based sauce) and a combination platter (beef taco, enchilada, quesadilla, and avocado dip). At dinner, we have been offered baked California lobster ($26) and *camarones enchiladas* (shrimp sautéed with pepper).

Lunch or dinner children's offerings include soft tortilla with chicken or beef, fried chicken, or grilled beef taco. Traditional Mexican desserts include flan or *capirotada* (bread pudding). Alone or with dessert, try Mexican coffee with Kahlua, tequila, and cream.

Dos Equis and Tecate beers, margaritas, and a full wine list also are available.

## Norway

**Kringla Bakeri og Kafé.** Open-faced sandwiches, pastries, cakes, $3 to $4.

This interesting kafé is located on the left side of the Norwegian exhibit, behind the replica of the church.

What else would you expect from a Kringla Bakeri than fresh kringles? All right: a kringle is a candied pretzel. Also available are *vaflers,* which are waffles covered with powdered sugar and jam and other interesting sweets. Sample the wonderfully-white rice cream pudding or chocolate ball, like a three-inch truffle.

Open-faced sandwiches ($3 to $5) are very well presented for a medium-to-small serving. Offerings include tongue, beef, smoked salmon, mackerel, and ham. And yes, there's a herring platter.

Chairs and tables are available outside, between Norway's Ancient Church and the shops at the pavilion.

**Early meals.** Oslo, the capital and major port of Norway, lies at the head of the Oslo Fjord. The earliest settlement was on the Akershus Peninsula, where a royal fortress was built about 1300. The building still stands, used for state banquets.

🏠 **Restaurant Akershus.** Buffet with hot and cold meat, cheese, pasta, and dessert. Lunch, $11.25 for adults and $4.25 for children; dinner $17.25 for adults and $7.50 for children. Reservations are available and necessary on busy days. Open from 11:30 A.M. to 3:30 P.M. for lunch, and 4:30 to 8:30 P.M. for dinner.

This restaurant is located inside a replica of the famous castle of Akershus in the Oslo harbor on the right side of the Epcot Norway exhibit.

Visitors are offered a version of a Royal Norwegian Buffet *koldbord,* or "cold table," with more than 30 items. You'll find more types of herring than you ever imagined possible, along with hot and cold smoked salmon, turkey, or mackerel. You can also find meatballs, scrambled eggs, lamb with cabbage, mashed rutabaga, hot smoked pork with honey mustard sauce, and more. Be sure to take advantage of the offer by the waiters and waitresses for guided tours of the *koldbord.*

Desserts, wine, beer, and soft drinks are a la carte; free refills are offered on soft drinks.

Akershus is an interesting excursion for the adventurous, although most children we know will find the offerings a bit strange and unappealing. Even some adults will consider the buffet to be an unending selection of appetizers without the main course.

The white stone walls and tile floors offer a pleasant, cool atmosphere for lunch or dinner. The rustic elegance of high ceilings and exposed wooden beams are enhanced by the appetizing odor of cabbage and vinegar.

## China

🍴 **Lotus Blossom Café.** Stir-fry, eggrolls, sweet and sour chicken, soup, and more, $2 to $6. Lunch, dinner.

This is a quality fast-food restaurant located near the entrance to the China exhibit beside the Nine Dragons Restaurant. It offers covered outdoor dining in a cafe or patio setting. The dining area is tastefully decorated; the food is better than most fast-food operations.

For the most variety for your money, try the combination platter for a sample of stir-fried beef with vegetables, egg roll, and fried rice. For a lighter meal, sample a bowl of soup for under $2. Chinese beer, tea, and soft drinks are available.

🏠 **Nine Dragons Restaurant.** Varied traditional Chinese cuisine in Mandarin, Cantonese, Kiangche, and Szechuan styles, plus appetizers. Lunch entrees range from $5 to $15; dinner entrees start at $15. The children's

**Goes great with chili dogs.** For an unusual treat, try the red bean ice cream offered as a dessert at the Nine Dragons restaurant in China.

menu offers three items. Reservations required at busy times. Open from 11 A.M. through the closing time for the park.

This is a palace-like, Oriental setting located near the entrance of the China exhibit, on the left side as you enter. Look up as you walk into the waiting area to see an interesting golden dragon hanging from the ceiling. An ancient robe hangs on the back wall of the waiting area.

As fancy as it is, the selection of food is no better than many average Chinese restaurants, and not as impressive as gourmet Asian eateries. Specialties include *kang bo* chicken and red bean ice cream.

Chinese beer as well as specialty drinks and Chinese cordials also are available.

### Village Traders

Village Traders. Located in a dead area (space for a new pavilion?) between Germany and China. A group of huts there offers vegetarian delights, including a "vegetable box" for $1.40 (you might call it a salad); the box with dips costs $2. A selection of fresh fruit is also available.

**One million bottles of beer on the wall. . . .** The famous Oktoberfest is celebrated in Munich, Germany, every October. Germany has the highest per capita beer consumption in the world, about 40 gallons per person per year.

### Germany

Biergarten. Traditional German fare including potatoes, pork, and bratwurst, served for lunch and dinner in all-you-can-eat banquet-style dining. The luncheon buffet, offered from 11:30 A.M. to 3 P.M. was priced at about $9.95 for adults, and $4.75 for children 11 and under; offerings include sausages, rotisserie chicken, salads, red cabbage, and potatoes. At dinner, the menu expands to include sauerbraten and smoked pork; prices increase to $14.75 for adults and $5.99 for children.

Located at the rear of the German exhibit off the Sommerfest courtyard, the Biergarten offers a loud and raucous atmosphere that gets louder as the evening wears on.

Once inside you'll feel like you are in a German beer hall at night. You'll dine at long tables, served by waiters and waitresses in alpine dress. The setting also includes simulated small-town shops and a stage for the nightly music performances.

Wash it all down with a huge 33-ounce stein of beer (up to $7.50) or German wine and sit back and enjoy the floor show of oompah music and other lively tunes. All in all, a lot of fun.

Sommerfest. Bratwurst und strudel und Black Forest cake und beer for about $2 to $4. Lunch, dinner, snacks.

Sommerfest offers German fast-food treats served at an attractive outdoor cafe located at the right rear of the German exhibit outside the Biergarten. You won't have any trouble finding this interesting and different establishment; follow the sharp odor of wurst and sauerkraut.

Select a German beer to accompany one of the sandwich offerings. Ask for sauerkraut and all the fixings with your bratwurst sandwich.

## Italy

[icon] **L'Originale Alfredo di Roma Ristorante.** Veal, chicken, pasta, and seafood entrees plus appetizers and dessert in an Italian atmosphere, with strolling musicians at dinner. Lunch entrees range from about $5 to $20; dinner entrees start at $15. Children's lunch and dinner entrees. Reservations are required; stop by the Earth Station on the day you wish to dine.

Enter by crossing the stone-paved square, beside the huge Neptune fountain and walled patio. The pink stucco exterior, complete with columns, stone benches, and lanterns, provides an appropriate atmosphere.

A semiformal decor with interesting wallpaper and upholstered seating welcomes you to the cool interior and pleasantly lively atmosphere. Check out the numerous photographs on the wall of the waiting area; you'll see many familiar personalities being served pasta.

**Originally elsewhere.** L'Originale Alfredo di Roma Ristorante is not the original Alfredo's, actually: the real thing is in Rome and is credited with the invention of the creamy pasta dish fettuccine Alfredo (noodles in butter and Parmesan cheese).

**Not invented here.** What could be more American than hamburgers, hot dogs, and chili? Well, actually, there are some doubts as to the lineage of hamburgers (as in Hamburg, Germany), hot dogs (a sausage, like those made in Frankfurt, Germany, but placed on a roll), and chili (influenced by Mexico well before Texas was a state).

The menu features a wide selection of freshly made pasta (including spaghetti, rigatoni, ziti, lasagna, and more) with various delectable sauces. In past years, entrees have included eight veal dishes, sausage, eggplant, chicken, and beef dishes. House wines available by the glass or by the liter.

## The American Adventure

[icon] **Liberty Inn.** Burgers, sandwiches, chili, and salads, $2 to $6. Lunch and dinner. Child's menu, $3.50 to $4. Indoor and outdoor seating with traditional stateside fare.

There's nothing here to startle a youngster or, for that matter, to educate the palate of an adult, but the food is acceptable and typical of what many American families eat most of the time.

The outdoor patio is a very pleasant, tree-shaded affair that includes umbrella tables and colorful landscaping. The inside dining room is very spacious and has large window walls to maintain a bright, light atmosphere, even late in the day.

Lunch and dinner offerings are essentially the same, with a few more options for dinner. For example, you can select a chicken breast sandwich served with french fries or fresh fruit for about $5 for lunch or dinner. At dinner, you can also choose a roasted half chicken with french fries and cole slaw for about $6. The evening offerings also include jambalaya, a southern stew that includes pork, shrimp, crawfish, chicken, sausage, vegetables, and rice. For the children there is fried chicken and hot dogs.

**Minimalist meals.** The Japanese style of raw or lightly cooked foods in small, elegantly prepared portions is said to be derived from that nation's historical situation of being overpopulated and short of both food and fuel.

**Sipping rice.** Sake, pronounced sah'-key, is a colorless, sweet alcohol, sometimes called rice wine. It is made from rice fermented with yeast. It is traditionally served warm.

## Japan

🍴 **Yakitori House.** Japanese fast food including beef, chicken, seafood, and salads, for about $3 to $8. Lunch, dinner, snacks.

Yakitori is located in the rear left portion of the Japanese exhibit, behind the fountain, within the Japanese gardens in a replica of the 500-year-old Katsura Imperial Summer Palace in Kyoto. Dine indoors or outside; the rock-walled patio with fragrant landscaping is a pleasant getaway for lunch or dinner. Imitation paper lanterns give the evening meal a pleasant glow.

The restaurant offers Japanese fast food, serving yakitori (skewered chicken basted with soy sauce and sesame), teriyaki chicken and beef, and guydon (a beef stew served over rice).

The Shogun Combo offers a good selection of foods, including beef teriyaki, seafood salad, and soups.

🍴 **Japanese Shaved Ice.** In hot weather, the snack bar on World Showcase Lagoon just to the left of the Japanese pavilion sells *kaki-jori*, which is your basic snow cone done Japanese style with tasty fruit syrups. Flavors include cherry, strawberry, honeydew melon, tangerine, or mixed for $1.50.

🍸 **Matsu No Ma Lounge.** Exotic drinks, sushi, and more, from about $2 to $8. The lounge is located upstairs at the right side of the pavilion.

Here you can sample sake (warm rice wine), Japanese beer, or exotic mixed drinks. Nonalcoholic drinks include *Ichigo* (strawberries, pineapple juice, lemon), and *Mikan* (Mandarin orange and pineapple juice with lemon).

Appetizers include tempura, Kabuki beef or chicken, sashimi, and assorted Nigiri sushi.

🏯 **Teppanyaki Dining Room.** Table-prepared Japanese entrees of beef, chicken, and seafood. Lunch entrees from $5 to $15; dinner entrees start at $15. Children's menu available. Reservations are usually necessary; make them at the Earth Station on the day you want to eat.

Find this interesting restaurant on the second floor of the building on the right of the Japanese exhibit, above the Mitsukoshi Department Store.

An entertaining and tasty break from the hubbub of Epcot. Groups of diners are assembled around a hot table, facing a chef equipped with a set of sharp knives; he carries salt and pepper shakers in holsters. Depending on the luck of the draw, your chef may be a multilingual comic, playing games with the chicken, shrimp, and beef as he slices and stir-fries the food. Teppanyaki fare is fresh and simple, featuring vegetables and meat over rice.

The dining experience is definitely not for someone who wants a quiet, leisurely, and private time. But children—and adults who enjoy a floor show with their meal—are certain to have fun.

Dinner entrees are the same as for lunch, but the prices are higher and the portions slightly larger.

Before and during your meal, sample exotic alcoholic and nonalcoholic drinks. For example, the Sakura includes light rum, white curaçao, strawberries, and lemon juice.

Note that there are several teppanyaki-style Japanese restaurants just outside of Epcot, generally offering better prices and smaller crowds.

**Tempura Kiku.** Batter-fried meat and vegetables, sushi, sashimi, shrimp, scallops, lobster, and fried beef and chicken strips. Lunch entrees from $5 to $15; dinner entrees start at $15. Open from 11 A.M. to 3 P.M. for lunch, and from 5 P.M. to park closing for dinner.

Tempura Kiku is located upstairs at the right side of the Japanese pavilion, next to the Matsu No Ma Lounge. Exotic drinks from the lounge are available at the restaurant.

Reservations are not accepted; waits are rarely long.

## Morocco

**Restaurant Marrakesh.** Traditional Moroccan food. Lunch entrees from $10 to $15. Dinner entrees start at $15. Children's lunch and dinner selections. Reservations necessary in busy season; stop by the Earth Station or sign in at the podium at the front of the Morocco exhibit.

One of our favorite places at Epcot, this place really makes you feel as if you have traveled to an exotic place. When you arrive, wind your way through the Fez gate to the back of the Medina to find the Marrakesh amid the narrow streets and quaint shops.

Waiters in ankle-length *djellaba* robes, strolling musicians, and belly dancers provide an interesting and entertaining backdrop for a delightful meal. Even if you have to wait in the lobby briefly for your table, you'll be entertained by the music, native costumes, and decor.

**Veiled threat.** Belly dancing first came to America in 1893 at the Chicago World's Fair when a Syrian dancer who called herself Little Egypt scandalized viewers with what later came to be named the "hootchy-kootchy." Belly dancing is believed to have originated in Persia (now Iran) and is still popular throughout the Middle East.

The dining area, with its raised, segmented dining rooms that overlook a central entertainment area, adds interest to your meal.

Among the traditional delicacies you may be able to sample for lunch are *meshoui* (lamb roast in natural juices with rice, almonds, raisins, and saffron) and *couscous* (rolled semolina) steamed with garden vegetables, chicken, or lamb. You might also consider ordering one of the sampler plates with small portions of various offerings for yourself or to share with someone.

The dinner menu is similar, but with more variety and larger portions. Try the Tangier sampler for a selection of items, including specialties marinated in spices such as ginger, cumin, paprika, garlic with olives, and pickled lemon. It's all topped off with some delicious honey-sweetened pastries or crepes.

## France

🍴 **Boulangerie Patisserie.** French pastries and fresh croissants, priced from about $2 to $4. Breakfast, snacks.

This quaint bakery shop is across the narrow French street from the Bistro de Paris.

A wonderful place to grab breakfast or a sweet snack any time of the day. The bakery is managed by the Chefs de France, which is as tasty a recommendation as can be found at Epcot.

Any of the assorted tarts, apple turnovers, quiche Lorraine, and chocolate treats is good. Dark, flavorful coffee makes a good accompaniment for the sweet treats.

🍷 **Bistro de Paris.** Traditional French cuisine in a light, quiet setting. Dinner and lunch (in peak season only). Dinner entrees start at about $15 and rise from there. Children's menu.

Reservations are available and necessary on busy days.

Upstairs over the Chefs de France, this bistro is entered through a rear door at the back of the building. A bistro is an intimate little cafe or pub, and that's what the designers of the Bistro de Paris had in mind in this lighter and (usually) quieter version of Chefs de France. The same master chefs designed the menu, which includes a variety of appetizers, soups, entrees, and desserts.

Specialties include grilled beef tenderloin with mushrooms, glazed onions, and green peppercorn sauce.

Appetizers and entrees vary by season and are occasionally changed. In recent years, offerings have included appetizers such as salad of duck liver pâté at $14, *gratin d'escargots de Bourgogne* (casserole of snails in herbal butter) at $7.50, cream of lobster soup ($4.50), or a mixed green salad with true Roquefort dressing and walnuts at $7.50.

Entrees have included a sautéed breast of duck with cherries and red wine sauce for $20, and a rack of lamb with vegetables for two is $48.

At least 10 dessert items are available and have included fruit and sherbet with raspberry sauce, and vanilla creme in a puff pastry shell topped with caramel sauce.

🍷 **Au Petit Cafe.** French cafe fare from soup to quiche, $4 to $14.50. Children's offerings, about $4. Lunch, dinner, snacks.

This is a Parisian-style sidewalk cafe located to the left of Chefs de France. You'll find it through the smell of fresh flowers coming from the many hanging baskets that adorn the posts that support the awning over the patio.

The World Showcase is not quite the Champs-Elysées, but the little sidewalk cafe here with its formal black-jacketed waiters gives a nice taste of the time-honored people-watching stations on the streets of Paris.

The menu includes traditional onion soup with cheese, *coq au vin,* and sautéed strip steak with Bordelaise sauce. Moderately priced offerings include such familiar items as quiche Lorraine and salads. Luncheon entrees range from $5 to $15; dinner plates begin at $15.

Fruit sorbets, ice cream, pastry shells filled with light cream and chocolate sauce, and ice cream soufflé with Grand Marnier sauce round out the menu.

No reservations are accepted, and the waiting lines can become quite long on busy days.

[▲] **Chefs de France.** Traditional French cuisine. Lunch, $8 to $15. Dinner from $15. Children's lunch and dinner menu. Reservations are suggested.

Chefs de France is located on the ground floor of the large building at the left of the entrance to the France exhibit, to the right of the Au Petit Cafe outdoor dining area.

*C'est merveilleux!* Right here in Epcot, just across the way from umpteen hot dog and pizza stands, is a restaurant nearly as fine as any in France.

**Recipe for success.** The chefs of France who are behind the restaurant of the same name are Paul Bocuse and Roger Vergé, operators of two of the country's finest restaurants, and Gaston LeNôtre, considered a national treasure for his pastries and desserts.

Enter this intriguing restaurant under the red awning off of the stone-paved street of the France exhibit. The building is of classic French architecture with stone walls and a metal roof. Inside is an elegant French dining room complete with fresh tablecloths, paintings, and chandeliers; table service in elegant continental style with a bustling, active atmosphere. Pleasant and helpful personnel speak French (English, if you insist) and are ready and willing to help you make selections.

To the right of the main dining room is a pleasant, glassed sunroom that provides bright, sunny dining in a dark green and wood tone motif.

Lunch and dinner meals include 10 or more salads and appetizers and about as many entrees. All of this comes at only a slightly high premium, compared to other Epcot table-service restaurants.

Menu items change from season to season. On recent visits we have seen filet of snapper and spinach baked in puff pastry with lobster cream sauce, sautéed tenderloin of beef with raisins and brandy sauce, and chicken breast marinated with herbs and baked in puff pastry.

As you might expect, desserts are worth drooling over, with plenty more than a dozen selections. We have dreamed about Crème Caramel (baked French custard with caramel sauce).

Beer and wine by the glass or carafe also are made available.

## United Kingdom

[▲] [Y] **Rose & Crown Pub and Dining Room.** English pub fare in a pleasant atmosphere. Lunch entrees from $5 to $15, and dinner from $15. Chil-

ort. Tea dates back several thousand years to ancient China and Tibet. It was introduced into England in the 1600s and soon thereafter into the American colonies by British merchants in the East India Company. The classic English breakfast tea is a Chinese black tea called Keemun. The popular Earl Grey tea is a black tea flavored with bergamot or lavender oil.

dren's menu. Lunch, dinner, snacks. Traditional afternoon tea at 4 P.M. Reservations for the dining room are recommended and necessary on busy days; no reservations are accepted for the pub.

Located across the street from the main portion of the United Kingdom exhibit, the Rose & Crown is an interesting British dining experience. Very ordinary pub food in England seems very exotic in Orlando. On previous visits, we have been offered steak-and-kidney pie, lamb and barley soup, chicken and leeks, and fish and chips. The dinner menu expanded to include mixed grills of pork, beef, and veal kidney. A selection of sweets, such as traditional sherry trifle, was also available.

There is a decent selection of beers, stouts and ales, including Bass from England, Tennent's from Scotland, and Guinness Stout and Harp ale from Ireland. They're sold by the pint and "yard" for those with powerful thirsts.

The decor is appropriately rough and dark, with elements of both city and country drinking establishments in the United Kingdom. Frosted and etched glass adds an elegant interest to this beautiful setting.

The pub, which can become quite crowded, offers appetizer-sized portions of the dinner menu along with beers and mixed drinks.

## Canada

**Le Cellier Restaurant.** Reopened in August of 1995, the cafeteria-style eatery features Canadian specialties including Torierre Pie, smoked beef brisket, chicken and meatball stew, smoked beef brisket sandwich, pemeal bacon sandwich, Canadian cheddar cheese soup, carved Steamship Round, and maple syrup pie. Lunch entrees are priced from $7.50, and dinner from $9.50.

# EPCOT CENTER

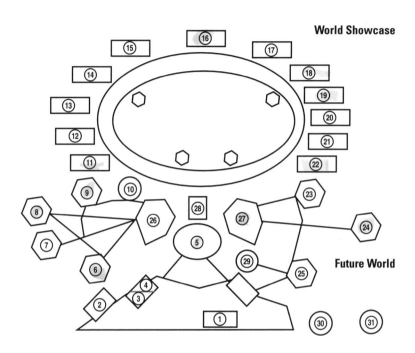

**World Showcase**

**Future World**

1. Monorail Station
2. Pet Care Kennel
3. Banking
4. Strollers
5. Spaceship Earth
6. Universe of Energy
7. Wonders of Life
8. Horizons
9. GM Test Track
10. Odyssey Center (under construction)
11. Mexico
12. Norway
13. China
14. Germany
15. Italy
16. The American Adventure

17. Japan
18. Morocco
19. France
20. International Gateway
21. United Kingdom
22. Canada
23. Journey Into Imagination
24. The Land
25. The Living Seas
26. Innoventions East
27. Innoventions West
28. Fountain of Nations
29. Lockers
30. Disabled Parking
31. Bus Parking

# INNOVENTIONS AT EPCOT CENTER

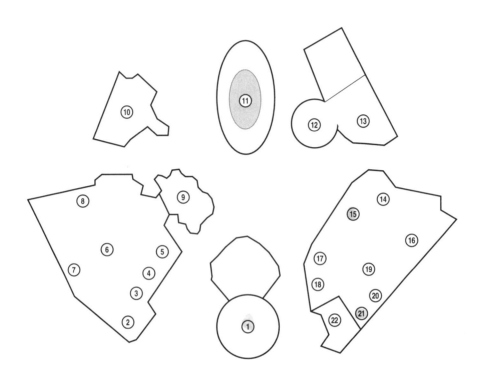

① Spaceship Earth
② Guest Relations/Earth Station
③ Hammacher Schlemmer
④ General Electric
⑤ Apple Computer
⑥ General Motors
⑦ Magic House Tour
⑧ Oracle
⑨ Electric Umbrella
⑩ Centorium
⑪ Fountain

⑫ Fountain View Espresso
⑬ Pasta Piazza
⑭ Videonics
⑮ Sega of America
⑯ IBM Corp.
⑰ Bill Nye
⑱ AT&T
⑲ Eclectronics
⑳ *Discover* Magazine
㉑ Lego
㉒ Epcot Discovery Center

# Chapter 8
# Disney-MGM Studios

Let's go to the movies: The Disney-MGM Studios Theme Park is the newest major park at Walt Disney World, opening in 1989. Its tone sits somewhere between the silly fun of the Magic Kingdom and the entertaining education of Epcot Center.

**Audience wanted.** Stop by the Production Information Window just inside the gates, or the Guest Services Window outside the turnstile early in the day to see if there are any available tickets for taping of television shows at the studios. Tickets are free and offered on a first-come, first-served basis.

While the Magic Kingdom draws most of its themes from fairy tales and works of fiction, the Disney-MGM Studios Theme Park allows guests to step into some of the greatest—or at least the most popular—movies and television hits of the 20th century. Disney also pushes hard for its recent hits, including *Aladdin, Beauty and the Beast, The Little Mermaid,* and *Honey, I Shrunk the Kids.* The hottest new attraction at the park is a spectacular ride destined to become one of the big draws of all of Walt Disney World for adults and older kids, the **Twilight Zone Tower of Terror.**

**Fishy statue.** Note the statue between the Studio Catering Co. and the Special Effects Tour. It's the actual mermaid fountain from the 1984 film *Splash.*

How does Disney-MGM Studios compare to Universal Studios Florida? In our judgment, the Disney operation—like everything within Walt Disney World—offers a more polished and better planned experience than almost anywhere else we know. Universal Studios is larger and has several rides and attractions that are considerably wilder and more entertaining than anything that Disney offers. If you have the time, we suggest you visit both Disney-MGM and Universal; if you are on a very tight schedule and must choose between the two parks, we'd suggest Disney-MGM if you are with young children and Universal for older parties.

The overall theme of Disney-MGM Studios seems to be "Nothing is what

ES

OW

**Twilight Zone Tower of Terror**

**The Great Movie Ride**

**SuperStar Television**

**Star Tours**

**Voyage of the Little Mermaid**
*(adults are excused)*

**The Magic of Disney Animation**

**Honey, I Shrunk the Kids Movie Set Adventure**

**Jim Henson's Muppet\*Vision 3D 4D**

**Backstage Studio Tour**

it appears to be." This will be apparent from the moment you spot the park's distinctive Earffel Tower (a set of mouse ears atop a 130-foot-tall water tower) to when you first see the very realistic New York street scenes or see some of the inside magic of the studio production tours.

Also visible from the road is the new Twilight Zone Tower of Terror, a creepy derelict hotel. It's fun to think of the Tower as a counterpoint to the squeaky-clean real hotels spread throughout Walt Disney World.

Be sure to find time to stroll **Hollywood Boulevard** near the entranceway—we suggest coming back to this area at midday when lines are longest at the attractions. The boulevard is a constant street theater. Pretty girls may be approached by "producers" handing out their business cards. Would-be actresses looking for work will give you the eye; vain stars will expect you to swoon at their feet. Actors perform skits and gags from old silent films. The street actors stay in character all of the time they are "on"; for fun, try asking one of them for directions, or some personal questions about their careers. Also new is a second street of shops and restaurants, **Sunset Boulevard.**

And, especially if you arrive late or are visiting on a crowded day, be sure to stop by the **Studios Tip Board** at the top end of Hollywood Boulevard. A chalkboard here will tell you how long the waits are for many of the attractions at the park; the hosts are kept up to date by walkie-talkie reports from head counters. You may need to alter your Power Trip based on unusual conditions.

One more note: the layout of the park seems to make it one of the hottest areas of Walt Disney World. Be sure to bring a hat and suntan lotion in season.

About the future: Disney-MGM may receive a major new draw if a version of the fantastic Fantasmic! music and light show is imported from Disneyland, a possibility for 1997 or later. A new attraction that may arrive is Roger Rabbit's Hollywood, off Sunset Blvd. And a new film for Star Tours is said to be on the drawing boards. Plans for 1998 or later include a Virtual Reality attraction, perhaps based on the Aladdin demonstration project which had been showcased at Epcot in 1995.

# Power Trip #1

## For Adults and Adventurous Kids

Arrive early. This tour allows time for a quick fast-food lunch and a more leisurely dinner. Stop by the **Production Information Window** just inside the gates on the right side to see if there are any tickets for tapings of television shows.

Head up Hollywood Boulevard and turn right and head down Sunset Boulevard to the **Twilight Zone Tower of Terror**, the new first stop on our Power Trip. If the lines are short and you are so inclined—if you can pardon that pun—check into the hotel again before the lines reach intolerable lengths later in the day.

Once your stomach is back in its customary position, zoom out of Sunset Boulevard and back to Hollywood Boulevard; make a left at the first corner along Echo Lake. Note the Hollywood & Vine and '50s Prime Time Cafe as possible dinner stops; you may want to make a reservation as you go by.

The goal is **Star Tours**. (Pass by the Indiana Jones Epic Stunt Spectacular—it'll wait for later.)

After Star Tours, make a sharp left turn and head for **Jim Henson's Muppet\*Vision 3D 4D**, a treat for all ages. While you're in the area, check out Mama Melrose's Ristorante Italiano, another interesting food stop, or the Sci-Fi Dine-In Theater Restaurant, a must-see eatery; make reservations early for these dining options.

The next stop is **The Great Movie Ride** at the top of Hollywood Boulevard. (Along the way, you have passed by the Monster Sound Show and SuperStar Television.)

Continue moving in a counterclockwise direction through the archway to the studio section of the park.

It should be time for lunch now; the Soundstage Restaurant is in the studio area and is as good a fast-food stop as any other.

Go next to **The Magic of Disney Animation** tour; don't let youngsters talk you out of this visit—they'll enjoy the Peter Pan movie in the preshow and you'll want to see the artists at work.

At this point, you have visited all of the attractions with the largest lines. Backtrack or continue in a counterclockwise direction to see shows like the **Indiana Jones Epic Stunt Spectacular** (consult the daily schedule for show times), **SuperStar Television** and **The Monster Sound Show**.

Remember that crowds at many rides and restaurants will be shorter during the afternoon parade; check the schedule on the day you arrive.

In season, the spectacular **Sorcery in the Sky** fireworks show is presented over the lake at dusk.

# Power Trip #2

## For Young Children and Adults with Them

This tour skips two rides that may be too wild for youngsters: Twilight Zone Tower of Terror and Star Tours.

Arrive early. Make restaurant reservations for lunch or dinner.

Head up Hollywood Boulevard and go straight to **The Great Movie Ride.** When you're through, enter into the studio section of the park and join the line for **The Voyage of the Little Mermaid** stage show.

The next stop is the **Backstage Studio Tour.**

Now cross over the top of the park to visit the **Honey, I Shrunk the Kids Movie Set Adventure** and one of the outdoor stage shows including **Ace Ventura—Pet Detective Live in Action** and **Beauty and the Beast.** The new Hunchback of Notre Dame show may be appropriate for some younger visitors.

It's time to go inside for some inspired silliness at **Jim Henson's Muppet*Vision 3D 4D**, a treat for all ages.

Go next to **The Magic of Disney Animation** tour.

Depending on the ages of your children, you may want to visit shows like the **Indiana Jones Epic Stunt Spectacular** (consult the daily schedule for show times, and be aware that there are some loud noises and flashes in the show), **SuperStar Television,** and **The Monster Sound Show.**

In-season, the spectacular **Sorcery in the Sky** fireworks show is presented over the lake at dusk.

## Attractions at Disney-MGM Studios

**WOW** **Twilight Zone Tower of Terror.** Behold the mysterious Hollywood Tower Hotel, a relic of Tinseltown's golden age.

You'll approach the hotel across its beautifully landscaped grounds; if the waiting line extends outside the building, you are in for a lengthy wait.

Even before you enter the lobby of the abandoned hotel, there are signs of impending danger high on the side of the 199-foot-tall building: a sparking electrical sign hangs above a gaping hole in the tower walls. (The hotel is the tallest structure at Walt Disney World.)

Legend has it that an entire guest wing was once attached to that damaged wall. What happened to the wing? And more important, what happened to the people in the tower when it disappeared?

Well, you'll receive a not-too-subtle hint of what lies ahead as you see an out-of-control elevator cage plunge past you through exposed doorways high on the outer wall.

Once inside the hotel, you'll enter the lobby where you will see the concierge's table and the front desk. On the left side you'll see a dusty, interrupted mah-jongg game and a stack of newspapers from the 1930s. Many of the furnishings of the lobby came from old hotels in Hollywood and Los Angeles, including the famed Jonathan Club, an L.A. landmark built in the 1920s.

Eventually, you'll make it to the bellhop's podium where you will be assigned to one of the four libraries. (Warning: if you're prone to claustrophobia, you may feel uncomfortable in the library; then again, if the library scares you, then the elevator definitely will terrify you.)

The introduction begins in the darkened hotel library as a flash of lightning energizes a television in the corner. Our host Rod Serling (long dead, but that doesn't matter in the Twilight Zone) tells the story of the dark and stormy night—Halloween of 1939, to be exact—when the guests disappeared from their elevator and stepped into a nightmare.

"This elevator travels directly to . . . The Twilight Zone."

When the lightning bolt struck, service in all the main elevators of the building were lost; only the creaky old service elevator still functions.

And then the library doors open to reveal the entrance to the hotel's basement, a creepy world of boilers, generators, and electrical boxes. It even smells like a basement.

**Bottoms up.** The drop in the Tower of Terror is about 40 feet, and the elevator cab is actually driven downward by high-power motors so that it travels faster than it would in free-fall. The rest of the way down, the cab travels in what the engineers call controlled deceleration. That means putting on the brakes.

And, by the way, the drop is advertised as a 13-story drop but the top floor is the twelfth. Ah, but you got on the elevator in the basement.

There's another waiting line down in the basement; the line splits into left and right queues that head to one or the other of the two elevator shafts in the building. The rides are the same, although the shaft to the right offers a brief view of the park from the top, while the left shaft overlooks the Disney road system.

The cars seat 22 passengers with three rows. If you want to sit in the front row of the car, you'll need to camp out on one of the spaces marked 1 or 2 in front of the elevator; to snag the center seat on the top row—a seat with an unobstructed view and a seat belt instead of safety bar to hold you in place, you'll want to ask for seat four in Row 5. The elevator operator at the door may be able to help you with your choice.

The doors of the elevator will open on the first floor where you will see a happy family and bellhop suddenly struck by lightning; the view changes to a star field. Your car will move forward into the lights and the shaft.

When you arrive at the "fifth dimension" you will look out at what seems to be an elevator shaft. Wait a minute! Are you going up or sideways? And who are those people who seem to have hitched a ride in your elevator? They seem like ghostly doubles of you and those around you.

Finally, you are in the vertical elevator shaft in the most severely damaged part of the hotel; your cab rises up higher and higher. At each floor, you can catch glimpses of the happy theme park outside. At the very top, you will reach the damaged elevator motors; they are sparking and flashing ominously.

The door opens for a view of the park—guests down below will be able to see the elevator cab hanging in space for a few seconds. We won't spoil it for

**Instant photography.**
When you are about to ride the elevator up the tower, the ghost of Rod Serling will greet you. Even more scary, his living representatives will attempt to sell you photos taken as the bottom fell out. Actually, the pictures are snapped at the moment of the first, false drop.

you even if we do tell you there are a few false drops before the big one.

How good is the ride? Well, it definitely is worth a 🔳WOW🔳 in this *Econoguide*. But it is a very short experience once you are in the elevator, about two minutes with just ten seconds or so of drop. Personally, I wouldn't want to wait in line for two hours for two minutes of ride and ten seconds of thrill.

In fact, Disney went back and retooled the ride a bit in early 1996, adding a "randomizer" to the drop sequence that adds a few extra ups and downs to the experience and just a bit of uncertainty for veterans of the ride.

On busy days, be sure to get to the park early and ride the Tower of Terror immediately, especially in the summer and in holiday periods. On one of my visits in March, the official opening hour for the Disney-MGM Studios was 9 A.M. but the gates opened at 8:30 A.M. and people poured into the park. We were on the ride by about 8:40, off by about 8:45, and back on ten minutes later. By 11 A.M., the wait was up to nearly an hour. But during the midday parade, the lines fell away and the wait was a reasonable 10 minutes.

**Going my way?**
The Great Movie Ride brings to Disney-MGM the same "moving theater" cars first introduced at the Energy pavilion at Epcot.

🔳WOW🔳 **The Great Movie Ride.** A celebration of some of the most famous movies of our time within a reproduction of the famous Mann's Chinese Theater in Hollywood.

The sidewalk outside of the ride includes hand- and footprints from all sorts of celebrities minor and major. Look carefully to find Pee-Wee Herman, dated 1984 before he became persona non grata at Disney. Leonard Nimoy's handprint gives the V-shaped Vulcan "Live long and prosper" salute.

The interior of the Chinese Theater is a bittersweet reminder of how full of marvel were the grand theaters of the early years of movies and how ordinary are our local quintupleplex mall theaters. In the lobby, you'll find what may be the world's most expensive slippers: Dorothy's ruby shoes from the 1939 MGM classic *The Wizard of Oz*. You'll also find a carrousel horse from the 1964 *Mary Poppins* movie, and a portion of the set from the 1979 *Alien* film.

Your first stop is a waiting area in a theater that is continuously showing original trailers from some of the most beloved movies of all time, including *Singin' in the Rain, Fantasia, Footlight Parade* with Jimmy Cagney, Joan Blondell, and Ruby Keeler, and a stark preview of *Alien*. You'll go within all of those movies and more in the ride to come.

Your moving auditorium will be presided over by a host or hostess who will narrate the tour. The excitement begins soon, when your leader will be hijacked by a 1920s gangster or a Wild West desperado (depending on which set of seats you are in). Don't worry, though: the good guys will prevail later on in the ride.

In addition to the West and old Chicago, you will visit a re-creation of the "By a Waterfall" scene (with more than 60 Audio-Animatronic dancers) from Busby Berkeley's *Footlight Parade.* You will also travel into and through the Nostromo spaceship, home of the Alien himself; an extended *Raiders of the Lost Ark* set, including wriggling robotic snakes; the jungle world of *Tarzan;* Mickey Mouse's *Fantasia;* and finally a drive down Oz's Yellow Brick Road.

The last stop on the ride is a high-tech theater that will surround you with the sound and images of a well-done short film with some of the best-known scenes of all time. See how many stars and films you can recognize as they fly by.

The lines for this attraction build at midday. If the lines extend outside of the building, we'd suggest you come back at another time; there is still a lengthy queue within the theater. The ride itself takes about 20 minutes once you're seated.

**Fly it again, Sam.** According to the Hollywood myth-makers, the Lockheed Electra 12A on display in the *Casablanca* set was actually used in the real movie, a happy accident.

**The heart of darkness.** The spaceship that is invaded by a murderous alien—the most chilling scene of the Great Movie Ride—was named "Nostromo." That name comes from a 1904 book by the Polish/English novelist Joseph Conrad who spent much of his early life as a seaman on a succession of freighters.

**WOW! SuperStar Television.** Casting for the show goes on in the waiting area about 15 minutes before show time; if you want to be picked, the best position is down front. If you want to avoid your moment of fame, hang back and try to blend into the wallpaper—which may or may not work when the "casting director" comes down off the stage and walks among the audience. There will be calls for couples young and old, singles of both sexes, and even youngsters.

The 30-minute show moves quickly from one setup to another, with the cast members sharing electronic space with some of television's old and new stars: reading the news with Dave Garroway on the original *Today Show* in 1955, on the set of the *Howdy Doody Show,* a guest appearance as a singing group on *The Ed Sullivan Show,* a cameo appearance on *Gilligan's Island*, and more. One lucky woman will get to appear in one of the most famous scenes of the *I Love Lucy* show—the candy factory scene. Some of the couples will trade cracks with Woody from *Cheers,* and others will make appearances on *The Golden Girls* and the *Tonight Show.* A recent addition is a bit where a guest gets to play the part of Tim "Tool Man" Taylor in a skit from *Home Improvement.* Finally, some lucky kid (of whatever age) will get to hit a game-winning home run in a televised baseball game.

Outside the SuperStar building, you'll find the **Academy of Television Arts and Sciences Hall of Fame Plaza** honoring television legends. The Academy was founded in 1946, the same year network television was born; the real Hall of Fame is located at the Academy's headquarters in Hollywood. Plaques in Orlando honor Red Skelton, Bill Cosby, Mary Tyler Moore, Sid Caesar, Rod

**Behind the screens.** The trick behind the SuperStar Television show is the use of "color key" technology allowing electronic insertion of images or backgrounds. Some of the old television scenes have had elements "matted" out.

The same technology is used at Universal Studios in the Screen Test Home Video Adventure attraction, where visitors can pay to place themselves into the action on a videotape.

**Sounds like . . .** The Foley Stage is named after the acknowledged creator of the Hollywood sound-effects stage, Jack Foley. The same sort of devices were used in adding sounds to live radio dramas of the 1930s and 1940s.

The work of the audio engineer is called "sweetening" and includes the use of sound filters, the addition of echo, and the inclusion of sound effects.

Serling, James Garner, Andy Griffith, Milton Berle, Danny Thomas, Barbara Walters, Carol Burnett, and, of course, Walt Disney.

**The Monster Sound Show.** An odd name for a funny show—don't let the title scare away youngsters. This is an entertaining introduction to the use of sound effects in film. Four visitors will be chosen from the audience to make sounds for the film inside.

While you're waiting for the next show, enjoy the introduction by David Letterman of Foley Stage artistry. When you enter, Dave warns visitors that anyone who breaks anything will be attacked by security guards in mouse suits.

Inside, the audience will view a short film starring Chevy Chase and Martin Short (a Short-short?) that takes place inside a pretend haunted house, complete with the sounds of thunder, rain, and all sorts of things that go bump in the night. Next, recruits from the audience operate some of the tools of the soundmakers as the now-silent film scrolls by on the overhead screen. And finally, the often-miscued new version is projected.

Don't pass by the interactive discovery areas at the end of the show, either. **SoundWorks** gives you that favorite special effect of them all—a bunch of buttons to push. The **Earie Encounters** section allows you to play with some of your favorite sci-fi sounds; the **Movie Mimica** booths let you dub in your voice for Roger Rabbit.

**Indiana Jones Stunt Spectacular!** A huge covered outdoor theater, but it still fills up within 10 or 15 minutes of afternoon showtimes, even earlier on busier days. It's a good place to park at the busiest, hottest times of the day. The best seats are in the center of the theater; they are filled first and it is from this section that the "casting director" usually selects a dozen or so "extras" to participate. All must be over the age of 18; there's a ringer among them— see if you can spot him or her. The extras don't have an awful lot to do.

The stunt show starts with a real bang as a double for Indiana Jones rocks and rolls across the huge stage; most of the later actions rely less on mechanisms and more on the skills of the stunt actors. It's a 30-minute world of Nazis, Arab swordsmen, fiery explosions, and bad jokes.

**WOW** **Star Tours.** "Whenever your plans call for intergalactic travel," say the travel posters, "please consider flying Star Tours to the vacation moon of Endor."

Disney builds the atmosphere and excitement beautifully from the moment you walk beneath the huge space machine outside; it continues as you walk through the indoor waiting area that simulates a gritty space garage. Our favorite flaky robots, R2D2 and C3PO, are the mechanics.

Most of the queue for Star Tours is inside the building; if visitors are lined up outside the building onto the plaza, you've got about a 45-minute wait; if the line extends outside and into the covered space "forest," you might want to plan your expedition to Endor for later in the day.

**Another big adventure.** The original voice of the robot pilot at Star Tours was none other than the exceedingly strange Paul Reubens, also known as Pee-Wee Herman. After Pee-Wee was, err, exposed as someone a bit out of the Disney mold, a new (less interesting) voice replaced his.

When your time comes, you will enter a 40-passenger simulator cabin and meet your pilot, Captain Rex. The doors will be closed and your seat belts tightly cinched before he informs you that this is his first trip. Too late— you're off. You'll make an uneasy takeoff and then blast (accidentally) into and then through a frozen meteor, stumble into an active intergalactic battle zone, and finally make a wild landing at your goal, the vacation moon of Endor.

This is quite a wild ride, at about the same level of twisting, turning, and dipping as the Body Wars show at Wonders of Life in Epcot Center. It's a short ride, but a bit rough for the very young; pregnant women and those with health problems are advised to sit this one out.

After the ride, note the travel posters for other Star Tour destinations, including lovely Hoth and Tatoine.

**WOW** **The Voyage of the Little Mermaid** is presented throughout the day at a theater that includes all sorts of bits and pieces of Disney magic, including snippets from the movie, more than 100 puppets, lasers, holographic projections, live performers, and Audio-Animatronic robots. The 15-minute show can draw huge lines on a crowded afternoon. If this film is a favorite of your youngsters, you would do best to head there early. Very young kids may become a bit startled by some of the special effects; prepare them ahead of time.

At the start of the show, the curtain becomes running water, and laser beams overhead create the effect of descending beneath the waves. Especially enchanting is the opening sequence of black-light puppetry.

**Beauty and the Beast Stage Show.** Off-off-Broadway, this 30-minute live-action show at the outdoor Theater of the Stars showcases live performers in fanciful and spectacular sets, costumes, and special effects.

All of your kid's favorite characters—and your own—are there: Belle, Gaston, Lumière, and Mrs. Potts among them.

Check the daily entertainment schedule for times.

**Short subject.** A lot of effort went into the animation of the Cronkite-Williams film, as well as into striking a balance between tall Walter and diminutive Robin—we suspect there was a soapbox somewhere, as well as some creative camera angles employed.

At the end of the film *Aladdin,* we see the Genie in yet another guise, dressed as your basic Walt Disney World tourist including a Goofy hat; it's the same getup worn by Robin Williams (voice of the Genie) in the film with Cronkite.

**Hunchback of Notre Dame.** A stage spectacular based on Disney's new cartoon of the same name, presented at the Backlot Theater near the Muppet*Vision show. The production replaced a "Pocahontas" show in mid-1996.

**WOW! The Magic of Disney Animation.** Disney cartoons are, after all, the foundation upon which the entire Disney empire was built. And this tour offers an extraordinary glimpse at the history and process of animation.

Disney-MGM Studios is a satellite operation of the main studio in Burbank; 75 artists work in Florida. Their first full work was "Roller Coaster Rabbit," a short that ran with the *Dick Tracy* feature film.

The tour opens with an exhibit of old and new animation cels, featuring the megahits *Beauty and the Beast* and *Aladdin,* as well as drawings from the archives. Check out the Oscar statue.

Next is an entertaining short movie starring one of the all-time odd couples: former newsman Walter Cronkite and present wild man Robin Williams in "Back to Never Land."

The best part of the tour comes last, when visitors are let loose in a glass-walled hallway where they can literally look over the shoulders of animators and technicians in the studios below. We found it hard to tear ourselves away from watching the detailed work; the animators work in shifts so that there is always someone at work during park hours, every day.

The self-guided tour can take about 30 minutes; lines build at midday, so making a morning or late-in-the-day visit is best. No photographs are permitted inside.

The gift shop after the tour offers actual painted cels from Disney movies—beautiful but quite pricey for objects that once were thrown out as trash. Some of the cels sell for several thousand dollars.

**WOW! Honey, I Shrunk the Kids Movie Set Adventure.** A most inventive playground based on the hit movie about a mad inventor whose shrinking ray accidentally reduces his children and a few friends. Play areas include giant cereal loops, ants, spiders, a huge roll of film, and a leaky garden hose. The ground is carpeted in a spongy rubber.

It's a great place for youngsters to burn off some energy; be advised, though, that it is quite easy to lose a child in the playground. The best strategy is to station an adult by the single exit from the playground, rather than chasing through the various adventures.

**WOW! Jim Henson's Muppet*Vision 3D 4D.** We have to admit that we passed by this attraction the first few times we brought our kids to the studios—Bert and Ernie and Kermit the Frog seemed a bit too silly, even for an eight-year-old. Were we ever wrong!

The fun begins once you enter the theater, which is designed as Muppet World Headquarters. Pause just inside the entrance to read the office directory on the wall. Listings include the Institute of Heckling and Browbeating—Statler and Waldorf, Curmudgeons-in-Chief; the Sartorial Accumulation Division, run by Miss Piggy, of course; and the Academy of Amphibian Science, under the tutelage of Kermit the Frog. The security desk at the door advises that the guard will be back in five minutes, but the key is under the mat.

The preshow area for Muppet*Vision includes a wonderfully goofy collection of packing cases with equipment for the Muppet Labs (Tongue Inflators, Gorilla Detectors, and Anvil Repair Kits) and roadshow suitcases for the Muppet band, Dr. Teeth and the Electric Mayhem, including paisley bell bottoms, Nehru jackets, Beatles boots, and love beads. There's a big pink trunk that bears the label, "Miss Piggy Satin Evening Gowns"; below that is "More Satin Evening Gowns," and finally, "The Rest of the Satin Evening Gowns." Another favorite: a cargo net filled with orange and green cubes and labeled "A-Net-Full-Of-Jello" in a tribute to original Mouseketeer Annette Funicello.

**Playing soon.** Disney animators are at work on an update to one of Walt Disney's most beloved—and most avant-garde—works: *Fantasia*. The new film, tentatively called *Fantasia Continued*, is expected to include some of the most famous segments of the original film, including the "Sorceror's Apprentice," "Night on Bald Mountain," and "Nutcracker Suite." (I don't know about you, but I can't watch a ballet company performing the "Nutcracker" without seeing a hippo in a tutu.) New segments are expected to include classical classics such as "Pomp and Circumstances" and the "Carnival of the Animals."

But the real fun is within the beautiful 584-seat theater, which is decidedly more opulent than your neighborhood quintupleplex. There's a robotic all-penguin orchestra in the pit (they took the job just for the halibut) and a private box at the front for Waldorf and Statler. The film includes some marvelous 3-D special effects as well as flashing lights, a bubblemaker, smell-o-vision, and a surprise from the skies, as well as a live actor and a cannon.

Don't pass this extraordinary multimedia show by. If you don't have a kid with you, you can pretend you're with the ones in front of you in line.

And when you leave, be sure to check out the statue outside: It's Miss Piggy as the Statue of Liberty.

**WOW Backstage Studio Tour.** Disney-MGM Studios is a working movie lot, and the 25-minute backstage shuttle tour is a great way to see some of the real—and not-so-real elements of moviemaking. Films and TV shows under production vary, but have included in recent seasons *Star Search, Mickey Mouse Club,* professional wrestling shows, and bits and pieces of major films including *Honey, I Blew Up the Baby.*

The large trams run continuously, and lines are generally short in the

**Fill 'er up.** The oil field at Catastrophe Canyon bears the markings of Mohave Oil, a fictitious company that is also represented at the old-timey Oscar's Super Service Station on Hollywood Boulevard.

**Historic sign.** To the right of the entrance to Inside the Magic: Special Effects and Production Tour you will see a small steel sign that tells you that you are at the corner of Mickey Avenue and Dopey Drive.

This street sign is similar to the one located at the Walt Disney Studios in Burbank, originally installed for the 1941 movie "The Reluctant Dragon." The sign soon became a company landmark.

For many years the Disney studios posed its stars in front of the sign; you'll see an example near the reproduction, showing Walt Disney with Rosalind Russell.

morning and late in the day. Remember this: the left side of the cars (the first person into each row) is the wet side, no matter what the guide says at first. (Not very wet, by the way—more of a splash than a soaking.)

As you pull out of the tram station, you will first pass by the **Car Pool**, which includes some of the vehicles used in your favorite movies. In recent years, the lot has included a futuristic vehicle from *Blade Runner* and an assortment of gangster cars from *The Untouchables* and *Dick Tracy*. The trams next pass through the **Costuming** shops.

Carpenters and designers at the **Scenic Shop** construct just about anything and everything for the movies; you'll also glimpse the huge stock of lighting fixtures for filmmaking. The interior of the 747 was used for scenes in *Passenger 57*; it is part of an actual plane retired from the Delta Airlines fleet.

The backlot of Disney-MGM Studios includes a **Residential Street** with some familiar sights— you may recognize the homes from *Golden Girls, Empty Nest,* and other television and movie settings. These are empty shells, of course, and are used for exterior shots; interior filming is performed within soundstages in California or elsewhere.

At the end of the street, you'll make a right turn past the **Boneyard**, home of some of the larger props from former movie productions. Look for the trolley from Toontown in *Who Framed Roger Rabbit* and the UFO from *Flight of the Navigator,* among other props. A recent addition is a Gulfstream airplane owned by Walt Disney and used in 1964 during the scouting for land for Walt Disney World in Florida.

And finally, it is on to a demonstration of large-scale special effects in the area known as **Catastrophe Canyon,** which simulates a working oil field in a narrow desert canyon. We won't spoil the fun except to point out that the "set" includes hydraulic shaker tables, a series of tanks storing 70,000 gallons of water, and flames, and explosions, and . . .

The tour ends at the **American Film Institute Showcase** where sets, props, costumes, and items from major films are on display. Our favorite items here include the cheesy little minature saucer used in the 1955 sci-fi classic, *The Day the Earth Stood Still.* You'll also see storyboards from *Toy Story* and a giant sneaker that was supposed to be that of baby Adam Szalinski in Disney's 1992 film, *Honey, I Blew Up the Baby*.

Lines build by midday; come early or late in the day to avoid a long wait.

**Inside the Magic: Special Effects and Production Tour.** Ever wonder how they can re-create a fierce naval battle without hiring—and sinking—an entire navy? How they got those kids to ride on a bee in *Honey, I Shrunk the Kids*? You'll learn the answer to these and other questions in the special effects tour, a one-hour (no bathroom break) walking tour.

**Water Effects Tank.** This pool, home of the "Miss Fortune" tugboat and other miniature or partial boat sets, demonstrates how technicians use fans, explosions, and a 400-gallon splash tank to re-create a raging storm and a battle at sea. Two volunteers from the audience will get to play captains courageous.

**Special Effects Workshop and Shooting Stage.** A technician will demonstrate how miniatures and matte paintings are combined in thousands of hours of work to produce extraordinary special effects for films like *Dick Tracy* and *Cocoon*. Two lucky kids from the tour will get to demonstrate a wild bee ride—all of the action is in the computer-controlled camera, not the bee.

**Soundstages I, II, and III.** Depending on production schedules, you may get to see sets, rehearsals, or even scenes in production at one of the soundstages; no photography is permitted in this section of the tour. The stages are often used for Disney Channel television productions.

Next you will see a cute film starring Bette Midler, called "The Lottery," that demonstrates the use of special effects and post-production editing. The 2½-minute short required the efforts of a crew of 100 and five days of shooting at the Orlando studios.

**Post Production Editing and Audio.** Some of the tricks of the editors and "Foley Artist" sound technicians are demonstrated, with the aid of Mel Gibson, C3PO, and R2D2, among others.

**The Walt Disney Theater.** Finally, you'll enter a theater for previews of coming Disney and MGM films, introduced by company CEO Michael Eisner.

**Toy Story Parade.** *Toy Story*, the first computer-drawn feature cartoon, was a big hit for Disney in 1995, and so is the spectacular parade that celebrates its characters at the Disney-MGM Studios. How's this for a turn-about: huge walking figures with human beings inside, replicating computer-drawn characters given voice by human actors.

The parade steps off daily down Hollywood Boulevard to the circle in front

**Two pants, one jacket.** Tailors at the costume shop make as many as 12,000 costumes a year. Disney claims the world's largest working wardrobe with more than 2.5 million items available. Among articles on display is a hot red dress from *Pretty Woman* and Michael Jackson's "Captain EO" suit.

**Time pieces.** Watch carefully when Disney honcho Michael Eisner sits down in the theater next to his company's symbol. Eisner wears a Mickey Mouse watch; the corporate mouse wears an Eisner timepiece.

When is a set not a set? It's a bit of a stretch to call the decorations at the Soundstage Restaurant "sets." As an animated movie, *Aladdin* was entirely based on drawings and had no actual sets.

**KEY:**

[🍴] = Fast food

[🍸] = Pub

[🏠] = Full-service restaurant

of The Great Movie Ride, and then toward Echo Lake before it exits between Star Tours and the Backlot Express restaurant.

The stars of the parade are pull-string cowboy Woody and his friend Buzz Lightyear, who sits atop a 20-foot-high rocketship. Woody's pet Slinky Dog—who just can't seem to keep himself together—trots alongside. And there is Mike, the Rockin' Robot Radio Tape Recorder; Woody uses him to broadcast to the crowds along the parade route.

You'll also meet walking-around representatives of favorite toys including Mr. Potato Head, Hamm, and the Barrel of Monkeys.

**Sorcery in the Skies.** A spectacular laser and fireworks show, choreographed to classical and Disney music (which are not the same), presented in peak season when the park is open late. The finale of the show includes a gigantic inflatable Mickey dressed as the Sorcerer's Apprentice. The best view of the show is from near the Chinese Theater, but you can also see the fireworks and hear the music from the parking lot—a good place to beat a quick getaway with the kids.

## Eating Your Way Through Disney-MGM Studios

Disney-MGM Studios includes some of the more interesting eateries at Walt Disney World. Be sure to check when you arrive for Early Value Meals offered at some of the restaurants, and for special meal deals for youngsters under the age of 9.

[🍴] **Disney-MGM Studios Commissary.** Behind SuperStar Television. A large fast-food cafeteria offering basic fare including burgers, large hot dogs, chicken breast sandwiches, and stir-fry chicken, with prices ranging from about $4 to $5. Children are offered hot dogs, chicken strips, and more for about $4.

[🍴] **Starring Rolls Bakery.** A small bakery almost hidden along the right side of the Brown Derby. A good place to stop for a quick breakfast, or anytime during the day for dessert. Offerings include bagels, small loaves of bread, croissants, pastries, donuts, muffins, and cheesecake, with prices from about $2 to $4.

[🍴] **Min and Bill's Dockside Diner.** On Echo Lake, near SuperStar Television. Belly up to the hatchway in the S.S. *Down the Hatch*, moored at a dock on the studio pond. Snack offerings include nachos with cheese, fruit cup, danish, soft yogurt, and ice cream sodas, with prices from about $2 to $3.

[🍴] **Dinosaur Gertie's Ice Cream of Extinction.** Across from the Indiana Jones Stunt Spectacular! Cold treats from within the belly of a dino, or so it appears. Some of the same items can be purchased from wagons around the park.

🍴 **Backlot Express.** In the Studio Shops between Star Tours and the Indiana Jones Stunt Spectacular! An interesting setting for a burger and hot dog fast foodery, set among the props of the Studio Shops. Offerings include charbroiled chicken with flour tortillas, burgers, hot dogs, chili, and chef's salad, with prices ranging from $4 to $7. Make good use of the condiment bar, which includes about two dozen toppings.

🍴 **Soundstage Restaurant featuring Aladdin.** Within the Studios area, across from the Voyage of the Little Mermaid. A cavernous fast-food eatery offering four distinct types of fare. The building includes "sets" from *Aladdin*, and characters from the movie make appearances there. All of the restaurants offer a children's peanut butter and jelly meal for about $1.50.

**Sandwiches, Soup, and Salads** offers exactly what its name promises. Its Northern Bean Soup is available served within a hollowed-out sourdough bread bowl for about $2.50; a combination sandwich goes for about $6.

**Bar-B-Que** offers a barbecue beef, chicken, or pork sandwich for $4 to $5; a smoked turkey leg is sold for about $4.

**Pizza and Pasta** sells individual deep dish pizzas, linguine with a variety of sauces, and a pasta and vegetable salad, each for about $4.

**The Catwalk Bar** up above the Soundstage Restaurant offers bar fare including peel-your-own shrimp for $8 and nachos with red bean salsa for about $2, along with a nice selection of beers and California wines.

🍴 **Studio Catering Co.** Off the streets of New York, next to the *Honey, I Shrunk the Kids* playground. It's an outdoor fast-food restaurant under a corrugated tin roof. Just outside is an ice cream and sundae bar.

🏛 **The Hollywood Brown Derby.** At the end of Hollywood Boulevard, near the entrance to the studios. A replica of the Hollywood landmark, featuring an art deco interior with drawings of stars on the walls. Lunch includes the famous Cobb salad introduced at the original Brown Derby, as well as corned beef and cabbage, and pasta with seafood; prices range from about $9 to $18. Dinner entrees include baked grouper, filet mignon, and sautéed medallions of veal, with prices ranging from about $15 to $24. Also

**Movie souvenirs.** If you are a movie fan, Sid Cahuenga's One-of-a-Kind shop near the entrance gate at Crossroads of the World offers large color posters for many classic movies from Disney, MGM, and other studios (we found *Bambi, Sleeping Beauty,* and *Pinocchio* for about $15 each). Also available are small lobby cards for about $3 and even original press kits for major motion pictures.

**Stetson steaks.** The Brown Derby was the "in" restaurant and night spot of Hollywood in the 1930s. Owner Bob Cobb reportedly told his friends that food was all that mattered—in fact, he said, his menu would be so good that people would eat out of a hat. So he built his restaurant in the shape of a derby.

**On the cover of *Rolling Stone*.** The Cover Story shop offers visitors the chance to be on the cover of one of more than a dozen well-known national magazines. After you choose the ego trip of your dreams, a costumer will help you into appropriate garb and help you pose for the cover. Most color covers cost about $17 to $20.

offered are appetizers including snails, fried Camembert, and pasta with wild mushrooms.

The child's menu includes pasta, burgers, fried fish, chicken, and pizza for about $4.

🏛 **Hollywood & Vine "Cafeteria of the Stars."** At Hollywood and Vine, on the main gate side of Echo Lake. An old-style cafeteria with a hot table and an art deco interior. Offerings include the Serenade of Life—a shrimp, chicken, and fruit salad; Backlot Ribs, and Cahuenga Chicken, for about $9 to $11. The child's menu includes chicken, fried fish, tenderloin tips, and peanut butter and jelly sandwiches, from $3 to $6.

🏛 **'50s Prime Time Cafe—Tune In Lounge.** Along Echo Lake, near the Indiana Jones Stunt Spectacular! Step right into a kitchen of the 1950s; Mom will greet you at the door, and your waitress will stand by to make sure you clear your plate. Luncheon appetizer offerings include Mom's Chili over angel hair pasta for about $4, Dad's Bachelor Chili for about $2.50, and fried zucchini for about $3. Entrees include Magnificent Meatloaf, Chicken Pot Pie, Granny's Pork Roast, and the All-American Burger, for about $8 to $15.

Dinner offerings include Auntie's Roasted Lamb and a charbroiled T-bone steak, with prices ranging from about $13 to $23. Book a reservation early to assure a seat.

🏛 **Mama Melrose's Ristorante Italiano.** In the streets of New York near the Muppet*Vision theater and Star Tours attractions. A very attractive eatery. Much more than your basic pizzeria, you'll enjoy the wood-fired pizza oven smell as you enter.

"Tutta La Pasta Che Puoi Mangiare" (all the pasta you care to eat) costs about $10.50; grilled tenderloin of beef goes for $14. Other offerings include fresh fish, vegetable lasagna, and chicken marsala. Your basic (small) pizza sells for about $9.50. There are also vegetarian, ham, Mexican, and other varieties. The child's menu includes spaghetti, pizza, hot dogs, and chicken strips, for about $4 to $6. A children's special is priced at $3.99.

There are 292 seats available, but things can become quite hectic between 1 and 3 P.M. Reservations are accepted.

🍴 **Disney's Toy Story Pizza Planet Arcade.** A pizza parlor with a collection of the latest in video games—or is it the other way around? Located near the entrance to Star Tours.

🏛 **Sci-Fi Dine-In Theater Restaurant.** Behind Monster Sound and across from Star Tours. Ya gotta see this place—it's a must-see eatery, among the most unusual settings of any restaurant anywhere. Each group of diners is shown to their table—inside a little convertible—by a parking attendant. Each four-seat car with 1955 license plate faces a large drive-in movie screen showing coming attractions for weird and wonderful science fiction movies of the 1950s and 1960s. Reservations are essential.

On a recent visit, the films included *Cat Women of the Moon* starring Victor Jory, *Devil Girl from Mars* (a creature without mercy), *The Horror of Party Beach* (teenagers, beach, rock 'n' roll, bikers, and atomic monsters) and Peter Graves in *It*, and the original trailers for *Attack of the 50 Ft. Woman.* (The girl in one of the horror films says to the guy she is with, "I expected to be frightened on my wedding night, but not like this.")

The reel of trailers also includes a few newsreels; it runs about 45 minutes before repeating itself, which is enough time to order, eat, and leave.

All in all, the Sci-Fi Restaurant is a hoot. The food is appropriate for a drive-in theater—very ordinary, but that's not really the reason you came.

Luncheon offerings include Journey to the Center of the Pasta, Attack of the Killer Club Sandwich, Return of the Killer Club Sandwich, Revenge of the Killer Club Sandwich, and Beach Party Panic (filet of fish, of course), with prices ranging from about $8 to $12. At dinner, look for some of the same dishes, plus Red Planet (linguine and tomato sauce) and Saucer Sightings (a rib-eye steak), priced from about $10 to $17.

In early 1996, Disney discontinued the free bowl of popcorn that used to adorn every dashboard; our waiter said the powers decided diners were filling up on the freebie and not ordering enough from the menu. Boo!

Unusual for a diner and very unusual for Disney, the eatery also offers beer to adults.

The child's menu includes grilled cheese sandwiches, chicken strips, burgers, and spaghetti, priced from $3.50 to $5.

⑪ **Sunset Ranch Market.** As you rush to or from the Twilight Zone Tower of Terror, don't overlook the attractive outdoor eatery on Sunset Boulevard. Included in this area is **Rosie's Red Hot Dogs**, **Catalina Eddie's** frozen yogurt stand, and **Echo Park** and **Anaheim Produce** fruit and vegetable stands.

# DISNEY-MGM STUDIOS

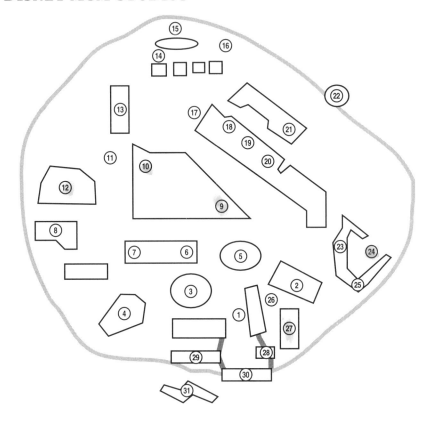

1. Hollywood Boulevard
2. Theater of the Stars
3. Echo Lake
4. Indiana Jones Epic Stunt Spectacular
5. Toy Story Parade
6. Superstar Television
7. The Monster Sound Show
8. Star Tours
9. The Great Movie Ride
10. Honey, I Shrunk the Kids Movie Set Adventure
11. New York Street
12. Jim Henson's Muppet Vision 3-D 4-D
13. Special Events Stage
14. The Backlot
15. Catastrophe Canyon
16. Residential Street

17. Inside the Magic
18. Soundstage I
19. Soundstage II
20. Soundstage III
21. Production Center
22. Earffel Tower
23. Voyage of the Little Mermaid
24. Backstage Studio Tour
25. The Magic of Disney Animation
26. Sunset Boulevard
27. Twilight Zone Tower of Terror
28. Lockers/Strollers
29. First Aid
30. Guest Relations
31. Entrance Plaza
32. Pet Care Kennel

# Chapter 9
# Disney Water Parks

On hot New York City summer days when I was a kid, we sometimes pried the covers off fire hydrants and turned them on: an instant water park!

Over the years, the idea of a water park has grown. All over America you'll find 100-foot towers of fiberglass and steel, lubricated with rushing water. Beneath them you will find large swimming pools with wave machines.

But once again, leave it to Disney to take what has become the ordinary water park and make it extraordinary. It's all in the setting.

Disney's watering holes, the new Blizzard Beach and the venerable Typhoon Lagoon and River Country, are state-of-the-watery-art. They are a great way to cool off and have a ton of fun on a hot summer or summer-like day—a season which in Florida can extend from March and sometimes February through December.

If you've got an all-parks admission ticket, it's not a bad idea to plan on splitting your day into thirds: start at one of the theme parks in the morning, break away to a water park in the heat and crowds of the afternoon, and then head back to a theme park in the evening for more rides and the nightly fireworks or parade.

The water parks have fast food eateries. You can also bring your own lunch in a cooler; no bottles or alcohol are allowed.

If you're on an a la carte plan, jump at the chance to unwind at a water park on the hottest day of your trip. And don't overlook Wet 'n Wild, an independent park near Universal Studios.

## Blizzard Beach

You are, of course, perfectly willing to suspend disbelief—that's why you are at Walt Disney World in the first place. So you'll have no problem getting this concept: after a freak storm dumped a ton of snow on Orlando, Blizzard Beach was planned as Florida's first ski resort. Unfortunately, temperatures quickly returned to normal.

And so, what we've got here is a ski resort for swimmers. Blizzard Beach

**Electricity overhead.** Thunderstorms can come up quickly and powerfully in Florida, especially in the late afternoons of hot days. Lifeguards will clear the pools and slides of Typhoon Lagoon or Blizzard Beach if a storm is near, and they may even close the park if necessary.

**Whoa!** It's you against gravity as you plunge down the flumes at River Country, Typhoon Lagoon, and Blizzard Beach. You can somewhat control your speed, though, by the way you lie down.
**Fastest:** Lie on your back with your hands over your head. Arch your back so that only your shoulders and heels touch the track.
**Fast:** Lie on your back with your hands crossed on your chest and your ankles crossed.
**Slow:** Sit up.
**Slowest:** Walk back down the stairs.

is built around 90-foot **Mt. Gushmore**, which is served by a chairlift to the top of the ski jump. This is no bunny hill, either; nearly all of the 17 slides are a few notches above the level of Typhoon Lagoon on the other side of Walt Disney World.

The 42-acre park is located north of Disney's All-Star Sports Resort, across World Drive from Disney-MGM Studios.

**Summit Plummet.** This is the big one, the ski jump starting 120 feet up. (It actually begins from a platform 30 feet above the top of Mt. Gushmore!) As far as we know, it is the highest free-fall water slide in the world. Sliders may reach a top speed of 55 mph down the 500-foot-slide at an angle of 60 degrees; the slide passes through a ski chalet on the way down. From below, it looks as if skiers . . . err, sliders . . . are heading off a ski jump at the top of the mountain. For those in training for the water slide Olympics, there's a timing clock at the bottom to report your results.

If you make it to the top of Mt. Gushmore but don't have the courage to take the plummet, there's an easier slope to the bottom: **Slush Gusher**, a double-humped slide about half the length and speed but still a spectacular plunge.

Another way off the top is **Runoff Rapids**, an inner tube ride that includes a dark section within a pipe.

**Snow Stormers** is a twisting and turning inner tube slide that looks like a slalom ski course. "Snowmaking" jets spray water over the course as you bounce your way to the bottom.

**Ski Patrol Training Center.** Activities for the hotshots include the **T-bar** at the **Ski Patrol Training Center**, where you can hang on to an overhead trolley for a trip over—or into—a pool. You'll also find the **Thin Ice Training Course** which presents a pathway across treacherous icebergs in the pool. And the **Krinkle Tin Slide** is an enclosed water pipe that deposits sliders into a deep pool.

**Teamboat Springs.** A record-setting five-person, 1,500-foot raft ride through waterfalls.

**Toboggan Racer.** An eight-lane competitive waterslide; unlike the other slides, this one puts riders head-first on a mat. Nearby is another mat slide,

**Snow Stormers;** this trio of flumes races down the mountain on a switchback course through slalom gates.

**Melt Away Bay.** A 1.2-acre wave pool at the base of Mt. Gushmore.

**Cross Country Creek** circles the park, pushing visitors on inner tubes on a half-mile circuit; the creek passes through an ice cave where the "icicles" melt onto the paddlers below.

For the youngest visitors, there's **Tike's Peak** with miniature versions of Mount Gushmore's slides and a snow castle fountain.

The new Blizzard Beach is sure to be a hot draw and may attract crowds beyond your tolerance during busy times of the year; a contrarian approach calls for taking advantage of Typhoon Lagoon instead. Disney planners will close admission to the park once the lot is full; after that, only guests at Disney resorts arriving by bus will be admitted; come early during peak times. Note that during the off-season in the early months of the year, Blizzard Beach is closed on Sundays.

## Typhoon Lagoon

According to Disney legend, this was once a beautiful tropical resort until a rogue typhoon roared through. What was left standing was knocked down by an earthquake. Oh, and then there was a volcanic eruption. (Sounds like a lovely place to vacation.) But the villagers refused to give up, and they rebuilt their paradise in and among the ruins.

The fabulous water slides are built into realistic miniature mountains; the huge wave pool has a sandy beach; and the river rafting ride passes through jungle canopies, a rain forest, and caves. There is hardly any sign of the artificial nature of the park—the water that cascades down the mountainside emerges from rivers and creeks without a pipe in sight.

**Mount Mayday** is one of the tallest peaks in Florida, even if it is a Disney-created simulation. It rises some 90 feet into the air and is topped by the wreckage of the shrimp boat, **Miss Tilly.** The smokestack on the boat erupts in a plume of water every once in a while, adding to the cascades all around.

The namesake central pool is **Typhoon Lagoon,** which is almost three acres in size. Every 90 seconds, you can catch the world's largest man-made waves, walls of water as high as six feet tall. You'll hear a thunder-like rumble as the

**Up before down.** As enjoyable as Typhoon Lagoon is, be aware that there is quite a bit of climbing involved in using the slides. There is a bit less climbing if you use the ski lift at Blizzard Beach, but you can expect long lines at busy times there.

**Slip, sliding away.** According to local myth, more than a few women have lost their bikini tops on the old Kowabunga. Always trying to please, Disney has built a little viewing stand at the bottom. We spent part of our afternoon there—strictly for research purposes—but the only lost articles we observed were sunglasses.

By the way, we'd strongly recommend wearing an eyeglass strap or carrying your glasses in your folded hands when you ride one of the slides. You should also use plenty of suntan lotion.

**Lockers.** Small lockers rent for $5; larger spaces for $7. You can use the key over and over during your day at the park. When you are ready to leave, return the key to receive a $2 deposit back.

wave is generated and a scream from the bathers as the water is released. Two sheltered pools, **Whitecap Cover** and **Blustery Bay**, serve the less adventurous and have shallows for young children.

Hang on to your bathing suit as you drop 51 feet at speeds of up to 30 mph, down the 214-foot-long **Humunga Kowabunga** water slide. Do we actually pay good money and wait in line for the privilege of falling this far, this fast? The moment of truth will come when you reach the top; try not to stop and consider the folly of it all. Just lie down on your back, cross your ankles, and fold your arms over your chest. Once you've survived, come back another time and try the slide with your eyes open.

Or, try the nearby **Storm Slides.** The trio of body slides, **Rudder Buster, Jib Jammer,** and **Stern Burner,** crash through waterfalls, caves, and geysers. Each of the slides is somewhat different—on a busy day you'll have to take the slide assigned to you by the lifeguard at the top of the stairs. Our favorite is the center slide, which passes through an unexpected dark tunnel midway down the hill. Top speed on the slides is about 20 mph.

**Mayday Falls** and **Keelhaul Falls** send you down a slide on a large inner tube on a tour through caves, waterfalls, and more. Mayday is the taller and longer ride, about 460 feet in length. Keelhaul is shorter, about 400 feet, but includes sharper twists and turns.

Entire families can go for a relatively tame white water adventure at **Gangplank Falls.** Your circular boat will work its way down the mountain in and among waterfalls and obstacles. Don't say the wrong thing to the person who loads your raft at the top of the slide—with the flick of a wrist, he or she can send your raft under the waterfall at the loading zone. The rafts can hold up to five or six persons, and you may end up with strangers if lines are long.

For the youngest swimmers, **Ketchakiddie Creek** features water slides, boats, squirting animals, and other toys for children only.

And finally, you can take a tour on the lazily flowing **Castaway Creek** that circles the park for almost half a mile; it takes about 30 minutes to circle completely around. If the traffic gets too thick or if the float is *too* lazy, you can get out and walk in the three-foot-deep creek or even leave and cross the park to your starting place.

Perhaps the most unusual attraction at the park is the **Shark Reef**, where guests get to strap on a snorkel (provided) and float through an artificial coral reef in and among small nurse and bonnethead sharks, and thousands of other colorful little fishies. We're assured that these are peaceful creatures. In fact, naturalists worry more about visitors damaging the fish with their suntan lotions and other pollutants; you'll be asked to take a shower first. It's an absolutely captivating experience and highly recommended.

Lockers and sometimes-crowded changing rooms and showers are available along the right side of the lagoon as you face Mt. Mayday. You can also rent towels. During the summer, the park is open into the evening; in spring and fall, it often closes as early as 5 P.M. Typhoon Lagoon typically closes for maintenance in January or February.

We have found that dragging a towel and shirt around the park is more of a nuisance than it is worth—you can't bring the towel up the waiting line for slides, and the exits are usually not in the same place as the entrances. If it's warm enough to go swimming, you might want to do without a towel. Although you are allowed to wear water shoes and glasses, you should take care to hold on to both in the water and on slides.

The snack bars in the park include **Lowtide Lou's, Leaning Palms, Typhoon Tilly's,** and **Let's Go Slurpin'**. Items range from about $3 to $5 for your basic burger, chicken, and fried fish dishes; you can also get soft drinks, beer, and ice cream.

There's also a gift shop, **Singapore Sal's Saleable Salvage**, where you can buy bathing suits, T-shirts, and souvenirs. They also have suntan lotion; you can save a few dollars or more by shopping at a drug store outside the park.

Note that during the off-season in the early months of the year, Typhoon Lagoon is closed on Saturdays.

## River Country

**River Country** is Disney's version of Huck Finn's swimmin' hole. Get there by driving to the Fort Wilderness parking lot and taking the Disney bus from there to the park. Or you can hop a short boat ride from the Magic Kingdom across Bay Lake.

The walk from the bus stop to River Country takes you past the small Fort Wilderness **Petting Zoo,** a pleasant shaded area with goats, sheep, horses, and other animals. Admission to the zoo is free; there is a $2 charge for pony rides, with an adult leading the very docile pony around the track.

**Bay Cove** at the heart of River Country includes rope swings, a ship's boom, and other interesting ways to fly out over and into the water below. Bay Cove is actually a part of Bay Lake, which is itself connected to Seven Seas Lagoon at the Magic Kingdom. Across the cove from the beach are the **Whoop 'n Holler Hollow** corkscrew flume rides. Also emptying into the cove are the inner tube rafts coming down **White Water Rapids,** which despite its name is actually a rather slow, 330-foot-long meander.

Be aware that there is a health warning about swimming in Bay Lake—and most every other pond or lake in the state of Florida. Swimmers are advised not to swim underwater near the bottom of the pond because of the presence of certain bacteria and algae that thrive in the warm waters.

The **Upstream Plunge Pool** is a large heated swimming pool including **Slippery Slide Falls,** a pair of water chutes that end about seven feet above the water; you're on your own for the rest of the way down.

River Country is a pleasant break from the crowds at higher-energy water parks like Typhoon Lagoon and Blizzard Beach; parents can watch their children from the comfort of the sandy beach. From the beach, you can see Discovery Island and across Bay Lake to the monorail, the ferryboats, and a distant peek at Space Mountain.

In the summer, though, the park can become quite crowded, and the gates

**Night slide.** Consider ducking out of the Magic Kingdom or Epcot some hot summer afternoon for a cooling dip as the sun goes down. River Country is open until 8 P.M. during summertime, and ticket booths have in past years offered lower-cost tickets after 3 P.M.

**Man-made discovery.** Discovery Island was completely invented by Disney, with tons of earth and stone brought in to create the land. At first, the Disney concept was a re-creation of *Treasure Island,* complete with a sunken pirate ship just offshore. The ship is still there, but the eventual theme is more natural.

**Kids on tour.** Youngsters between the ages of 8 and 14 can take a 4-hour guided tour of Discovery Island in the summer months (most of June, July, and August). The Chip 'n Dale Rescue Rangers Kidventure at Discovery Island costs about $32. Call (407) 824-3784 for information and reservations.

are sometimes shut before noon; they'll reopen in late afternoon, and the park stays open late in season.

You don't need to pay a parking charge for River Country; head for the Magic Kingdom, and move all the way to the rightmost toll booth. Tell the attendant you are going to River Country and bear right after the toll plaza.

## Discovery Island

**Discovery Island** is Disney's 11-acre zoological park, stocked with a fascinating collection of wild animals, both native to Florida and from far away. The island is a serious preserve where the animals roam free, and we humans come to visit.

There are more than 100 species of animals and 250 species of plants on the island. Among the birds you will meet as you walk the paths on the island are tame cockatoos, macaws, toucans, American flamingos, Australian kookaburra, scarlet ibis, trumpeter swans, African crowned cranes, sandhill cranes, small demoiselle cranes, southern bald eagles, brown pelicans, snowy egrets, great blue herons, and hornbills.

The bald eagles are native to the Florida wilderness; the ones on the island are injured and cannot survive on their own. The brown pelicans on Discovery Island are a successful reclamation of a species endangered by generations of harmful DDT spraying.

Animals on the island include muntjac, miniature deer from southeast Asia; alligators; Galápagos tortoises, and Patagonia cavy rodents.

Animal Encounters are presented at three areas on the island several times each morning and early afternoon; they include Feathered Friends, Birds of Prey, and Reptile Relations.

Boats for Discovery Island leave from River Country, Disney's Fort Wilderness Resort and Campground, Disney's Contemporary Resort, Disney's Polynesian Resort, Disney's Grand Floridian Beach Resort, or the Magic Kingdom. The park is open from 10 A.M. to 7 P.M. in the summer and until 5 P.M. the rest of the year.

# TYPHOON LAGOON

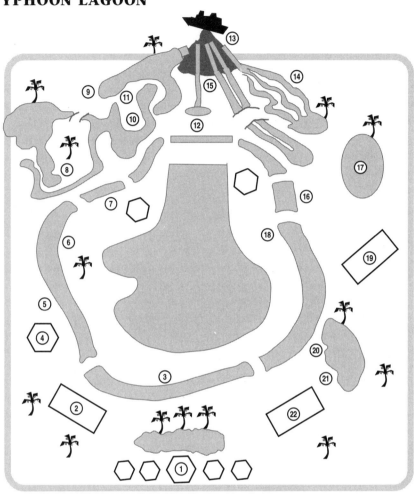

1. Entrance
2. Leaning Palms
3. Castaway Creek
4. Swiss Family Treehouse
5. Starfish entrance to creek
6. Rain Forest
7. Shell entrance to creek
8. Ketchakiddee Creek
9. Keelhaul Falls
10. Gangplank Falls
11. Mayday Falls
12. Forgotten Grotto
13. Mt. Mayday
14. Storm Slides
15. Humunga Kowabunga
16. Shark entrance to creek
17. Shark Reef
18. Snail entrance to creek
19. Typhoon Tilly's
20. Sea Horse entrance to creek
21. High & Dry Towels
22. Singapore Sal's Souvenirs

# Chapter 10
# Nightlife and Disney Shopping

## Pleasure Island

Merriweather Adam Pleasure, also known as MAD Pleasure or the Grand Funmeister, disappeared in 1941 on a circumnavigation expedition of the Antarctic. By 1955, his beloved home island was in disrepair; the coup de grace was administered by a rogue hurricane.

The six-acre island languished in ruins until it was rediscovered by Disney archaeologists, who painstakingly rebuilt the town.

If you believe that story, perhaps you'd like to join the Pleasure Island Histerical Society, whose plaques dot the landmarks of Pleasure Island, which is located next to Disney Village. Even if you don't, a visit to Pleasure Island is a worthy nighttime entertainment.

It's New Year's Eve every night of the year at the nightly **New Year's Eve Street Party.** The celebration begins at 11:45 P.M. and includes music, dancers, confetti, and fireworks.

**Designated drinkers.** Note that the drinking age in Florida is 21, and visitors to Pleasure Island who are not obviously over that age will be required to show proof of their birthdate; once "carded," you'll receive a wristband you can wear for the rest of the evening. There is, however, no requirement that you buy any drinks in any of the clubs—just say "no" and you'll be left alone to watch the shows.

Other special events at Pleasure Island include a spectacular **Mardi Gras** parade each spring; for the past several years, Disney has brought in the famed Caesar's Krewe from New Orleans.

**Mannequins Dance Palace.** A contemporary club with a rotating dance floor and a high-tech (recorded) sound, light, and dance show presented several times each night. There are also a whole bunch of strange and wonderful mannequins scattered about, bubble machines, and more. You must be 21 to enter.

**Pleasure Island Jazz Company.** A new club celebrating America's native

**We're impressed.** On one of our visits, a sign at the entrance to the parking lot read, "Impress your date. Use our Valet Parking services." Actually, though, you might consider it worth the fee to use the valet in bad weather since the outlying parking spaces for Pleasure Island can seem like they are in the next state.

**Half the pleasure.** You can enter Pleasure Island during the day without paying a ticket; this will allow you to visit the shops and restaurants for free. Guests who are within the gates at 7 P.M. can stay at Pleasure Island and see all of the outdoor shows without buying a ticket, although a Pleasure Island ticket is required to enter any of the clubs. The clubs generally open at 8 or 8:30 P.M.

musical form with live performances in an old warehouse stacked with amusement park and carnival equipment.

**Rock & Roll Beach Club.** Live bands perform the classics of rock; a DJ spins stacks of vinyl—well, stacks of CDs anyway—during breaks. Be sure to check out the second floor where there is a selection of pool and air hockey tables and some video and pinball machines; check out the shark hanging from the ceiling with a bikini top in its teeth. Menu items include pizza by the slice.

**Neon Armadillo Music Saloon.** Live country-and-western music and southwestern style food. Opens about 7 P.M., with first show at 8 P.M. Offerings include tortilla chips with salsa, chicken fingers, wings, and burgers.

**8TRAX.** If you can remember what an 8-track tape player was, you've got the basic concept of this celebration of the '70s (The Doors, Iron Butterfly, Janis Joplin, bell-bottoms, bean bag chairs, and lava lamps). It includes your basic disco mirror ball, fog machine, and a small dance floor. You must be 21 to enter. This place, by the way, is notable because of the apparent struggle Disney has gone through in search of an acceptable dance club at Pleasure Island. It began as something called Videopolis East but apparently ran into some unruly behavior problems; next it became CAGE, an underground music and video dance club with almost 200 video monitors. That didn't work either, and so now it's back to the '70s.

**The Adventurers Club.** Five strange rooms filled with strange actors and you, their guests. Stick around and see what happens. The Adventurers Club is one of the most entertaining "performance spaces" you'll find at Walt Disney World. According to the cover story, this is the place where Mr. Pleasure stored all of the strange items he brought back from his journeys; it's enough fun just to cruise among them. You'll likely meet the curator, the maid, and other oddball friends of Pleasure who will share their stories, and you'll be invited to enter into the library for an oddball show, including the "Balderdash Cup Competition," the "Curator's New Discovery," the "Second Annual Radiothon Talent Show," the "Maid's Sing-a-long", and the "Bon Voyage Party."

**The Comedy Warehouse.** This place is a hoot, presenting an evening of improvisational humor, with somewhere between a PG and R rating—by

Disney standards it can get downright risqué. (I'll leave it to the comics to express themselves, but on one of my visits the skit—directed by instructions called out by the audience—progressed to a love scene on the beach in which Ariel the mermaid lost her strategically placed seashells and was revealed to be a man.) There were even a few gentle jibes at Disney, including a fake movie poster on the wall advertising a film called *Dumbo, First Blood*.

There are several shows each night; the club is small and seats are often filled well before showtime. If you want to sit through two sessions, you'll have to exit and get back in line for a later show. From time to time, television crews tape comedy specials here. When a "name" comedian is appearing there may be an extra charge for admission.

As at all of the clubs in the park, you will be approached by a waiter or waitress but you do not have to purchase anything if you don't want to. Drink prices include small beers for about $3, up to a 60-ounce pitcher for $9. Special drinks include Laughter Punch, made with Midori, rum, and pineapple juice. Sodas, popcorn, pretzels, and banana splits are also available.

There is no cover charge or age restriction to visit Pleasure Island during the day, or at anytime to enter the restaurants. The shops open at 10 A.M. The ticket gates go up at 7 P.M., charging $16.91; after 7 P.M., visitors under the age of 18 must be accompanied by a parent. (You don't need a ticket to visit the **Portobello Yacht Club** or the **Fireworks Factory** for meals or drinks.)

If you're planning a lengthy stay at Walt Disney World with regular visits to Pleasure Island, consider buying a World Hopper ticket which includes admission to the nighttime revelries as well as the Disney waterparks. Or, think about buying an annual pass to Pleasure Island, priced at just under the cost of three individual visits.

## Planet Hollywood

**Planet Hollywood**'s three-story 400-seat restaurant near Pleasure Island is one of the busiest eateries on the planet. The club, which has several major film stars among its owners, including Sylvester Stallone, Arnold Schwarzenegger, Bruce Willis, and Demi Moore, is a cinema equivalent to the Hard Rock Cafe chain. (Not at all coincidentally, there is a Hard Rock restaurant at Universal Studios Florida across town.)

The restaurant is decorated with movie and TV scripts, artifacts, and costumes and the sounds of music and film clips echo throughout. Surprisingly, the food is above average including huge Caesar salads, Cajun chicken breast, hot wings, burgers, and pizza. Entrees start at about $10.

## Pleasure Island Restaurants

The major restaurants on Pleasure Island are located outside the turnstiles between Pleasure Island and Disney Village and can be visited without purchasing a ticket.

**Hill Street Diner.** Cheese steaks, personal pizzas, hot ham and cheese. About $5.

**Fulton's Crab House.** By the shores of Disney's inland sea is a new

**KEY:**

[🍴] = Fast Food

[🍸] = Pub

[🏠] = Full-service
restaurant

seafood restaurant, replacing the Empress Lilly. Fulton's Crab House promises to change its menu daily to reflect the latest and greatest seafood available in season. (They'll even post the air freight bills on the wall!) Entrees, from about $15 to $35, include Nantucket Bay Scallops, Mustard Crusted Trout, and Fulton's Cioppino. Appetizers begin with a well-stocked oyster bar, and also include such delicacies as alderwood smoked salmon with potato crostini lemon chive cream.

[🏠] **Portobello Yacht Club.** A first-class northern Italian eatery, with offerings ranging from thin-crust pizza cooked in a wood-fired oven ($7 to $8) to steak, chicken, and fish dishes. Lunch salads, priced from about $5 to $8 may include *insalata Caesar di pollo* (Caesar salad with chicken). A sample of lunch entrees (from about $7 to $10) includes *panino di vitello* (veal flank steak, charcoal grilled and served open-faced over sourdough toast with wild mushrooms in rosemary sauce) and angel hair pasta with smoked chicken, sun-dried tomatoes, olive oil, garlic, and pesto. The same salads and pizzas are available at dinner as appetizers, and entrees range in price from $13 to $16 for pasta and $17 to $23 for steak and chicken. A child's menu is also available. Open from 11:30 A.M. to midnight; call (407) 934-8888 for reservations.

The club is outside the gates of Pleasure Island and a ticket is not required to enter; Pleasure Island visitors can come and go if they hold on to their ticket for the evening.

[🏠] [🍸] **Fireworks Factory.** A brick-walled warehouse setting, filled with piles of boxes on the south side of the Buena Vista Lagoon. Lunch offerings include meatloaf, $7; BBQ trio (beef, pork, chicken), $10; burgers, $7 to $8; sandwiches, $6 to $9; salads, $3.50 to $10. For dinner, entrees start at $15 and include catfish, crabcakes, chicken, ribs, meatloaf, and steaks. Appetizers include Super Smokehouse Wings and Sizzling Catfish. The bar promises 32 types of beer, including bottles from a selection of American microbreweries.

## Disney Village Marketplace

When the going gets tough, the tough go shopping, and the Village Marketplace is one of Disney's most interesting collections of shops. You can drive to the Village and park in the huge parking lot (it adjoins and mixes with the spaces for Pleasure Island), or you can take a water taxi from the Port Orleans Resort, Dixie Landings Resort, or the Disney Vacation Club. The stores are open from 9:30 A.M. to 10 P.M.

Of course, there are lots of shops selling T-shirts, sweatshirts, and hats with pictures of Mickey or Minnie, but perhaps the single largest collection is at **Mickey's Character Shop.** For the sporting fan, **Team Mickey's Athletic Club** offers Disney paraphernalia for fans and players.

It's Christmas all the time at the **Christmas Chalet**, where you can purchase American and European ornaments and Disney holiday merchandise.

Other shops for children of all ages include **You and Me Kid**, with an assortment of toys, games, gifts, and clothing.

At **Toys Fantastic**, you'll find guess-what from guess-who, plus a selection of Barbie toys. **Eurospain** sells an interesting collection of hand-crafted Spanish crafts. **Great Southern Craft Co.** offers Americana.

**Harrington Bay Clothiers** and **Resortwear Unlimited** offer sportswear for men and women, respectively. **The City** has hot trends in apparel for young men and women.

**Cristal Arts** offers cut glass curios, ready-made or customized. **Discover** offers toys, educational items, and gifts with an environmental edge. **2R'S** is a bookstore with a coffee shop, or is it the other way around?

And Disney has disclosed plans for an expansion of the Village Marketplace with additional shops and restaurants including a **House of Blues**, **Rainforest Café**, and an eatery called **Lario's** launched by singer Gloria Estefan.

### Disney Village Restaurants

🍴 **Minnie Mia's Italian Eatery.** Lunch, dinner. An informal cafeteria featuring pizza, pasta, chicken, and seafood. Pizza by the slice or pie; lunch items about $5, dinner from $5 to $15. Open from 11:30 A.M. to 10 P.M.

🍴 **Lakeside Terrace.** Lunch, dinner. A large fast-food restaurant with tables across from the lake. Burgers, hot dogs, fried fish, barbecued chicken, $2.50 to $5.

🏠 **Chef Mickey's Village Restaurant.** Breakfast (9 to 11 A.M.), lunch (11:30 A.M. to 2 P.M.), and dinner (5 to 10 P.M.). A pretty setting along the lake, featuring Disney music and settings. Chef Mickey himself will stroll among the tables at dinnertime. Breakfast goes for $2 to $7; luncheon offerings include soup, salad, sandwiches, and entrees from $6 to $10, and the dinner menu offers pork chops, steak, and seafood from $10 to $18. The children's menu includes burgers, pasta, and fish from $3.50 to $6.50. For reservations, call (407) 828-3900.

🏠 **Cap'n Jack's Oyster Bar.** Lunch, dinner. A little bit of Cape Cod in a pretty setting on a shack built into the village lake. Lobster tails, crab claws, clams, chowder, frozen margaritas. $5 to $15. Child's menu features pasta, $4. Open from 11:30 A.M. to 10 P.M.

### A Movie Theater, Too

And in your spare time, if you'd like to catch a flick, there is the **AMC Pleasure Island 10 Theatres.** Not just Disney movies, either, and not just G and PG ratings. The complex sometimes offers a discount ticket in conjunction with Pleasure Island admission. Call (407) 827-1300 for show times.

### Hot Night Spots at Disney Hotel Plaza

**Giraffe.** A funky dance club featuring New Wave and contemporary rock played by a DJ nightly. Happy hour nightly until 9:30 P.M. Hotel Royal Plaza.

**Laughing Kookaburra.** Soft rock and disco dance club, with live bands most evenings at 10 P.M. Happy hour nightly until 8 P.M. Buena Vista Palace.

**Top of the Palace Lounge.** An elegant lounge with live jazz and cabaret music on the 27th floor, it provides a spectacular view of fireworks at the theme parks. Buena Vista Palace.

**Toppers.** A jumping dance club featuring modern rock spun by a DJ. Another excellent spot to watch the fireworks. Happy hour until 7 P.M. nightly. Travelodge Hotel.

# Chapter 11
# Walt Disney World Seminars

Feeling bad about taking your kids out of school for a vacation at Walt Disney World? How about giving them a little homework, Mickey-style?

Feeling too old to leave your job at the law firm to spend a week with Mickey and Minnie? How about coming to the Disney Institute to take a course on art or music? (While you're there, you can still sneak in a few circuits with Dumbo the Flying Elephant.)

Disney offers a range of educational seminars for youngsters and adults. You might want to discuss some of the options with your children's teachers.

## Should You Take Your Kids Out of School?

In the best of all worlds, probably not. There are enough interruptions in the normal school year as it is. However, if work and school vacation times do not coincide, or if you are taking our advice seriously and trying to avoid crowds, there are ways to work with your schools.

We'd suggest you meet with your children's teachers to determine if there are particular times when an absence of a few days (wrapped around or including a weekend or minor holiday) will not make a big impact on schoolwork. Consult your school calendar in search of local holidays or "workshop" half-days.

See if you can coordinate special assignments for your children. If there is an upcoming unit on Mexico, for example, perhaps they could be assigned to produce a special report with research performed at Epcot Center's Mexican pavilion.

## Wonders of Walt Disney World

Here's a chance for kids from ages 10 to 15 to engage in a guided learning adventure; parents will receive a six-hour break for themselves, too.

Each of the programs is a backstage exploration of one of the Walt Disney World theme parks; participants receive a special book, classroom materials, and follow-up activities, as well as lunch at a park restaurant. Call (407) 354-

1855 for information and reservations. In 1996, prices were $79 per program; a ticket to one of the theme parks is not included or required during the tour period; the child will require a ticket to reenter the park after the tour is over. The groups—limited to 14 persons—leave from the entrance of the Disney-MGM Studios and run from 9:30 A.M. to 3:30 P.M.

### Keys to the Kingdom

Go beneath the streets of the Magic Kingdom to see the famous Utilidor underground tunnel system, visit rehearsal and behind-the-scenes areas at some of the live shows of the park, and visit up to five attractions—waiting in regular lines. Register for the four-hour tour at City Hall for 10 A.M. departures. Cost is $45; admission to the Magic Kingdom is not included. Call (407) 824-4521.

### Backstage Magic

A seven-hour peek behind the curtain at Walt Disney World including an exploration of the Utilidor system beneath the Magic Kingdom, backstage areas at all three parks, and special dining and entertainment. Cost is $150 for guests 16 and older, and the tour is offered Mondays and Wednesdays. For reservations call (407) 939-8687.

## Chip 'n Dale Rescue Rangers Kidventure at Discovery Island

Special programs for children from 8 to 14 years teach about ecology and animal behavior. The four-hour classes, which include lunch, cost about $32. Call (407) 824-3784 for reservations.

### Dolphin Exploration and Education Program (DEEP)

A three-hour dolphin study at The Living Seas at Epcot. Tickets for visitors ages 16 and older are $45. For reservations call (407) 939-8687.

### Night Under the Sea (NUTS)

Kids from ages 7 to 11 can sleep with the fish at The Living Seas at Epcot. Admission is $125, which includes a souvenir T-shirt and sleeping bag, snacks, and breakfast with Disney characters. For reservations, call (407) 939-8687.

### Scout Spirit Days

Merit badge activities including bird, reptile, and amphibian studies, cinematography, and environmental studies. For reservations call (800) 833-9806.

## Disney Learning Adventures for Adults

An in-depth exploration of some of the wonders of Epcot Center for visitors over the age of 16. Call (407) 824-4321 for schedules, information, and reservations. 1996 prices were about $20 per program; a ticket to Epcot Center is also required.

## Hidden Treasures of World Showcase

A three-hour walking tour to explore the art, architecture, costumes, customs, and culture of the nations of Epcot.

## Gardens of the World

Explore the green side of the World Showcase in a three-hour walking tour led by a Disney horticultural expert.

# The Disney Institute

One of Disney's principal goals in recent years has been to find ways to attract older visitors to Walt Disney World. Mickey and Minnie can only go so far once adults loose the excuse of bringing their children to the park.

Disney has had great success with its golf courses and other outdoor activities. Other expansions have seen such facilities as Sports Center Disney.

Now the attention has moved to the mind: In early 1996, the Disney Institute opened at an attractive new campus near the Disney Village Resort. The Institute began with an ambitious catalog of 80 courses with 27 studios, a broadcast-quality performance center, an outdoor amphitheater, cinema, teaching garden, and closed-circuit television and radio stations.

Courses included:

**Entertainment Arts.** Learn to take nature photographs, shoot better home videos, learn about broadcasting, write your own episode for an ongoing Disney Institute soap opera.

**Story Arts.** An exploration of animation using traditional and state-of-the-art computer facilities.

**Design Arts.** Tour Walt Disney World Resort hotels and learn about architecture, interior design, and decorative arts.

**Culinary Arts.** Each student has an individual cooking station for lessons on gourmet and international dishes.

**Environment.** Learn about organic gardening and landscaping, using Walt Disney World as a classroom.

**Sports and Fitness.** Golf, tennis, rock climbing, canoe tours of Walt Disney World waterways, aerobics, and more.

Facilities at the Institute include a full-service spa, saunas, whirlpools, steam rooms, massages, body therapies, and facials.

The programs are aimed at singles, couples, and families with older children. Youth programs include park scavenger hunts, rock climbing, and bird watching.

Housing for programs is at the Institute, in bungalows and one- or two-bedroom townhouses.

All this does not come cheap. Rates for week-long courses run from $1,550 to $2,023 per person for double occupancy with full meals and a one-day ticket to a Disney park, plus $840 to $951 per youth in the same room.

For information, call (800) 282-9282.

# Chapter 12
# Inside the World of Disney

## Coming Soon: Disney's Animal Kingdom

It all started with a mouse, so it seems perfectly logical that Disney should extend its Walt Disney World empire to include its own fanciful animal park.

According to the Imagineers, Disney's Animal Kingdom will celebrate all animals that ever or never existed. It is scheduled to open in the spring of 1998 with a combination of thrill rides, exotic landscapes, and close encounters with wild animals—real and imagined.

Construction was due to begin in September of 1996 on 500 acres on the western edge of Walt Disney World.

Centerpiece of the park will be the giant Tree of Life, 14 stories tall—about the height of Spaceship Earth at Epcot. It will be hand-carved by Disney artists with a tapestry of animal forms representing the diversity of animal life on Earth.

Guests will visit three major sections of the park: the real, the mythical, and the extinct.

The "real" world will include herds of live animals, including giraffes, zebras, lions, hippos, and elephants; there will be links to Disney stories, of course. Most of the animals for Disney's Animal Kingdom will be born in zoological parks or rescued from endangered habitats, according to the company.

The "mythical" world is home to unicorns, dragons, and other magical creatures from legends, fairy tales, and storybooks.

The world of the extinct animals, of course, will use Disney's Audio-Animatronics to bring back the giant dinosaurs of the Cretaceous era for a thrill ride. (The Cretaceous era follows the Jurassic era in geological dating; across town, Universal Studios Florida will introduce its Jurassic Park theme area as part of its massive Universal's Islands of Adventure expansion due to open in 1999.)

## Inside the World of Disney

According to *Amusement Business* magazine, Disney owned the top four spots

**Land sakes.** In 1993, the Walt Disney Company struck a deal with the Florida Department of Environmental Regulation that resulted in the establishment of the **Disney Wilderness Preserve** on 8,500 acres of newly acquired land south of Walt Disney World. The company also created permanent conservation easements of 7,500 acres already owned by Disney. The purpose of the deal was to attempt to balance out wetlands lost to development within the park.

Under terms of the agreement, the Nature Conservancy will own and manage the preserve, while Disney will fund education programs, restoration activities, and management of the site. Residents of the land include woodstorks, Florida scrub jays, gopher tortoises, and one of the largest groups of nesting bald eagles in the Southeast.

among American amusement and theme parks in 1995. For the first time in many years, though, Disneyland in California edged ahead of the Magic Kingdom in Florida, mostly on the strength of the fabulously successful Indiana Jones ride in Anaheim.

The magazine estimated that Disneyland drew about 14.1 million visitors in 1995, up 38 percent from the year before. The Magic Kingdom drew about 12.9 million, a 15 percent boost. In third place was Epcot, and the fourth spot went to Disney-MGM. Universal Studios Florida owned fifth place.

Overall, Disney parks accounted for about 30 percent of all theme park visitors in the United States.

Of all the Disney parks around the world, though, Disneyland Tokyo holds the number-one position for attendance, the magazine says.

## The Disney Rest Stop

Disney and the American Automobile Association are experimenting with a rest stop in South Carolina on Interstate 95, a primary route for tourists driving south to Orlando.

The "Disney Stop" is expected to open by the end of 1996 and include a restaurant, travel center, and auto service station. The second phase of the project may add a hotel and shopping center.

The design concept is a re-creation of a small town of the 1950s and 1960s, with oversized icons like those at the All-Star Resorts at Walt Disney World.

The stop is in Hardeeville, about 20 miles from Hilton Head Island, where Disney plans a time-share project in the future.

## Disneyland Paris

Its Disney's newest theme park, yet it feels like an old favorite. It's in a country where they don't speak English, yet everyone understands each other. Its financial problems have been front-page news around the world, yet it can offer some great bargains for the careful traveler. Disney renegotiated the financing package in 1994, which seems to have saved the park for the foreseeable future. In that same year it sold about 25 percent of ownership of the park to Saudi Prince Al-Waleed bin-Talal al-Saud; Disney retains 40 percent ownership.

I visited Disneyland Paris (it was originally called Euro Disneyland) in Marne-la-Vallée near Paris in the spring of 1994; my wife and I were able to convince our preteen son and daughter to come to Europe for a week in London and a week in Paris with the promise of two days at Disneyland Paris as a reward for good behavior. As it turned out, the kids absolutely *loved* London with its museums and theaters, and were intrigued by incredible sights such as the Cathedral of Notre Dame in Paris, the palace of Versailles, and the ancient city of Provins, all within an hour of Marne-la-Vallée. Oh, and they liked Disneyland Paris real well, too.

**Mouse mouths.** Walt Disney himself performed the voices of Mickey and Minnie in the earliest cartoons, including *Steamboat Willie*, which was the first Mickey Mouse cartoon with sound—but not the first movie starring the rascally rodent. That honor went to *Plane Crazy*. The current voice of the Mickster is Wayne Allwine.

The cost of the trip in off-season (similar to Walt Disney World, with lowest prices in winter and parts of the fall and spring) was just slightly more than a trip to Orlando. Winter airfares from the East Coast to Paris or London usually drop to about $400 round-trip.

Disneyland Paris is not a big draw for Americans, with only a few percent of visitors from this country. However, enough visitors from the United Kingdom and other non-French-speaking nations, plus the international allure of Disney makes it possible to get around the park without speaking French. The staff at the hotels within the park is multilingual, and guidebooks and signs are available in English.

If you do speak French, though, it's a bit of fun to see Disney Francified: the centerpiece of the park is *Le Château de la Belle au Bois Dormant* (Sleeping Beauty's Castle); favorite rides in Fantasyland include *Blanche-Neige et les Sept Nains* (Snow White and the Seven Dwarfs).

There are some significant differences at the park; European tastes call for less subtle entertainment, sometimes much more explicit than at the American parks.

Beneath the castle is *La Tanière du Dragon* (The Dragon's Lair), with a rather scary, mechanical creature who comes to life every few minutes. *Indiana Jones et le Temple du Péril* in Adventureland is Disney's first real roller coaster, a wild ride through an archeological dig among the ancient ruins of the Lost City. Phantom Manor in Frontierland is scarier than its cousins in Florida and California. And Big Thunder Mountain is faster and wilder, disappearing into a tunnel under the river at one point.

But there are also some very refined, European touches in the park. We were enthralled by *Le Visionarium*, a Cinematronic 360-degree theater presenting a beautifully produced film about French science fiction author Jules Verne, in a spectacular time-travel adventure that soars through Europe. A version of that film opened as *The Timekeeper* in the Magic Kingdom's New Tomorrowland in 1996.

It was also a kick to see the familiar Star Tours, with a French-speaking R2D2 and C3PO.

New for 1995 was *Space Mountain: De la Terre à la Lune,* a spectacular new version of Space Mountain that extends the Jules Verne theme of a rocketship from the earth to the moon with a roller coaster that includes some upside-down spirals and twists and turns that are well beyond anything at an American Disney park.

Just outside the gates to the park is Festival Disney, a little of home in a cross between Pleasure Island at Walt Disney World, Church Street Station in Orlando, and CityWalk at Universal Studios in Hollywood. Under a starfield made up of tiny lights on wires, you'll find a collection of restaurants (Annette's Diner, Key West Seafood, Los Angeles Bar & Grill among them), nightclubs, and bars (Billy Bob's Country Western Saloon, Hurricanes, Rock 'n' Roll America, and The Sports Bar), and boutiques, all with an American theme.

And absolutely not to be missed is Buffalo Bill's Wild West Show, one of the best dinner theaters I have ever seen. The show is loosely based on an actual touring company brought to France by Buffalo Bill. Four ranchers compete in competitions with herds of buffalo, longhorn steer, and dozens of cowboys on horseback. Included is an Old West meal including chili, barbecued chicken and beef, and dessert. The show is located next to Festival Disney and there are two performances per night at busy times.

Hotels in the park include:

**Disneyland Hotel.** A luxury reproduction of a turn-of-the-century Victorian palace, right at the entrance to the park.

**Hotel New York.** A first-class hotel with architectural touches of Manhattan in the 1930s, including a jazz club, an outdoor skating rink (winter months) styled after Rockefeller Center, and more.

**Newport Bay Club.** A moderate-class hotel, modeled after a seaside resort in New England.

**Sequoia Lodge.** A moderate-class reproduction of a Rocky Mountain resort.

**Hotel Cheyenne.** An economy hotel styled after an Old West town, complete with dirt roads, wooden sidewalks, and bunkhouses.

**Hotel Santa Fe.** Another economy hotel, paying tribute to the pueblo architecture of the American southwest.

**Davy Crockett Ranch.** A wilderness retreat in a forest, very much like Fort Wilderness in Orlando; it offers 498 rental cabins plus camp sites.

There's also a 27-hole championship golf course, swimming pools, and . . . Paris, just up the road. Future plans call for expansion to include a studio attraction like Disney-MGM Studios in Florida, although this and other new expenditures may have to wait until the park's finances are straightened out.

If you decide to go to Disneyland Paris, check with a capable travel agent for special packages offered by Disney; not all packages, though, are better than putting together your own arrangements. If you visit in off-season, you may be able to obtain bargain rates at one of the hotels in the park.

We chose to make Disneyland Paris our base, venturing north to Paris and Versailles and southwest to Provins; you could also stay in Paris and commute down to the park quite easily. We were able to purchase off-season airfare of about $400 and a hotel room within the park for a bargain basement price of about $45 per night. Car rentals are slightly more expensive in Europe than in America; you can save money by renting a vehicle with manual transmission. Tickets to Disneyland Paris are about the same as at the American parks.

Disneyland Paris is located about 20 miles east of Paris in Marne-la-Vallée. Direct shuttle bus service is available from Orly or Charles de Gaulle airports in Paris; or you can drive from Paris on the A4 motorway or take the new high-speed railway line that leads to a station directly at the gate to the park.

## Tokyo Disneyland

*Hai, Mickey-san.* If ever proof was required of the global impact of American popular culture, it came with the opening of Tokyo Disneyland in 1983. The park, which is owned by a Japanese company under license to Disney, is located six miles outside of Tokyo. It includes familiar Disney attractions as well as new shows such as Pinocchio's Daring Journey, The Eternal Seas, and Meet the World.

Instead of Main Street, U.S.A., you'll find World Bazaar as the gateway to Adventureland, Fantasyland, Tomorrowland, and Westernland. Adventureland attractions include the Jungle Cruise, Enchanted Tiki Room, and Pirates of the Caribbean. In Westernland you'll find the Mark Twain Riverboat, Tom Sawyer Island, The Golden Horseshoe Revue, and Country Bear Jamboree, among other lures.

Fantasyland includes the Pinocchio ride, plus It's a Small World, Haunted Mansion, Snow White's Adventure, and the Mickey Mouse Revue. There are also venerable favorites like Dumbo, the Flying Elephant, and Cinderella's Golden Carrousel.

Tomorrowland includes yet another Space

**Real Disney dollars.** Over the past decade, the Walt Disney Company has been one of the highest fliers of Wall Street. In April of 1994, the company opened its first Broadway show, an adaptation of its film hit *Beauty and the Beast.* The most expensive Broadway production ever, it immediately set a record with the highest single day ticket sale in the history of the Great White Way.

Disney's hockey team, the Anaheim Mighty Ducks of the NHL (we're not kidding), has been a box office and merchandising success even if its skaters sometimes seem to look like the kids in the Disney movie of the same name.

And also in 1994, Disney announced its interest in getting into the cruise line business, disclosed plans to build a residential resort in Vero Beach, Florida, and expanded its network of Disney Stores around the nation to 268.

All this in pursuit of the company's announced goal of a 20 percent annual growth in profits. Since 1984, annual revenue has grown from $1.5 billion to $8.5 billion; investors who came in before the rise saw the value of their shares go up tenfold.

**Suspended animation.** A recurring rumor about dear old Walt Disney is that he chose to be cryogenically frozen when he died of lung cancer in 1966, in hopes of a defrost in another day and age. Actually, according to the company, he went to the other extreme and was cremated before burial at the famous Forest Lawn Memorial Park in California.

Mountain as well as Meet the World, an attraction based on Japanese history and the country's influence on the rest of the world.

## Home Sweet Disney

Disney Development's newest project, **Celebration**, opened in mid-1996 on some 4,000 acres in the Reedy Creek area of Osceola County at the south end of the still-growing borders of Walt Disney World off I-192. The planned community includes schools, a medical center, an office complex, over 8,000 homes, recreational facilities, and a huge open-air shopping mall,

By the way, Disney reportedly considered offering some homes within Walt Disney World itself until legal types figured out that the residents would end up having political power within the kingdom of the mouse, which is technically an independent governmental entity. Today, a handful of Disney employees do live in the park, under the close watchful eye of the company.

## Ahoy, Mickey

**The Disney Cruise Line** is due to set sail in 1998, with the introduction of the new *Disney Magic*. A second vessel, the *Disney Wonder*, is set to begin service in November of the same year.

Disney plans week-long experiences that will include three or four days at Walt Disney World and three or four days at sea with stops in the Bahamas and at a private island. The vessels were expected to sail from Port Canaveral on Florida's east coast, about an hour away from Orlando.

The ships, built at a shipyard in Trieste, Italy, are supposed to feature a "classic exterior design reminiscent of the majestic transatlantic ocean liners of the past." We don't recall the Queen Mary offering Disney character breakfasts and shows, though.

Wanting to maintain its wholesome image, Disney has decided not to offer gambling on board and will instead have a "family lounge," a teen club, and an activities center for young children. A theater will offer live productions and Disney films. Adults will, though, be able to attend stage shows and nightclubs.

# III
# Universal Studios Florida

## Chapter 13
## Universal Studios Florida

It was 80 years ago that movie legend Carl Laemmle began to allow visitors—at 25 cents a head—to come to his studios to watch silent movies being made.

The tours at Universal Film Manufacturing Company in Hollywood were stopped when sound was added to film, but in 1964 the renamed Universal Studios reopened its doors to visitors.

Universal's Hollywood lot became the third most popular tourist attraction in the nation; visitors board trams that take them in and around the historic backlot and soundstages of Universal City and along the way into some very special attractions based on some of the movie company's greatest hits.

In 1990, Universal moved east to Florida with the opening of its gigantic Orlando studios. Here are a few things to understand about Universal Studios Florida:

- It is a working studio, producing motion pictures, television shows, and commercials.

- The 444-acre site is more than 20 years newer than most of Walt Disney World, and as such includes some of the most spectacular and state-of-the-art rides and attractions anywhere in the world, well beyond Pirates of the Caribbean.

- The designers abandoned the Universal Studios Hollywood model of a single ride made up of a dozen or so elements in favor of a Disney-like park with lots of walking and, alas, lots of waiting on busy days. And the waits can be longer than those at any other area park.

**Universal Studios Tickets** (In effect in the spring of 1996. Prices include tax.) Call (407) 363-8182 for latest prices.

**One-Day Studio Pass**

| | |
|---|---|
| Adults (10 and older) | $40.81 |
| Children (3 to 9) | $32.86 |

**Two-Day Studio Pass**

| | |
|---|---|
| Adults (10 and older) | $58.30 |
| Children (3 to 9) | $46.64 |

**Celebrity Annual Pass** (Good for one year)

| | |
|---|---|
| Adults (10 and older) | $73.14 |
| Children (3 to 9) | $62.54 |

**Respect for elders.**
Senior citizens should
stop by guest services to
pick up a VIP sticker
that entitles them to
preferred seating
at several of the shows,
including the Wild, Wild,
Wild West Stunt
Show and the Animal
Actors Stage.

**Value Pass.** In 1996,
Universal Studios, Sea
World, and Wet 'n Wild
came together to offer a
five-day, three-park pass.
It was priced at $89.95
plus tax for adults, and
$72.95 plus tax for
children 3 to 9 years old.
It's a good deal if you are
planning to visit all three
parks. You can also save
about the same amount
. . . with a bit more
flexibility . . . using the
discount coupons from
all three parks that are
included in this edition
of the *Econoguide*.
**Parking:** $5 for cars and
$7 for recreational
vehicles and trailers. If
you've incurably gone
Hollywood, valet parking
is available for $11.
**Information:**
(407) 363-8000.

Here's our bottom line: Universal Studios is
worth a day out of the tour of any vacationer in
Central Florida, but it also requires the most
careful planning for the date of a visit and a
schedule within the park.

The best times to come to Universal Studios
are the same as for other area attractions. Arrive
between September and November, between
Thanksgiving and Christmas, or in mid-January
and you may be able to walk around like you
own the place. Show up during Christmas break,
Easter vacation, or mid-summer and you'll meet
what seems like the entire population of Manhattan or Boston or Cleveland in front of you
in line.

Universal Studios is open 365 days a year.
Hours of operation of the park are adjusted based
on projections for attendance and are subject to
change. Check with the park before you make
plans for late evenings.

Also note that some of the shows are opened
on a staggered basis. When you first walk in the
door at a quiet time of year you may find that
some of the shows don't offer performances
before 11 A.M. or noon; head for the rides first.

The park is located near the intersection of
Interstate 4 and the Florida Turnpike in Orlando.
The main entrance is about one-half mile north
of I-4 at exit 30B—Kirkman Road (Highway 435).
Another entrance is located on Turkey Lake
Road.

From Orlando International Airport: Take 528
West (the Bee-Line Expressway) toward Tampa
and Walt Disney World. Watch for signs to Interstate 4 East (to Orlando); take Exit 29 (Sand Lake
Road) and pass under the interstate to the second traffic light at Turkey Lake Road. Turn right
onto Turkey Lake and travel about one mile to
the Universal Studios entrance on the right.

From Walt Disney World: Take I-4 East to Exit 29 (Sand Lake Road). Turn
left onto Sand Lake and pass under the interstate to the second traffic light,
Turkey Lake Road. Turn right onto Turkey Lake and travel about one mile to
the Universal Studios entrance on the right.

Universal Studios sells VIP Tours through its guest relations desk. For $90
each plus tax, a group of as many as 15 people will have their own guide for

a four-hour half-day with the privilege of breaking through any line in the park. For $900 plus tax, you can hire an "exclusive" tour with up to 15 people you choose. Neither tour includes lunch. As expensive as the tours are, they might begin to make sense if you are forced to visit the park on a day when all of the major rides have 90-minute waits. There are about a dozen tour guides available; Guest Services usually requires 48 hours notice before a tour. Reservations must be made at least 72 hours in advance and prepaid; call (407) 363-8295.

Universal Studios Florida is jointly owned by MCA, Inc., and The Rank Organization. Rank's worldwide interests include the famous Pinewood Studios in England, one of the world's largest film libraries, video production, and film processing facilities and hotels, restaurants, and recreational services. MCA in turn is a unit of the Seagram Company Ltd.

## Move Over, Mickey?

Universal Studios Florida is the theme park–come-lately in Orlando, but it has gone through explosive growth since its opening in 1990, drawing millions of visitors and a great deal of attention for some of its spectacular rides like Back to the Future, E.T. Adventure, Kongfrontation, and Earthquake.

The park is basically a one-day stop, something that most visitors fit in and among the days spent at Walt Disney World. And as good as the park is, very few tourists journey long distances to Orlando just to see Universal Studios Florida.

But all that is due to come to an end in 1999 with the completion of **Universal City Florida**. The expansion will add more than 600 acres or about three times the developed acreage of the current park. Part of the expansion will be accomplished by replacing much of the existing parking lot with multistory parking garages, and the rest will expand onto new property to the south toward Interstate 4 and Turkey Lake Road.

Most guests will park in the garage and take

**Upgrading your ticket.** If you decide that you want to come back for a second day at Universal Studios, visit Guest Relations to upgrade your ticket to a two-day pass. You must do this on the day of purchase of the original ticket. During the off-season, Universal sometimes offers a "second day free" promotion. And if you are a regular visitor to Orlando, you might want to consider buying a Celebrity Annual Pass; in 1996, Universal actually lowered the price for the pass to a level slightly less than the price of two day passes.

**Triple A.** Most of the gift shops and several of the sitdown restaurants within Universal Studios will give a 10 percent discount to AAA members; bring your card.

**Dog days.** You can safely park your dog, cat, bird, shark, or ape at the Studio Kennel next to the main entrance plaza for a $5 per day fee. Guest must provide food and return periodically to walk their pet.

## MUST-SEES

**Terminator 2 3-D**

**Back to the Future . . . The Ride**

**E.T. Adventure**

**Animal Actors Stage**

**Earthquake— The Big One**

**Jaws**

**Kongfrontation**

**Hitchcock's 3-D Theatre**

**The Funtastic World of Hanna-Barbera**

**Nickelodeon Studios**

**The Gory, Gruesome & Grotesque Horror Make-Up Show**

a "people-mover" to the new E-Zone complex and from there to one of the two Universal theme parks.

At the heart of the expansion will be **Universal's Islands of Adventure**, a second theme park with its own entrance gate and separate admission charge.

The park will include:

• **Seuss Landing**, a lineup of wacky and outrageous rides inspired by Theodor Seuss Geisel's characters in books including "The Cat in the Hat," "Green Eggs and Ham," "How the Grinch Stole Christmas," "One Fish Two Fish Red Fish Blue Fish" and others.

• **Isla Nubar**, home of *Jurassic Park*. Director Steven Spielberg's film will come to life for guests who visit the island.

• **Popeye** and his cartoon shipmates from Sweethaven will find a new home port. Popeye will be joined by the likes of **Olive Oyl, Swee' Pea, Wimpy,** and **Brutus** with rides, shows, and attractions.

• **Spider-Man**, the X-Men, **The Incredible Hulk,** and other Marvel Comics super heroes will be permanent residents of the islands with new rides and shows.

In January of 1998, Universal is due to open another major new area, the **E-Zone,** a 12-acre entertainment complex offering live music, electrifying dance clubs, and specialty restaurants.

The E-Zone is based on the successful City-Walk complex at Universal Studios Hollywood in California. The two-tiered promenade includes realistic streetscapes wrapping around a four-acre lagoon with waterfalls and interconnecting waterways. A set of brilliantly colored 10-story towers, icons, and free-form sculptures will identify the E-Zone's skyline from miles away. Elements already announced include:

• **Bob Marley—A Tribute to Freedom.** A one-of-a-kind celebration of music and culture based around the music and philosophy of Jamaican musical legend and cultural icon Bob Marley.

• **All New Hard Rock Cafe Orlando.** The

world's largest Hard Rock Cafe (replacing the existing eatery at Universal Studios) will include a spectacular new restaurant and gift shop, along with Hard Rock's first live concert venue capable of seating up to 2,000 people.

• **Shaq's Place.** A unique sports-themed entertainment complex based on the world of NBA superstar Shaquille O'Neal, concentrating on sports, music, and people and including a lounge inspired by Shaq's own high-tech game room and a nightclub that features a "half-court" dance floor.

• **B.B. King's Blues Club.** A combination blues house and supper club featuring live performances by R&B artists.

• **Cineplex Odeon Megaplex.** A 16-screen, 5,000-seat theater with its own set of eateries, cafes, and shops.

• **E! Entertainment Television Production Center.** A studio for tapings and live celebrity interviews for the cable television network.

• **Marvel Mania.** A restaurant with a comic-book theme.

• **NASCAR Café.** Food, fun, and fast cars, including a pit-crew wait staff.

**Emeril's of New Orleans.** Where chef Emeril Lagasse will bring his creole-based "kicky cuisine" to the East Coast for the first time with a restaurant built around an open kitchen allowing guests to watch their gourmet meals being created.

• **Pat O'Brien's.** The only replica of New Orleans' legendary watering hole, the original home of dueling pianos, the "flaming fountain" patio, and the famous "Hurricane" drink.

• A "floating" outdoor theater on the E-Zone's lagoon for special shows and concerts.

As an extension of Universal Studios Florida, the E-Zone was also designed to serve as a location for films and television shows produced there.

Other additions to Universal City Florida will include:

• Expansion of the studio facilities for television and movie production.

• Five different themed hotels, with more than 4,300 rooms. Each of the hotels will be designed to double as a backlot set for motion picture and television production. The first two hotels will be open in 1999 and a second pair in 2005. A 300-unit golf lodge and villa community will also open in 2005.

• More than 300,000 square feet of meeting and conference space, equipped with satellite uplinks and downlinks for video feeds and teleconferencing.

**Production schedule.** To find out what is "in production" at the studios, call the Guest Services office at (407) 354-6356.

**Shopper's pass.** Need to grab a quick souvenir on your way to the airport? You can purchase a Shopper's Pass at the Guest Services window; you'll put down a deposit equal to a full-price ticket, which will be refunded if you return to the window within an hour.

**Universal on the Web.** Visitors to the Internet's World Wide Web can check out the latest news from Orlando at http://www.usf.com.

• An 18-hole PGA golf course, set amid a 300-unit golf villa community, and a championship tennis facility with a professional level center court stadium for major competitions.

In the preliminary plan, many of the hotels, attractions, shopping, dining, entertainment, and recreation areas will be interconnected by waterways. Winding rivers and canals with rocky shorelines will weave through the property, again themed for use in television and movie production. Water taxis and ferries, as well as trams and motor coaches and a vast people-mover sidewalk system will carry guests throughout the resort area.

# Power Trip #1

## Head for the Future

Lines at some of the more popular attractions can build to as much as 90 minutes on busy days; the Power Trip puts you on a fast track for the major magnets in the morning with a more leisurely pace for the rest of the day.

The spectacular new **Terminator 2 3-D** show, the **Jaws** ride, and the older but wilder **Back to the Future** simulator are the biggest draws at the park; therefore the smartest plan is to head for one of them as soon as you arrive at the park—and the earlier the better. Make your first right turn on Rodeo Drive and go directly to Terminator 2 3-D; if you're in the first crush of visitors you should be able to meet your robotic fate within half an hour. When the show lets out, continue up Hollywood Blvd. to Sunset Blvd. and head directly for Back to the Future. Lines should still be at manageable levels in the morning. When you're back to the present, continue around the lagoon to Jaws.

Warning: in our judgment, many young visitors and some older ones may find these rides to be too wild; if you're not up to the journey, go instead to the **E.T. Adventure** as your first stop.

When you are through with your early targets, you can check out the lines at the ride you missed, or make plans to come back late in the day.

Continue around the lagoon in a counterclockwise direction to **Earthquake—The Big One** and ride the subway to San Francisco. Exit that ride and continue to **Kongfrontation.**

Now, head to the front of the park and **The Funtastic World of Hanna-Barbera**, where you will probably find a growing line. It's worth the wait for youngsters; adults may choose to pass it by, especially if they've been to The Future already.

Youngsters will certainly want to visit **Nickelodeon Studios.** We also recommend to adults **Alfred Hitchcock: The Art of Making Movies.**

You have now seen the major attractions of the park. Check the daily schedule for show times and then make a second tour to visit **The Gory, Gruesome & Grotesque Horror Make-Up Show**, the **E.T. Adventure** if you missed it the first time around and if the lines are at a reasonable length, the **Ani-**

mal Actors Stage, the **Wild, Wild, Wild West Stunt Show, Ghostbusters**, and the "**Murder, She Wrote**" **Mystery Theatre**.

The **Dynamite Nights Stunt Spectacular** is worth a peek. At the same time, though, while it's on and drawing thousands to the sides of the lagoon, it's a pretty good time to duck into one of the major shows for a second ride or to catch one you've missed. Go back to Back to the Future or Jaws now.

# Power Trip #2

## Counter-Revolutionary

Here's an alternate plan for use on the very busiest days. It works especially well when you have a full day and the park is open late.

Start by going clockwise, against the crowds sprinting for Terminator 2 3-D, Jaws, or Back to the Future. Instead, your first stop should be one of the big draws near the entrance to the park. Try **Kongfrontation**, then **Earthquake** and then, depending on length of line, visit **Ghostbusters, Alfred Hitchcock**, and **The Funtastic World of Hanna-Barbera**. By this time, the park should be pretty crowded; have an early lunch. For the rest of the afternoon, visit the less-crowded shows including **Nickelodeon, "Murder, She Wrote," the Wild, Wild, Wild West Stunt Show, Animal Actors Stage**, and **The Gory, Gruesome & Grotesque Horror Make-Up Show**.

**Don't say you weren't warned.** Back to the Future is described as a "dynamically aggressive ride." Visitors suffering from maladies including dizziness, seizures, back or neck problems, claustrophobia, motion sickness, and heart disorders, as well as pregnant women, are advised to sit this one out. The ride also won't work for persons of a certain size or shape who cannot fit into the seats and safety harness. We suspect you know who you are.

**Meeting spot.** If you're planning to do a baby swap, ask for advice from one of the attendants on the proper place to wait. And, if you need to meet someone after the ride, pick a specific spot like the Jules Verne Train, since there are two exits from the building.

Have an early dinner. As the rest of the visitors collapse from waiting in lines all day, use the evening to see the biggest draws: **Terminator 2 3-D, Jaws, Back to the Future**, and **E.T. Adventure**, plus any other shows you missed in the morning.

## Attractions at Universal Studios Florida

### Expo Center

**WOW** **Back to the Future . . . The Ride.** Dive into the world of the record-breaking movie trilogy, *Back to the Future* in Universal's incredible simulator adventure. This is about as wild a ride as anything you'll find in Florida, with the possible exception of the real Space Shuttle. There is absolutely nothing like it at Walt Disney World.

**Coming attraction.** If you have really sharp eyes and a good sense of balance, keep an eye out during your wild Back to the Future ride for the movie poster on the wall in Hill Valley; it advertises *Jaws 19.*

**We assume they've changed the sheets.** Outside the pavilion toward the front of the park, take a look at the Garden of Allah Villas. This is a reproduction of what is believed to be the world's first motel, built in California by Alla Nazimova, a Russian-born silent picture star who lost her job when the talkies started—it seems she could not speak English. The Garden was the sometimes home for many Hollywood stars, including Lauren Bacall and John Barrymore.

**You're being watched.** We took a backstage tour of Back to the Future, visiting the computer rooms and the security "tower" where operators monitor all 12 cars in each theater using see-in-the-dark video cameras. They are able to turn off individual cars if anything goes wrong or a rider becomes ill or faints.

It seems that weird Doc Brown is back home conducting new time travel experiments. He has created his newest vehicle—an eight-passenger Time Vehicle that is faster and more energy efficient than anything before . . . or since. That's the good news. The bad news is that Biff Tannen has broken into the Institute of Future Technology and threatens to end the universe as we know it! It's up to you to jump into your own DeLorean and chase down Biff.

Surrounded by images and sound and buffeted by the realistic motion of your flight simulator, you will soar into Hill Valley in the year 2015, blast back to the Ice Age for a chilling high-speed encounter with canyons of sheer ice, explode into the Volcanic Era for a once-in-a-lifetime encounter with a Tyrannosaurus rex and then through a volcano and over the edge of a molten lava fall.

This is a state-of-the-art attraction that combines a spectacular 70-mm Omnimax film with simulator ride vehicles (bearing Florida license plates "OUTTATIME"). The 80-foot-diameter domelike screens of the Omnimax theaters occupy all of the viewer's peripheral vision, making the screen seem to vanish and taking the viewer into the scene.

The Institute of Future Technology in the waiting area features actual props from the *Back to the Future* movie series, including hoverboards (futuristic skateboards without wheels) and the all-important flux capacitors for time travel.

Check out the bulletin board in the waiting area where you will see the names of some of the visiting scientists with offices in the building. They include Thomas Edison, Albert Einstein, and Francis Bacon.

There are actually two identical rides in the building, each with its own set of 12 eight-seater DeLoreans and movie dome. Each area has cars on three levels with three cars at the top, five in the middle, and four at the bottom.

Universal insiders say that the very best experience can be had by sitting in the front row of the center car on the second tier; dispatchers call it Car 6. This particular vehicle is in the absolute center of the movie dome and you cannot easily see any surrounding cars which might distract from the illusion.

At about the midway point of the waiting line visitors will be divided among three rampways, one to each level. If you can at all arrange to go through portal number two to the middle level, you have a one-in-five chance of ending up in magic Car 6.

If you are concerned about getting motion sickness, you may want to try to get onto the lower level of the ride. (I prefer a Dramamine in the morning and Car 6.)

When you enter the holding room for the simulator, try to maneuver next to the door to get a seat in the front of the car. (Some visitors find the small waiting room a bit confining; you can ask the attendant to leave the door open if you feel it necessary. Trust us: a much more intense experience is coming.)

As you wait to board your simulator, pay attention to the little movie about time travel safety; we enjoyed watching crash dummies "Fender" and "Bender" at work. When you feel a rumble beneath your feet, you'll know the car is returning to its base.

**Don't wait twice.** If you're in line for a ride and it breaks down and must be shut, ask one of the attendants for a "comp" ticket that will allow you to skip lines that may build up later in the day.

**From 2001 to the Future.** The director of the Back to the Future ride-film was renowned movie special effects designer Douglas Trumbull, who created special effects for hits including *2001: A Space Odyssey,* and *Close Encounters of the Third Kind.* The 4-minute 70-mm movie portion of the ride took two years to make and cost as much as a feature film. Elaborate hand-painted miniatures were created for the filming.

The preshow film and the movie shown in the ride itself were made specially for the simulator. Doc Brown (Christopher Lloyd) and Biff Tannen (Thomas Wilson) took part in the movie, but Marty McFly (Michael J. Fox) is nowhere to be seen. According to rumors, Fox asked for too much money.

The glass case in the preflight waiting room includes some juicy little details for fans of the film. In the famous Car 6, you'll find a notepad discussing the results of various flights in which Doc Brown reports he discussed the theory of electricity with Benjamin Franklin and philosophy with Mark Twain. On one of the flights, Brown reports he attended a presidential inauguration, noting that "she is quite a woman."

The DeLoreans themselves rise about eight feet out of their garages at the start of the movie. Once in the air, four actuators drive the car—three for vertical movement and one for fore-and-aft movement. Although it may feel as if your car is soaring and dropping hundreds of feet, the entire range of movement for the vehicle is about two feet.

To give the feeling of traveling through space, the cars are surrounded with a fog made from liquid nitrogen.

On a busy day, lines easily reach to 90 minutes or more. Remember that the crowd you see out on the plaza is only about half the backup—there are internal walkways and hallways as well. Each ride takes about 4½ minutes, with about 96 persons entering each of the two simulator theaters at a time. By the end of the day on a quiet day, there may be no line at all. But it still takes 15 minutes or so to walk into the gate, up the stairs, into a waiting room for one of the simulators, and into your seat.

How long can the lines get at Back to the Future? Well, let's just say that this is the first waiting line I have ever seen with a beer vendor halfway to the entrance.

Before or after you join the line, check out the large prop to the left of the building. The Jules Verne Train was used in the closing scene of *Back to the Future III,* when Doc Brown returns from 1885 in this steam engine adapted to become a time machine.

**WOW! E.T. Adventure.** One of the best-loved movies of all times is given life in this imaginative ride which begins where *E.T.* left off. You will share a bicycle with our favorite extraterrestrial in a voyage across the moon to save E.T.'s home, a planet dying for lack of his healing touch.

The huge miniature city beneath your bicycle includes 3,340 tiny buildings, 250 ultra-compact cars, and 1,000 street lights. The stars above include some 4,400 points of light. The music for the ride was written by Academy Award–winning composer John Williams, who was also responsible for the movie score.

As marvelous as the ride itself is, don't overlook the incredible fantasy world of the waiting area. It will start when you register at the door and are cast as an actor in the coming adventure; be sure to hold on to the special card you are given until it is collected as you climb onto your bicycle.

The entrance line wends its way through a mysterious redwood forest populated with all sorts of human and otherworldly creatures. All around you, government agents search for E.T.

Finally, you are at your bicycle. As with most of the other rides at Universal, the E.T. ride has been subtly improved over the years. The beginning is now much scarier as your bicycle is pursued by police cars with searchlights. Nicer effects include a gorgeous star field using fiber optics; throughout the rest of the ride the colors have been brightened. New fog and smoke effects were also added. It's the same wonderful ride it used to be, only better.

Higher and higher you climb, until the city looks like a toy beneath you. Director Steven Spielberg created a phantasmagorical cast of new characters for the adventure, including Botanicus, Tickli Moot Moot, Orbidon, Magdol, Horn-Flowers, Tympani Tremblies, Water Imps, Big Zoms, Gurgles, Squirtals, and Churtles. Will you arrive home at the Green Planet in time?

Well, yes: and the celebration begins as E.T.'s friend the Tickli Moot Moot laughs again, Orbidon sparkles, and Magdol sings. Baby E.T.s will dance and play all around you, and E.T. will thank you . . . personally.

**WOW** **Animal Actors Stage.** And you think you've a right to be proud when Bowser rolls over the third time you ask? Wait until you see the professionals at work—they've pawed and clawed their way to the top of animal show business.

I was especially impressed with the cat who opens the show. Yes, that's right: a trained domestic cat. He runs out onto the stage, gives the audience a glance, and then climbs up the wall, jumps into a basket, and sits there waiting for a dog to pull him up by rope. Then the cat runs across a catwalk and pushes down a sign

**Mr. Ed, unmuzzled.** We hope we're not going to shatter any heartfelt illusions, but we trust you realize that Mr. Ed does not really talk. His trainers fill his mouth with peanut butter before he goes on stage, which makes him want to move his jaws any time his bit is loosened.

that says "Welcome to the Animal Actors Stage." I don't know about yours, but our family cat Friskey would never stoop so low as to perform tricks for mere humans.

The cast of animals changes over the months. On one visit, the stars included Lassie (actually, one of many collies who have held that name over the years), Benji, and even a horsing-around Mr. Ed.

Most of Universal Studios Florida's dogs and cats were rescued from the pound before they went on to stardom. Benji has appeared in four movies— three bearing his name, plus *Oh, Heavenly Dog!* with Chevy Chase. He has twice been named the Animal Actor of the Year by the American Guild of Variety Artists. We've also seen stars of *Ace Ventura* and *The Flintstones*, and bit parts played by raccoons, skunks, and a sea lion.

The open-air stadium will accommodate 1,500 people for its 25-minute show; it is a good place to take an afternoon break when lines are longest at the most popular attractions and the sun is at its hottest.

**Fievel's Playland.** Now here's *serious* entertainment for the very youngest visitors to Universal Studios, and a good place to burn off some energy.

The playground, based loosely on the series of *An American Tail* animated movies, is located between the E.T. Adventure and the Animal Actors Stage and (don't tell the kids) in the shadows of the replica of the Bates Motel on the hill.

The playground is padded with a soft absorbent surface to protect kids who might fall. It includes a carnival-like air pillow for jumping, a 30-foot climbing net, and a kids-only water slide.

Actually, the sign at the water slide has a measuring post at about 40 inches that says: "If you ain't this tall, bring an adult." Another sign warns that the slide will give you wet breeches, and this is quite true. The slide itself, on a small raft, is short and not nearly as wild as bigger rides at water parks. The line for the slide can become quite long, and parents who do not accompany their kids will probably want to park themselves at the bottom of the slide to retrieve them.

It might be possible to let your kids run loose at the playground while an adult waits in line at E.T.; I'd suggest you keep them out of line for the water

**Would you love him anyhow?** The original concept for Barney was as a teddy bear but became a dinosaur on the advice of creator Sheryl Leach's young son.

**Backstage at the earthquake.** We took an exclusive tour into the control room and observed the computer controls for the sophisticated ride. You can see the room along the right side of the train in the catastrophe station; it's the operator who runs out with a megaphone at the end of each adventure.

**Out of business.** On the streets of San Francisco, note the impressive facade of Ferries & Cliff, which was one of the biggest department stores in that city at the turn of the century. It collapsed in the great earthquake of 1906 and was never rebuilt, except at Universal Studios.

slide, though, since it would be impossible to retrieve them quickly if they were way up in the queue.

**A Day in the Park with Barney.** This interactive musical show and hands-on educational playground stars the ubiquitous purple dinosaur, his best friend Baby Bop, and her big brother BJ. The theater-in-the-round teaches life lessons through song, dance, and play. Adults are excused unless accompanied by an insistent youngster.

## San Francisco/Amity

**WOW** Earthquake—The Big One. Why in the world would any sane human being want to travel all the way to Orlando, fork over a not-small number of hard-earned bucks, and then wait in a long line for the privilege of walking right into a devastating earthquake?

Well, it has to be because this ride is devastating fun. This spectacular attraction is based on the motion picture *Earthquake,* which was the first movie in history to win an Academy Award for special effects.

Six visitors—usually three women, a man, and two kids—are picked as extras and "grips" for a demonstration of movie special effects. The kids get to fulfill a child's fantasy: dropping (foam) boulders on a bunch of adults; the male extra is in for a surprise dive.

Before the action, you'll see a short film about some of the special effects used in the film. Most interesting is probably the miniature city constructed for one of the most spectacular scenes in the movie. It took six months to build at a cost of about $2.5 million, and about six minutes to destroy; the actual sequence in the movie takes even less than that.

We'd suggest you move all the way across the rows in the demonstration area so that you can move quickly to the train for your choice of seats. When the demonstration is over, you will enter into a realistic re-creation of a subway station in Oakland and board a train heading to Embarcadero Station in San Francisco.

The front of the 200-seat train is to your left; the best car for the ride is the second car from the front. The first row of each car has a somewhat blocked view; try to grab a seat in the middle. The right side of the train (the far side of the row as you get in) has the best view of the flood; the left side of the train (where the last person in the row gets on board) is closest to the explosions and the train crash.

The train pulls out of the station and under the bay. Right away something goes very wrong. The train begins to shake violently, lights flicker, and the ceiling starts to collapse. The street above your head caves in, and a huge propane tanker truck crashes its way toward you. But that's only the beginning: another train bears down on you at high speed aiming for a head-on crash. Finally, a huge tidal wave races your way.

Cut!

**Amity Games.** Down by the waterfront, there's a movie set version of a boardwalk, complete with games of chance including **Short Shot** basketball, **Milk Can Menagerie, Hoop Toss, Shark-Banger** (a version of the familiar whack-a-mole game), **Muffin Tin,** and **Dolphin Dash.**

**WOW! Jaws.** Just when you thought it was safe to go back to Florida, Universal Studios went and opened **Jaws,** a spectacular new ride based on the movie classic that kept millions out of the ocean 20 years ago.

It's always the Fourth of July in the picturesque seaside resort of Amity. You can walk the boardwalk and try your hand at carnival games or stop for a seafood snack. And, of course, you are going to want to hop on board the Amity Harbor tour boat for a peaceful jaunt.

The five-minute cruise starts out innocently enough. The vicious little shark that had previously terrorized Amity hangs—dead—from a hook in the village. So what could possibly go wrong?

Well, okay, we imagine you have guessed what happens next. Your boat will motor gently around the corner, past a picturesque little lighthouse to find the wreckage of a tour boat just like the one you are in. A moment later, the harbor explodes with terror as a 32-foot, three-ton killer great white shark decides to invite you all to lunch. His lunch, that is.

**Heavy effects.** The special effects of this ride are among the most spectacular ever created for an amusement park. To begin with, the rocking and rolling of the simulated earthquake would actually register a whopping 8.3 on the Richter scale. The mega-tremor releases 65,000 gallons of (recycled) water every six minutes. The falling roadway slab weighs 45,000 pounds.

Perhaps most interesting is the fact that the tracks themselves remain stable; all of the rocking and rolling takes place with lifters within the train itself.

**Back from the past.** Check out the photos along the walls of the preshow area. Universal researchers uncovered a treasure trove of photos from the family of a survivor of the 1906 San Francisco earthquake.

*Le regole, per piacere.* If you're reading this book, you probably speak English, but you might be interested to know that each booth at Amity Games has a book with the rules of the game translated into French, Spanish, Portuguese, Italian, and German.

**Vital stats.** The Jaws ride employs space-age underwater technology never before used in an amusement attraction.

The 7-acre lagoon holds 5 million gallons of water and there are eight boats. Much of the New England memorabilia scattered about was found in Gloucester, Massachusetts, and surrounding fishing towns.

The 32-foot shark is made of steel and fiberglass, with a latex skin; its teeth are made of urethane. When it attacks it moves through the water at realistic shark speeds of 20 feet per second, with thrusts equal to the power of a 727 jet engine.

**Land line.** How long is that line for Jaws? Here is a formula to estimate the wait: there are eight boats, each capable of holding 48 visitors, and the ride takes six minutes. Allowing two minutes to load and unload, that means each boat will carry about 336 passengers an hour. The eight boats, then, will move about 2,688 victims per hour across Amity Harbor.

By the way, the Jaws boat ride may be shut down if an electrical storm is in the area.

It starts with a quick glimpse of a dorsal fin that zips past and then under your boat. Then he comes back!

Your boat captain will attempt to save the day, firing rifle grenades in a desperate attempt to stop the attacker. Somehow he will steer the boat into the safety of a deserted boathouse. Hah! Suddenly there's a loud crash on the side of the boathouse and the wall all but comes down with the force of Jaws breaking through.

Now it's a race for life as the boat is chased by the frenzied creature. This time the captain's shots hit a chemical tank along shore and the lagoon fills with burning fuel as he attempts to break for safety on a barge that carries the main power supply cable to Amity Island.

Once again the shark attacks, but this time he grabs hold of the main power cable: instant fish fry! At last, you're safe . . . right?

By the way, some young visitors may find the explosions and the hot steam that envelops you at the end of the ride to be very frightening; the fright level of the Jaws ride has been ratcheted up a few notches for 1996.

The left side of the boat is definitely the place to be for the more adventurous traveler; that's the side closest to the explosions, fire, Jaws, and . . . water. By the way, when the ride first opened, Universal set decorators included a pair of mouse ears in the shark's mouth, but the top brass decided it was too scary for youngsters . . . and Disney.

**Dynamite Nights Stunt Spectacular.** A wild demonstration of explosive movie stunts, performed on the lagoon. There's no waiting line for the show—just pull up a piece of the railing. In peak season the show is presented more than once each day; check the daily schedule for show times. There's a story line for those who care about such things: something about a high-energy shootout with desperate drug dealers.

**Wild, Wild, Wild West Stunt Show.** Guns blaze, cowboys brawl, and dynamite creates instant urban renewal in Universal's re-creation of a 19th-century western town. Hollywood stunt players demonstrate how they simulate the dangerous action.

The show, held in a 2,000-seat arena, is short, intense, and suitable for kids of all ages, although some of the explosions and gunfire are a bit loud. There's a little story about a rough and tough "Ma" and her gang of boys; the guys in the white hats win, but not before there's a terrific battle down in the corral, up on the roofs, and even out on the ropes that hold the sign ("Square Dance and Hanging, Saturday Night") across Main Street.

## New York

**Ghostbusters Spooktacular.** Who ya gonna call? Yeah, we know, but return visitors to Universal Studios are gonna get a different and much better version of the live-action and special effects spectacular than first was presented here.

Here's the story: the Ghostbusters are offering franchises to Universal Studios visitors to allow them to bust ghosts in their own home towns. Check out the flyers on the wall:

"Big bucks! Get rich today.

Come to a fantastic free business seminar.

It's the cash bonanza of a lifetime!

Come to Ghostbusters headquarters in Engine Company 89.

Get in on the ground floor. Trust us, you won't be sorry.

For more information, call 1-800-555-BUST."

Only $29,999, and MasterCard and Visa are, of course, accepted.

The preshow, under the direction of a Rick Moranis look-alike, is well done. Check out some of the details in the products on the wall, including Ghost Motel (better than Roach Motel, we guess). Listen to the messages on the answering machine, too; one of them sounds very much like Elvis.

**President Wasserman.** The statue at 5th Avenue and Canal Street in the simulated streets of New York may appear to be Abraham Lincoln at first glance, but actually represents an insider moviemaking joke. The face on the statue is actually that of Lew Wasserman, the chairman of MCA, the parent company for Universal Studios; he is discreetly holding a pair of glasses behind his back, out of camera range.

**Pool room.** The lagoon at Universal Studios is actually a 15-million-gallon pool with a gunite bottom.

**Bottoms up.** There is a block of seats at the Wild, Wild, etc. show that is marked "splash zone." Sit there if you are overdue for a shower. The water doesn't come from the "well" on the stage, though; that's a stunt pit, about six feet deep and padded on the bottom with a trampoline.

For the preshow, they select three volunteers from the front row of standees—a kid, a man, and a woman. My son Willie was chosen and placed on a stool and given a double handful of slime to juggle.

There are some interesting little details within the preshow area. On the

**Ghostly magic.**
Ghostbusters
Spooktacular features
what Universal calls the
largest single magic
illusion ever created,
requiring 2,300
computer cues, 11 tons
of liquid nitrogen, and a
unique laser system
generating both visible
and nonvisible light.

**Expensive stains.** The
New York streets are
made of concrete; a
mold was applied to
make the roads appear
to be constructed of
cobblestones. All of the
cracks in the road,
bubble gum on the
sidewalks, and rust stains
on the stone (styrofoam,
actually) walls were
applied by artists.

left wall, you will find a display of ghost identi-fication charts. Creatures listed include Spindle Fingers, described as a "mobile exoskeletal aggressor," also known as Handyman or Bones. The suggested trap involves a dozen Chinese finger traps.

The Jailbird is an "ectolarcenous cranial morph," also known as Light Finger Lee or Roller Noggin. To trap him, use a trail of coins leading into the vault, and then slam the door.

And, of course, there is Slimer, a "free floating class B phantasm," also known as Onion Head or Spud. To capture him, use a frankfurter or a Twinkie on a string.

On the same wall, you'll even find a City of Orlando occupational license for Ghost-busters, Inc. There is also a collection of newspaper articles of great accomplishments of the Ghostbusters including clippings from tabloid newspapers with headlines like, "My Septic Tank Is Haunted by My Dead Husband's Ghost." A handwritten note on that one read, "We flushed him out."

After the preliminaries, you're into the main theater. A huge transparent shield protects the audience of nearly 500 from the goings-on—and also serves as the medium to carry some of the special effects. The best seats in the house are at the middle-right side in the back, offering an unobstructed view of the Sta-Puft Marshmallow Man and other treats.

Spirits swirl, strange howls echo, and dark clouds gather overhead. The Terror Dogs suddenly crackle with energy and beams of light strike the temple doors. The vault of Gozer cracks open, and all hell seems to break loose as the she-devil takes the stage. You know the question, right? Who ya gonna call?

That's right, the Ghostbusters. Actors playing the roles of Spengler, Venkman, Zeddmore, and Stantz take the stage. Gozer blasts our heroes with ectoplasmic power; they fight back with bursts from their neutronic wands. A Terror Dog comes to life. But the gooiest mess is yet to come when the Marshmallow Man emerges from his jar.

**Screen Test Home Video Adventure.** Here's your chance—for an additional charge of about $30—to put yourself right on the screen with *Star Trek*, *King Kong*, and *E.T.*

You can choose between a short Star Trek scene in which you will trade lines with stars William Shatner and Leonard Nimoy or film a highly fictional version of "Your Day at Universal."

After selecting their screen test, guests enter one of seven production studios where they will take their cues from a director. The studios are painted a special shade of blue that can be blanked out by Universal's Ultimatte 6 system, computer-controlled cameras, and video technology and replaced with fantastic scenes much like the way special effects are added to real movies.

It is an amazing process, and the final result will astound even the most technically sophisticated or jaded visitor. Most visitors choose the Star Trek scene, but we will always treasure our "Day at Universal" tape, especially the scene where *we* escaped from *within* the Earthquake set.

When you exit the adventure, you will take with you an 8- to 10-minute VHS videotape to show over and over again at home. Versions for European PAL, Secam, and Hi-8 players are also available.

Attention Trekkies: there's a souvenir store in the lobby of the Screen Test Home Video Adventure with everything you ever wanted to buy for your *Star Trek* collection, including videotapes, books, T-shirts, jackets, and Enterprise uniforms. More? How about Star Trek ties, calendars, figurines, holograms, and magnets?

**WOW** Kongfrontation. It's the big banana himself, and you are a helpless captive in New York's Roosevelt Island tram. In fact, you're so close you can smell the bananas on his breath.

The 4½-minute adventure begins as you walk through a beautifully constructed replica of a Manhattan subway station, complete with advertising posters appropriately redecorated with graffiti. Up above are a series of television sets, and as you move through the building watch for news bulletins about the wild escapades of the famous ape.

The Big Apple has been turned into a war zone, with wrecked cars, burst water mains, and massive fires. As your 60-seat tram makes a turn, you arrive at the Queensboro Bridge to find the big guy hanging from the supports. Uprooting telephone poles as if they were toothpicks, he reaches for your tram . . . until a helicopter makes a brave attempt to distract him.

Phew! You're safe. But are you, really?

The Kongfrontation set is based on Manhattan's lower west side in 1976, the setting for the remake of *King Kong* starring Jessica Lange and Jeff Bridges. Pay attention to the little details along the way—peek into some of the win-

**Medical news.** If you are prone to dizziness or upset stomach on wild rides like Back to the Future or The Funtastic World of Hanna-Barbera, you might want to take one or two Dramamine motion sickness tablets at the start of the day (before you take any rides). They work like a charm. Check with your family doctor first if you are taking any other medications or if you have any allergies or unusual conditions. And be aware that the pills may make you a bit sleepy; you may want to assign a designated driver for the end of the day.

**Write if you get work.** When the park was first opened, Universal hired a graffiti artist from New York to decorate the walls of the tram waiting area. Since then, a lot more has been added by amateurs.

**Kong's coat and other details.** King Kong, the biggest computer-animated figure ever built, wears a 7,000-pound fur coat. Standing four stories tall and weighing six tons, he has an arm span of 54 feet. The rescue helicopters are molded from real National Guard OH6 choppers.

dows of the tenements and see schoolkid drawings, posters, and boxes of food.

New Yorkers will note that the moviemaking magic ignores a few Big Apple facts. You enter into the ride through a replica of Penn Station which is on the west side of Manhattan; within, though, is the Roosevelt Island Tram, which is on the east side.

This is a must-see show, but be forewarned that lines can build by midday. Go early or late.

**Beetlejuice's Graveyard Revue.** This is the ultimate in graveyard rock, a tuneful singing and dancing show presented in a shaded outdoor amphitheater and starring everybody's favorite creep, Beetlejuice, and a monstrous cast of characters including Wolfman, Dracula, Frankenstein, the Phantom of the Opera, and the Bride of Frankenstein.

The background music is tape recorded, but the singing and dancing is live and very entertaining, although the very young and older adults may find it a bit loud. Pay attention to some of the inside jokes: Beetlejuice takes a gander at the creepy old horror set and comments, "Hey, it looks like Tim Burton's summer home."

We especially enjoyed the stage performance of the "Banana Song" from

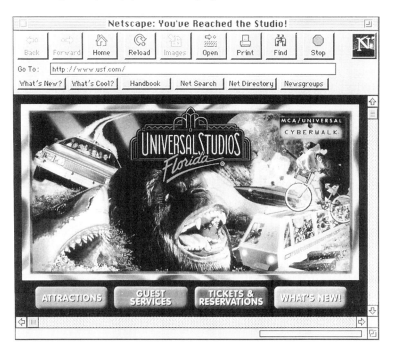

*Universal Studios Florida web site at http://www.usf.com*

the movie, with Beetlejuice dancing with a pair of shrunken head dummies.

The Beetlejuice Revue is even better at night; the crowd is a little more rowdy and the lighting effects look especially impressive against the dark sky. Check the schedule for the hours of performance.

Beetlejuice is a character on loan from Warner Bros., while the rest of the awful actors are from Universal classics.

**Made in Florida.** Films shot at the Orlando studios have included *Psycho IV: The Beginning*; Sylvester Stallone's *Oscar*, and *Problem Child 2*. Even the unlamented (by some) New Kids on the Block made a music video here. Other television projects include dozens of commercials and numerous Nickelodeon series.

**The Blues Brothers in Chicago Bound.** They may be headed for the Windy City, but you'll find these two stand-ins for those strange rhythm and bluesmen performing on a stoop in New York's Delancey Street. Check the daily schedule for their next appearance.

**Namco Coney Island** and **Namco Space Station.** As if you needed any more excitement, there is a pair of state-of-the-art video arcades in the New York section with a good selection of current games. Pricing is a little sneaky: you must change your real money into tokens to play the games, and the basic rate is three tokens for a dollar. Most of the current games cost at least two tokens. It's easy to think 50 cents when you are spending 67 cents. The token exchange rate does improve a bit if you are going to spend a serious amount of time and money at the arcade; you can purchase 80 tokens for $20 or 38 for $10.

## Production Central

**Murder, She Wrote Mystery Theatre.** Solving a murder is easy; getting a script from paper to the screen is the really difficult part. Step into the world of the popular television series and become the executive producer. You'll watch as technicians race against time to complete the editing, scoring, and special effects of the latest episode within budget and on time.

This is your chance to see if you've got what it takes to be a movie executive. Can you make essential decisions in split seconds? Can you direct the movie and the crew? You'll have to choose a murder weapon, the bad guy, the caper, and even the guest star. You'll supervise the editing, select the takes, and add sound and special effects. Six "volunteers" will be selected—usually from front rows—for the sound effects room. When all the work is over, you'll be able to view the final results on the big screen.

This attraction is a sometimes entertaining and sometimes silly lesson in the critical world of postproduction—the painstaking work that goes on in editing rooms after scenes have been shot. The real *Murder, She Wrote* series often goes from story development to broadcast in just 15 days.

Lines for this attraction can build at midday; unless you're a serious fan of the television series, we'd prefer waiting in line for the Hitchcock show or coming back later.

**Hitchcock's 3-D Theatre.** At a theme park that celebrates the art of

**Check it out.** In the Bates Motel replica at the end of the tour, notice that the key to room #1 is missing. Even more interesting is what you'll uncover if you move the painting to the left of the check-in desk! The shop also offers some of the more unusual souvenirs of the park: Bates Motel towels and bathrobes.

Hidden behind an "employees only" door in the Bates Motel is a "Wall of Fame" with autographs of some of the celebrities who have toured the attraction. Signatures include those of Michael Jackson and Anita Baker.

**Hitchcock at Universal.** Hitchcock made 10 movies with Universal, beginning in 1934 with *The Man Who Knew Too Much* and ending with *Family Plot* in 1976. Universal was also the company behind his television series.

**Doubles.** One of Hitchcock's signatures was the fact that he always had a minor walk-on in his movies. In Anthony Perkins' film introduction to the *Psycho* set, pay attention early on when the technicians start to remove the set and lighting equipment; there is a Hitchcock look-alike walking off in the distance.

moviemaking, this show is the most serious exploration of the role of the director and a very entertaining stop.

Hitchcock, the king of cinema chills, made more than 50 motion pictures in his career, along the way creating some of the most famous scenes on film. From the dizzying heights of *Vertigo* to the terrifying shower scene of *Psycho* to the relentless aerial attack of *The Birds,* you will relive the terror—and learn the techniques behind Hitchcock's brilliance. Personal opinion here: the Hitchcock show, especially the assemblage of great clips shown in the theater, demonstrates moviemaking at its highest art form, while the *Murder, She Wrote* show across the way celebrates television at its most pedestrian.

The "filmstrip" that wends its way around the preshow area includes the names of all of Hitchcock's films. One volunteer will be chosen from the waiting line to participate in a re-creation of the shower scene. Sorry, girls, but the winner will almost always be a young man of average height, wearing tennis shoes. The reasons for the specifications will become apparent later.

Enter the 258-seat **Tribute Theater** for a giant screen film journey through many of Hitchcock's movie and television works, including a portion of the rarely seen 3-D version of *Dial M for Murder.* (The movie was filmed in 3-D, but while it was still in production the public fascination with 3-D seemed to have passed and the movie was released in a standard version.) You're also in for a surprise conclusion, courtesy of some of the flying fiends of *The Birds.*

Next, it's on to the **Psycho Sound Stage.** Anthony Perkins, who created the role of creepy motel owner Norman Bates, is your filmed host for a reenactment of one of the most terrifying scenes ever filmed. You'll see the scene as an unimaginative director might have shot it, and then learn how the master did it. The presentation includes actors (including a pretty model in a body stocking for the shower), our volunteer, reproductions of the *Psycho* house and the Bates Motel set, and clips from the movie.

Finally, you'll visit a fascinating interactive

area where you can explore more of Hitchcock's technique. Actor James Stewart will be your guide in an exploration of the visual shocks of *Vertigo*. John Forsythe will assist you in the reenactment of the murder on a carrousel in *Strangers on a Train*. And Norman Lloyd, who played the villain in *Saboteur* and later produced Hitchcock's television shows, will lead you up the gigantic torch of the Statue of Liberty, the climactic scene in that film.

Be sure to climb the stairs for a fascinating simulation of the famous apartment building scene in *Rear Window*. You'll be able to peer through binoculars at a wall of windows, each showing a different scene—in one of them, a murder takes place.

Back downstairs, Shirley MacLaine narrates a presentation about Hitchcock's famous cameos—his brief appearances in each of his films. Note the lifesize mannequin of the director in the room; the master was only about 5'3" tall.

The first two acts, including the Psycho Sound Stage, may be too intense and frightening to youngsters. You might choose to go directly to the final, interactive area. You can also enter into the gift shop and the interactive area without waiting in line for the show itself.

**WOW** **The Funtastic World of Hanna-Barbera.** Yabba-dabba-doo. Children won't need to be persuaded, but adults: don't pass this one by. This show combines a wide-screen cartoon with state-of-the-art simulators—it's a wild ride for children of all ages. Think of it as a Junior Back to the Future.

Each group of eight seats in the 96-seat auditorium is actually a flight simulator without the cabin, offering an unusual glimpse at the technology—that is if you can take your eyes off the screen during the show. Remember the view when you ride the much wilder Back to the Future attraction, which uses similar technology.

The adventure begins with a three-minute preshow that introduces us to Bill Hanna and Joe Barbera, the rarely seen artists who launched some of our best-loved *non*-Disney characters, including Yogi Bear, the Flintstones, the Jetsons, Scooby Doo, and more. Their work has garnered eight Emmys and seven Oscars.

Hanna and Barbera will introduce us to the story of the adventure that lies

**Rapid cutting.** The shower scene in Alfred Hitchcock's original *Psycho* is made up of 78 different shots, edited in rapid sequence to simulate the violence of the attack. However, the knife is never shown piercing the skin. Hitchcock chose to shoot the film in black and white to lessen the gore. The "blood" is actually chocolate syrup, since stage blood photographs as grey in a black and white print.

**Studio lingo.** As you walk through the backlot, try to spot the differences between three types of movie fake construction. A *facade* is a false front that has nothing behind it. A *shell* includes a front, back, and side but contains no useable interior space. Finally, a *practical set* is a shell that can be used for moviemaking or other purposes. For example, Louie's Italian Restaurant is within a practical set of a New York bank building.

**Back door.** You don't have to wait in the sometimes-lengthy lines to the ride in order to get to the nifty play area of Funtastic Adventures. Enter through the Hanna-Barbera Store. This is a good place to let the kids burn off some energy in the rain or at the end of the day.

ahead, if such things really matter. It seems that Bill and Joe have decided to make Elroy Jetson their star of the future. But along comes that diabolical dog Dastardly, who kidnaps Elroy. It's up to you, Yogi, and Boo Boo to rescue him.

While you are in the preshow area, if you listen carefully, you can hear from the other side of the door the screams of the people who are already riding. When it is your turn, the doors will open and you will be ushered into the auditorium full of simulator cars—it's an unusual opportunity to see the motion of a simulator ride, since the mechanisms are usually hidden from view.

Yogi will lead the entire audience—seated in its simulators—to a giant spaceship for a blastoff into the stratosphere and then back down into Bedrock for a prehistoric tussle with Fred, Wilma, Barney, Pebbles, Bam-Bam, and the entire Flintstones family. From there it is on to Scooby Doo's weird world and eventually the fantastic future of the Jetsons.

The four-minute trip is every bit as silly as it sounds, but an exhilarating ride all the while. Lean back for the best ride. By the way, the auditorium includes a row of seats down front that don't move; the elderly, the very young, pregnant women, and those with back problems are advised to sit there. By the way, if you get queasy here, you will get sick at Back to the Future.

The fun and learning doesn't stop after Elroy is rescued, either. An interactive play area allows you to play with sound effects, color your own cartoon cel with an electronic paintbox and even see yourself as a cartoon character shrunk in size to play in Pebbles' dollhouse.

**The Boneyard.** The storage place for some of the largest props from recent movies. In recent visits, we have seen the houseboat from *Cape Fear*, the Love Rock from *Problem Child 2*, and some of the topiary from *Edward Scissorhands*.

**Production Studio Tram Tour.** Don't confuse this short tram ride with the tour/demonstration at Disney-MGM Studios or the lengthy tour that is the heart of the Universal Studios Hollywood theme park. This open-air tour takes you in and among the same sets you can walk through by yourself; you may pick up a few interesting details from the narrator's spiel. A quick jaunt into the studio area itself gives a great view of blank walls and closed doors and a few glimpses at some of the production "shops" and storage areas.

**WOW** **Nickelodeon Studios.** If you have children, they'll already know the way to The Network for Kids once they spot the 17-foot-tall **Green Slime Geyser** out front; it's the planet's only known source of the stuff.

This is a real working television studio, producing nearly 300 episodes per year of Nickelodeon favorites such as *Legend of the Hidden Temple*, *Welcome Freshmen*, *Make the Grade*, *Fifteen*, *Clarissa Explains It All*, *Hi Honey I'm Home*,

*Eureeka's Castle, Nickelodeon Weinerville, Nick Arcade,* and of course, *Double Dare, Super Sloppy Double Dare,* and *Family Double Dare.*

And, you Eeediot! There's *The Ren & Stimpy Show,* the cult classic cartoon, as well as other animated shows including *Rugrats* and *Doug,* and classics such as *Dangermouse, Looney Tunes & Merrie Melodies, Inspector Gadget,* and *Count Duckula.*

Squarely aimed at an audience of children from ages 2 to 15, the channel is on the air from 6 A.M. to 8 P.M. daily, reaching into more than 60 million homes. Nick at Nite fills the dark hours with reruns of classic situation comedies for children of all ages. Nickelodeon, which began in 1979, is owned by MTV Networks, which is itself owned by Viacom International.

Check out some of the funny signs overhead as you wait in line for a Nickelodeon tour or a television taping. One particularly interesting one offers translations of common proverbs from

**Inside slime.** Try as we could, we were unable to obtain the secret recipe for Gak and Slime. We can tell you, though, that slime is the stuff that is poured over people while gak is dumped. And slime sorta tastes like applesauce while gak is a bit like butterscotch pudding gone wrong.

Just in case you were wondering, more than 7,000 kids have been slimed with more than 40,000 gallons of green slime through the end of 1994, plus at least one famous adult, movie director Steven Spielberg.

English to foreign tongues. For example, in English you might say, "Don't waste your breath"; in France you would say (in French), "Save your saliva." An American might observe that something is "nothing to lose sleep over"; in Hawaii you could say, "It's a heap of relish made of octopus liver." And finally, "All that glitters is not gold" is translated in Haiti as "not all hair is real."

Admission to the Nickelodeon studio tour is free to Universal Studios visitors. You'll be invited to tour the production facilities and the two large sound stages for the cable television network. From glassed-in catwalks above the stages, you can watch episodes being rehearsed or taped as well as look in on control rooms, make-up rooms, and the "kitchen" where slime, gak, and other concoctions used in the various game shows are made.

At the end of each studio tour, kids and their families enter the **Game Lab,** where the youngsters can try out some of the stunts used on the shows; the kids, by the way, get the best seats while their parents are segregated into the bleachers. And, of course, at least one kid will get slimed!

The Game Lab is sponsored by Sega, and the video game maker tests unreleased video games with kids in the waiting lines.

If you or your kids are hoping to be in the audience for the taping of one of the game shows, stop by early in the day and see if they are handing out tickets alongside the door to Stage 18. You can also call the Nickelodeon operator and ask to be connected to the "hotline" number to find out about tapings: (407) 363-8586. Most taping is done on weekdays.

The odds are not great: there are only a few hundred seats for each taping

**Eek, a mouse!** They don't like to see Mickey and friends walking around at Universal; some of the strolling characters will offer you rewards for turning your Disney hats backwards. On one recent visit, the Groucho Marx look-alike was giving $1 in free arcade games.

**Instant stardom.** Who gets picked to be a contestant on a Nickelodeon show? Shy guys and gals need not apply. Casting directors look for kids with enthusiasm and a clear speaking voice.

and they are usually snapped up by the first few hundred youngsters through the gates.

Your child's chances of appearing as a contestant on a Nickelodeon show are pretty slim; most participants are drawn from the Orlando area because they must be available on short notice to meet the schedules of the producers.

From time to time, the studios are used for other productions; at the time of one of our visits, the soundstage was being set up to record a country music performance for VH-1, a sister network to HBO and Nickelodeon that specializes in music videos for adults.

## Hollywood

**Terminator 2 3-D.** He's back . . . and with a vengeance. Universal's newest major attraction is a tour-de-force of film and computer special effects that puts the audience in the middle of an epic battle between and among the fearsome "cinebotic" robots, live actors, and the reunited stars of *Terminator 2:* Arnold Schwarzenegger, Linda Hamilton, Robert Patrick, and Eddie Furlong along with director James Cameron and special effects wizards from the series. In this newest "Terminator" adventure—which begins in the present day and jumps to the Los Angeles of 2029 covered in the film—Cyberdyne Systems, the dreaded creators of Skynet and its fearsome Terminator cyborgs, has moved its corporate headquarters to Universal Studios Florida's Hollywood Boulevard.

Guests will twist and turn in their seats as menacing Cyberdyne Systems "T-70" cinebotic warriors train their sights on random targets throughout the theater, firing across the theater. The audience will leap back in three-dimensional shock when the T-1000 Terminator "cop" from the *Terminator 2* movie morphs to life before their very eyes, then cheer with relief as Schwarzenegger's T-800 cyborg literally charges off the screen to save the day astride a Harley Davidson "hog" that actually lands on the stage.

And we don't want to spoil the fun, but you'll want to hold onto your seats for the jaw-dropping finale. You'll understand what we mean when your feet are back on solid ground.

Since the audience is in the present day, the story uses T-70 cinebots, a design of robots not seen in the movies which take place several decades in the future. The six T-70s each stand eight feet tall; they rise from their hiding places along the walls of the theater with the aid of a sophisticated hydraulic system.

This is the first time interlocking three-dimensional images are projected onto multiple screens, surrounding guests in 180 degrees of action. For its climactic third act, the film opens up from one 50-foot center screen to simultaneous projection on three screens, arranged at 60-degree angles for a sense of enveloping the audience. Spanning 165-feet, Terminator 2 3-D enjoys the distinction of being the world's largest 3-D installation and the first to use the triple screen setup.

**Lucy, I'm home!** The original TV show was unusual in that the creators worked with three or four permanent sets that stood side-by-side in the studio, avoiding the flimsy looking sets typical of television shows at the time. The permanent setting also allowed for more advanced lighting, allowing cameras to move quickly from one area to another. All of the sets were painted in carefully chosen shades of gray to control the contrast of the finished black-and-white film.

Live action portions of the film took place in a two-week shoot at Kaiser Eagle Mountain, an abandoned steel mine in Desert Center, California, rebuilt in spectacular fashion to resemble Los Angeles after a nuclear war. More than 100 cars, trucks, and buses were hauled in from wrecking yards and strewn about the one-million-square-foot location set. The background consisted not of mockups but of actual buildings that were blown up during filming, lending a scale authenticity that surpassed many big-budget Hollywood action flicks.

Additional scenes were shot on a Los Angeles soundstage, where an elaborate 24-foot "miniature" of Skynet, the pyramid-shaped headquarters of Cyberdyne Systems was constructed. Through the magic of cinema trickery it will appear to be 800 feet tall on screen.

The show has a seating capacity of 700, and can accommodate about 2,400 guests per hour for the presentation which runs just a bit over 14 minutes. Much of the waiting area for the show is within the Cyberdyne building; if lines extend out onto the street you may want to come back later in the day.

According to the experts we consulted during the final preparations for the show, the best seats for the 3-D effects are from the middle to the back of the theater; the best seats to see the live action, including the arrival of the Harley on stage, is up front.

**Lucy: A Tribute.** On the left side of Rodeo Drive, keep your ears open for the world's largest indoor collection of Lucy screams. If you are a fan of Lucille Ball and everyone around her, you'll be enthralled at this collection of photos, scripts, and memorabilia and a continuous showing of episodes from her television show. Among my personal favorites is Lucy as part a barbershop quartet.

There is a diorama showing how the original television show was filmed in front of a live audience. The show was photographed (on 35-mm black-and-white film) on one large set; episodes were edited and combined for the final show.

We don't know very many other places in the world where you can see a collection of Desi Arnaz's conga drums or view some of the original scripts from *I Love Lucy*.

There's also a *Lucy* trivia quiz including questions like, "What was the biggest laugh in Lucy history?" Here's a hint: the answer involves Lucy, Ricky, a bunch of raw eggs, and a wild and romantic dance. You figure it out.

Desi Arnaz was born Desiderio Alberto Arnazey Acha III in Santiago, Cuba, in 1917. The son of a Cuban senator, he lived in great luxury until the Cuban Revolution of 1933 when the family left the country. Arnaz worked at various jobs, including cleaning bird cages for 25 cents.

Eventually, he got a job in a band and soon became one of the leading band leaders in New York. Signed to the lead in the New York musical "Too Many Girls," he played a Latin football player. When he went to Hollywood to play his role in the movie version of the musical, he met the studio ingenue Lucille Ball, and in late 1940 they began a bicoastal marriage.

After World War II, looking for a way to work together in Los Angeles, Lucy and Desi hired the writers of Lucy's radio show *My Favorite Husband* and produced a pilot for *I Love Lucy*. Their new company, Desilu Productions, became the largest television and film production company in Hollywood. Arnaz died in 1986. Lucy passed on in 1989.

**WOW** **The Gory, Gruesome & Grotesque Horror Make-Up Show.** It's nearly all in the name; they left out "gross."

Most everyone loves a good monster or horror movie. Here's your chance to learn some of the secrets behind the special effects. For example, where else would you find the recipe for gore: shrimp sauce, oatmeal, and red dye.

Among the devices demonstrated in the lively 25-minute film and live show is the teleportation scene from *The Fly*, somewhat humorously re-enacted on stage.

A film clip explains how Meryl Streep is turned around in her body in *Death Becomes Her*, a special effect that involved blue-screen technology. Streep was videotaped walking backward wearing a blue bag over her head, and then her face was electronically superimposed onto the bag for the effect.

One extra from the audience—usually a woman—gets her arm sliced open and suffers other simulated indignities. She is usually selected from one of the front rows.

Some children may find the GG&G show too gory, gruesome, and grotesque: parents be warned.

There are 355 seats in the theater, and visitors are often turned away at midday; go early or late on busy days.

**AT&T at the Movies.** An interactive electronic playground that may interest some visitors; it does have buttons for kids to push and, it is a good place to duck in out of the rain or the sun and enjoy a few Epcot-like science and computer games.

The **Movie Make-Up** screen is similar to an exhibit at the Imagination pavilion of Epcot; you pose yourself in front of a TV camera and then apply different ears or mustaches or beards or other facial adornments.

Nearby is what may be the world's largest working telephone, a booth where the entire family can enter to place a speakerphone call (on your dime, not theirs).

And there is the **Dawn of Sound** where you can listen to some of the most famous early sound clips of all time, including Al Jolson, news clips from Prohibition, the early talkies, and of all things, a bit of *Steamboat Willie*—the first Mickey Mouse cartoon with sound.

## Special Events

Most any day in the summer and during holiday periods the rest of the year you can expect a high school or college marching band to high-step around the park at mid-morning. And Universal Studios also regularly throws itself a party for special events; call (407) 363-8000 for calendar updates.

**New Year's Eve Celebration.** A blazing fireworks show and other seasonal entertainment welcome the new year.

**Spring Break and Daytona Speed Week.** The park offers special discounts to college students during spring break.

**Mardi Gras at Universal Studios Florida.** Presented each year from early March through early April, and featuring 15 full-size floats direct from the streets of New Orleans, more than 200 costumed street performers including stiltwalkers, fire-eaters, unicyclists, and 10 marching bands. In addition, more than 150 elaborately costumed characters—many of them guests selected from the audience will ride on the floats. The parade will take place nightly at closing time. In addition, major musical groups will perform on stage each Saturday during the Mardi Gras celebration, and the park's restaurants will add New Orleans favorites including crawfish, jambalaya, and étouffé.

**Fourth of July.** A special fireworks show, with music from E.T., Back to the Future, and other movie favorites.

**Halloween Horror Nights.** Hundreds of monsters, maniacs, and mutants crawl out from the backlot from mid-October through Halloween.

## Eating Your Way Through Universal Studios

There are some interesting choices for food at Universal Studios, including a variety of foreign and ethnic foods and a spectacular branch of the Hard Rock Cafe.

We include general price ranges in our listings and mention specific prices for some items. Even where we use specific prices, however, you should consider this an approximate amount. Pricing on food is subject to change.

Some of the best meal deals include a slice of pizza for about $3 at the Food Court or a beef hot dog from one of the street stands for about the same price.

**Something old, something new.** The *Psycho* House on the hill is an empty shell best seen by walking to the left of the park entrance to the Hard Rock Cafe. Note that the house has both an old and a new facade. An old and weathered side faces into the studios, while a freshly painted side faces Kirkman Road. *Psycho IV* was one of the first major motion pictures filmed at Universal Studios Florida, and the producers needed a new view of the house for flashback scenes as well as a dilapidated version for the updated story.

**KEY:**

 = Fast food

 = Pub

 = Full-service restaurant

**Veggies.** Looking for something other than a burger for lunch? Many of the restaurants in Universal Studios have vegetarian offerings; pick up a current listing at Guest Services when you arrive.

Here are a few meatless meals: **Louie's Italian Restaurant** has cheese pizzas, ravioli, and pasta; at **Studio Stars,** you can order a variety of salads and can also dine on *penna a la amatriciana* or chive fettuccine (request them without chicken or pancetta); at **Café La Bamba,** request a meatless taco; at **Lombard's Landing,** they serve a Veggie Burger as well as ravioli with pesto and a steamed vegetable basket.

**Movies, anyone?** The International Food Bazaar is the only place at Universal Studios where they actually show real movies; shorts and classics appear on television monitors above the tables.

## The Front Lot

 **The Fudge Shoppe.** Just like the sign says—no more, no less—The Fudge Shoppe is located beside the Studio Store across from the main Universal entrance. This is a good stop to get something special for the road or for a quick sweet treat on your way into the grounds.

The bonus: you can watch fudge being made. A wide selection of types and flavors is offered. Each third-of-a-pound slice sells for about $3. The store also offers fresh-squeezed lemonade.

 **Beverly Hills Boulangerie.** Gourmet-style sandwiches and pastries, from about $2 to $6.

At the corner of Plaza of the Stars and Rodeo Drive just inside the gate, the Boulangerie offers a selection of sandwiches, sweet treats, and drinks.

You'll appreciate the attractive presentation of pastries and the intimate round tables and metal chairs; a pleasant setting for a quick quality treat.

For a special sandwich, try the smoked turkey with avocado and sprouts. Sandwiches include smoked turkey, ham, and swiss combos, as well as a vegetarian health sandwich, and a selection of soups.

Sweets include cherry turnovers, cheese danishes, overstuffed muffins, macadamia chip cookies, flavored croissants, hazelnut eclair, and key lime pie, for about $2 to $3. There's also a huge chocolate chip cookie for $1.99.

To quench the thirst, select from a variety of beers, wine, and domestic or imported champagne.

## Expo Center

 **International Food Bazaar.** Gyros, brats, burgers, pizza, and more, $2 to $8.

In the rear of Expo Center, next to the Back to the Future ride, this food court offers American, Chinese, German, Italian, and Greek fast food. The advantage of this eatery is evident to families: everyone in the party should be able to indulge his or her own tastes in one place.

The Italian stand offers individual slices of

pizza for about $3; whole pies go for $14 to $15, which is a better deal, relatively speaking. Lasagna is $6.

From the German selections (about $3 to $7), we liked the German bratwurst platter served with sauerkraut and french fries, grilled chicken and muenster sandwich, bratwurst on a bun, and beef goulash.

The American section had entrees from about $5 to $8, including Southern fried chicken, barbecue pork sandwich platter, Philly cheese steak platter, and burgers.

From the Greek menu, you can select such traditional specialties as gyros or *spanakopita*, each about $5.

The Chinese offerings include a variety of dishes priced from about $2 to $7 including egg rolls, won ton soup, sweet and sour chicken, shrimp lo mein with scallops, and stir-fried vegetables and chicken with lemon sauce. The stand also offers Tsingtao beer from China.

For dessert (priced from about $2 to $3), black bottom pie from the American section and baklava from the Greek counter caught our eye. If that's not enough, check out the German Black Forest cake, the Italian amaretto mousse, or one of the frozen yogurt or ice cream offerings.

**Animal Crackers.** Hot dogs, burgers, chicken fingers, hoagies, and yogurt, about $3 to $6.

You'll find this quick food shop next to the E.T. Adventure at the edge of the Expo Center nearest to Hollywood.

Stop here for a hurried lunch or snack to keep you going on to the next section.

**Hard Rock Cafe.** American favorite fare from burgers to pies, salads, and steaks. Entrees $8 to $16.

Approach this interesting dining experience from inside the park via the walkway past the Bates Motel; visitors can also eat at the cafe without buying an admission ticket to the studios by entering from the parking lot side. (If you're coming from the studios, be sure to get your hand stamped at the gate so you can return to the park.)

The restaurant will close sometime in 1997 to be reborn larger and louder as part of the new E-Zone complex at Universal City.

The food here competes with a huge collection of pop memorabilia including original Beatles clothing, the huge motorcycle from the film, *Rebel Without a Cause,* and "mom's" dress from *Psycho IV* (filmed at Universal Studios Florida). Notice the script of *Psycho IV* under the glass beside a number of autographed photographs.

You'll likely enjoy the unusual atmosphere and the good food, but don't plan on being able to carry on a normal conversation while you eat. The background music here is loud, loud, loud rock 'n' roll. For a little quieter atmosphere, ask for the fireplace room; the decor is nice, and the sound's a little more subdued.

Appetizers, ranging from about $3 to $10, include Mom's Chicken Noodle Soup, Bordertown Guacamole & Chips, and Love Me Tenders. Salads, priced from about $8 to $10, include chef, chicken, and tortilla shell.

Club sandwiches ($8 to $9), barbecue platters ($9 to $10), and burgers ($7 to $10) are among the main offerings of the menu. If you want a little more to eat, try the Texas-T, a 16-ounce T-bone steak ($16), or one of the daily seafood specials that are priced according to the day's catch.

## Hollywood

🍴 **Mel's Drive-In.** Burgers, hot dogs, salads, chips, and drinks in a 1950s diner, modeled after the eatery from *American Graffiti.*

You can't miss Mel's. Just look for the garish pink and blue building with its large neon sign on the corner of 8th and Hollywood Boulevard. Unless you are a child of the '50s, you may not immediately appreciate the true beauty of the pink and white 1956 Ford Crown Victoria parked next to an absolutely cherry 1957 black Chevrolet out front.

Inside a sock-hop theme prevails, with period music and booths with individual juke box selectors. Check out the old 45-rpm records pasted to the wall and the pedal pushers worn by the attendants.

Notice we didn't say "waitresses." Forget the personal, at-table service you knew in the '50s, because you have to stand in line to retrieve your fast food here. You'll also have a lot of company in line at this popular place.

If you're lucky, an a cappella singing group will come into your dining area to entertain you with some doo-wop favorites.

As for the food, the menu is authentically limited: Mel's charbroiled double burger, about $4; hot dog, $3; and a chili dog for about $3.50. French fries, onion rings, or a garden salad are all about $2. Finish up with cherry or apple pie ($2.50 plain; $3.50 a la mode).

🍴 **Café La Bamba.** Mexican fast food and an all-you-can-eat buffet, $5 to $8. Child's buffet, $4.

Find La Bamba on Hollywood Boulevard next to the Horror Make-Up Show and across the corner from Mel's. Here you'll find attractive outdoor dining on glass-topped, circular tables with wrought iron chairs. The patio includes an attractive, bubbling fountain.

You can enter La Bamba through this patio or under the large, green awning to the left of the patio. Inside you'll find a cool, tropical interior.

While you can choose entrees (priced from about $4 to $10) including Tex-Mex and ranchero burgers or chicken tostada salad, the best buy of the day for hungry visitors is the all-you-can-eat buffet. For about $8 ($4 for children) you get a wide selection of enchiladas, soft tacos, corn tacos, bean and cheese burritos, quesadillas, beans, rice, and more. Separate bars are available for a variety of alcoholic and soft drinks.

When it is over, leave room for margarita mousse, flan, or churros for dessert.

🍴 **Schwab's Pharmacy.** A classic old-time drugstore fountain just waiting to be discovered.

Hard to miss, on Hollywood Boulevard next to the Brown Derby Hat Shop. Look for the giant blue neon sign, and walk into the bright white drugstore fountain area.

This is a typical 1950s drugstore with a few booths and seating around a curved counter. Soda jerks in blue jeans, white shirts, and classic paper hats take your order and prepare the treats while you watch. The walls are decorated with vintage photos from the original Schwab's in Hollywood and some of its famous patrons.

If you remember the '50s with its custom, handmade ice cream treats (or even if you don't), you'll have a hard time selecting from the familiar Schwab's offerings. Cones go for about $2 for a single scoop, $3 for a double. We liked the creamy, chocolate malt, made in the classic metal cup, poured into a thick, footed glass, and topped with whipped cream and a cherry. We also wished we had some room for one of the ice cream floats and sodas.

Main courses include hot dogs, chips, and soda.

Schwab's is also a good place to pick up an emergency supply of aspirin, Tylenol, Rolaids, or cough drops—some of which you may need after the treats you go through.

### San Francisco/Amity

🍴 **Boardwalk Snacks.** Hot dogs, chips, fruit, and drinks. On hot days, this is the place to go for an emergency Slush Puppy.

For a quick, takeout snack or light meal on the go, stroll into the Boardwalk on the small wharf on Amity Avenue. The shop offers a nautical theme with outdoor dining on picnic tables with a view of the lagoon.

Kids will love the traditional corn dogs—a meal on a stick—or a jumbo hot dog for about $3.50. Chili or sauerkraut toppings are available for the hot dogs. Kids may enjoy chicken fingers for $5.50. Serious boardwalk fans will enjoy the potato knishes and colorful cotton candy.

🍴 **Chez Alcatraz.** Quick seafood treats and drinks. Located over the water on the first wharf in San Francisco/Amity, this walk-up stand gives you a chance to sample shrimp cocktails, clam chowder, soft drinks, or beer and wine while you watch the activities in the lagoon.

An interesting crab salad called a "Conewich" gives you a one-handed shot at seafood salad on the go, or you can try a crab cocktail. Entrees range in price from about $3 to $6.

Alcatraz offers outdoor seating on park-like benches, no tables.

🍴 **Richters Burger Co.** Richter, as in Richter scale, and as in The Big One (a $6 burger with fries), The San Andreas (chicken breast on bun with fries), and The Trembler (a hot dog platter with fries). Entrees range from about $5 to $8. Located directly opposite the entrance to Earthquake, the tables in the back have a view of the lagoon.

🍴 **San Francisco Pastry Company.** San Francisco–style pastries and sweets, plus espresso and cappuccino and the best selection of beers at any casual restaurant in the park.

At the front of Pier 27, on The Embarcadero across from Earthquake: The Big One. The European cafe design opens off of brick-paved streets and the patio overlooks the lagoon. Select your treats inside, then settle into the high-backed iron chairs at imitation marble tables and enjoy.

The Pastry Company artfully displays a variety of pastries and other desserts in a lighted case. In fact, once you move across the attractive tile floor and step up to the brass rail beside the display case, it will be hard to keep from overloading on the tasty offerings.

Our pick of the case is the chocolate or strawberry mousse or the fruit tart. But you can't go wrong with the fudge supreme, cheesecake, or the eclair. The smell of espresso and cappuccino add to the atmosphere. Beers include Anchor Steam from San Francisco.

🍴 **Pier 27.** Barbecue, hot dogs, clam chowder, beer, and chips.

You'd almost have to know this little eatery was here or find it by accident tucked into the back of Golden Gate Mercantile on Pier 27.

Draft ($2.50) and imported bottled beer ($3.50) complement the limited but rather nice selection of barbecue pork sandwiches ($3.75), clam chowder ($2), or hot dogs ($2.50).

You sit on high, padded stools at square tables that you may share with others after selecting your food from the service counter.

🏠 **Lombard's Landing.** Steak, pasta, and seafood served in an elegant 1800s warehouse, this is, by most visitors' accounts, the most attractive restaurant in the park with a nice view of the lagoon. Lunch entrees range from about $8 to $15 for adults and $3.50 to $5 for children. Dinner entrees start at about $15 and reach to about $22 for adults and $5 to $8 for children.

If you time your visit perfectly, you will have a front-row view of the stunt show in the lagoon; the best seats would be out on the balcony overlooking the water.

Located on the wharf next to the Pastry Company, Lombard's entrance is marked by a bright blue awning. Inside, the warehouse has been upgraded with jade green, simulated marble tables, fish fountains, and aquariums. Notice the exposed iron work and wooden beams with bright copper bases.

The large "port hole" aquarium in the center of the rear dining room is not to be missed. And while you select your food you can read the newspaper reproduction of the story of the great San Francisco Earthquake of 1906.

Menus we have seen on our visits include appetizer selections such as melons in honey ginger sauce, shrimp cocktail, and a Fruits-of-the-Sea bucket filled with clams, oysters, and mussels.

Entrees for lunch include fish and chips, grilled chicken, crab cakes, New York strip steak, or chicken and chive fettuccine. The signature sandwiches include the Lomberger (a hamburger on a sourdough bun with swiss, cheddar, or boursin cheese), a fried grouper sandwich on sourdough with a dill *rémoulade* sauce, and a veggie burger on a seven-grain bun.

The catch of the day can be grilled, blackened, or sautéed; fish selections include swordfish, red snapper, tuna, salmon, and lobster.

Children can choose from pasta with tomato sauce and meatballs ($3.50), chicken and noodles ($5), or a quarter-pound hot dog ($4).

Many of the same entrees are available for dinner at slightly higher prices; other dinner entrees we have seen include cioppino with lobster claws and stuffed veal.

Dessert specialties, priced from about $3 to $5, include Boston cream pie, San Francisco Foggie (deep chocolate brownie topped with vanilla ice cream, caramel sauce, whipped cream, and sliced almonds), and a *tiramisu* torte (capuccino flavored torte of mascarpone and cream).

## Production Central

**Studio Stars Restaurant.** Salads, pasta, seafood, and chicken. Entrees $7.50 to $16.50.

You'll find the Stars next to the Murder, She Wrote Mystery Theatre on 57th Street. The attractive, modern entrance is under a pink awning. A large polygon skylight in the center of the dining room gives an open, bright atmosphere to the restaurant. Notice the large color transparencies of Universal stars that line the walls. Some outdoor seating is available.

When things get crowded, request one of the smaller "sunrooms" off of the main dining room at either side of the entrance for a possibly quieter, less hurried meal.

On a recent visit, the menu included *penna a la amatriciana* (small tube-shaped pasta with imported olive oil, sun-dried tomatoes, pancetta, and a touch of hot pepper) for $10.50; chive fettuccine with grilled chicken for $11.50; seafood fettuccine for $12.95; angel hair pasta with baby artichokes, tomatoes, olives, garlic, and herb for $11.25, and Caribbean pork (grilled jerk-marinated pork loin with spicy rice with fried plantains and vegetables) for $12.95. Grilled breast of chicken, $11.25. Sandwiches included Rodeo Drive tuna melt for $7.95, a gourmet burger for $7.95, and a grilled mahi sandwich for $9.25. Appetizers included fried green tomatoes for $4.25.

A particularly good deal, offered at various times of the year, is an all-you-can-eat buffet priced at $9.95 for adults, and $4.95 for children.

## New York

**Louie's Italian Restaurant.** Italian antipasto, pizzas, salads, and more.

Located right on Universal's 5th Avenue at Canal Street, Louie's offers a wide selection of Italian specialties from antipasto to pizza, soups to salads, plus pasta and ices. You can also buy beer.

The dining area here is very large and open with studio-type lighting. The high ceiling and large front windows give an open, bright atmosphere. Two serving lanes offer the same fare on either side, but veteran Louie's visitors say the left side usually is shorter. (Do most people automatically seek the right side because they are right handed? Who knows.)

The portions are large and the food fresh. Pizza is available by the slice for about $3 or by the pie. The pizza is large and has very thick crust.

**Finnegan's Bar and Grill.** Traditional Irish fare including stews and meat pies, $5.50 to $14.

Finnegan's occupies a prominent position on 5th Avenue across the street from Kongfrontation. In movie-set style, the corner Regal Café is just another entrance to Finnegan's.

This is a typical New York City community bar, complete with brick-paved sidewalk and awning-covered entrance. The neon signs in the windows add to the festive saloon atmosphere. The pressed tin ceilings are high and accented with hanging lights and slow-moving fans.

Lighter items include a Blarney baguette filled with your choice of roast beef, corned beef, ham, or turkey with wedge fries for $7.75, and a Shamrock steak sandwich for $8.50. It's St. Patrick's Day every day here, including Irish Stew with lamb, potatoes, and fresh vegetable for $7.95. And there is London Times fish and chips (fish fillets in ale batter with fries and malt vinegar), served on the front page of the London Times for $9.25.

Full dinners include a Yorkshire rib eye steak with fresh vegetables and a giant Yorkshire pudding popover with red bliss potatoes for $12.95.

A children's menu featuring burgers, fried fish, ham and cheese, and chicken fingers is also offered.

The bar side of the eatery includes a handsome antique wooden bar. Besides a nice selection of beers, you can also order a potato and onion web with malt vinegar for $4.95 or breaded and fried jalapeno peppers stuffed with cheddar cheese and fresh salsa for $4.50.

# UNIVERSAL STUDIOS FLORIDA

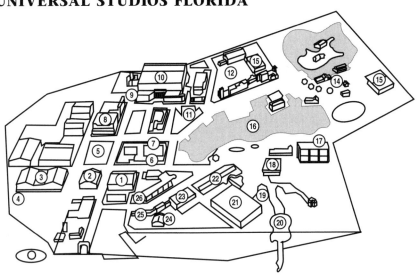

1. Hitchcock's 3-D Theatre
2. The Funtastic World of Hanna-Barbera
3. Nickelodeon Studios
4. Production Studio Tram Tour
5. The Boneyard
6. Murder, She Wrote
7. The Adventures of Rocky and Bullwinkle
8. Ghostbusters
9. Screen Test
10. Kongfrontation
11. The Blues Brothers
12. Beetlejuice's Graveyard Revue
13. Earthquake—The Big One
14. Jaws
15. Wild, Wild, Wild West Stunt Show
16. Dynamite Nights Stunt Spectacular
17. Back to the Future . . . The Ride
18. Animal Actors Stage
19. Fievel's Playland
20. Hard Rock Cafe
21. E.T. Adventure
22. AT&T at the Movies
23. Gory, Gruesome & Grotesque Horror Make-Up Show
24. Terminator 2 3-D
25. Guest Services
26. Lucy: A Tribute

# SEA WORLD

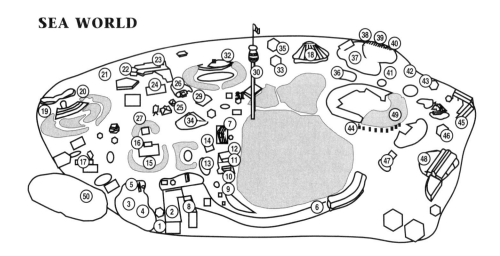

## Exhibits

⑧ Sand Sculpture
⑨ Pelican Exhibit
⑩ Spoonbill Exhibit
⑬ Dolphin Community Pool
⑭ Tropical Rain Forest
⑮ Flamingo Exhibit
⑯ Tropical Reef
⑰ Stingray Lagoon
⑳ Manatees: The Last Generation?
㉑ Special Exhibits
㉒ Friends of the Wild
㉓ Penguin Encounter
㉗ Tide Pool
㉚ Sky Tower
㉜ Pacific Point Preserve
㉟ Terrors of the Deep
㊱ Flamingo Lagoon
㊲ Clydesdale Hamlet
㊵ Anheuser-Busch Hospitality Center
㊶ Midway Games Area
㊷ Play Area
㊸ Radio Control Boats & Trucks
㊹ Shamu: World Focus
㊺ Shamu's Happy Harbor
㊻ Sand Sculpture
㊽ Wild Arctic

## Shows

⑥ Atlantis Water Ski Stadium:
  Baywatch at Sea World
⑦ South Seas Revue: Hawaiian Rhythms
⑱ Nautilus Theatre: Big Splash Bash
㉙ Sea Lion & Otter Stadium:
  Hotel Clyde & Seamore
㉞ Sea World Theatre: Window to the Sea
㊾ Shamu Stadium: Shamu: World Focus
㊿ Key West at Sea World

## Restaurants and Shops

⑤ Treasure Isle-Ice Cream
⑪ Polynesian Luau
⑫ Bimini Bay Cafe
⑲ Manatee Cove Gifts
㉔ Mama Stella's Italian Kitchen
㉕ Buccaneer Smokehouse
㉖ Florida Citrus Growers' Plaza
㉙ Chicken 'n Biscuit
㉛ Waterfront Sandwich Grill
㉝ The Smokehouse
㊳ The Deli
㊴ Label Stable
㊼ Mango Joe's

## Services

① Ticket Plaza
② Guest Relations
③ Sea Safari Tours
④ Special Services

# IV
# Sea World

## Chapter 14
## Sea World

Four-fifths of the earth's surface is water, and almost five million Orlando visitors a year swim upstream to Sea World, the world's most popular marine life park.

Located 10 minutes south of downtown Orlando and 15 minutes from Orlando International Airport at the intersection of I-4 and the Beeline Expressway, Sea World is open every day from 9 A.M. to 7 P.M., with additional hours during the summer and holidays. Call 351-3600 for park information.

Sea World has a decidedly different feel from Walt Disney World and many other attractions in Central Florida. Most of the scheduled events take place in outdoor theaters that seat 3,000 to 5,000 people. With rare exceptions, you don't wait in line here; you simply walk into the theater 15 or 20 minutes before the event and pick a seat. When the theater is full, you are told to return for another scheduled show.

Sea World estimates it will require about eight hours to see the entire park. We recommend that you see all of the shows first and then spend remaining time visiting areas that are not regulated by the clock. If you really want to see it all, plan on arriving at opening time (usually 9 A.M.) and staying through dusk.

One very interesting effort by Sea World is the free computer-prepared map offered at the information desk to the left of the main entrance. This map is keyed to your time of arrival and includes a suggested itinerary to help you see as much of the park as possible without time conflicts. The schedule of events and show times is based on your arrival time.

Where possible arrive for any presentation at least 15 minutes ahead of the show time. This gives you the best chance at getting the seat you want and it lets you view the preshow activities offered at some of the theaters. Most shows are 20 to 25 minutes. We found that you can usually make the next show on your computer-suggested schedule, even if there are only 5 or 10 minutes between shows.

Although Sea World presentations tend to start on time, unless the theater

# MUST-SEES

**Key West at
Sea World**

**Key West
Dolphin Fest**

**Wild Arctic**

**Shamu's
Happy Harbor**
*(adults excused)*

**Manatees: The Last
Generation?**

**Mermaids, Myths &
Monsters**

**Window to the Sea**

**Hotel Clyde
and Seamore**

**Baywatch at
Sea World**

**Shamu:
World Focus**

**Shamu: Close Up!**

**Big Splash Bash**

**Terrors of the Deep**

is full you can always slip in a couple of min-utes late if you need to without disturbing the show.

Saturdays and Sundays are usually the busiest days of the week at the park, with Mondays through Thursdays the quietest. A big day's attendance would be about 15,000 visitors.

As you enter the park, stop to consider the introductory plaque near the entrance that quotes the African Environmentalist Baba Dioum: "For in the end, we will conserve only what we love, we will love only what we understand, and we will understand only what we are taught."

## Power Trip

Begin your Sea World tour by stopping at the information counter to the left of the entrance gate. Ask for your own personalized park map and show schedule. This computer printout will guide you through an efficient schedule based on your time of arrival.

Notice that many of Sea World's shows and events occur only a few times each day. Decide which of these you definitely want to see (consult our must-see suggestions), then work the schedule.

We recommend that you see the scheduled shows in the order they occur from your arrival time; then spend the rest of your day viewing continuous view exhibits. This may sound inefficient, but the Sea World property isn't all that large; you can crisscross a few times if you need to.

Here's one scenario: If you are visiting on a busy day, go directly to the new **Wild Arctic** section to avoid lines. Then backtrack to the Sea World Theatre for the **Window to the Sea** presentation to get a good orientation to the park. Next, move quickly to the **Mana-tees: The Last Generation?** exhibit area. From there it's an easy jog to the Whale and Dolphin Stadium in the northeast corner of the park for the **Key West at Sea World**

Show. Depending on your time of arrival, you may have time to pass through the **Penguin Encounter** after the Discovery show. Penguin Encounter is a continuous view show; after this brief look, you can come back if you want to.

After viewing the **Hotel Clyde and Seamore** show at the Sea Lion & Otter Stadium, pass by one of the lagoon-side restaurants for a sandwich on your way across the lagoon to the Atlantis Water Ski Stadium for the new **Baywatch at Sea World Ski Show**. Don't worry if lunch takes a little longer than you'd like; simply sit dockside and you can see the start of the ski show from the back side of the lake.

After the water show, move into the Shamu Stadium (on the same side of the lagoon) for **Shamu: World Focus**. Before or after the show, depending on the timing, visit the **Shamu: Close Up!** research pool.

The afternoon may be the best time to visit the new Key West at Sea World. Then make your way back across the lagoon for **Terrors of the Deep**. Check out the current show and schedule in the **Nautilus Theatre**. Pass by a couple of the "touch-and-feed" pools such as Stingray Lagoon or the Dolphin Community Pool. Take time out for rest and snacks, walk through the Tropical Rain Forest (beside the dolphin pool), and end your day at the **Shamu Night Magic** finale at Shamu Stadium.

| Sea World Tickets (prices, which include taxes, were in effect for the summer of 1996) | |
| --- | --- |
| **Day Pass** | |
| Adult | $39.95 |
| Child (3 to 9) | $32.80 |
| **Parking** | |
| $5 for cars, $7 for RVs | |
| **Sky Tower** | $3.00 |
| **Two-Day Pass** | |
| Adult | $44.95 |
| Child (3 to 9) | $37.80 |
| **Sea World Annual** | |
| Adult | $74.15 |
| Child, Senior | $63.55 |
| **Sea World/Busch Gardens** (Two days) | |
| Adult | $70.10 |
| Children | $56.55 |
| **Sea World/Busch Gardens Wild Card Annual Pass** | |
| Adult | $116.55 |
| Children | $105.95 |
| **Discounts** | |
| AAA members 10 percent | |
| Military or dependent 15 percent | |
| Seniors 15 percent | |
| Handicapped 50 percent | |
| **Aloha! Polynesian Luau** | |
| Adult | $29.95 |
| Junior (8 to 12) | $19.95 |
| Child (3 to 7) | $9.95 |
| plus tax and gratuity | |

## Attractions at Sea World

### 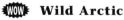 Wild Arctic

The Wild Arctic has arrived in balmy southern Florida, with the biggest new development in the history of any Anheuser-Busch Theme Park, a combination of a state-of-the-art simulator ride and an impressive re-creation of the wonders of the frozen north.

The adventure begins with a thrilling "flight" over the frozen north in the jet helicopter *Borealis* or *Snow Dog* to the remote Base Station Wild Arctic, surrounded by the beauty of the Arctic and kicking up snow at takeoff in a race to outrun an approaching storm.

As the chopper flies out of the hangar, the Arctic landscape unfolds. The

**Value Pass.** In 1996, Universal Studios, Sea World, and Wet 'n Wild came together to offer a five-day, three-park pass. It was priced at $89.95 plus tax for adults, and $72.95 plus tax for children 3 to 9 years old. It's a good deal if you are planning to visit all three parks. You can also save about the same amount . . . with a bit more flexibility . . . using the discount coupons from all three parks that are included in this edition of the *Econoguide.*

journey is relaxing—at first—as the sweeping vista is filled with frozen mountains, glacier peaks, and clouds. The craft's diving and banking levels out over the sea, and passengers are treated to a spectacular view of narwhals, walruses, and other marine life.

Unsettled briefly by buffeting winds and blinding fog banks, the jet helicopter swoops toward the pack ice for a closer view of polar bears. The radio crackles a warning: the blizzard is bearing down.

Following the frigid Franklin Strait, the helicopter skims low over the Arctic sea. At Larsen Sound, a huge glacier fills the horizon. Gently touching down on the ancient frozen floe, visitors absorb the beauty . . . until a deep rumbling starts, and the copter starts to tumble into a deep crevasse. The copter smacks into the sea just as the rotors reach full thrust. The pilot makes a spectacular escape through the close walls of an ice cavern and eventually makes it to the base station.

There are three helicopter simulators in the Wild Arctic building, each seating 59 people. The attraction accommodates up to 1,800 guests per hour when all three simulators are in operation. Handicapped access is provided. High-definition video laser disk projectors provide the visual stimulation, backed up by 1,200 watt, six-channel laser-disc sound systems.

Each cabin moves six ways—yaw, pitch, roll, heave, surge, and sway. Sometimes the cabin moves as much as nine feet, and in some directions it moves at speeds up to 24 inches per second.

Stepping from the simulator, guests enter a chilly passageway into a frozen wonderland of **Base Station Wild Arctic** with ice walls, where they will encounter some of the real animals that live at the North Pole.

Forget you're in Florida and buy into the story: The base station was built by modern scientists around the decrepit hull of a 150-year-old British exploration ship frozen in the ice for all these years, a unique vantage point for viewing Arctic sea life, including polar bears, beluga whales, walruses, and seals. The viewing position allows views of the animals above and below the water as they forage for food, dive, swim, and interact with Base Station workers.

High-tech equipment sits in and around the ship's remains with measuring devices next to old anchors and video receivers perched on old shipping crates. The base station makes extensive use of computers and touch-screen monitors to allow guests to communicate with reports from field researchers, and guests can use computers to communicate with research base "scientists." You'll be able to gauge your own ability to hold your breath against polar bears

(2 minutes), beluga whales (20 minutes), walruses (25 minutes), and the local champion, harbor seals (27 minutes).

The Arctic is a mystery to most people, assumed to be a frozen desert. Instead, it is a vast, ever-changing ocean, teeming with life and closely linked to the rest of the planet.

Among the animal stars of Wild Arctic are Klondike and Snow, a pair of polar bears. Abandoned by their mother at birth, the bears were hand-raised by experts at the Denver Zoo. Weighing about 1.3 pounds at birth, they already weighed several hundred pounds at the start of 1996 and were on their way to adult weights of about 1,800 pounds for males like Klondike and 900 pounds for females like Snow. Lack of space at the zoo demanded the bears be relocated, and in late 1995 the pair were brought to Orlando. They live in a special enclosure that includes a chilly pool stocked with fish (the cubs had never seen live food and had to learn how to fish for themselves). The bears' hunting instincts are further satisfied with morsels randomly hidden in nooks and crevices of the habitat.

**The missing bookstore.** Visitors who may have come to Sea World a number of years ago often made a special trip to the huge Harcourt Brace Jovanovich children's and science bookstore just outside the gates of the park. HBJ, which used to own Sea World, sold out to Anheuser-Busch and closed the bookstore, alas.

Polar bears are among the most beautiful and dangerous of animals, and are found only in the Arctic. The animals are born white; coats yellow in the summer sun, and turn white again after a spring molt. The hair itself is hollow to trap warm air, oil coats their fur, and a thick layer of fat provides insulation from the cold. When awake, polar bears spend much of their time stalking or feeding on seals, walruses, and sometimes even beluga whales.

Beluga whales, sometimes called "sea canaries," are born gray and turn white as they age, making a natural camouflage from predators among the icebergs and ice floes. They weigh from 1,500 to 3,300 pounds and measure from 10 to 15 feet. Like other toothed whales, belugas "echolocate," sending out sonar-like sounds to find breathing holes in the ice and to locate prey such as squid, octopi, shrimp, and a variety of other bottom-dwelling fish.

Walruses have one pair of flippers in front and a second in back. A thick layer of fat, called blubber, helps regulate heat loss.

Harbor seals are usually solitary, and rarely interact other than to mate. They prefer shallow areas of estuaries, rivers, and places where sandbars, beaches, or rocks are uncovered at low tide. Males can be as much as six feet in length and weigh 110 to 330 pounds; they feed on a diet of fish, shrimp, squid, and octopus. The seals are preyed upon by killer whales, sharks, Steller sea lions, and polar bears; young harbor seals are also sometimes prey to coyotes and eagles.

Children may explore polar bear dens (without the bears), or pop their heads through openings in a simulated ice floe, just as they saw the harbor seals doing before them.

**Life of a dolphin.**
Bottlenose dolphins
inhabit temperate and
tropical waters
throughout the world,
and are the most
common dolphin species
along the United States,
from Cape Cod to the
Gulf of Mexico. They live
in groups called pods or
herds, varying in size
from 2 to 15 animals; the
members of the pod rank
themselves and establish
dominance by smacking
their tails against the
water, butting heads,
and other actions.

The pool contains some 900,000 gallons of manufactured seawater, maintained at a cool 50 degrees in a two-story habitat that stands above and below the surface.

🔲**WOW** **Key West at Sea World.** Sea World's newest area showcases the island beauty and funky tropical charm of the southernmost city in the United States, with a mix of New England and Bahamian architecture, framed by stands of palm trees, hibiscus, and bougainvillea. Visitors stroll along river rock and pathways and board-walks; restaurants feature Caribbean cuisine. Street performers and vendors and perhaps a tightrope walker brighten the landscape.

The five-acre site on the park's east side, along-side "Manatees: The Last Generation," opened in mid-1996.

Naturalistic animal habitats allow up-close encounters and interaction with bottlenose dolphins, sleek stingrays, and one of the world's few saltwater-adapted reptiles, the sea turtle.

The largest section of the new area is **Dolphin Cove**, home to more than two dozen inquisitive bottlenose dolphins, the species most often seen in the coastal waters of the Gulf of Mexico and off Key West.

A wavemaker moves chilled seawater through the deep 600,000-gallon pool, creating tides that ebb and flow onto a wading beach where school

*Dolphin Cove, Sea World*
© *Sea World of Florida 1995*

groups and guided tours can wade into the surf to interact with the dolphins. There is also an area where guests can touch and feed the animals. And an underwater viewport allows glimpses of the dolphins below the surface.

At **Sea Turtle Point**, visitors can come up close to threatened and endangered species of sea turtle including the green, loggerhead, and hawksbill. The hunting of sea turtles was a major industry in Key West until federal laws protecting the animals were enacted in the 1970s.

**Stingray Lagoon**, a longtime favorite at Sea World, was nearly doubled in size as part of the new area. The pool features a variety of graceful rays, including cownose, Southern, roughtailed, Atlantic and yellow stingrays, as well as guitar fish. Visitors are encouraged to touch and feed the 200 or so rays. These fascinating creatures swim close to the edge of the pool where you can easily rub their rubbery skin and feel their fins; their poison sacs have been removed, and these stingrays are used to humans. A new nursery cove will exhibit newborn rays.

In Key West, many rays are found in the shallow waters surrounding the island. These fish, relatives of the shark, often burrow into the sand at the water's edge.

Also part of the new area is **Duval Street**, Sea World's version of the main street of Key West; the row includes shops, restaurants, and entertainment with a Southern Florida theme.

**WOW** **Shamu's Happy Harbor.** If you asked an active, adventurous kid to come up with the design for the ultimate outdoor playground, he or she might come up with something just like this. Shamu's Happy Harbor is, quite simply, one of the most spectacular playgrounds we have ever seen. In the learned opinions of the kids we asked, it stands head and shoulders over Fievel's Playground at Universal Studios; Honey, I Shrunk the Kids Movie Set Adventure at Disney-MGM Studios; and Tom Sawyer Island at the Magic Kingdom. We cannot imagine higher praise.

And higher is the word that comes to mind first. The central feature of the three-acre playground is a pair of gigantic nets that each extend about 40 feet in the air. The netting—actually double netting to prevent accidents—winds back and forth and makes turns like flights of stairs. Way up at the top is a tire swing, safely allowing youngsters to fly out as if into space.

The base of the net lets out into a long slide. Down below is **Pete's Water Maze**, a pirate ship with water cannon, a large sand play area, and other activities. On very hot days you might want to dress your children in bathing suits and let them cool off on the small wet slides there.

Parents can park at the bottom of the net and keep an eye on their kids as they climb; a snack bar serves the area. Most of the area is under a roof, blocking the sun and some rain.

If all of this is too rambunctious for your young ones, they can explore Boogie Bump Bay, a special area for small ones that includes bubble bikes, a mini-ball crawl, an air bounce, a fence maze, and many other activities appropriate to their size.

**Hold the dressing, please.** The favorite food for the manatees is romaine lettuce. The salad bill represents one of the bigger expenses of the park. If you're in the viewing area at one of several feeding times, watch as the manatees use their flippers almost as hands to grab the lettuce.

**Close enough for us.** The fish that you see in the manatee ponds that look at first glance like an alligator are something called alligator gar *(lepisosteus spatula).* From the side, they look ordinary but from the top and bottom they certainly could fool all but the bravest.

**WOW** **Manatees: The Last Generation?** Sea World is doing its part to answer the question it poses with a "no."

This is a fascinating 3½-acre attraction that winds through a river-like setting, filled with the gentle manatee giants as well as turtles, fish (including tarpon, gar, and snook), and birds. A seamless, 126-foot-long acrylic panel permits underwater views. Nearby is a nursing pool built for manatee mothers and their babies.

The area includes the **Manatee Theater**, which presents a special film using Bi-Vision technology with stunning underwater footage to make it seem as if you are completely surrounded by manatees.

The manatee is an air-breathing marine mammal; when it submerges, special muscles pinch the nostrils tightly closed to keep the water out. If you look carefully, you will also see sparse hair on the manatee's skin. Manatee calves nurse from their mothers.

In the wild, an adult manatee dines exclusively on plants; a full-grown specimen may eat each day as much as 100 pounds of sea grass, water hyacinths, and other types of plants.

All of the manatees on display have been rescued from their only natural enemy—man. Most have been injured by boat propellers, fishing nets, or plastic items thrown in the water by boaters. Adults are released back into the wild once they are able to survive there. Orphans will probably spend the rest of their lives in the park.

Also on exhibit are some of the vehicles and equipment used by Sea World's Beached Animal Rescue Station. Since 1973, the park's marine animal experts have rescued more than 100 manatees found seriously injured, ill, or orphaned in the wild. The crews are also called upon to help at dolphin and pygmy sperm whale strandings.

One of the slogans in the manatee area is "Extinction is forever. Endangered means we still have time."

**Pacific Point Preserve.** This re-created coastal setting for California sea lions and harbor and fur seals is a great way to get up-close and personal with some of the most amusing aquatic creatures we know.

Able to swim at birth, a harbor seal pup stays close to his mother for short nursing periods. The female's fat rich milk helps the pup to more than double its weight by the time it is four to eight weeks old. Then the pup is weened, goes its own way, and fends for itself.

You'll be able to purchase a package of smelt to feed the seals. Washing stations are nearby to help remove the smell of smelt from your hands.

**Anheuser-Busch Hospitality Center.** Sea World is owned by brewer Anheuser-Busch (which also owns Florida attractions Busch Gardens and Adventure Island), and the new Hospitality House offers a bit of the corporate message along with free samples of the company's beers.

Set amid tropical lagoons and lush foliage, the center includes a display of antique brewery equipment, including a turn-of-the-century Studebaker wagon used for hauling more than six tons of Budweiser beer behind a team of Clydesdale horses.

Adults can sample Anheuser-Busch products including Budweiser and Michelob beers. A separate counter offers soft drinks and snacks at the going Sea World prices.

**Bigfoot.** Think your feet are tired at the end of the day? A Clydesdale horseshoe measures 20 inches end-to-end and weighs about five pounds.

**Clod reins.** The driver of an eight-horse hitch pulling a beer wagon like the ones at Sea World must wrestle more than 40 pounds of reins to control the horses.

An outside terrace offers a quiet, shady spot for sampling and resting and also provides a good view of the associated gardens and waterfalls, and the Clydesdale paddocks close by.

Ten or more of the giant Clydesdale work horses are on display at any given time, either in the outside paddock or in indoor stalls near the Hospitality Center. These huge horses, the symbol of Anheuser-Busch, are sometimes dressed in elaborate harnesses and hitched to their famous wagon to march in procession through the park.

## Shows

**WOW! Mermaids, Myths & Monsters.** Sea World's spectacular new nighttime show that combines fireworks, lasers, laser-graphics animation and water-screen technology, choreographed in time to festive music.

Presented in the lagoon with visitors in the Atlantis Water Ski Stadium, the backdrop for projected images is a 60-foot screen of water.

**WOW! Window to the Sea.** A good introduction to the themes of Sea World, and worth a stop before you begin your day or for a break on a hot or rainy day. Window to the Sea is a multimedia overview of the Sea World park, including a tour of the facilities and a description of the naturalist's philosophy.

The show opens with multicolored dancing water fountains that move in time with music. When the curtain rises behind the water fountain, you see a computer room set with aquariums, consoles, and large display screens.

In a simulation of a global video linkup, the moderator introduces researchers who are participating in Sea World projects everywhere. In an interview with biologist Dr. Jeanie Clark, for example, the Alvin deep-sea submersible is introduced and we see the "discovery" of new deep-sea creatures.

All of the interviews are on tape, of course, but the production is so well

**Sea food.** Each dolphin eats about 20 pounds of fish a day, much of it as part of a performance reward during the show. Dolphin skin feels like a wet inner tube.

**Don't mess.** Stingrays are venomous versions of ray fish, which have a winglike pectoral fin which they use in swimming. They usually lie partly buried in the sand. If they're stepped on or otherwise touched, they will lash out with their tail and try to drive a spine into their attacker; the spines are attached to poison glands. The resulting wound can carry venom to the heart and nervous system of the victim, affecting its ability to breathe. In the United States, stingrays extend as far up the Atlantic Coast as Cape Hatteras.

**Lion school.** How do the trainers make a sea lion appear to talk? Watch for a trainer's inconspicuous snapping together of thumb and forefinger. This clues the sea lion to move its mouth while a recorded voice makes it appear to talk. Also, listen for repeated sentences that may include hidden vocal commands.

done you'll feel that a whole crew of world-renowned researchers is standing by to talk with you live.

**Whale and Dolphin Stadium.** As part of the celebration of Sea World's new Key West area, the **Key West Dolphin Fest** opened in mid-1996. The show is presented in a stadium facing a large tank. You'll see dolphins swimming, flipping, and splashing in a variety of stunts with their trainers and with a young volunteer and his or her family from the audience.

On the trainer's command the dolphins "dance" in time to the Key West–style music or stand up in the water to take a "bow" after they have done well. Among our favorite feats are Dolphin Powerboating, when two dolphins push a trainer around the tank by placing their noses on the bottom of his or her feet, and Dolphin Water Skiing, when the trainer, riding with one foot on each dolphin, holds a loose harness around each animal and goes for a ride.

Perhaps the most spectacular trick is the Bouncing Trainer, when the whale surfaces with a trainer balanced on its nose, pushing him or her about 20 feet into the air.

In addition to dolphins, this show features a pair of **pseudorca crassidens**, or false killer whales. Their beautiful, solid black color and smooth features make them unusual performers. These fast swimmers and fun performers are up to 25 feet long.

Before and after the show you can walk up to the glass on the tank, nose to nose with the dolphins, but visitors are asked not to touch or slap the side. Be aware that the stairs to the seats in the stadium are quite steep and might pose a difficulty for some people; the easiest seats are at the bottom, where you may get a bit wet, or at the top where you are the farthest away.

**WOW** **Hotel Clyde and Seamore.** If your hotel in Central Florida is anything like the cozy little inn run by sea lions Clyde and Seamore, we'd suggest you move on down the road. Sea World's aquatic clowns' fun-silly show at the 3,000-seat Sea Lion and Otter Stadium is one of the most popular attractions at the park.

The humans in this show are more than mere characters: they are skilled animal handlers who are chosen for both their animal knowledge and their acting skill. The stars are the sea lions, a tiny otter, and the only trained walrus we've ever seen.

Depending on the time of day and season, much of the stadium may be facing the sun; come early to find a shaded area. The first four rows are marked as splash zones; we're talking about little spurts, nothing like the tsunamis at Shamu Stadium. Early arrivals also get to watch the talented mime make fun of late arrivals, one of the most popular minishows at Sea World.

**Pelican Exhibit.** On the left side of the walkway toward the Atlantis Stadium is a small spectacular collection of pelicans. Among the birds you will see there are American white pelicans, denizens of marshy lakes and the Pacific and Texas coasts; they winter chiefly in coastal lagoons from Florida and southern California south to Panama. Unlike Florida brown pelicans, white pelicans do not dive for their food. Instead they fish in groups, capturing their prey cooperatively by forming a crescent and beating their wings and driving the fish into shallow water where they use their large pouched bills to catch and then swallow their meal.

**WOW** **Baywatch at Sea World.** The thrills-and-bikinis television series bursts from the small screen to the big lagoon.

David Hasselhoff, who plays Lieutenant Mitch Buchannon on the TV show narrates the show and sings the theme song. As guests enter the 5,200-seat Atlantis Water Ski Stadium on Sea World's 17-acre lagoon, they encounter what seems to be a typical lazy stretch of beach, inhabited only by a few rollerblading kids and beachcombers. But within moments, the calm is broken as a reckless speed boater crashes into a buoy and is thrown into the water; a dramatic rescue effort follows.

Baywatch at Sea World bombards guests with an onslaught of jet ski, water ski, and aerial stunts, acrobatics, pyrotechnics, and musical numbers.

**WOW** **Shamu: World Focus.** The majestic, mysterious killer whale mostly lives in a world unto itself, traveling in pods from frigid waters off the coast

**Backstage at the ski show.** After you've seen this show once, come back for the next showing, but view it from the gift shop in the middle of the walkway over the lagoon. Here you can see some of the backstage preparations for some of the special events.

**Watered down.** The first four rows of the stadium, especially toward the center of the arena, are the wet seats. The views from anywhere are good, but the best seats are mid-stadium within the first 10 rows.

**Rock fish.** The show opening involves sea lions and an otter who appear to perform all by themselves. They're not that smart: their trainers are actually hidden behind rocks high up on the set. Look carefully and you will be able to see fish for the animals fly out of the rocks where the trainers wait.

**Whale school.** Many of the whale's actions are prompted by trainers' hand signals. For example, when the trainer holds up an open hand toward the audience, the whales face the audience and open their mouths. Also listen carefully for the faint sound of high-pitched training whistles during the show.

**Whale wisdom.** Whales are aquatic mammals and not fish, though they are good swimmers. Killer whales can remain submerged up to 12 minutes before surfacing for air. Newborn killer whales weigh about 300 pounds. Star of the show Shamu is 17 feet long and weighs about 5,000 pounds.

By the way, Shamu receives a physical examination once every two weeks including a blood test and measurements.

of Iceland to warmer climates near the tip of South Africa. On islands near Argentina, researchers have observed them hunting in packs, and have called them the "wolves of the sea."

But killer whales have also shown an unusual capacity for sharing special relationships with man.

The new main show at Sea World is Shamu: World Focus. The 5,200-seat Shamu Stadium, just down the hill from the Atlantis Water Ski Stadium and on the same side of the lagoon, was built around a 5-million-gallon saltwater tank that is home to the entire Shamu family of killer whales, including Baby Namu.

Hosted by actress Jane Seymour, the show combines rare video footage with live action featuring the Shamu family of killer whales. The video show is presented on the large ShamuVision screen at center stage; members of the audience will share top billing with Shamu as cameras pan the seats. The main television camera is to the right as you are seated and most of the people chosen to be up on the screen are on the left side of the stadium.

But the stars of the show are the black-and-white members of the Shamu family. The youngest killer whale weighs in at a mere 1,000 pounds, while the largest weighs some five tons—10,000 pounds.

Shamu is a willing teacher in the new show, demonstrating his sensitivity to touch as the video screen shows whales at a place called Rubbing Rock Beach in Johnson Strait where killer whales rub against the stones.

The best seat in the stadium—if you don't mind getting wet—is in the first six rows. Here you will be able to see under the water through the glass wall of the tank, as well as the show up above. If you prefer to stay dry, sit toward the front of the second bank of seats, in the middle of the stadium. You'll have a good view of the video screen and of the platform where the whales frequently beach themselves during the show.

Don't say we didn't warn you: The lower 15 rows are marked as the splash zone. That may seem like a bit of overkill—it does not seem possible that a whale can send water up that high over the glass. And in fact, for the first three-quarters of the show only those brave souls in the very closest seats are likely to be splashed by one of the animals as it passes by.

But don't congratulate yourself too soon. The conclusion of the show is one wet finale. Wet as in water that washes over the top of the glass in a spectacular wave and soaks the people in those front 15 rows. Water. Wave. Soaks. 55-degree saltwater. Actually, it's two waves. Get the picture?

One problem with the stadium shows at Sea World is that when one of the presentations lets out, a large number of people are deposited onto walkways leading toward the restaurants. If you are planning to eat after a show, head directly to a restaurant or even consider sending someone ahead to place an order.

**WOW** **Shamu: Close Up!** Sea World's new 1.7-million gallon killer whale research facility allows visitors to get closer than ever to Shamu and his friends. It also allows scientists further opportunities to study the development of killer whales. The habitat is located alongside the Shamu stadium and includes shallows that will encourage the whales to engage in some of their favorite activities: back scratching and tummy rubbing. Special devices include a huge scale, capable of measuring weights up to 40,000 pounds in five-pound increments.

**WOW** **Big Splash Bash.** Sea World's latest aquatic song-and-dance extravaganza is presented at the new **Nautilus Theatre.** The show features a cast of 14 performers sharing the stage with fountains, fire, fog, bubble tubes, a rain curtain, and even a flood. The show moves from a 1920s Coney Island cabana with period songs to a 1990s beach party and the Beach Boys to the Lost Continent of Atlantis and the Bermuda Triangle.

The 2,400-seat theater has been rebuilt, enclosed, and air-conditioned.

**South Seas Revue.** The "Hawaiian Rhythms" troupe performs songs and dances of the Polynesian isles on the beach at Atlantis Lagoon. Visitors sit on wooden benches over the sand, in front of a palm-shaded theater. Along with the music you will learn a little about Polynesian culture and the music of different locations.

If you're the uninhibited type, you can join hula dancers—male and female—on the stage for an impromptu hula lesson.

## Continuous Viewing Exhibits

A number of Sea World exhibits are open all day without scheduled events. You can enter them for a quick walk-through or a leisurely study. The premier facilities of this type at Sea World include Key West at Sea World, Terrors of the Deep, Penguin Encounter, and Tropical Reef. You'll see a number of other interesting places as you walk through Sea World, including a tropical rain forest, Stingray Lagoon, Harbor Seal Community, and more.

**WOW** **Terrors of the Deep.** A unique collection of dangerous sea creatures. You will find yourself immersed in the secret hiding places of menacing eels, venomous fish, hungry barracuda, and . . . sharks. The creatures in this exhibit all can be potentially dangerous, it is true, but the message of this exhibit is clear: "Respect them, don't kill them." For example, sharks have a bad reputation for attacking humans, but there are few documented instances of wanton attack. As with most injurious encounters between

**Shark tunnels.** The clear viewing tunnels can support the weight of 372 elephants, which is more than strong enough to keep you and the 450 tons of water above you apart.

One of the scenes from the film *Jaws 3-D* was shot inside the shark tunnel.

**Bad PR.** Sharks have gotten a great deal of bad PR. Two times more people die of bee stings each year than succumb to shark attacks.

**Last exit.** If you are claustrophobic and choose to avoid the tunnel, simply exit to your left through the unmarked door beside the tunnel entrance. You can wait for the rest of your party at the end of the line.

**Hungry sharks?** Sharks eat only about once a week. Check with the park for the current feeding schedule; if you can make it, you will understand what the term *feeding frenzy* really means. This is not an experience for the squeamish.

humans and sea creatures, these attacks usually are the result of mistaken identity: the human was mistaken for food.

A short video at the start of this exhibit gives you some excellent background; don't rush through. The shark movie and aquarium portion of the show are timed to give you about 25 minutes to view the tunnel area and the other displays. If you rush through these sections you'll have to stand in line waiting your turn for the shark theater. The entire show takes about 40 minutes, including the film and the walk-through.

Sea World's education department occasionally schedules sleepovers within the tunnels for school groups.

The first aquarium in this exhibit focuses on eels—more than 500 of them in a 10-foot-deep tank full of artificial coral that looks like the real thing but is easier to maintain.

One of the really interesting facets of this exhibit is the acrylic tunnel at the bottom of the aquarium that allows you to walk through the tank to view the "terrors." Among the creatures you'll see are moray eels (some more than six feet long), spotted morays, and purple-mouthed eels.

Grouper, snapper, lookdowns, and jacks—predatory fish native to the same ecosystems inhabited by eels—also are housed there.

A high-tech system simulates the currents and wave action of the reef, and a single light source is placed to simulate the sun.

After the walk through the first tunnel, you next encounter venomous lionfish and scorpionfish. The graceful lionfish will captivate you with their movement and the colors of the fins that hide their dangerous spines. The scorpionfish show their ability to camouflage themselves as they blend in with the sand and wait for an unsuspecting meal to swim overhead.

A separate tank showcases clown fishes, with beautiful but highly poisonous spines. Also on display are nasty surgeon fish. When agitated, they will sweep their tails and threaten antagonists with their spines; a swipe from one of the razor-sharp extensions can seriously slash another fish or injure a fisherman attempting to remove them from nets or hooks.

There's also a collection of barracuda, creatures that ordinarily feast on fish, squid, and shrimp, attacking with a single swift strike at speeds of as much as 28 miles per hour. Viewed from the side the barracuda is hard to miss, but from the front the slender fish is nearly invisible. Barracuda attacks on humans are rare and accidental. Murky water makes it hard to see and barracuda are apt to confuse shiny objects such as jewelry for fish; swimmers in tropical waters are advised not to be between the fish and the sunny surface of the water.

The final stop on the journey comes when you descend 15 feet below the surface to the territory of the shark through a six-inch-thick clear acrylic tube. You'll travel the 125-foot-long shark-filled habitat on a PeopleMover, as dozens of nurse, brown, bull, and sand tiger sharks swim overhead and in front.

Among the shark skeletons on display is a set of jaw bones from a 16½-foot male great white caught in western Australia.

**Hot house.** When it's snowing in the penguin exhibit, these fascinating animals are swimming in 55-degree water. That's cold to us, but compared to the 32-degree refrigerated air of their enclosure, it is relatively warm.

**Penguin and eggs.** If you see groups of penguins huddled along the back wall of the exhibit, chances are they are hatching eggs. Sea World has a very successful penguin breeding program.

**Penguin Encounter.** The largest and most technically advanced exhibit of its kind, it is the home to hundreds of penguins (from the Antarctic) and alcids (from the Arctic). The science center goes beyond entertainment to educate guests about the need to protect and preserve polar life.

So realistic that it even snows inside, this exhibit moves you past living Arctic and Antarctic displays on a 120-foot PeopleMover. Tempered glass provides an unobstructed and unobtrusive view above and below the water of stately king penguins, gentle gentoos, and bounding rockhoppers.

At the alcid exhibit, you come face-to-face with more than 100 puffins, buffleheads, smews, and murres from the Arctic. While not related to penguins, they are considered their ecological counterparts.

Sea World animal experts match temperature and daylight as closely as possible to the animals' native territory so that their seasons change as they would if they were living in the wild.

After the ride past the live exhibits, you enter a hall with many fascinating, lighted displays. Press on the kid-sized handprints within each display to hear a recorded message about what you are seeing.

The largest penguins at Sea World of Florida are the king penguins from Antarctica; at Sea World California they have a colony of emperor penguins, which are the largest in the world.

And be sure to stop at the Sea World Learning Center just past the moving walkway. A globe depicts Antarctic explorers. You will see Scott's expedition of 1910 to 1913, and his somewhat friendly adversary Amundsen's from

**Pool world.** The Atlantis Lagoon covers 17 acres and has an average depth of 12 feet. The deepest part of the lagoon is 20 feet.

**Lock and run.** Pay lockers are located to the right of the entrance next to Key Hole Photo and are offered at the rate of $1 per use. Leave things here you don't want to carry all day.

1910 to 1912. Further back is Drake's route around South America from 1578 to 1579, and Cooke's expedition from 1712 to 1715 which was the first known circumnavigation of Antarctica—marked on the map as Terra Incognita.

**Tropical Reef and Caribbean Tide Pool.** More than 1,000 tropical fish live in the 160,000-gallon exhibit, the largest South Pacific coral reef display in the United States. The Caribbean Tide Pool gives you close-up views of tropical fish and invertebrates such as sea urchins, crabs, starfish, and anemones. Seventeen smaller aquariums contain exhibits including sea horses, octopi, and clown fish.

**Sky Tower.** This 400-foot needle tower can be seen from miles around Sea World, marking the park location and helping you find your way in. Once inside the park, you can ride a sit-down, circular elevator to the top for a panoramic view of Sea World and much of Central Florida.

Admission to this ride is not included in the daily park pass. The elevator may not operate during heavy winds or other bad weather.

Take your Sea World map on this 5½-minute ride; it will help you orient yourself to the layout of the park as well as other attractions in the area such as Disney World, which you can see from your rotating, 400-foot perch.

There is rarely a long line at this ride, even though you must buy a separate ticket and wait your turn for the elevator. We estimate the average wait is between 5 and 10 minutes.

**KEY:**

🍴 = Fast food

🍸 = Pub

🏠 = Full-service restaurant

## Eating Your Way Through Sea World

In this section we offer a quick reference to Sea World restaurants. While we give price ranges, you should consider these approximate because food prices are subject to change. All Sea World restaurants offer a range of Pepsi soft drinks from about $1 to $1.55. A good treat on a hot day is a frozen frosty lemonade.

In general, Sea World food offerings are a bit simpler than you will find at Epcot or Universal. Menus are more limited (fewer different offerings at each restaurant), but the food generally is of high quality, and the portions are large.

By the way, watch out for marauding seagulls too. They are quite capable of swooping down and grabbing some of your food if you are eating at one of the outdoor restaurants.

 **Spinnaker's Cafe.** Hamburgers and sandwiches, $5 to $6. Interesting salads and desserts, $2. Separate nonsmoking section.

The large inside dining room is decorated in a nautical motif including ships' lanterns and flags.

The California Light (offered in several places throughout Sea World) is a turkey breast sandwich with sprouts and cheese. The clam chowder is acceptable ($3), and the fruit salad is a cool alternative to hamburgers.

The real forte at Spinnaker, however, is desserts. Select from Black Forest cake, key lime pie, cheesecake, strawberries and cream, and other delectables for about $2 each.

**Mama Stella's Italian Kitchen.** Near the Penguin area, this pleasant restaurant offers spaghetti for about $5 and pizza for about $4. You can also purchase a garden salad for $2 and garlic bread for $1.

Enter this attractive restaurant via a weathered wooden boardwalk that overlooks a small landscaped lagoon full of flowering shrubs and trees. Seabirds are everywhere around this area, which extends around three sides of the restaurant. Indoor seating is also available, although the noise level of active children may drive you back outdoors.

For a full taste of this restaurant's offerings, try the Italian sampler platter, or order eggplant Parmesan, spaghetti, pizza, or salads.

At the outside corners of this restaurant, find frosted fruit coolers and soft serve ice cream. Ice cold fruit flavored drinks range from $2 to $5; soft serve ice cream treats are $2 to $3.

**Mango Joe's.** Chicken or beef fajitas, fried fish, and club sandwiches, priced from about $5 to $7. Children's meals include chicken or steak fingers served with french fries for about $4. The chicken fajitas at Mango Joe's are quite good. About those "fingers": they are grilled pieces of meat, not fried; we'd vote them among the best snacks at the park.

**Bimini Bay Cafe.** Seafood sandwiches ($7 to $8) and platters ($10 to $13). Entree salads and fruit, $6 to $8. For a different appetizer, try the Key West Conch chowder. Child's sandwich plate, $4. Domestic and imported beer about $3.

Pleasant Polynesian or tropical atmosphere with bright "sunshine" colors. The glass-enclosed dining room overlooks Atlantis Lagoon and offers a cool getaway for lunch; the tasteful decor has the feel of a hotel or resort restaurant rather than your typical theme park eatery.

Outside the Bimini, beside the Hawaiian Rhythms show, you'll find a large kiosk that offers drinks and very light snacks. Buffalo wings or fish fingers, $6; french fries, $2. Coffee, beer, and mixed drinks. A small stage nearby sometimes features musical performances.

**Aloha! Polynesian Luau Dinner and Show.** Polynesian luau and show, adults, $30; ages 8 to 12, $20; ages 3 to 7, $10.

A South Seas adventure. Seating begins at 6:35 P.M. and is limited. Reservations required. Call (800) 227-8048 or (407) 351-3600, or stop by the information desk to the left of the main Sea World entrance.

The meal varies but usually consists of salads, seafood such as mahimahi with piña colada sauce, pork loin, sweet and sour chicken, rice, vegetables, and dessert. One cocktail or beer is included in the price of the meal.

🍴 **Dinner with Shamu.** A "backstage" buffet with Shamu and animal trainers at Shamu Stadium. Offerings include beef bourguignonne, chicken Dijon, mahimahi with piña colada sauce, salads, desserts, and beverages. A children's menu includes macaroni and cheese casserole. Adults $24.95, and children (3 to 12) $9.95. Seating is limited; tickets are sold inside the front entrance.

🍴 **The Smokehouse.** Chicken and ribs. Entrees, $5 to $7.

Picnic-style barbecue platters served with chicken or ribs, coleslaw, and roll. Umbrella seating available dockside overlooking the Atlantis Lagoon. Building has a weathered, seaside appearance; umbrellas are an attractive yellow. A pleasant place to rest and eat. You even have a back-door view of the ski show from the lagoon-side seats.

You can watch chicken and ribs being grilled through a large window beside the serving line. The chicken and ribs are slow hickory smoked, then grilled just before they are served. The chicken will have a slight pink color inside even though it's fully cooked.

You will be drawn to this restaurant by the smell of wood smoke and barbecue sauce during meal times. Stacks of split hardwood outside the restaurant add to the atmosphere.

🍴 **Waterfront Sandwich Grill.** Hamburgers and sandwiches, $4 to $6. Child's plate, $4.

Adjacent to Atlantis Lagoon, behind The Smokehouse. It shares dockside seating with The Smokehouse and offers a good view of the Sky Tower and Atlantis Lagoon. Inside is an attractive nautical layout.

🍴 **Chicken 'n Biscuit.** Fried or baked chicken, $4 to $6. Child's menu. Domestic beer, about $3.

A large chicken emporium, offering fried or baked birds. The indoor seating is somewhat close together, and when crowded the restaurant is a little noisy. Take your food outside when you can.

# V
# Dinner Shows


## Chapter 15
## Dinner Shows


If you're on vacation, why should the entertainment stop when you sit down to eat?

That's the thinking behind one of the fastest-growing industries in Orlando and the surrounding area—the dinner show. You can eat a Chinese meal while being entertained by Asian acrobats; you can pull apart a chicken with your bare hands while knights on horseback joust for your entertainment.

There are more than a dozen major dinner shows inside and outside Walt Disney World. In our experience, nearly every one of them has something to offer.

Prices for adults generally range from about $25 to $40 and usually include all courses and drinks; be aware that almost every show offers discounts from the listed price (you'll find some coupons in this book). You may be able to buy cut-rate tickets to dinner shows from ticket booths in hotels or on tourist roads; shop around a bit for the best deal.

One word of warning: most of the shows try to pad their nightly take with all sorts of appeals, including photos taken before you enter, photos taken at your table, souvenir booklets, flags, and other items. If you're not in the market for extra trinkets, just say no.

Call for hours of performance for any show; at the busiest seasons, some theaters will have two shows in a night.

### Within Walt Disney World

The dinner shows at Walt Disney World resorts generally require advance reservations and purchase of tickets. Call (407) 934-7639 for reservations; most times of the year you'll need to do this weeks or even months before arrival. Guests at hotels within the park get a head start for reservations, too. Prices and times are subject to change.

**Hoop-Dee-Doo Musical Revue.** Pioneer Hall in Disney's Fort Wilderness Resort. (407) 939-3463, or (407) 824-2803 on the day of the show.

A Western singing and dancing show, featuring all-you-can-eat chicken, ribs, corn, and strawberry shortcake. This is a hugely popular, raucous, thigh-slappin', hee-haw of a show; if that's the sort of entertainment you like, this is a fine example. Entertainment includes piano and banjo music, terrible jokes and gags, and an audience-participation washboard finale. Mixed in is a bit of improvisational humor as cast members sing songs about guests in the audience.

The large hall has two levels; the best seats are at the front of the balcony or a few rows back from the stage on the main level. Seats are assigned at the time of the reservation.

Veterans observe that although this is an all-you-can-eat adventure, the courses (including fried chicken, BBQ ribs, and strawberry shortcake) come and go pretty quickly and there is a show to watch, too. Disney also trimmed a half hour off the starting time of the late show by shortening the overall performance and turn-around times a bit. Seatings at 5, 7:15, and 9:30 P.M. Adults, $36; children (3 to 11), $18.

If you're not already at Fort Wilderness as a guest and plan to use Disney transportation, you'll need to leave about an hour before your show time to make connections to the resort and walk to the Pioneer Hall, which is located near the beach on Bay Lake. There is also a parking lot at Fort Wilderness if you have a car.

**Polynesian Luau.** Disney's Polynesian Resort. (407) 939-3463 or (407) 824-4321.

An all-you-can-eat feast featuring barbecue pork ribs, roasted chicken, mahimahi, fruit, and drinks including frozen piña coladas, accompanied by island singers, hula dancers, fire acts, and other entertainment.

There's a partial roof over the dining room, with the stage open to the sky; mosquito repellent is worth adding to your preshow preparations in bug season. The show is much more dramatic when it is dark; the early show in summer is presented while it is still light. (By the way, it is possible to see portions of the show from the courtyard of the Polynesian Resort without paying for a seat and meal.)

Make reservations early. Guests at park resorts can reserve seats when they reserve their rooms; others can make reservations within 30 days of the day of the show.

Seatings are at 6:45 and 9:30 P.M. Adults, $33; juniors (12 to 20), $25; and children (3 to 11), $17.

**Mickey's Tropical Luau.** Disney's Polynesian Resort. (407) 824-4321. A Polynesian revue for the short set, featuring Disney characters dancing along with guys and girls in grass skirts. Presented at the Polynesian Resort daily at 4:30 P.M. A full dinner is included. Adults, $29; juniors (12 to 20), $22; and children (3 to 11), $13.

## Nearby Walt Disney World

**American Gladiators Orlando Live!** West Irlo Bronson Highway (U.S. 192), two miles east of I-4. (407) 390-0000, (800) 228-8534. A live 90-minute show based on the wild "sports" featured in the television show of the same name. Events include The Assault, Joust, Breakthrough & Conquer, Powerball, The Wall, and Whiplash. Dinner and show: Adults, $39.95; children (2 to 12), $21.50. Show only: Adults, $27.95; children, $15.95.

**Arabian Nights Dinner Attraction.** 6225 West Irlo Bronson Highway (U.S. 192), east of the intersection with I-4 in Kissimmee. (407) 239-9221. (800) 553-6116. A prime rib dinner at the Palace of the Horses. One of Central Florida's largest live dinner shows, including more than 100 horses in a 1,200 seat indoor arena. Adults, $34.95; children (3 to 11), $19.95. *Discount coupon in this book.*

**Capone's Dinner & Show.** 4740 West Irlo Bronson Highway (U.S. 192). (407) 397-2378. A musical comedy review with guns and an unlimited Italian buffet with beer, wine, sangria, and Rum Runners. Adults, $29.50; seniors, $19.95; children (12 and under), $14.75. *Discount coupon in this book.*

**Medieval Times.** 4510 West Irlo Bronson Highway (U.S. 192), near Route 441 in Kissimmee. (407) 396-1518 or (800) 229-8300. Come to dinner as the guests of the royal family in the 11th century. The feast includes spectacular pageantry, dramatic horsemanship, swordplay, falconry, sorcery, and a jousting contest. The meal—which is served without silverware—includes a hearty vegetable soup, whole roasted chicken, spare ribs, potato, and dessert, plus beer, wine, and soft drinks.

Medieval Times is one of the old-timers among dinner theaters, dating back 11 years in Florida, 25 years in Spain, and nearly 1,000 years in history. Twenty-five years ago, Jose De Montaner converted his farm in Majorca, Spain, into a barbecue dinner show and then a medieval-theme show for tourists. There are now Medieval Times dinner attractions in Buena Park, California (near Disneyland); Lyndhurst, New Jersey; Schaumburg, Illinois; Dallas, Texas; and Toronto, Canada.

The troupe includes more than 30 horses and several dozen players, "slaves," and "serving wenches." New members of the Medieval Times troupe serve a four-to-six month apprenticeship, improving their riding, martial arts, and tumbling skills.

The entertainment takes place in the 1,000-seat Great Ceremonial Hall; seats are not reserved—arrive early for the best seats (down low at midcourt). The show begins with some demonstration of horse training and riding skills, including the Carousel, a display of intricate horse maneuvers. Practice sessions for the fights begin with wooden sticks and progress to the real weapons used in the show, including five-pound, one-handed swords and 18-pound axes.

The tournament games begin with knights on horseback with lances galloping at full speed toward three-inch hoops suspended from posts; the next challenge is horseback javelin toss. The final confrontation pits knights against each other in jousting tournaments and hand-to-hand fighting.

Alongside the theater is the **Medieval Life** exhibit, an extraordinary collection of artifacts brought over from Spain and other parts of Europe; see the write-up in the attractions section of this book.

Adults, $31.95; children (3 to 12), $21.95. Tickets include admission to Medieval Life. *Discount coupon in this book.*

**Wild Bill's Wild West Dinner Show at Fort Liberty.** 5260 U.S. 192 in Kissimmee. (407) 351-5151, (800) 883-8181. Step back into the Old West. The dinner show, hosted by Miss Kitty, features western specialty acts, native Comanche Indians, and the comical soldiers of E Troop. Also featuring the **Brave Warrior Adventure Wax Museum** and a **Wild West Trading Post.** Adults, $31.95; children (3 to 11), $19.95. *Discount coupon in this book.*

## International Drive/Universal Studios Area

**Aloha Polynesian Luau at Sea World.** 7007 Sea World Drive. (407) 363-2195, (800) 227-8048 in Florida. Eat, drink, and be entertained by the Hawaiian Rhythms troupe. (Located at the perimeter of Sea World, you do not require a ticket to the park to enter the luau.) Adults, $29.95; juniors (8 to 12), $19.95; children (3 to 7), $9.95. Served from 6:30 to 8:30 P.M. nightly. *Discount coupon in this book.*

**King Henry's Feast.** 8984 International Drive, Orlando. (407) 351-5151, (800) 883-8181. Dine in the Great Hall and be entertained by dueling knights, magicians, and performers on stage. Your meal, which includes tankards of beer, wine, or soft drinks, is brought by singing serving wenches. Adults, $31.95; children, $19.95. *Discount coupon in this book.*

**Mark Two Dinner Theater.** 3376 Edgewater Drive. (407) 843-6275, (800) 726-6275. Live Broadway shows, preceded by buffet dinner featuring prime rib. Open Wednesdays through Sundays; some matinee performances. Tickets are priced from $32.50 to $37.50. Tables surround the stage on three sides; the closest tables are rows LA, LB, MB, MC, RA, and RB.

**Sleuths Mystery Dinner Show.** 7508 Republic Drive, off International Drive behind Wet 'n Wild. (407) 363-1985, (800) 393-1985. Step into the scene of the crime. Mix with the characters, search for clues, and help track down the culprit. You'll also eat dinner along the way. One, two, or three shows per night. Adults, $35.99; children (3 to 11), $24.33. *Discount coupon in this book.*

## Disney Character Meals

For reservations at character meals at Walt Disney World properties, call (407) 939-7741.

**Aladdin's Breakfast Adventure.** Aladdin, Princess Jasmine, Jafar, and the Genie, at the Soundstage Restaurant at Disney-MGM Studios each morning from 8:30 to 10:30 A.M. Adults, $12.95; children, $7.95. Reservations necessary and ticket to Studios required.

**Baskerville's Character Breakfast Buffet, Baskerville's Character Dinner.** Grosvenor Resort. Breakfast offered 8 A.M. to 10 A.M. on Tuesdays, Thursdays, and Saturdays; $8.95 for adults and $4.95 for children. Dinner Wednesdays featuring prime rib buffet; $14.95 for adults and $5.95 for children.

**Cape May Café Breakfast.** Admiral Goofy and crew at the Beach Club Resort, from 7:30 to 11 A.M. daily. Adults, $12.95; children, $7.95.

**Character Breakfast Stampede with Chip 'n Dale.** A Disney world at Artist Point in the Wilderness Lodge hotel, served daily from 7:30 to 11:30 A.M. Adults, $12.95; children, $7.95.

**Chef Mickey's Breakfast à la Disney.** Seatings at 7:30, 9, and 10:30 A.M. Adults, $12.95; children (3 to 11), $7.95.

**Chef Mickey's.** With a name like that, you probably can guess who shows up for dinner between 5:30 and 10 P.M. nightly. Disney Village Marketplace. Menu items range from about $12 to $23.

**Contemporary Café Rescue Rangers Character Breakfast and Dinner Buffet.** Breakfast from 7:30 to 11:30 A.M. at the Contemporary Resort with your friends Goofy, Pluto, and a few others. Adults, $12.95; children (3 to 11), $7.95. Dinner from 5 to 9:30 P.M. Adults, $16.95; children, $7.95.

**Concourse Steakhouse Character Breakfast.** Winnie-the-Pooh, Tigger, Eeyore, and breakfast, from 7 to 11:30 A.M. Adults, $12.95; children $7.95.

**Country Fair Character Breakfast.** Hilton. Sundays from 8:30 to 10:30 A.M. Adults, $14.95; children, $9.95.

**Disney's Polynesian Resort.** Commune with Minnie and others at the Papeete Bay Verandah from 7:30 to 10:30 A.M. Reservations suggested. (407) 824-1391. Adults, $10.95; children (3 to 11), $7.95. Sunday brunch 11 A.M. to 2 P.M. Adults, $14.95; children (3 to 11), $7.95.

**Disney's Yacht and Beach Club Resorts.** Ahoy, it's Admiral Goofy and his crew for breakfast at the Cape May Café, from 7:30 to 11 A.M. Adults, $12.95; children (3 to 11), $7.95.

**Fireworks Factory Bang Up Breakfast.** Roger Rabbit and friends, with seatings at 7:30, 9, and 10:30 A.M. Adults, $12.95; children, $7.95.

**Garden Grill Character Experience.** Breakfast, lunch, and dinner at The Land pavilion of Epcot Center. Breakfast from 8:30 to 11 A.M., from 7:30 A.M. on Tuesdays and Fridays. Adults, $14.95; children, $7.95. Lunch from 11:15 A.M. to 4 P.M. Adults, $16.95; children, $9.95. Dinner from 4 to 7:30 P.M. Adults, $16.95; children, $9.95. Epcot admission ticket required.

**Garden Grove Café Character Dinner.** Rafiki and Timon appear Wednesdays and Saturdays, and Winnie-the-Pooh and Tigger visit on Thursdays. Order from menu.

**Garden Grove Character Breakfast.** Walt Disney World Swan. Wednesdays and Saturdays, 8 to 11 A.M. Buffet at $12.50 for adults and $6.95 for children; menu items also offered.

**Harry's Safari Bar & Grille Character Brunch.** Walt Disney World Dolphin. Sundays from 8:30 A.M. to noon. Adults, $15.50; children, $9.25.

**Liberty Tree Tavern Character Dinner.** Daily from 4 P.M. Adults, $19.50; children, $9.95. Magic Kingdom admission required.

**Mickey's Tropical Luau.** Daily dinner at the Tangaroa Terrace of Disney's Polynesian Resort at 4:30 P.M. Adults, $30; children (3 to 11), $14.

**Minnie's Menehune Character Breakfast.** Buffet at 'Ohana, Polynesian Resort, from 7:30 to 11:30 A.M. daily. Adults, $12.95; children, $7.95.

**1900 Park Fare Character Breakfast Buffet.** Disney's Grand Floridian Beach Resort. Breakfast with Mary Poppins and friends, from 7:30 to 11:30 A.M. daily. Adults, $14.95; children, $9.95.

**1900 Park Fare Character Dinner Buffet.** Buffet dinner with Mickey and Minnie from 5:30 to 9 P.M. daily; adults, $19.95; children, $9.95.

**Olivia's Cafe Breakfast with Winnie the Pooh.** Disney Vacation Club. Sundays and Wednesdays from 7:30 to 10:30 A.M. $11.50 for adults and $7.50 for children.

**Once Upon a Time Breakfast.** King Stefan's Banquet Hall in Cinderella Castle, with Cinderella, Captain Hook, and friends. Daily from 8 to 10 A.M. $14.95 for adults and $7.95 for children. Magic Kingdom ticket required. Reservations required.

**Ristorante Carnevale Character Brunch.** WDW Dolphin. Sundays only, from 8:30 A.M. to 12:30 P.M. Adults, $14.95; children, $7.95.

**Soundstage Character Breakfast.** A daily buffet with characters from *Aladdin* and *Pocahontas* at the Soundstage Restaurant within the Disney-MGM Studios. Daily from 8:30 to 10:30 A.M., and from 7:30 A.M. on Sundays and Wednesdays for Surprise Mornings guests. Adults, $12.95; children, $7.95. Admission ticket to Disney-MGM Studios required.

**Under the Sea Breakfast.** At the Coral Reef Restaurant at The Living Seas Pavilion, featuring Mickey in the tank in diving equipment plus Minnie and friends. Daily from 8:30 to 10:30 A.M. $14.95 for adults and $7.95 for children. Admission ticket to Epcot required.

**Watercress Café Character Breakfast.** Buena Vista Palace, Hotel Plaza. Sundays from 8 to 10:30 A.M. Order from menu.

**Wilderness Lodge Character Breakfast at Artist Point.** Goofy, Pluto, Chip 'n Dale, and friends for a buffet breakfast daily from 7:30 A.M. to 11:30 A.M. Adults, $13.50; children, $8.25.

## Arenas and Legitimate Theaters

**Bob Carr Performing Arts Centre.** A 2,500-seat theater located in downtown Orlando's Centroplex, used for touring Broadway shows, opera and ballet companies, and other performers. For event information, call (407) 849-2001.

**Citrus Bowl Stadium.** Seating for 70,000 for sporting events (including the Florida Citrus Bowl Classic on New Year's Day), rock concerts, and other events. Located west of downtown Orlando. (407) 849-2500.

**Civic Theatre of Central Florida.** Several small theaters used for off-Broadway-type and family theater productions. Located in Orlando's Loch Haven Park. (407) 896-7365.

**Tupperware Convention Center.** One of the area's most popular venues for big-name entertainment, at the Tupperware headquarters on the Orange Blossom Trail in Kissimmee. (407) 847-1802.

# VI
# Golf, Horses, Biking, Major League Spring Training, and Bungee Jumping

## Chapter 16
## Sports and Recreation Within Walt Disney World

Depending upon your point of view, Walt Disney World is either three theme parks surrounded by 99 holes of golf, or a country club so huge it includes three theme parks.

Either way, it's one version of golfing heaven—ever on the search for a cute phrase, Disney has taken to calling it "The Magic Linkdom." It's a way for mom and dad and even junior to come to Walt Disney World without having to spend all their time in the company of a bunch of cartoon mice.

But wait, perhaps you prefer tennis, horseback riding, swimming, fishing, biking . . . just about any popular form of recreation can be found within the park boundaries.

### Walt Disney World Golf Courses

There are five championship-level 18-hole golf courses within the World, plus the 9-hole Oak Trail practice course. Two of the courses are good enough to be stops on the PGA Tour.

Greens fees are $95 including a required cart for the five 18-hole courses; twilight rates (after 3 P.M.) are $45. At Oak Trail, a walking course, the fee is $23 for adults for 9 holes and $31 for 18 holes. Pro Shop: (407) 824-2288.

For information and reservations, call the Walt Disney World Master Starter at (407) 824-2270 between 8 A.M. and 5 P.M.; guests at resorts in the park can reserve tee times 30 days ahead of time, while others can request a starting time seven days in advance. You may also be able to reserve a starting time on the same day you want to play by calling the Pro Shop at each course directly.

Instruction is available through the **Walt Disney World Golf Studio** at the Magnolia driving range. The fee is $50 for a lesson, or $100 for a playing lesson. Private lessons with assistant pros are also available at $30 per half hour. Call (407) 824-2270 for reservations.

**Courses, rated.** According to the pros at the courses, here are the difficulty levels from most difficult to easiest:
1. Osprey Ridge
2. Palm
3. Magnolia
4. Eagle Pines
5. Lake Buena Vista

**No word on mouse ears.** Disney enforces a dress code requiring golf attire that bans T-shirts and short shorts.

You can rent a set of Titleist clubs for $20 at the Pro Shop; shoes and driving range balls are also available.

**Magnolia.** At the Shades of Green (formerly the Disney Inn). Named for the more than 1,500 magnolias on the course, this course plays to 6,642 yards from the middle tees and is the setting for the final round of the Walt Disney World/Oldsmobile Golf Classic. There's water on 10 of the 18 holes. The **Garden Gallery** offers breakfast, lunch, and dinner. The **Disney Golf Studio** offers lessons and videotape analysis. Pro Shop: (407) 824-2288.

Championship Par: 72. Yards: 7,190. Slope: 133. Forward Par: 74. Yards: 5,414. Slope: 123. Weekday and Weekend Fee: $95, cart included.

**Palm.** Considered the second most difficult course at Walt Disney World, it is included among *Golf Digest's* top 25 resort courses. It plays to a relatively short 6,461 yards from the middle tees, but water and sand seem to be almost everywhere. The 18th hole has been rated as the fourth toughest on the PGA Tour. Also located at Shades of Green, it shares the Garden Gallery and Pro Shop with the Magnolia course.

Championship Par: 72. Yards: 6,957. Slope: 133. Forward Par: 74. Yards: 5,398. Slope: 124. Weekday and Weekend Fee: $95, cart included.

**Lake Buena Vista.** A wide open and heavily wooded course that reaches to 6,655 yards, extending from the Disney Village Clubhouse. Located at Disney's Village Resort near the Hotel Plaza resorts. The **Lake Buena Vista Restaurant** in the clubhouse serves breakfast, lunch, and dinner. The **Lake Buena Vista Golf Studio** offers lessons and analysis. Pro Shop: (407) 824-3741.

Championship Par: 72. Yards: 6,829. Slope: 128. Forward Par: 73. Yards: 5,176. Slope: NA. Weekday and Weekend Fee: $95, cart included.

**Osprey Ridge.** By most accounts the most difficult course at Walt Disney World, it was designed by acclaimed golf course architect Tom Fazio. Osprey Ridge includes a circulating 18-hole routing with holes that play in every direction. The course extends 6,705 yards from the middle tees, including some remote tropical settings. Some of the tees, greens, and viewing areas are as much as 25 feet above grade; much of the earth was moved from the excavation at nearby Eagle Pines. The namesake "ridge" plays an important role in the course: you'll climb the ridge for the tee for Hole 3, the green for Hole 12 is built into its side, and the green for Hole 16 is atop it. Located at the Bonnet Creek Golf Club, it includes the **Sand Trap Bar & Grill**, a lunch spot with a view of the greens. The **Bonnet Creek Golf Studio** offers lessons and analysis. Pro Shop: (407) 824-2675.

Championship Par: 72. Yards: 6,957. Slope: 133. Forward Par: 74. Yards: 5,398. Slope: 124. Weekday and Weekend Fee: $95, cart included.

**Eagle Pines.** Eight of designer Pete Dye's courses are included in *Golf* magazine's top 50. Unlike the high mounds and ridges of Osprey Ridge, this new course offers a low profile, although many balls will end up in the surrounding pines. Eagle Pines plays 6,224 yards from the middle tees and is considered a bit more forgiving than the other courses. Dye included a lip on the edge of fairways along water hazards to reduce the number of wet balls. The course shares the Bonnet Creek Golf Studio, pro shop, and Sand Trap restaurant with Osprey Ridge.

Championship Par: 72. Yards: 6,772. Slope: 131. Forward Par: 72. Yards: 4,838. Slope: 110. Weekday and Weekend Fee: $110, cart included.

**Oak Trail Executive Course.** At the Shades of Green (formerly the Disney Inn). A 9-hole, 2,913 yard, par 36 course with small rolling greens and elevated tees. It's no pushover, though, with some of the most difficult greens at Walt Disney World. No golf carts are allowed.

Championship Par: 36. Yards: 3,000. Slope: NA. Forward Par: 36. Yards: 3,000. Slope: NA. Weekday and Weekend Fee: $95.

---

**More, you say?** In addition to the Walt Disney World courses, there are dozens of municipal, public, and semi-private golf courses in and around the Disney area in Orange County. Here is a selection. All phone numbers are in the (407) area code.

**Buena Ventura Lakes Golf Club West.** Kissimmee. Public 18 holes. 348-4915.
**Crystal Brook Golf Course.** Kissimmee. 847-8721.
**Cypress Creek Country Club.** Orlando. Semi-private 18 holes. 351-2187.
**Dubsdread Golf Course.** Orlando. Municipal 18 holes. 246-2551.
**Eastwood Golf & Country Club.** Orlando. Semi-private 18 holes. 281-4653.
**Falcon's Fire Golf Course.** Kissimmee. 18 holes public. 239-5445.
**Grand Cypress Resort.** Orlando. Resort 45 holes. 239-4700.
**The Greens.** Orlando. Public 18 holes. 351-9778.
**Hunter's Creek Golf Club.** Orlando. Public 18 holes. 240-4653.
**International Golf Club.** Orlando. Resort 18 holes. 239-6909.
**Kissimmee Golf Club.** Kissimmee. Public 18 holes. 847-2816.
**Marriott's Orlando World Center.** Orlando. Resort 18 holes. 239-4200.
**Meadow Woods Golf Club.** Orlando. Semi-private 18 holes. 850-5600.
**MetroWest Country Club.** Orlando. Semi-private 18 holes. 299-1099.
**Monastery Golf & Country Club.** Orlando. Public 18 holes. 647-4067.
**Orange Lake Country Club.** Kissimmee. Semi-private. 239-1050.
**Rosemont Golf & Country Club.** Orlando. Semi-private. 298-1230.
**Ventura Country Club.** Orlando. Semi-private 18 holes. 277-2640.
**Wedgefield Golf & Country Club.** Orlando. Semi-private 18 holes. 568-2116.
**Winter Park Municipal.** Winter Park. Municipal 9 holes. 623-3339.
**Winter Pines Golf Club.** Winter Park. Public 18 holes. 671-3172.
**Zellwood Station Country Club.** Zellwood. Semi-private 18 holes. 886-3303.

## Golf Tournaments

Each October, the PGA Tour comes to Orlando for the Walt Disney World/Oldsmobile Golf Classic, which therefore is a good time to come to watch but not to play. If you've got the scratch, though, you can pay about $5,000 for a one-year membership in the Classic Club. Each member gets to play with one of the pros in the tournament for three of the four days of the contest. For details, call (407) 828-2250.

The Classic can draw more than 100,000 participants and 200,000 spectators; this is not the time to come to Walt Disney World for a few casual rounds of golf. Hotel reservations also are somewhat difficult to obtain at this time.

Nearly 400 other tournaments of all types take place each year.

## Fantasia Gardens Miniature Golf and Fantasia Fairways

It was only a matter of time before Disney Imagineers put their hands and pruning shears to work creating a miniature golf course; it seems more than obvious, and besides, companies outside of Walt Disney World were making money with their own courses.

In 1996, then, Disney debuted Fantasia Gardens Miniature Golf with two 18-hole courses near the Swan, Dolphin, and BoardWalk resorts. The garden settings of the courses draw their influence from various classic and classical sequences from the Disney classic, *Fantasia*. They include "The Pastoral Symphony," "The Nutcracker Suite," "The Dance of the Hours," and "The Sorcerer's Apprentice."

Alongside is Fantasia Fairways, a par 3 and 4 putting course with exaggerated contours, water hazards, and sand traps.

## The Walt Disney World Speedway

The Walt Disney World Speedway, a $6 million 1.1-mile course to the left of the access road to the parking lot for the Magic Kingdom, hosted the first Disney World Indy 200 in late January of 1996, drawing tens of thousands of fans and creating a major slow-speed traffic jam. Visitors who wanted to go to the Magic Kingdom during the race had to park at Epcot or other outlying lots and take buses or the monorail to the gates.

The event consisted of Thursday and Friday practice and qualifying sessions and the race itself—with a $1 million prize—took place on Saturday.

The new speedway, with 51,000 seats, is expected to be a regular stop in the new Indy Racing League.

Disney officials were said to be exploring additional ways to use the track, with possibilities including a race driving school allowing visitors to take their turn at the wheel of a race car or ride along with a professional driver.

## Sports Center Disney

Lace up your sneakers, Mickey: work is underway on Walt Disney World's $100 million sports complex, including a 7,500-seat baseball stadium that beginning in 1998 will be the spring training home of the Atlanta Braves.

The sports complex is expected to be completed by 1997, between the Disney-MGM Studios and Typhoon Lagoon.

Also on the sports front is the ESPN Sports Club at Disney's BoardWalk Resort. The combination bar, studio, and arcade is expected to open in July of 1996. Visitors will be able to observe production and telecast of ESPN shows as well as watch live sports action on more than 50 monitors. Plans were also underway to add interactive technology to permit visitors to predict or suggest strategies for games underway around the world.

The Amateur Athletic Union moved to Walt Disney World in 1995, leaving its former headquarters in Indianapolis. The AAU annually hosts more than 100 national tournaments and supervises dozens of leagues. The Disney-AAU alliance calls for as many as 60 amateur sporting events per year, bringing an estimated 35,000 athletes to Orlando and Walt Disney World. And the new facility will be the home for the AAU Junior Olympic Games every four years.

The sports complex will include the baseball stadium, a number of practice and Little League fields, tennis courts, soccer fields, and a fieldhouse with six basketball courts.

Disney also says it expects the center to help the entire Central Florida area in its efforts to attract major league teams and professional sports facilities. College, high school, and youth-league teams, amateur and senior athletic groups, and individual professional and leisure-time athletes will be invited to share in training, games, and sports camps.

**Boating away.** The Kissimmee Waterway, a 50-mile-long series of lakes, connects Lake Tohopekaliga with Lake Okeechobee and, through that body of water, with both the Atlantic Ocean and the Gulf of Mexico. There are boat ramps at Granada (2605 Ridgeway Dr.) and Partin Triangle Park on Lake Tohopekaliga, and at Sexton on Fish Lake (2590 Irlo Bronson Memorial Hwy. [I-192]), all in Kissimmee.

**Hunting and fishing licenses.** Fishing (fresh and saltwater) and hunting licenses for persons over age 16 may be obtained from the Osceola County Tax Collector's office. More information is available from the Florida Game and Fresh Water Commission at (800) 282-8002 or the Florida Marine Patrol (saltwater fishing) at (800) 342-5367.

Planned future sports activities include soccer, golf, indoor and beach volleyball, rugby, indoor and outdoor tennis, basketball for men and women, football, baseball, men's and women's softball, track and field, martial arts, badminton, fencing, gymnastics, aerobics, cardiovascular conditioning, table tennis, weight lifting, body building, roller hockey, wrestling (free-style, Olympic, sumo, and Greco-Roman), handball, squash, racquetball, lacrosse, field hockey, and other sports.

Plans are also being made for home run derbies, basketball slam dunk competitions, volleyball spiking contests, quarterback challenge, and other made-for-television sports events. The new center could also be the site of preseason training camps in some professional sports, according to the company.

Disney has indicated in past years that later phases of the project could include a hockey rink, an Olympic-size pool for swimming and diving competitions, a sports dormitory, a cycling track, miniature golf, bowling, and more.

And Disney was wooing the U.S. Volleyball Association in hopes that the group will move its headquarters from Colorado Springs to Orlando, too. Finally, some sources say Disney may submit a bid for the Summer Olympics for 2004 or 2008.

## On the Water

### Walt Disney World Marinas

Walt Disney World offers the country's largest fleet of pleasure boats, more than many navies of the world. There are three major areas: the Seven Seas Lagoon, which sits between the Magic Kingdom and the Ticket and Transportation Center and is surrounded by the monorail; Bay Lake, the largest body of water, which includes Discovery Island; and the Buena Vista Lagoon, a 35-acre body of water that fronts on Pleasure Island and Disney Village.

Marinas are located at the **Contemporary Resort, Fort Wilderness, Polynesian Resort, Grand Floridian, Caribbean Beach, Yacht Club**, and **Beach Club.** There is also a boat rental station at the **Disney Village**, where a variety of boats are available for rental to day visitors as well as guests at Disney resorts. In the summer, waiting lines for boats can be lengthy at midday.

Guests at some of the Disney resorts can purchase a pass that includes unlimited use of boats during their stay; if you're planning to make use of Disney's navy more than twice during a weeklong stay, the pass will save you money.

**Water Sprites.** Small and low-powered, they're still zippy enough to be a lot of fun. They rent by the half hour for about $11; children under 12 are not allowed to drive. Available at Contemporary, Polynesian, Grand Floridian, Fort Wilderness, and Disney Village.

**Water Skiing.** A powerboat with driver and equipment is available at Fort Wilderness, Polynesian, Grand Floridian, and Contemporary marinas. The rate is about $70 per hour. For information, call (407) 824-2621.

---

**Water, water everywhere.** Not to drink, but to swim in, boat and water-ski on, and parasail over. In addition to the offerings within Walt Disney World, there are numerous places for aquatic recreation in the Orlando area.

**Turkey Lake Park** offers sand beaches, swimming pool, and nature trails. For general information, call (407) 299-5594. You can reach **Turkey Lake Park Boat Rentals** at (407) 677-5554.

You can rent a houseboat for cruising on the St. John's River through **Hontoon Landing Marina** at (800) 248-2474.

**Ski Holidays** offers parasail thrill rides, jet-ski rentals, and water-ski charters on a private 400-acre lake adjoining Walt Disney World. Contact them at (407) 239-4444.

Experienced divers can explore the Atlantic or Gulf Coasts or inland springs with equipment rented from **The Dive Station.** Call them at (407) 843-3483.

**Slow Boats.** Pontoon Flote Boats putter around, very slowly, from Disney Village and most of the resort marinas. Rentals cost about $35 per hour. Also available for about the same price are Canopy Boats, 16-foot V-hulls with an outboard.

**Sailboats.** Wind-powered vessels, from little two-seater Sunfish and speedy Hobie Cat catamarans to heavier six-seater Capris are offered at Contemporary, Polynesian, Grand Floridian, Fort Wilderness, Yacht Club, and Beach Club marinas. Prices range from about $10 to $15 per hour.

**People-Power.** One-person pedal boats, for about $8 an hour, are available at most marinas. Canoes for canal paddling can be rented at the Fort Wilderness Bike Barn for about $4 per hour, or $10 for the day.

## Fishing Within Walt Disney World

Although Bay Lake is well-stocked with bass, fishing opportunities are somewhat limited within Walt Disney World.

Guests at Fort Wilderness or Disney Village can fish from the shore or on any of the canals. Equipment is available for rent at the Bike Barn (rods and reels) or at the Fort Wilderness trading posts (cane poles and lures).

Twice a day an escorted fishing expedition leaves the Fort Wilderness marina; the price is about $110 for two hours and $25 for each additional hour for a party of up to five persons and includes all gear. Call (407) 824-2621 for information and reservations.

There's a two-hour catch-and-release fishing safari that leaves twice daily from **Cap'n Jack's Marina** at the Disney Village Marketplace. Call (407) 828-2461 for reservations.

Finally, there is the **Fishin' Hole on Ol' Man Island** at Disney's Dixie Landings Resort hotel. The hole is stocked with bass, blue gill, and even catfish; they'll provide bamboo poles and bait. After all that, though, you'll have to return the fish to the pond after you catch them; this fishin' hole is just for sport. The cost is about $3 per hour, with a family rate of about $10 for up to six people.

## Swimming

Guests at Disney resorts are surrounded by water, with swimming encouraged almost everywhere. There are more than five miles of white sand beach along the shores of **Bay Lake** and **Seven Seas Lagoon**. Both waterways were engineered by Disney; the sand was mined from beneath the lake muck during construction.

Beaches can be found at Contemporary, Grand Floridian, Caribbean Beach, Fort Wilderness, Polynesian, Yacht Club, and Beach Club resorts. At certain times of the year, though, swimming may be restricted because of environmental or health concerns because of algae and natural bacteria growth; check with the resort for information.

All of the hotels within Walt Disney World offer swimming pools, some more exotic than others. For example, water slides can be found at the Polynesian and Caribbean Beach Resorts.

Use of these pools is restricted to guests at Disney resorts, although we have never seen a swimmer "carded" for a guest pass. Day guests looking for cooling water are encouraged to visit River Country, Typhoon Lagoon, or Blizzard Beach.

# Out and About
## Tennis Courts Within the Park
There were, at last count, 27 lighted courts within Walt Disney World at various resorts. The largest tennis facility is at the Contemporary hotel, including backboards and an automatic ball server for practice. Other courts can be found at Shades of Green, the Yacht Club, Beach Club, and the Swan and Dolphin resorts. A pair of clay courts can be found at the Grand Floridian.

Courts can be reserved no more than 24 hours in advance, with fees from $10 to $12 per hour at the Contemporary, Grand Floridian, Swan, and Dolphin. Tennis is free at the Disney Inn, the Village Clubhouse, Fort Wilderness, Yacht Club, or Beach Club. Call the resorts for reservations; racquets and balls can be rented or purchased at some of the resorts.

A tennis clinic is offered at the Contemporary Resort. The course includes video recordings of your game.

## Horseback Riding
Trail rides for resort guests and day visitors depart from the Fort Wilderness campground several times a day. Riders must be at least nine years old; the horses are very gentle, and experience is not required of riders. The rides cost about $13. Call (407) 824-2832 between 8 A.M. and 3:30 P.M. for information and reservations.

## Biking Within Walt Disney World
More than eight miles of bicycle paths can be found at Fort Wilderness and at the Disney Village Resort; other places to bike include some of the spread-out resorts like Caribbean Beach. In an unusual departure for Disney entertainment, use of the paths is free—that is, if you bring your own bike. You can pick up maps wherever bicycles are rented.

Rental bikes can be engaged at the Bike Barn at Fort Wilderness, the Villa Center at Disney Village or the marina at Caribbean Beach. Rates are about $3 to $5 per hour or $6 to $10 per day; tandems (bicycles built for two) can be rented at the Bike Barn.

**Port Orleans** and **Dixie Landings.** A 2.5-mile tour around the Carriage Path and along the riverfront. Dixie Landings: rent single or tandem bikes at **Dixie Levee** near the marina. Port Orleans: single or tandem bikes at **Port Orleans Landing** near the marina.

**Fort Wilderness Resort and Campground.** More than eight miles of roads and trails in and among forests, beaches, trails, waterways, and boardwalks. Single and tandem bikes are available at the **Bike Barn.**

**Disney's Village Resort** and **Disney Vacation Club.** Easy riding along the golf course, waterways, and residential streets of the resort. You'll have to share the road with cars, buses, golf carts, and joggers. At this location, bicycles are available for rental only to guests at a resort within the park. Village Resort: rent single bikes at the **Reception Center.** Vacation Club: single and tandem bikes at **Hank's Rent 'n Return.**

**Disney's Caribbean Beach Resort.** A leisurely, flat circuit around Barefoot Bay Lake, including bridges to Parrot Cay Island and other interesting destinations. Rent single bicycles at the **Barefoot Boat Yard.**

## Disney Health Clubs

**Olympiad Health Club at Contemporary Resort** includes Nautilus gym equipment, sauna, and individual whirlpools. Open to resort guests and day visitors for $5 fee, $10 including whirlpool baths. Open daytime hours, closed Sunday. Call (407) 824-3410 for appointments and information.

Other clubs, open to guests only and each charging a daily or vacation-long fee, include **St. John's Health Spa** at the Grand Floridian, **The Magic Mirror** at the Shades of Green, the **Ship Shape Health Club** at the Yacht Club and Beach Club, a facility at the Lake Buena Vista Club, and **The Body by Jake** club at the Dolphin.

# Chapter 17

# Outside Walt Disney World: Participant and Spectator Sports

### Major and Minor League Baseball

Spring Training is a dream fulfilled for the serious fan and an enjoyable sojourn for the casual observer. You are so close to the superstars of baseball, the young hopefuls trying for a one-in-a-million spot on a major league roster, as well as some of the greats of yesteryear soaking up the spring sunshine as coaches. Listen to the enthusiastic chatter of the ball players—talk of "taters" (home runs) and "hacks" (swings) and "beep" (batting practice).

There are two parts to Florida's Grapefruit League: the training and the not-quite-prime-time practice games. Pitchers and catchers arrive in Florida in mid-February to work themselves into shape with exercise and steadily lengthening throwing sessions. Their teammates usually arrive a week or two later. In general, the teams can be found at their practice fields each morning until early afternoon; check with the Spring Training sites before heading out. At most parks there is no admission charge for the workouts, and you will be able to wander in and among the superstars.

Most teams invite many of their upper-level minor league players as well as promising rookies to their camps; you'll see uniform numbers as high as 99.

Practice games begin about March 1, and most of the early games take place in the afternoon. Toward the end of the season, in early April, some games may be scheduled under the lights. Teams tend to concentrate on playing nearby neighbors to cut down on travel time; some of the games are "split squad," meaning that half of the large preseason roster may be playing elsewhere at the same time.

Ticket prices range from about $5 to $12. You can usually obtain tickets as late as the day of game, except for the more popular matchups, like Yankees vs. Mets or Mets vs. Red Sox.

If you're a golfer, you might want to check out a course near one or another of the training camps; many players and coaches share that sport and can be found on the links in the afternoon.

Once the big leaguers depart, many leave behind their minor league farm teams who play a full summer season in the Florida League.

The four closest spring training camps to Orlando are used by the Houston Astros, Kansas City Royals, Florida Marlins, and Detroit Tigers.

And the Atlanta Braves have announced plans to move their Spring Training operations to Sports Center Disney within Walt Disney World beginning in 1998. The Braves were lured away from their former base in West Palm Beach, their springtime home for 34 years. According to the team, they signed a 20-year lease with Disney World.

## Closest Spring Training Camps

**Houston Astros.** Osceola County Stadium, 1000 Bill Beck Boulevard, Kissimmee, FL 34744. (407) 933-2520. Tickets $5 to 8. The **Osceola County Stadium and Sports Complex** is also the summer home of the Florida State League Osceola Astros at the Class A professional level. The complex includes a 5,120-seat stadium plus four other practice fields as well as clubhouse and training facilities.

**Kansas City Royals.** Baseball City Stadium, 300 Stadium Way, Davenport, FL 33837. (407) 839-3900 or (813) 424-2500. Tickets: $5 to $9.

**Florida Marlins.** Space Coast Stadium, 5600 Stadium Parkway, Melbourne, FL 32940. (407) 633-9200. Tickets: $9 to $12.

**Detroit Tigers.** Joker Marchant Stadium, Lakeland Hills Boulevard, Lakeland, FL 33801. (813) 499-8229. Tickets: $5 to $8.

## Other Grapefruit League Teams

**Atlanta Braves.** Municipal Stadium, 715 Hank Aaron Drive, West Palm Beach, FL 33401. (407) 683-6100 or (407) 839-3900. Tickets: $6 to $12. 1997 will be the last season here for the Braves before they move to Walt Disney World.

**Baltimore Orioles.** Fort Lauderdale Stadium, 5301 N.W. 12th Avenue, Fort Lauderdale, FL 33309. (305) 776-1921. The O's took over the Yankee's longtime home for the 1996 season.

**Boston Red Sox.** City of Palms Park, 2201 Edison Avenue, Fort Myers, FL 33901. (813) 334-4700. Tickets: $5 to $9.

**Chicago White Sox.** Ed Smith Stadium, 12th Street and Tuttle Avenue, Sarasota, FL 34237. (813) 954-7699 or (813) 953-3388. Tickets: $4 to $10.

**Cincinnati Reds.** Plant City Stadium, 1900 South Park Boulevard, Plant City, FL 33566. (813) 752-1878. Tickets: $4 to $7.

**Cleveland Indians.** Chain O' Lakes Stadium, Winter Haven, FL 33880. (407) 839-3900 or (813) 287-8844. Tickets: $5 to $8.

**L.A. Dodgers.** Holman Stadium, Dodgertown, 4101 26th Street, Vero Beach, FL 32961. (407) 569-6858. Tickets: $5 to $8.

**Minnesota Twins.** Lee County Sports Complex, 14400 Six Mile Cypress Parkway, Fort Myers, FL 33912. (800) 338-9467 or (612) 338-9467 in Minnesota. Tickets: $6 to $9.

**Montreal Expos.** Municipal Stadium, 715 Hank Aaron Drive, West Palm Beach, FL 33401. (407) 689-9121. Tickets: $6 to $12.

**New York Mets.** Thomas J. White Stadium, 525 N.W. Peacock Boulevard, Port St. Lucie, FL 34986. (407) 871-2115. Tickets: $6 to $8.

**New York Yankees.** Tampa's Yankee Stadium, a new 10,000-seat home for the Yankees beginning with the 1996 season. Call (800) 969-2657 for ticket information.

**Philadelphia Phillies.** Jack Russell Memorial Stadium, 800 Phillies Drive, Clearwater, FL 34615. (813) 442-8496. Tickets: $7 to $8.

**Pittsburgh Pirates.** McKechnie Field, 1750 9th Street, West Bradenton, FL 34205. (813) 748-4610. Tickets: $5.50 to $8.50.

**St. Louis Cardinals.** Al Lang Stadium, 180 2nd Avenue S.E., St. Petersburg, FL 33701. (813) 894-4773. Tickets: $6 to $7.

**Texas Rangers.** Charlotte County Stadium, 2300 El Jobean Road, Port Charlotte, FL 33948. (813) 625-9500 or (813) 624-2211. Tickets: $5 to $7.

**Toronto Blue Jays.** Dunedin Stadium at Grant Field, 311 Douglas Avenue, Dunedin, FL 34698. (813) 733-0429. Tickets: $6 to $8.

### Major League Wanna-Bes

**Chet Lemon's School of Baseball.** 333-3010. Lake Mary. A year-round instructional camp for ages 6 and up, taught by professional ball players.

## NBA Basketball

The **Orlando Magic** of the National Basketball Association plays to packed houses at the Orlando Arena from November to April of each year.

The arena, which opened in 1989, seats 15,291 for basketball and includes a spectacular videoscreen used for replays and special encouragements to the fans.

For ticket information, call (407) 896-2442; to purchase seats by phone through TicketMaster, call (407) 839-3900. According to the team, although most every game is a sellout, there are likely to be a few seats available if you call ahead of time; the most difficult times to get a ticket are during the same winter and spring holiday times when the theme parks are crowded. Tickets are very difficult to obtain, especially for matchups against the powerhouses of the NBA, including Chicago and New York; seats range in price from about $20 to $80. If you are especially determined to see a game you may have to use the (expensive) services of a ticket broker.

And if you want to pick up a character T-shirt that doesn't have mouse ears, you might want to visit the **Orlando Magic FanAttic**, a store selling official clothing and other items. It is located in Orlando at 715 North Garland, near the intersection of I-4 and Highway 50. Call (407) 649-2222 for details.

## IHL Hockey

Professional hockey in Orlando? That's the concept, although time will tell if the Orlando Solar Bears can make a go of it as the southernmost member of the International Hockey League. The team plays its games in the Orlando Arena in a season that runs from late September through mid-April.

Tickets are sold by TicketMaster, at (407) 839-3900.

## Arena Football League

The Orlando Predators play a 14-game schedule at the Orlando Arena from mid-April through August. The league features eight-man "Ironman" football on a 50-yard indoor field; with the exception of the quarterback and an offensive specialist, players must play both offense and defense. Tickets are priced from $10 to $33, and regularly sell out. (407) 648-4444.

## Greyhound Racing

**Melbourne Greyhound Park.** (407) 259-9800. Melbourne. Put your money on the dogs. Evening races Monday, Wednesday, Friday, and Saturday; matinees Monday, Wednesday, Saturday, and Sunday.

**Sanford-Orlando Kennel Club.** (407) 831-1600. 301 Dog Track Road, Longwood. Racing from November 1 through May 2, nightly at 7:30 P.M. except Sunday, and matinees Monday, Wednesday, and Saturday at 12:30 P.M. General admission, $1; clubhouse, $2.

**Seminole Greyhound Park.** (407) 699-4510. Casselberry. Racing nightly except Sunday; matinees on Monday, Wednesday, and Saturday.

## Roller and Ice Skating

**Rock on Ice, Ice Skating Arena.** (407) 352-9878. 7500 Canada Avenue, off International Drive near Sand Lake Boulevard. Spectacular lighting, sound, a DJ . . . and indoor ice skating. *Discount coupon in this book.*

**Skate Reflections.** (407) 846-8469. 1111 Dyer Boulevard. Roller skate to the latest music on 17,000 square feet of solid maple floor.

## Fishing

**All Pro Bass Guide Service.** (407) 847-9919. Half-day or full-day trips in Kissimmee and Stick Pond; all tackle provided and transportation available.

**Backcountry Charter Service.** (407) 668-5516. Inshore saltwater trips on the Indian River near the Kennedy Space Center and on the St. John's River.

**Bass Anglers Guide Service.** (407) 656-1052.

**Bass Bustin' Guide Service.** (407) 281-0845.

**Bass Challenger Guide Service.** (407) 273-8045, (800) 241-5314.

**Cutting Loose Expeditions.** (407) 629-4700, (800) 533-4746. Fresh and saltwater expeditions.

**Florida Deep Sea Fishing.** (813) 360-2082. St. Petersburg Beach.

**Flying Fish Fishing Adventures.** (407) 366-7372. Ocean sportfishing.

**J & B Central Florida Bass Guide.** (407) 293-2791.

**Pro-Sport Bassin' Guide Service.** (407) 275-0633.

## Horseback Riding

**Grand Cypress Equestrian Center.** (407) 239-4608, (800) 835-7377. Orlando. Instruction and trail riding.

**Horse World Poinciana Riding Stables.** (407) 847-4343. Kissimmee. Trail riding, hayrides, pony rides, and farm animals. Open daily at 9 A.M. Adults, $30 to $40; children (5 and under riding double), $8.

## Rodeo

**Kissimmee Rodeo.** Kissimmee Sports Arena. (407) 933-0020. 959 South Hoagland Boulevard. Every Friday from 8 to 10 P.M. Adults, $10; children, $5. *Discount coupon in this book.*

**Silver Spurs Rodeo.** (407) 628-2280. Kissimmee. The largest rodeo east of the Mississippi, with bull and bronco riding, steer wrestling, and more, is held for one weekend in mid-February and early July only.

## Bungee Jumping

The Orlando area features more bungee-jumping establishments than you could shake a tourist at; it's a very changeable industry, with cranes or towers moving from one open lot to another. If this is the sort of thing you're looking for, cruise Irlo Bronson Highway or International Drive, and take a look up.

## Boating and Cruises

**Airboat Rentals U-Drive.** 847-3672. 4266 West Vine Street, Kissimmee. Adults, $22 per hour. Airboats, electric boats, and canoes available for rental and use in a cypress swamp.

**Rivership Romance.** (407) 321-5091. 433 North Palmetto Avenue, Sanford. Adults, $30; children, $20. Cruises on 110-foot vessel on the St. John's River. Three-to-four-hour luncheon cruises priced at $30 to $40 for adults, and $20 to $30 for children. Dinner cruises Friday ($41 for all tickets) and Saturday nights ($46 all tickets).

**Toho Airboat Excursions, Inc.** (407) 344-1334. 3701 Big Bass Road, Kissimmee. Guided tours in Florida wilderness; night alligator hunts available. Adults, $13; children, $6.50.

## Blimps, Hot Air Balloons, and Sightseeing Flights

**Airship International Ltd.** (407) 351-0011. 301 Dyer Boulevard, Kissimmee. Adults, $99. A tour by blimp over central Florida, departing daily from Kissimmee Municipal Airport.

**Balloons by Terry.** (407) 422-3529. 3529 Edgewater Drive, Orlando. All tickets $100 to $150. A tour by hot air balloon.

**Central Florida Balloon Tours.** (407) 294-8085. Winter Park. Adults, $160; seniors, $140; children, $100. Hour-long tours over attractions and countryside; champagne and picnic breakfast served.

**High Expectations Balloon Tours.** (407) 846-1110. 312 Chiquita Court, Kissimmee. Adults, $120; children, $75. Champagne balloon flights over Orlando.

**Kissimmee Aviation Services.** (407) 847-9095. 3031 W. Patrick Street. Aerial tours of central Florida. All passengers $41 for one to three persons for half-hour flight; $82 for one-hour flight.

**Orange Blossom Balloons.** (407) 239-7677. Lake Buena Vista. One-hour champagne flights over central Florida, followed by breakfast buffet. Adults, $150; seniors, $125; children, $100.

**Rise & Float Balloon Tours.** (407) 352-8191. 5767 Major Boulevard, Orlando. Adults, $150; children, $85.

**Skyscapes Balloon Tours.** (407) 856-4606. 5755 Cove Drive, Orlando. Adults, $125; children, $75.

**Vintage Air Tours.** (407) 932-1400, (800) 835-9323. 310 Dyer Boulevard, Kissimmee. Aerial tours in DC-3 aircraft.

# VII
# Attractions and Shopping
# Away from the Theme Parks

## Chapter 18
## Church Street Station, Gatorland, Splendid China, and Other Attractions

### Orlando-Kissimmee Attractions
Major Attractions in Orlando and Kissimmee
   Church Street Station
   Gatorland
   Green Meadows Farms
   Kennedy Space Center
   Medieval Life
   Movie Rider
   Ripley's Believe It or Not!
   Splendid China
   Wet 'n Wild

**Church Street Station.** When you've maxxed out on rides and exhibits at Disney World, take a drive into Orlando for a visit to Church Street Station. This is a restored historical section of the city set up for live entertainment, shopping, and dining. The Station has been open for business for more than 20 years. In its typical fashion, the Walt Disney Company has "adopted" the concept for its own Pleasure Island complex within the park; Church Street is aimed at a slightly older crowd and has a more adventurous edge to it.

Actually, **Church Street Station**—located in one block of Orlando's downtown Church Street—is two facilities at once. You'll see one Church Street Station if you go during the day and a completely different and exciting facility after the sun goes down and the lights come up. Admission is free for lunch; there's a cover charge after 5 P.M. ($16.95 for adults, $10.95 for children 4 to 12). Annual passes are $29.95 for one, and $44.95 for a two-person pass.

The mood is high-energy with musicians roaming through the dining areas or performing on stage. The rooms generally are crowded, noisy, active, and fun. This is one place where you don't have to choose one restaurant or bar, you can "hop" around all evening for food, drink, and entertainment.

**Rosie O'Grady's Good Time Emporium** is about 90 years behind the time, a rip-roarin' saloon with antique brass chandeliers, etched mirrors, and leaded glass that celebrates the Gay 1890s to the Roaring 1920s. It's a place of strumming banjos, Dixieland jazz, bartop cancan girls, Charleston dancers, and singing waiters and bartenders.

**Apple Annie's Courtyard** is a grand Victorian garden domed by arched pine and cypress trusses from the circa-1860 St. Michael's Church in New Orleans, ornamented with hand-carved Viennese mirrors and brass chandeliers.

**Lili Marlene's Aviator's Pub and Restaurant** memorializes the sweetheart of World War I in a room of classic wood paneling, fireplace, and a wine cabinet brought from the Rothschild house in Paris from about 1850. It is open for leisurely lunch, brunch, or dinner. There is a Sunday Brunch Buffet from 10:30 A.M. to 3 P.M., priced at $9.95 for adults and $6.95 for children from 4 to 12.

The **Cheyenne Saloon and Opera House** is a magnificent showroom constructed from lumber from a century-old Ohio barn; it took more than 50 craftsmen nearly two-and-a-half years to construct; no nails were used. The Cheyenne includes an eclectic collection of artifacts, including six 1895 chandeliers from the Philadelphia Mint and an 1885 solid rosewood pool table from San Francisco. The restaurant features beef, pork, and chicken barbecue as well as buffalo burgers with all the fixings. A specialty is the Backyard Barbeque buffet, offered Fridays from 11 A.M. to 3 P.M. for $6.95 per person.

**Phineas Phogg's Dance Club** celebrates great balloonists of the past and present with sounds from the latest Top 40 hits.

The **Crackers Oyster Bar** serves fresh Florida seafood and pasta specialties; **Rosie O'Grady's** offers deli sandwiches and red hots (hot dogs).

For lighter and quicker fast-food fare, try the **Exchange Food Pavilion**, a small covered mall with interesting shops and food. And there is also the **Wine Cellar**, with more than 5,000 bottles of fruits of the vine. The Exchange also includes an unusual collection of shops. There is no admission charge to the Exchange at any time. Church Street Station is open every day from 11 A.M. to 2 A.M.

There are "street parties" at Church Street Station on a regular basis; check with the attraction for exact dates: January, **Boola Bowl**, a post-Citrus Bowl party; February, **Valentine's Day Dinner**, **Carnivale Street Party**; March, **St. Patrick's Day**; April, **Easter Brunch**, **IslandFest**; May, **Cinco de Mayo**, **Mother's Day Brunch**; June, **Father's Day Brunch**; October, **Mini Monster Mash**, **Halloween Street Party**; November, **Fallfest**, **Thanksgiving Dinner**; December, **Christmas Tree Lighting**, **New Year's Eve Street Party**.

To get to Church Street Station, take I-4 toward Orlando. Exit on Anderson Street, and follow the signs to Church Street Station. Open parking is available under the I-4 roadway, but you must pay in advance and if you overstay your promised time, you will get ticketed. A better choice is to follow the parking garage signs to the covered parking. You'll walk a little farther, but you'll avoid a ticket. Call (407) 422-2434. *Discount coupon in this book.*

**Gatorland.** This is about as real a place and as un-Disney a theme park as you are likely to find in Central Florida, and it is one of our favorite places in the world. It is, quite simply, a shrine to the alligator, and when they say they have the world's largest collection of the fascinatingly creepy creatures, they're not exaggerating: there are thousands of them at every turn in this 50-acre park.

Gatorland is one of the older attractions in Central Florida, dating back to 1949. Over the years, the park has grown from a handful of alligators with a few huts and pens into the Alligator Capital of the World and an active breeding station. You'll stroll along a boardwalk through a cypress swamp to see gators, herons, and dozens of other wild creatures. Other creatures on display include monkeys, snakes, deer, goats, talking birds, a 300-pound Galápagos turtle, and even a Florida bear. Brave visitors can even "pet" an alligator—a baby with his mouth taped shut.

Florida "Crackers" (the term comes from the sound made by bullwhips cracking over the heads of cattle) were the first alligator wrestlers—of necessity. They would often have to fight gators that had grabbed calves for a snack. At Gatorland, you'll see an exhibition of stunt wrestling in the 800-seat **Wrestlin' Stadium**. Another highlight is the **Gator Jumparoo**, where giant alligators as big as 15 feet and 1,000 pounds jump out of the water to be hand fed.

The park also includes an alligator breeding marsh, a three-story observation tower, the **Gatorland Express Railroad**, and the **Snakes of Florida** show. And one pen holds "Sawgrass," an 80-year-old 800-pound gator captured in the Everglades by Gatorland founder Owen Godwin in 1952.

Gatorland also offers a line of alligator boots, belts, wallets, and meat. Yes, meat: **Pearl's Smoke House** offers smoked alligator ribs, deep fried gator nuggets, and gator chowder. We tried the nuggets: they (of course) taste like chicken.

Open daily from 8 A.M. to dusk, visitors should allow several hours; to catch the full cycle of shows, we'd suggest arriving early or at lunchtime. Ticket prices in 1996, including taxes, were $12.67 for adults and $9.49 for children ages 3 to 9. Located at 14501 South Orange Blossom Trail (S.R. 441) in Orlando, about a 20-minute drive from Walt Disney World. (407) 855-5496, or (800) 777-9044 in Florida. *Discount coupon in this book.*

**Green Meadows Farm.** The ultimate petting farm for children of all ages, it includes a two-hour guided tour with introductions to more than 300 animals including pigs, cows, goats, sheep, donkeys, chickens, rabbits, turkeys, ducks, and geese. Everyone gets to milk a cow, and children can go for pony rides and a tractor-pulled hayride.

This is a lovely place for animal lovers of all ages to while away a warm afternoon; the farm setting could not be more different than a theme park with real oohs and aahs at every turn. On one of our visits, the tour came to a complete halt in front of a pen occupied by three-day-old Vietnamese potbelly pigs. My children fell in love with some of the exotic chickens, including a variety called *milles fleurs* ("thousand flowers") because of the intricate pattern on their back.

The farm is one of eight similar operations around the country, the brainchild of Bob and Coni Keyes of Waterford, Wisconsin. It started in Wisconsin when that farm began to allow visitors to come and pick vegetables and raspberries. It expanded from that to allow urban youngsters to get up-close to farm animals. There are now Green Meadows Farms in Texas, Illinois, California, New Jersey, and New York.

Special events at Green Meadows include **Haunted Halloween Hayrides** in October, **American Indians & Cowboys Too!** in November, **Santa's Magical Farm** from Thanksgiving through New Year's Day, and **Christmas Tours** from December 1 through 16.

Take I-192 east toward Kissimmee; turn right at Poinciana Boulevard; go five miles to the farm. Open every day but Thanksgiving and Christmas from 9:30 A.M. to 4 P.M. (407) 846-0770. Tickets $12; children under 2, free. *Discount coupon in this book.*

**John F. Kennedy Space Center Visitors Center.** (407) 452-2121 or (800) 572-4636 in Florida. Located off S.R. 405, NASA Parkway, seven miles east of U.S. 1. From Orlando, take S.R. 528 (the Beeline) to S.R. 407, about one hour total driving. From Atlantic Coast Florida, take Exit 78 off I-95. Follow signs for Kennedy Space Center.

The home base of America's Space Shuttle is the fifth most popular attraction in Florida. It's also one of the best tourist bargains anywhere.

The Space Center is about 55 miles from Orlando, and there's enough to occupy you for a full morning or afternoon. Parking and admission to all indoor and outdoor space exhibits are free. Here's your chance to climb aboard the *Explorer*, a full-scale replica of the Space Shuttle, accurate down to the switches in the cockpit. The **Gallery of Space Flight** includes a fabulous collection of spacecraft, moon rocks, and other items.

There are a pair of two-hour double-decker bus tours ($7 for adults and $4 for children from 3 to 11). The Red Tour includes good views of **Launch Complex 39** where the Shuttles are launched, the massive **Vehicle Assembly Building**, and other elements of current operations including facilities constructed for upcoming space station missions. (The first multinational launches for the space station are planned to begin in late 1997, with complete operation due about 2002.) The Blue Tour visits the historic **Cape Canaveral Air Force Station**, where the U.S. space program began in the 1960s.

Future plans may result in consolidation of the two bus routes into a single interconnected tour.

In late 1996, the center was due to open a new *Apollo/Saturn V* center showing a restored massive *Saturn* rocket—one of only three still in existence—and other artifacts of the *Apollo* program which took the first humans to the moon. In 1997, a motion-based simulator ride will be added, offering some of the sensations of flight.

Also offered are two spectacular IMAX movies, shown on the huge screen of the **IMAX Theater.** Shown are the 37-minute *The Dream Is Alive*, which shows astronauts living and working in space, and the 42-minute *Blue Planet*, which offers an environmental view of the Earth from 200 miles up.

The IMAX film format produces an image 10 times larger than conventional

35-mm film used in theaters. To share a view of Earth few humans have experienced, crews from five Space Shuttle missions were trained to operate the cameras. Movie tickets are about $4 for adults and $2 for children from 3 to 11 for each film.

In 1991, the **Astronauts Memorial** was dedicated to honor the 15 American astronauts who gave their lives in the line of duty (including the crew of the *Challenger* and the *Apollo 1* spacecraft as well as others killed in training accidents). The 42-foot-high Space Mirror is set by a quiet lagoon near the entrance.

The 140,000-acre space center itself is an interesting wildlife area with some 15 endangered species making their homes there. Watch for alligators in the many canals along the roadways; the cape is also home to numerous wild pigs.

The park tends to be less busy on weekends than weekdays and is open every day of the year except for Christmas Day, from 9 A.M. to dusk. The visitor center may be off-limits on launch days, and bus tour routes may be altered or canceled when rockets are being prepared or launched.

NASA's schedule hopes to have one Shuttle in space, one ready to go, and two in processing at any one time. If you are lucky, you may see one of the vehicles—mated to its external tank and rockets—moving down the 3½-mile road from the Vehicle Assembly Building to the launch pad on board a transporter. The entire assemblage weighs about 12 million pounds. Shuttles typically spend several weeks on the pad being prepared for launch. Most orbiters return for a landing on a special runway at the space center, making a signature double sonic boom as they cross over central Florida.

It is especially interesting to visit the center while a Shuttle is in orbit; the air crackles with radio transmissions to and from the orbiter and special displays track the progress of the current mission.

**Space Shuttle Launch Viewing.** Current information on launches is available by calling NASA at (407) 867-4636, or the Kennedy Space Center Visitor Center from within Florida at (800) 572-4636.

From outside the Space Center, the best places to watch a launch are along U.S. Highway 1 in the city of Titusville and along Highway A1A in the cities of Cape Canaveral and Cocoa Beach on the Atlantic Ocean.

A limited number of launch viewing passes that permit private cars to enter the Space Center and park at a site six miles from the pad are available for free by writing three months in advance to NASA Visitor Services, Mail Code: PA—Pass, Kennedy Space Center, FL 32899.

The visitor center at Kennedy Space Center sells about 1,500 tickets to board buses to a viewing site six miles from the launch pad; tickets for adults are $7, and for children 3 to 11 are $4. Reservations for tickets are taken about one week before launch at (407) 452-2121, extension 260/261; tickets sell out quickly for daylight launches. In addition, if there is an afternoon launch, you may be able to park at the Visitor Center and watch the blastoff from there.

**Medieval Life.** (407) 396-1518 or (800) 229-8300. 4510 West Irlo Bronson Highway, near Route 441 in Kissimmee. A little piece of ancient Spain, it includes a truly amazing collection of tools, personal items, and some of the darker elements of the Medieval times, including dungeons and torture chambers. This place is for real—an exhibit unlike most anything else in Central Florida or elsewhere in the United States.

Your visit will start at the architect's house, the home of one of the most respected members of the community; the craftsmen exhibits include authentically dressed tradesmen and artisans including potters, blacksmiths, millers, carpenters, and glassblowers.

Then—parents of young children be warned—it's into the dungeon where you'll see replicas and real instruments of torture including the garrote, iron torture masks called "branks," and the interrogation chair, a large wooden chair covered with sharp iron spikes used to "convince" a person charged with a crime to offer a confession. And be prepared to explain—or steer your kids around—a few real chastity belts.

Adults, $8; children (3 to 12), $6. Free admission with the Medieval Times Dinner Show available, too. *Discount coupon in this book.*

**Movie Rider.** (407) 352-0050. 8815 International Drive; 5390 W. Highway 92.

This is not your neighborhood cineplex; Movie Rider is a giant-screen, high-energy simulator theater wilder than most anything else in Florida. The 36-seat theaters are divided up into cars that move with the action on the 30-foot-high by 42-foot-wide screen. It's closest competition is "Back to the Future" at Universal Studios.

Your ticket buys you two features, each about three to five minutes long. A changing roster of films includes "Red Rock Run," a trip on a runaway mine cart within an active volcano; "The Rattler," a re-creation of the world's tallest and fastest wooden roller coaster at Fiesta Texas in San Antonio; "Dino Island," a journey back to a place time has forgotten; and "Supersonic Flight," a trip in a T-38 jet trainer.

All tickets are $8.95. Combination tickets with **Ripley's Believe It or Not!** are $14.95 for adults, and $12.95 for children ages 4 to 12. You can stay to watch the same pair of movies for a second showing for a half-fare ticket. Note children must be at least 42 inches tall to ride the movie. Open daily from 10 A.M. to midnight. *Discount coupon in this book.*

**Ripley's Believe It or Not!** (407) 363-4418 or (800) 998-4418. 8201 International Drive, one block south of Sand Lake Road. This is one strange place—something that will be immediately obvious when you look at the building; think of it as the leaning museum of Orlando and you'll get the idea. Among the oddities you'll find here are a replica of the Mona Lisa constructed out of toast, a 1907 Rolls Royce built from more than a million matchsticks, and extraordinary humans including the world's tallest man and Liu Ch'ung, the man with two pupils in each eye.

The Orlando branch of the chain of museums also includes a portion of the Berlin Wall, a reproduction of Van Gogh's self-portrait created from 3,000 postcards, and a Disasters Gallery.

And the Orlando Ripley's even made it into the *Wall Street Journal* in late

1995 with a "believe it or not" of its own: eight of the 20 staffers at the museum became parents in a single year, each after touching an African fertility totem in the office lobby. Add to the roster a delivery woman for an air express company.

This is a must-see for visitors with a taste for the bizarre; it's even stranger than a theme park celebrating a talking mouse. Allow about 90 minutes for a self-guided tour. Open daily from 9 A.M. to 11 P.M. Adults, $9.95; children (4 to 12), $6.95. Combination tickets with the nearby Movie Rider are $14.95 and $12.95. *Discount coupon in this book.*

**Splendid China.** A journey of 10,000 miles and 5,000 years within a 76-acre theme park that includes miniature replicas of The Great Wall of China, The Lunan Stone Forest, and The Forbidden City. Performances and exhibits include Chinese acrobats, artists, Mongolian wrestlers, and martial artists.

The park, which opened at the end of 1993, is a near duplication of the original Splendid China which is located in Shenzhen, China, near Hong Kong.

Areas of the park include **Suzhou Gardens**, a life-size replica of a commercial street in the "water city" of Suzhou in eastern China of 700 years ago; construction of the city included construction techniques utilized by the Chinese of the 12th and 13th centuries.

Near the entrance are some unusual **Tihu Stones**, rocks found in Tihu lake and other lakes in eastern China. The rock is much admired by the Chinese for its shou (slimness), lou (leaking), znou (folding), and tou (transparent) characteristics. The Chinese as a people greatly value mountain and water landscapes and go to a great deal of effort to create gardens to celebrate these themes; the Tihu stone is often used to re-create mountains in miniature.

**The Great Wall of China**, scaled down to a half-mile in length, includes six million replica bricks that were hand-laid by Chinese artisans. The Great Wall stretches 4,200 miles from east to west—wider than the entire continental United States. Beacon towers were built at regular intervals from which sentries could send smoke and fire signals if an enemy approached.

The grand 9,999-room **Imperial Palace** is the centerpiece of Beijing's **Forbidden City**. Built in 1420, it was the seat of power. The reproduction of the Forbidden City and Imperial Palace occupies a central location at the park.

The **Potala Palace** at the back of Splendid China is a reproduction of the Lhasa capital of the Tibet region, built in the 7th century by King Song Song Gombo for his bride. The 13-story palace atop a cliff has 1,000 rooms.

The spectacular **Leshan Buddha Statue** in Sichuan Province is located at a point where three rivers come together, creating turbulent waves and violent eddies that have caused many shipwrecks. More than a thousand years ago, a monk tried to end the disasters by carving a huge Buddha out of the hillside where the three rivers met. The 236-foot-tall statue was eventually completed. Two people can stand side-by-side in each of his ears, and more than 100 people can sit on each of his feet. When one of the Buddha's fingers was damaged, 5,000 bricks were used to mend it.

One of the most spectacular sights in the park is the re-creation of the

**Stone Forest.** Some 300 million years ago limestone was deposited in thick layers on the ocean floor; about 30 million years ago the seabed rose above sea level to reveal the stone, and over the following centuries the wind and rain have sculpted the limestone into a strange forest of nearly 66,000 acres. Some of the stone forest peaks have been given vivid names like "A Leisurely Stroller," "A Galloping Horse in the Sky," and "A Phoenix Combing Her Wings." Even in miniature, the reproduction towers over visitors.

The wonders of Splendid China also include the **Stone Sculptures of the Dazu Grottoes**, some 50,000 statues. Although they were completed as early as the 13th century, they remained hidden until 1939. Most of the statues are dedicated to Buddhism, but others represent Confucianism, Taoism, and the ordinary life of the times.

A now-vanished ethnic group created the **Cliffside Tombs of Eban** in southwestern China about 600 years ago; their beautifully preserved wooden coffins still hang on the cliffs, accompanied by paintings depicting horse racing, dancing, religious activities, and martial arts.

The **Dai Village** includes reproductions of the simple but efficient bamboo homes of the Dai people, which include advanced climate control. When the sun shines, the thatches of the roof curl upward and allow the sunlight in and the heat out; when it rains, the thatches absorb moisture and expand to seal the roof. Each April, the Dai celebrate a water festival in which every Dai man and woman takes a bucket of water and splashes each other in a joyous ceremony that is supposed to bestow good luck.

The **Guanyin Statue** is also known as "1,000 Eyes and 1,000 Hands." It celebrates the Bodhisattaba Buddha, a disciple of Buddha who was supposed to have sprouted all those eyes so that he could see all human anguish and all of the hands so that he could appease the suffering.

The **Terra Cotta Warriors & Horses** display reproduces another wonder of China: the 1974 discovery of a hidden cave with more than 8,000 life-size and individually carved statues of soldiers and horses. The "army" was a guard of honor for the spirit of Quin Shihuang.

Restaurants at Splendid China include the **Suzhou Pearl**, offering Cantonese, Mandarin, Mongolian, Chiu Chow, Peking, Szechuan, and Hunan cuisine. Informal dining is also available at **The Seven Flavors** cafeteria in Suzhou Gardens, **The Great Wall Terrace**, **Wind and Rain Court**, and **Pagoda Garden**.

Splendid China is open daily from 9:30 A.M. to 6 P.M. in the off-season, and from 9:30 A.M. to 9 P.M. during the summer, the Chinese New Year's period, and other holiday periods. When the park is closed at 6 P.M., the Suzhou Pearl restaurant remains open until 9 P.M.

At closing time, visitors will be admitted to the park to eat at one of the restaurants; during the day, you can purchase a ticket to go shopping and receive a refund for the ticket if you leave the park within a limited time.

The park throws itself a big two-week-long party for Chinese New Year's, which occurs near the end of January. Included are special athletic and musical entertainments and special dishes at the Suzhou Pearl.

At night the park takes on another dimension, with small white lights outlining the roof lines of the buildings in Suzhou Gardens, just as they do the buildings of the Forbidden City of Beijing.

Located at Splendid China Boulevard, two miles west of Disney World on U.S. 192. (407) 396-7111. Adults, $23.55; seniors, $21.20; children, $13.90. Annual pass adults, $53.40; children, $42.75. *Discount coupon in this book.*

**Wet 'n Wild.** (407) 351-9453. 6200 International Drive, just off I-4. It's all in the name in this large water park near Universal Studios.

Although it doesn't have the Disney "theme" magic, Wet 'n Wild does have some of the wildest—and most unusual—water rides anywhere around.

The newest, wettest, and wildest attractions at the park include **The Surge**, a five-passenger bouncing tube that twists and turns its way down a 600-foot path, and the **Fuji Flyer** tower. Other attractions include **The Bomb Bay** and **Der Stuka**, claimed to be the highest, fastest water slides in the world; the **Black Hole**, a 500-foot twisting, turning journey through darkness, time, and space; the **Surf Lagoon** wave pool; and the **Kids' Playground**, with smaller versions of the park's most popular rides.

Our favorite here is **Knee Ski.** You'll snap on a life vest and a helmet and then plant your knees in a surfboard; then hold onto the handle for dear life as you are launched out onto the lake and towed by an overhead cable around a half-mile course. We've yet to see someone make it completely around on the first try, but after a few exciting tries, most visitors master the Knee Ski. My 10-year-old daughter couldn't get enough of this unusual ride.

At **Wild One**, you and a friend ride on a pair of bouncy tubes pulled around the pond by a jet-ski. Open year-round, dependent on weather conditions. For most of the year, the park is open until 5 P.M.; from June until Labor Day, Wet 'n Wild is open until 9, 10, or 11 P.M.

Adults, $24.33; children and seniors (3 to 9, 55 and older), $19.03. Half-price admission is offered after 3 P.M. or 5 P.M., depending on closing time that day. *Discount coupon in this book.*

## Other Attractions in Orlando, Kissimmee, and Nearby

**A World of Orchids.** (407) 396-1887. 2501 Old Lake Wilson Rd., Kissimmee. Botanical gardens including an arboretum containing some 2,000 orchids which bloom throughout the year. Open daily 10 A.M. to 6 P.M. Tickets $9.58 with tax; children 15 and under, free.

**Congo River Golf & Exploration Co.** Orlando: (407) 352-0042. 6312 International Drive, next to Wet 'n Wild. Kissimmee: (407) 396-6900. 4777 West Highway 192, three miles east of I-4. A miniature golf course and more, with exploration games, an arcade, and go-carts (International Drive) or paddle boats (Kissimmee). Golf fees, $6.50 for 18 holes, $8.50 for 36 holes; children under 4 years old, free. Open from 10 A.M. *Discount coupon in this book.*

**Cypress Island.** (407) 935-9202. 210 E. Monument Ave., Kissimmee. Airboat and tour boats to an island with a two-mile nature trail, free-roaming exotic animals, and nighttime airboat gator safaris. Open daily from 9 A.M. to sunset. Adults, $18; children (3 to 12), $14 plus tax.

**Falcon Helicopter Service, Inc.** (407) 352-1753. 8990 International Drive.

Rides over Sea World, Universal Studios, Walt Disney World, and Orlando range from $20 to $150 per person with a minimum of two adult fares per flight.

**Florida Seaplanes.** (800) 359-7786. Scenic seaplane tours of Kissimmee, Sanford, and other areas of Central Florida. Special tours for Space Shuttle launches and landings. From Kissimmee, $70 per person for 30-minute flight. From Sanford, $90 per person for 40-minute flight.

**Flying Tigers Warbird Air Museum.** (407) 933-1942. At Kissimmee Airport, off I-192 on Hoagland Boulevard. An impressive collection of American warplanes in working condition or undergoing restoration by mechanics and artisans. The private collection features dozens of planes including a B-17 Flying Fortress bomber, P-51 Mustang fighter, and antique biplanes. Tour guides take you through the hangars. Open every day. Adults, $6; seniors (over 60), $5; children (under 12), $5. *Discount coupon in this book.*

**Fun 'n Wheels.** Orlando: (407) 351-5651. International Drive at Sand Lake Road. Kissimmee: (407) 870-2222. I-192 at Osceola Square Mall. The wheels include a Ferris wheel (in Orlando), bumper carts, boats, and small race cars; other fun includes miniature golf (in Orlando) and bumper cars (in Kissimmee). *Discount coupon in this book.*

**Fun World.** (407) 628-2233. Located at Flea World on Highways 17-92 in Sanford. Go-carts, miniature golf, midway rides including a Ferris wheel, pirate ship, midway games, and a video arcade with more than 350 machines.

**Haunted House at Old Town.** (407) 397-2231. 5770 West Irlo Bronson Highway. Two floors of spooks and special effects. Adults, $5; children 10 and under, $3.50. Open noon to 10 P.M. daily, Saturday until 11 P.M.

**Jungleland.** (407) 396-1012. 4580 West Irlo Bronson Highway, Kissimmee. Primates, cats, birds, unusual animals from around the world, and indigenous animals of Florida are among the more than 500 animals displayed on nine acres. Open daily 9 A.M. to 5 P.M. Tickets $10.65 with tax for adults; $7.44 for children 3 to 11.

**Kartworld Kissimmee/Orlando.** Orlando: (407) 345-9225. International Drive between Wet 'n Wild and Belz. Kissimmee: 396-4800. Highway 192, four miles east of I-4. Indy-style and double-seater go-karts on a nearly mile-long track that goes over and under bridges.

**Katie's Wekiva River Landing.** (407) 628-1482. 190 Katie's Cove, Sanford. Downstream canoe runs with equipment rental and shuttle service. Runs range from 6 to 19 miles.

**Malibu Grand Prix.** (407) 351-4132. 5901 American Way, Orlando. Grand Prix-style fun in scale models of racing cars.

**Monument of States.** Lakefront Park, downtown Kissimmee. Erected in 1943, the Monument of States is a 50-foot-tall solid concrete structure reinforced with 3½ tons of steel rails.

More than 1,500 stones represent every state in the nation and 21 foreign countries. Minerals and ores include gold and silver, plus chrome, cobalt, copper, iron, lead, platinum, and zinc. Stones include agate, alabaster, alva, coquina, coral, diamond-bearing rocks, feldspar, flint, Florida keystone, granite, limestone, marble, meteors, mica, petrified wood, petrified teeth and bones, quartz, sandstone, schist, slate, stalactites, stalagmites, and travatia.

**Mystery Fun House/Starbase Omega.** (407) 351-3356. Across from the main gate of Universal Studios at 5767 Major Boulevard in Orlando. A houseful of surprises including the Forbidden Temple, an Egyptian tomb, a miniature golf course, a video arcade and the "Ultimate Lazer Game—Starbase Omega." Fun House tickets are $8.43 with tax for all. Starbase Omega tickets are $6.95 for all. Miniature golf tickets are $5.95. Open from 10 A.M. to 9 P.M. daily; later in holiday periods. *Discount coupon in this book.*

**Orlando Science Center.** (407) 896-7151. 810 East Rollins Street, Orlando. A modern museum of hands-on science for adults and mostly children. Exhibits explore weather, engineering, animal life, and more. The **John Young Planetarium** offers daily shows. Adults, $6.50; children, $5.50. Open Monday through Thursday from 9 A.M. to 5 P.M., Friday from 9 A.M. to 9 P.M., and Sunday from noon to 5 P.M. Closed Thanksgiving and Christmas.

**Paintball World.** (407) 396-4199. Behind Old Town, off Highway 192 East, Kissimmee. A 60-acre paintball preserve with trenches, forts, bases, spectator areas, concessions, and a pro shop (honest!). Open Wednesday, Saturday, and Sunday from 8:30 A.M. to 5:30 P.M.

**Pirate's Cove Adventure Golf.** (407) 352-7378. 8601 International Drive in Orlando and (407) 827-1242. Exit 27 off I-4 at Lake Buena Vista. A clever pirate-theme golf course with two 18-hole challenges at each of its locations in the Orlando area. Adults, $5; children, $4. *Discount coupon in this book.*

**Pirate's Island Adventure Golf.** (407) 396-4660. 4330 West Irlo Bronson Highway, Kissimmee. Two 18-hole courses set in a tropical paradise. Adults, $5; children, $4. *Discount coupon in this book.*

**Reptile World Serpentarium.** (407) 892-6905. 5705 East Irlo Bronson Highway, St. Cloud. Cobras and other poisonous snakes. Open Tuesday through Sunday, 9 A.M. to 5:30 P.M. Adults, $4.25; students, $3.25; children 3 to 5, $2.25.

**River Adventure Golf.** (407) 396-4666. 4535 West Irlo Bronson Highway. All tickets $6.42; children under 4, free. *Discount coupon in this book.*

**St. John's River Cruises and Tours.** (407) 330-1612. A slow boat through the shallow backwaters of the St. John's River near Orlando. Full-day tours including Blue Springs State Park, $45 per person; two-hour tours daily except Monday, $12.84 per adult, and $6.42 for children.

**Terror on Church Street.** (407) 649-3327. 135 S. Orange Ave., Orlando. A ghoulish combination of high-tech special effects and live actors, imported from Europe and plunked down in Orlando. Open evenings from 7 P.M. until midnight or later; closed Monday. Admission, $12; children 17 and under, $10.

**Toho Airboat Excursions.** (407) 931-2225. Day and night tours on West Lake Tohopekaliga in Kissimmee, including alligator hunts. Daytime tours $15 for adults, $7.50 for children 7 and under.

**Trainland.** (407) 363-9002. Toy trains from the 1920s to the present, plus a gift shop for collectors. 82255 International Drive, behind Ripley's Believe It or Not. Adults, $6; seniors, $5; and children (3 to 12), $4.

**Tupperware World Headquarters.** (407) 847-3111. U.S. Highway 441, north of Kissimmee. The home base for the world's largest manufacturer of food containers that burp when they seal is set on 1,500 acres of beautiful gardens and lakes. A self-guided tour shows pictures of the manufacturing process plus (we couldn't make this up if we tried!) a museum of historic food containers dating back to 4000 B.C.

**Water Mania.** (407) 396-2626 or (800) 527-3092. 6073 West Irlo Bronson Highway. Catch a wave at this water park right on I-192 in Kissimmee, in and among many of the off-site hotels. The slides are not as artfully decorated as those at Typhoon Lagoon, but still wet and fun. There's the Banana Peel two-person raft plunge, the Rain Forest children's water playground, and the Anaconda family raft ride. Open year-round except for about November 27 to Christmas. Adults, $24.56; children (3 to 12), $19.21.

**Wings Over Florida.** (407) 920-3856. One-hour tourist flights over Walt Disney World, Sea World, Universal Studios, and area in twin-engine aircraft. Adults, $75; children (3 to 11), $40. Reservations required.

## Other Attractions Outside Orlando

**Bok Tower Gardens.** (813) 676-9412. Located in Lake Wales, about 55 miles south of Orlando, off U.S. 27 to Alt. 27. Florida's historic bell tower, centerpiece of a magnificent garden, is at Florida's highest point—all of 295 feet. Bok Tower Gardens was dedicated to the American people by Dutch immigrant Edward Bok, Pulitzer Prize-winning editor of the *Ladies' Home Journal*. Some of the 57 bronze bells weigh as much as 12 tons. The 128 acres of gardens include thousands of azaleas, camellias, magnolias, and other flowering plants. The gardens are home to a colony of wood ducks and more than 100 other species of birds. Adults, $4; children (5 to 12), $1.

**Cypress Gardens.** (941) 324-2111 or (800) 282-2123. Florida's first theme park, established in 1936, Cypress Gardens is home of the famous water-ski team, Dixie Belles in hoop skirts, and thousands of varieties of plants, birds, and other creatures. There's also much more in this lush, green park off U.S. 27 near Winter Haven, Florida, about 45 minutes from Orlando.

The famed botanical gardens include more than 8,000 varieties of plants from 75 countries.

One of the newer exhibits is the incredible **Wings of Wonder**, a walk-through glass conservatory that is home to more than 1,000 free-flying butterflies from more than 50 species. Two glass-enclosed chrysalis houses contain unhatched butterflies imported from farms in Ecuador and El Salvador, a practice which helps protect species that come from the rain forests. The conservatory is also home to a flock of green and neon iguanas, mandarin ducks from Asia, ringed teal ducks from South America, and South African cape teals.

Guests are encouraged to snip and sniff a wide variety of herbs, including oregano, garlic, mint, lemongrass, rue, mallow, and safflower in the **Herb and Scene Garden**. The **Vegetable and Fruit Garden** bursts year-round with crops including colorful burgundy queen cauliflower, tango onions, red Boston lettuce, sparkler radishes, and jade pagoda cabbage.

Nonedible but spectacular is the famed **Rose Garden**, which includes Europeana red, French Lace white, Summer Fashion yellow, and Angel Face lavender roses in appropriate seasons.

The park is perhaps best known for **The Greatest American Ski Show**, a water-ski extravaganza which showcases high-powered boat races and ski-jumping feats and a team of 56 skiers. Cypress Gardens' first water-ski show took place in 1943 when a group of local skiers gathered on Lake Eloise to entertain military troops on leave. Since then, skiers have recorded more than 50 world records, including the first four-tier human pyramid.

**Varieté Internationale** has a changing selection of performers. **Feathered Follies**, a bird review, features macaws, cockatoos, and Amazon parrots.

Other entertainment includes a magic show and an elaborate model railroad, **Cypress Junction**, which includes 20 high-speed model trains touring tiny replicas of U.S. landmarks on 1,100 feet of track. The **Pontoon Lake Cruise** is an electric boat ride through the man-made canals that wind through the 223-acre park.

In 1996, admission was adults, $29.63; children 6 to 12 were admitted free with a paying adult; and seniors (55 and older), $24.33.

For many years, Cypress Gardens was part of the Anheuser-Busch family that includes Sea World and Busch Gardens in Florida. In 1995, the park was sold to a group of its executives.

**Lion Country Safari.** (407) 793-1084. Located in West Palm Beach, off exit 99 of the Florida Turnpike, about 175 miles from Orlando. The nation's first drive-through zoo when it opened in 1967, the park includes more than 1,000 wild animals from all over the world, including giraffes, eland, bison, elephants, rhino, zebra, ostrich, and antelope, wandering free over hundreds of acres. Other areas include a petting zoo and an amusement area that includes paddleboats, a boat ride, and an old-time carrousel. A KOA campground is nearby. Open every day from 9:30 A.M. to 5:30 P.M.; convertibles must be exchanged for available rental cars to drive through the preserve.

**Silver Springs.** (904) 236-1212 or (800) 234-7458. Approximately 72 miles from Orlando; take exit 69 off I-75 to S.R. 40 East. Silver Springs has been drawing visitors to its natural beauties since the early 1800s. In the 1860s, steamboats explored the area. In 1878, Silver Springs became famous for the invention of glass-bottom boats for display of underwater wonders. Six of the original Tarzan movies were filmed at Silver Springs in the 1930s and 1940s; *The Yearling*, starring Gregory Peck and Jane Wyman, was filmed there in 1946. And more than 100 episodes of the *Sea Hunt* television series, starring Lloyd Bridges, were filmed at Silver Springs from 1958 to 1961.

Divers have mapped and explored what is said to be the largest spring system in the world, the source of up to 2 billion gallons of water daily. Discoveries at the site have included fossilized mastodon teeth dating back 10,000 years, a giant ground sloth claw, and a mammoth tooth from the Pleistocene period. In addition, several species of troglobitic life, including crayfish, have been found.

Visitors will cruise on glass-bottom boats on a tour that explores seven natural formations including **Mammoth Spring**, the world's largest artesian limestone spring. Creatures in the nearly pure spring include alligators, turtles, garfish, and largemouth bass. Along the riverbanks are great blue heron, cormorants, ibis, egrets, raccoons, and river otters.

The **Jeep Safari** takes passengers on a four-wheel-drive vehicle into a jungle home to free-roaming wildlife, including two-toed sloth, Brazilian tapirs, African waterbuck, and four species of deer. The highlight of the safari is a trip through a three-foot-deep pit teeming with alligators.

The **Lost River Voyage** explores an untouched cypress jungle. At Cypress Point, you may be lucky enough to meet Sonek, believed to be the world's largest American alligator.

New in 1995 was the **Tarzan Jungle Spectacular**, a choreographed stunt show, which includes some of the actions performed in the Tarzan movies. A spring and summer concert series in 1995 brought stars including Glen Campbell, Holly Dunn, and George Jones. From about Thanksgiving to New Year's Eve, Silver Springs celebrates with a **Festival of Lights**, a central Florida version of a winter wonderland. Apropos of nothing else, the park is also the home of **A Touch of Garlits**, a museum of antique and race cars honoring famed drag racer Don "Big Daddy" Garlits.

Restaurants at Silver Springs include the **Springside Restaurant**, **Billy Bowlegs**, **Springside Pizzeria**, and the **Deli**.

Nearby Silver Springs is the **Wild Waters** waterpark, which includes seven water flumes, the **Tornado** water ride, and a 450,000-gallon wave pool.

Silver Springs is open every day from 9 A.M. to 5:30 P.M., with extended hours in the summer and on holidays. Adults, $28.57; children, $20.09. *Discount coupon in this book.*

**Valiant Air Command Warbird Air Museum.** (407) 268-1941. Located near the Kennedy Space Center, on Tico Road in Titusville. Historic displays of aircraft and aviation memorabilia from World War I, World War II, Korea, and Vietnam. Adults, $6; children (12 and under), $4.

**Weeki Wachee Spring.** (904) 596-2062 or (800) 678-9335. North of Tampa on U.S. 19 at the intersection with S.R. 50. Mermaids abound at this water park on the Gulf Coast. Presentations include an underwater version of the original Hans Christian Andersen story, "The Little Mermaid," as well as a **Wilderness River Cruise**, a **Birds of the World Show**, and a petting zoo. Adults, $16.95; seniors, 10 percent discount; children, $12.95.

Next to Weeki Wachee Spring lies the **Buccaneer Bay** water park, open from April to early September.

# Chapter 19
# Shopping

To heck with mice, sharks, and whales—for some folks, the ultimate Orlando recreational activity is . . . shopping. And the millions of visitors to the entertainment attractions of Orlando have proved to be a tremendous lure to retailers.

Bring an empty suitcase with you and leave time for some of the shopping adventures listed here.

**192 Flea Market.** (407) 396-4555. 4301 West Vine Street (I-192) in Kissimmee. A full-time, free admission market with as many as 400 dealer booths under one roof. Disney souvenirs, jewelry, crafts, clothing, and more. Open daily from 9 A.M. to 6 P.M.

**Altamonte Mall.** (407) 830-4400. North of Orlando, east of I-4 on S.R. 436 in Altamonte Springs. Burdine's, JC Penney, The Gap, Cache, The Limited, Sears, and more than 175 specialty shops.

**Belz Factory Outlet World.** (407) 352-9600. Located at the north end of International Drive, past Kirkman Road. A huge collection of factory outlet shops, with more than 160 companies represented in two enclosed malls and four shopping centers, all within walking distance of each other. Manufacturers include L'eggs/Hanes/Bali, Maidenform, Totes, Polly Flinders, Bally, Bass, Stride-Rite, Mikasa, Adolfo II, Anne Klein, Geoffrey Beene, Jordache, Leslie Fay, Levi Strauss, Van Heusen, Oshkosh B'Gosh, Capezio, Dexter, Corning, Burlington Brands, Guess Jeans, London Fog, Danskin, Londontown, Harvé Bernard, and Young Generations. Open Monday through Saturday 10 A.M. to 9 P.M. and Sunday from 10 A.M. to 6 P.M.

**Dansk Outlet.** (407) 351-2425. 7000 International Drive.

**The Florida Mall.** (407) 851-6255. Intersection of Sand Lake Road (S.R. 482) and South Orange Blossom Trail (Hwy. 441). Belk Lindsey, Dillard's, Gayfers, JC Penney, Sears, and 170 specialty shops. Open daily from 10 A.M. to 9:30 P.M., and Sunday from 11 A.M. to 6 P.M.

**Kissimmee Manufacturer's Mall.** (407) 396-8900. I-192 near Kissimmee. Shops include American Tourister, Casual's Unlimited, Fieldcrest Cannon,

Geoffrey Beene Co., The Magic Shop, Nike Factory Store, Olde Times, Publishers Outlet, Totes Factory Store, Van Heusen, and Westport Ltd.

**Mercado.** (407) 345-9337. 8445 International Drive. A small but interesting collection of shops and eateries. Just as Disney's creative roller coaster packaging makes Space Mountain an above-average ride, the Mercado "package" makes this mall a different sort of shopping experience.

Mercado includes more than 60 unusual specialty shops, including Once Upon A Star (movie motif gifts and clothing); Kandlestix, Pet Palace, Krazy Kites, House of Ireland, Earth Matters (wildlife and marine-life clothing and accessories for the conservation-minded), Kitchen Magnetism (kitchen accessories and magnets for your refrigerator door), Space 2000 (air- and space-related clothing and gifts), and The Magic Shop.

Restaurants include Damon's—The Place for Ribs, Charlie's Lobster House, Bergamo's Italian Restaurant, The Butcher Shop Steakhouse, José O'Day's Mexican Restaurant, and the Blazing Pianos Red Hot Rock 'n' Roll Piano Bar.

In the Village Cafe food court, you'll also find The Greek Place, Wok 'n Roll, Sabor Latino, the All-American Grill, Gombadi Pizza, En La Frontera, The Sandwich Gallery, Chicken Magic, and Le Gelateria Molto. At Fat Tuesday's, they claim the world's largest selection of frozen drinks; there's also Cricketers Arms, an English pub.

At night, the grounds and shops are alight with twinkling lights, and free entertainment is presented in the courtyard.

Shops open from 10 A.M. to 10 P.M. daily; restaurants and bars close later. *Discount coupon in this book.*

**Quality Outlet Center.** 5527 International Drive, one block east of Kirkman Road. A small outlet center, it features shops selling products from companies including Arrow, American Tourister, Corning-Revere, Florsheim, Laura Ashley, Linens 'n Things, Magnavox, Mikasa, Royal Doulton, Villeroy & Boch, and Yes Brasil. Open Monday through Saturday from 9:30 A.M. to 9 P.M.; Sunday from 11 A.M. to 6 P.M.

# VIII
# Busch Gardens Tampa and Adventure Island

## Chapter 20
## Busch Gardens Tampa and Adventure Island

Busch Gardens opened as a hospitality center for the Anheuser-Busch brewery in Tampa in 1959, showcasing a collection of exotic birds and some of the Busch family's collection of African animals. In 1971, when the era of Florida as theme park began, the company began a massive expansion of Busch Gardens.

Today, the park is like stepping onto the African veldt—albeit a veldt with a monorail circling above and some of the most outrageous modern roller coasters and other rides on the horizon. New for 1997 is the spectacular Montu coaster in the new Egypt area of the park.

Busch Gardens is a welcome getaway from the concrete of Walt Disney World and environs, drawing 3 million visitors a year to its 355 acres, home to more than 2,800 animals representing nearly 320 species. The brewery that was the original reason for being for Busch Gardens Tampa was closed at the end of 1995; no plans have been announced for the use of the 17-acre parcel at the heart of the park, except that the land has been given to the park for future development.

The map of Florida looks so huge to many visitors that the thought of a drive from Orlando to Tampa seems like a day's drive; it's not. Measured from the intersection of I-4 and I-192, it's 70 easy miles at 65 mph to the gates of Sea World, about 75 minutes.

Although it is only about 70 miles away, it is on the other coast of Florida and sometimes in a different weather pattern than Orlando. One March day, we left Orlando in the rain and arrived to find the sun blazing in Tampa.

The busiest times of the year are similar to those of the Orlando attractions: June to Labor Day and Spring and Easter Breaks. Other times of the year bring large crowds of foreign visitors, including planeloads from South America and Brazil. Lines, though, rarely approach anything like those at Walt Disney World or Universal Studios Florida.

Operating hours are 9:30 A.M. until 6 P.M. Extended hours into the evening are offered in summer and over selected holiday periods.

# MUST-SEES

## Montu
*(the latest and greatest for coaster fans)*

## Moroccan Palace Theater
*(ice show fans)*

## Myombe Reserve: The Great Ape Domain

## Questor

## The Monorail

## The Scorpion
*(ever so slightly less intense than Kumba)*

## Kumba
*(number one for roller coaster fans)*

## The Python

## Congo River Rapids

## Claw Island

## Stanley Falls Log Flume

## Tanganyika Tidal Wave

Busch Entertainment Corp. operates entertainment parks, including Busch Gardens in Tampa and Williamsburg, Virginia; Sea World parks in Orlando, San Antonio, San Diego, and Aurora, Ohio; Adventure Island in Tampa; and Sesame Place in Langhorne, Pennsylvania.

From Orlando: Take I-4 West about 60 miles to Tampa. Exit to I-75 North and then take the Fowler Avenue off-ramp (Exit 54) and follow signs to the park.

# Power Trip for Summer and Holiday Periods

Begin your Busch Gardens tour by studying the schedule of entertainment you will be handed at the gate; some shows like the ice extravaganza at the **Moroccan Palace Theater** and **The Dolphins of the Deep Show** are put on numerous times during the day. Other presentations may be scheduled only once or twice. Adjust your Power Trip to include any must-see shows.

If you've got the heart and stomach for it, head immediately to Egypt to ride **Montu**. Lines are sure to be lengthy in the heart of the day, so visit early or late. Serious coaster fans will then want to move on to the Congo to ride **Kumba**, Busch Gardens' other thriller.

While you're in Kumba's neighborhood, check out **The Congo River Rapids**. We like all three of the major water rides at Busch Gardens; you might want to leave a dry sweatshirt in a locker for the occasional chilly day. Now try the awesome **Python** roller-twister-coaster. When you're through, the majestic tigers on **Claw Island** will probably seem tame, but they're certainly worth a visit.

Of the two remaining water rides, **Stanley Falls** may be more fun but the **Tanganyika Tidal Wave** is more dramatic. What the heck: ride 'em both.

For a different type of thrill, consider heading very early for the sign-up for the

Serengeti Safari tour into the animal preserve. This extra-charge trip sells out early; tickets are sold at the booth near the animal nursery.

If you are not in the mood for an immediate upside down rattle and roll, you can instead start your day by bearing right from the entrance toward Crown Colony to visit **Questor.** Once you return to earth, backtrack to the Skyride and Monorail station. We'd recommend a trip on the **Monorail** to explore the Serengeti Plain; come back later in the day for a Skyride if you have the time.

At busy times of the year, we'd advise you to now press on through Nairobi without stopping and head for the thrill ride areas, stopping in Timbuktu. If you've got the stomach for it you've got to ride **The Scorpion**; it'll set you up for even more of a wild ride later on. If a show is planned that matches your schedule, visit the **Dolphin Theater** now.

At this point, you will have ridden on all of the major rides. Now take a second, more leisurely circuit of the park and visit the animal exhibits and shows and finish with the **Skyride** and **Trans-Veldt Railroad.**

## Busch Gardens Attractions

### Morocco

A re-creation of the exotic city of Marrakesh, featuring unusual architecture and a wide range of demonstrations of Moroccan crafts, snake charmers, the Mystic Sheiks of Morocco marching band, and the Sounds of Steel, a five-man steel drum band.

**Busch Gardens 1996 Ticket Prices (Tax included) Prices are subject to change.**

| One-Day | |
| --- | --- |
| Adult | $36.15 |
| Child (3 to 9) | $29.75 |

| Twilight Pass (Sold 2½ hours before closing) | |
| --- | --- |
| Adult | $25.50 |
| Child | $20.20 |

| Busch Gardens Tampa/Adventure Island Combo | |
| --- | --- |
| Adult | $37.30 |
| Child | $31.75 |

| Busch Gardens Tampa/Sea World Orlando Combo | |
| --- | --- |
| Adult | $53.25 |
| Child | $43.80 |

| Parking | |
| --- | --- |
| Cars | $4.00 |
| Trucks, campers | $5.00 |

| Wild Card Annual Pass (Busch Gardens Tampa and Sea World Orlando) | |
| --- | --- |
| Adult | $109.95 |
| Senior/Child | $99.95 |

| Surf 'n Safari (Busch Gardens Tampa and Adventure Island Annual Pass | |
| --- | --- |
| Adult/Child | $111.75 |

**Marrakesh Theater.** Two 20-minute shows alternate daily.

**Sultan's Tent.** A snake charmer performs daily.

**WOW Moroccan Palace Theater.** "Hollywood Live on Ice" is the latest show performed several times daily in this 1,200-seat arena. Midday performances fill up within 20 minutes of show time. The 35-minute show features 14 skaters and two vocalists.

A singing director opens a silent film segment while video walls on both sides of the rink show closeups of the action stage. A horror film segment is introduced with dramatic smoke and fog; through the mist emerge a 17-foot-tall inflatable dinosaur, a werewolf, and 30 skeletons that come to light with the aid of special lighting effects. A rain curtain sets the effects for (of course) a version of "Singing in the Rain."

**Serious shoppers only.**
Busch Gardens offers a
plan for visitors who
want a quick shopping
spree at one of the shops
just inside its gates. Buy
your ticket, go forth and
shop, and be back at the
Guest Relations booth
within 30 minutes and
you will be given a
refund of your ticket.
(You'll have to pay for
parking, though.) We're
told that some visitors
make a mad dash from
the gate to the
Smokehouse restaurant
for take-out ribs or
chicken.

James Bond arrives on a hang glider . . . and leaves via helicopter. The finale of the ice show includes a towering staircase and fountain for the dancers.

One of the choreographers for the show is former Olympian Randy Gardner, who partnered with skater Tai Babilonia.

Serious shoppers may enjoy a visit to the brass store just past the ticket booths; an artisan/importer from Morocco offers an impressive display. And, if you like to pay to carry someone else's corporate slogan or ad campaign, check out the **Rabat Label** store, where you can buy just about any article of clothing or sporting equipment with one or another Anheuser-Busch logo on it.

**Tangiers Theater.** Site of weekday 12:30 P.M. broadcasts of *Harris & Co.,* a Tampa television talk and variety show starring Jack Harris. Park guests are welcome as members of the audience.

## Egypt

**WOW** **Montu.** The world's largest inverted steel roller coaster, soars across nearly 4,000 feet of track and includes four first-of-a-kind elements:

- The "Immelman," an inverse loop named after a famed German stunt pilot;
- The world's largest vertical loop on an inverted coaster, at 104 feet; and
- Two vertical loops slanted at 45-degree angles, known as a "batwing."

Other elements include a camelback maneuver that delivers three seconds of weightlessness, sweeping arcs crossing over and under the tracks of the Transveldt Railway, and a corkscrew finale.

There are three trains comprised of eight cars, each of which holds four passengers across for a total of 32 riders per train. The cars hang from the top and swing out from side to side; the foot platforms drop out when the train departs, leaving feet dangling below the car; at one point the swooping cars dive as close as 18 inches above the ground. The tracks dive into three Egyptian-theme tunnels below ground.

Peaking at speeds in excess of 60 miles per hour, Montu reaches a maximum G-force of 3.85 at certain points during the three-minute trip. Riders must be at least 52 inches tall.

The approach to the loading area for the ride is through a portal in a spectacular 55-foot-tall wall with hand-carved hieroglyphs.

Montu is named after a hawk-like Sun God worshiped by ancient Egyptians at Thebes. The ride is the centerpiece of Egypt, Busch Gardens' largest expansion and ninth themed area.

Visitors to Egypt will be able to tour a six-room replica of King

Tutankhamen's tomb as it looked when it was first discovered by archeologist Howard Carter in the early 1920s. Young visitors will be able to dig through a sand pit with buried artifacts of the ancient culture. The area also includes shopping bazaars for the older visitors. Items for sale at the **Golden Scarab** and **Treasures of the Nile** shops include hand-blown glass and cartouche painting on scrolls.

The Transveldt Railway tracks have been moved to bring them closer to Egypt, offering a glimpse of Montu from the safety of the cars.

## Nairobi

**WOW** **Myombe Reserve: The Great Ape Domain.** Busch Gardens' newest habitat, featuring six lowland gorillas and eight common chimpanzees in a tropical forest setting. Gorillas include Lash, a 15-year-old, 330-pound silverback male who was hand-raised by surrogates at the Cincinnati Zoo after his mother died. Also resident is a social group of five gorillas on a long-term breeding loan from Emory University in Atlanta, Georgia.

**Montu Mania**
Here are some of the specs on Busch's latest and greatest coaster:
**Track length:** 3,983 feet
**Maximum speed:** 60 mph
**Maximum G-force:** 3.85
**Maximum drop:** 128 feet
**Length of ride:** About three minutes
**Capacity:** About 1,710 riders per hour.

**Animal hospital.** The veterinary clinic includes operating rooms, X-ray, laboratory, and recovery areas, as well as brooder rooms for birds.

Visitors enter the three-acre habitat through dense foliage to a clearing with a glass wall where they can observe the chimps; passing through a bamboo thicket, guests will come upon the gorillas at the base of a mountain between waterfalls in a simulated tropical rain forest. (On cool days, boulders near the viewing areas are heated to draw animals.) There are chimp nests scattered in the trees, as much as 70 feet off the ground.

At each turn in the reserve, you will see educational displays that tell you about the lives of the gorillas, and how humans are threatening their natural environment. Some other things you'll learn: a young female uses blades of grass and stems to extract termites, a chimp delicacy; chimps, who eat mostly fruit, also use plants for medicinal purposes to kill parasites, fungi, and viruses; before chimps were observed using tools it was assumed that humans were the only ones to do so.

**Nairobi Station Transveldt Railroad.** The train offers some of the best close-up views of the animals on the Serengeti Plain between the Nairobi and Congo stations. Other portions of the track offer a tourist's eye view of the back sides of the Python and Scorpion roller coasters. The train is a ¾-scale replica of an actual African steam engine and cars; the engine is an unusual combination of energy sources, using propane gas to boil water for steam that powers an electric generator for the wheels.

**Aldabra Tortoise Habitat.** Opposite the train station, you'll find a collection of gigantic tortoises, including the Aldabra tortoise, often found on

**Vanishing gorillas.**
Gorillas, the largest living primates, are seriously endangered or in some cases on the brink of extinction in the tropical forests, woodlands, and mountain regions of Africa. Most threatened is the mountain gorilla subspecies; perhaps fewer than 450 remain.

**Coaster clinic.** If you are prone to dizziness or upset stomach from roller coasters, you might want to take one or two Dramamine motion sickness tablets at the start of the day (before you take any rides). They work like a charm. Check with your family doctor first if you are taking any other medications or if you have any allergies or unusual conditions. And be aware that the pills may make you a bit sleepy; you may want to assign a designated driver for the end of the day.

Aldabra Island in the Indian Ocean. Brought back from near extinction, Aldabras often weigh as much as 600 pounds when mature, and are now seen in large groups wallowing in mud or shallow lagoons.

In the same area, you may also see an African Spurred Tortoise, Africa's largest land tortoises. They span the continent along the southern fringe of the Sahara desert to the Red Sea.

**Serengeti Safari.** Twice a day, a small group of visitors can clamber on board an open flatbed truck for a one-hour visit behind the fences of the 60-acre **Serengeti Plain**, with close-up views of giraffes, zebras, hippopotamuses, and other animals. A park guide accompanies visitors on the truck. It's a fabulous opportunity for camera buffs and animal lovers of all ages. Tickets, which sell out quickly from a booth near the animal nursery, are priced at $20 for adults, and $14 for children from 5 to 9 years of age.

**Animals.** As close as you can get to some of the animals, and some special treats for the children. You'll find an unusually attractive **Petting Zoo**, but don't overlook the fascinating **Nairobi Station Animal Nursery**, home to Busch Gardens' newest and littlest arrivals including tiny birds, alligators, and snakes, set in a replica of a yesteryear African hospital.

The **Elephant Wash** is just what it sounds like: ponderous pachyderms stand still for showers several times a day; nearby is a small enclosure where guests can climb onto a seat on the back of an elephant for a short ride.

## Crown Colony

**WOW** **Questor.** Set sail on a truly amazing adventure in this spectacular high-tech simulator voyage along with the eccentric inventor Sir Edison Fitzwilly on a harrowing mission in search of the elusive Crystal of Zed. You'll bore down into the earth, dodge stalagmites in a dark cavern, and blast back to the watery surface just in time to plunge over a raging waterfall—all this without leaving your seat or even moving very far. Be warned, though, that passengers will experience more G-force than a roller coaster drop.

The somewhat fanciful waiting area includes pipes marked "coolant to flaxilator," a meter for the Jurbilium capacitor (energy units measured in Jurbs), as well as blueprints and drawings of Fitzwilly's invention.

We found the ride somewhat similar—although a bit goofier—to the Star Tours simulator at Disney-MGM Studios. There are two, identical simulators, each seating 60 travelers for a four-minute ride. On busy days, we'd suggest heading for Questor early or late in the day.

**The Skyride.** An open cable car ride from the Crown Colony to the Congo and back, passing above the Serengeti Plain and then deep into deepest, darkest amusement park–land with good views of the Scorpion and the Congo River Rapids. A lovely way to see the park on a lovely day; when it is not lovely, the ride can be a bit chilly, and it is shut down in high winds and inclement weather.

**WOW The Monorail.** An ultra-modern train that hangs from an overhead single rail for a nearly silent 10-minute cruise in and among the zebras, rhinos, ostriches, and other animals of the Serengeti Plain. The track drops down low for close-up views of some of the residents.

The driver of the train, which can carry about 72 persons in its six air-conditioned cabins, will fill you in on all sorts of things you always wanted to know—like the fact that more people are killed each year by river hippos than by crocodiles.

**Animals.** Some of Anheuser-Busch's famous corporate symbols can be visited in their stables at the **Clydesdale Hamlet.** The largest adults can be as large as six feet at the shoulder and weigh about a ton.

## Serengeti Plain

The largest open area of

*Aldabra Tortoises, Busch Gardens Tampa Bay*
© *Busch Entertainment Corp.*

the park, an 80-acre natural setting featuring more than 800 animals in free-roaming herds of camels, elephants, zebra, giraffes, chimpanzees, rhino, Cape buffalo, gazelles, greater kudus, and hippos. Ride the Monorail for the closest views; the Trans-Veldt Railroad also circles the Plain, while the Skyride passes overhead.

## Timbuktu

**WOW** **The Scorpion.** It goes up to the top of its tower, then down and to the left at 55 mph before entering a full 360-degree loop into a series of corkscrew descents that put you on your side.

The Scorpion is by most accounts in the middle between Python and Kumba on the wildness meter.

Parental Guidance: The exit to the ride is in a different area from the entrance.

You must be at least 42 inches tall to ride, and in good physical condition.

**Carousel Caravan.** A most unusual merry-go-round, featuring desert camels and Arabian horses.

**The Phoenix.** A dry boat ride that gives new meaning to the term "rock 'n' roll." The platform moves forward and then backward with increasing power until riders make a complete pass up and over the top a few times. This is a bigger and wilder version of the pirate ship rides common at many amusement parks.

Other rides here include the **Sandstorm**, an aerial whip; the **Crazy Camel**, a collection of children's rides, an electronic arcade, and a group of carnival games of skill.

**Dolphins of the Deep Show.** Bud and Mich (sounds vaguely commercial, doesn't it?), with their sea lion sidekick and their trainers, demonstrate their speed and agility in an entertaining show at the Dolphin Theater.

In front of Dolphins of the Deep Theater, be sure to locate the Floss Silked Tree. Native to South America, in late fall the leaves shed and large showy flowers appear. At the peak of color, the canopy is a mass of pink orchid blossoms. When flowering is over, pear-shaped fruits appear that explode when they are ripe, sending a silky cotton material floating to the ground.

## Congo

**WOW** **Kumba** means "roar" in a dialect of the African Congo. It might have been better to call it "aiyeeeee!" or some other such scream. Kumba is one of the largest and fastest steel roller coasters in the country, reaching speeds in excess of 60 mph and putting as much as 3.75 Gs on the bodies of its lucky riders.

The coaster includes several unusual elements, including a diving loop, which plunges riders into a loop from a height of 110 feet; a camelback, a maneuver that creates three seconds of weightlessness while spiraling 360 degrees; a 108-foot vertical loop, the world's largest; a cobra roll which turns passengers upside down as they twist around a spectator bridge; and more ordinary super-coaster thrills including an oblique loop, a vertical spiral, and a double corkscrew-shaped twist.

But the ride itself is even wilder than its description—longer and with more twists and turns than three or four ordinary coasters put together. Riders are securely locked into place with an overhead harness and are seated four across. The outside seats give the best view—that is, if you are able or willing to turn your head while moving.

But before I scare you off, consider the fact that Kumba's roar is much worse than its bite. You are moving so fast that you hardly realize that you are on your head or your side or your back. And if it makes you feel any better, know that my nine-year-old daughter led the family onto the ride one morning; she rode it once with me and her big brother, a second time with her brother, and a third time by herself when we all insisted on a rest.

**Kumba-yah!** Here are the vital specs for Kumba, one of the largest and fastest steel roller coasters in the country.
**Track length:** 3,978 feet
**Maximum speed:** 60 mph
**Maximum G-force:** 3.75
**Maximum drop:** 135 feet
**Length of ride:** 2:54
**Capacity:** about 1,700 riders per hour.

The ride is very nicely integrated into the bushes and trees of the park, with many of the dips and turns in the bushes. You can walk beneath much of the track, too, which offers a great view for spectators and bragging rights to successful riders.

You must be at least 52 inches tall to ride and in good physical condition. Did I mention that I started that day with two Dramamine tablets?

**WOW** **The Python.** Only at a park like Busch Gardens would a roller coaster like the Python have to settle for second-class status behind Montu and Kumba. The Python includes wicked twists and turns and a 360-degree *double* spiral, and cars reach speeds of more than 50 mph as they travel some 1,200 feet. All that said, the Python is a very short ride; you'll be back at the loading station before your heart has returned from your throat.

If you're a little uncertain about your roller coaster credentials, you may want to try your stomach at Python, then move on to Scorpion, and then make it all the way to Kumba and finally to Montu.

You must be at least 48 inches tall to ride.

**WOW** **The Congo River Rapids.** Riders sit in a 12-passenger circular air raft and are let loose on a churning whitewater trip in an artificial river with rapids, logs, and other boats in the way. We'd tell you to sit at the back of the boat to avoid getting soaked, but the darned thing keeps turning around. The ride won't get your heart pounding quite as fast as one of the flume trips, but it's still a lot of fun. Riders must be at least 38 inches tall, or at least two years old and accompanied by an adult.

By the way, on the footbridge overlooking the rapids beneath the Kumba track there is a coin-operated water cannon aimed at the rafts below. Put a quarter into the **Congo Water Blasters** and add a little extra water to the passengers below.

Other rides in this area include the **Ubanga-Banga Bumper Cars**, the **Monstrous Mamba** octopus ride, and more kiddie rides.

**WOW! Claw Island.** Here's your chance to get as close as you may ever want to a rare white Bengal tiger.

## Stanleyville

**WOW! Stanley Falls Log Flume.** Over the edge of a 43-foot plastic cliff in a hollowed-out log. Lines build at midday; visit early or late in the day to avoid long waits.

**WOW! Tanganyika Tidal Wave.** Go for a pleasant little cruise through lush, tropical foliage. Sounds relaxing . . . that is, until your 20-passenger boat plunges over the edge to fall 55 feet into a splash pool. The result is a huge wave—really huge—that wets the passengers but can really *soak* observers standing in the wrong place on the walkway below.

For a great view of the tidal wave, climb the bridge and stand within the glass-walled tunnel. If you are riding, the back of the boat gets wet the least.

You must be at least 42 inches tall to ride.

**Animals.** Orangutans.

**Stanleyville Theater.** Daily variety shows in season.

**Zambezi Theater.** Improvisational comedy presented several times daily in season. Resident zanies are the **Congo Comedy Corps.**

## Land of the Dragons

**Land of the Dragons.** Busch Garden's new children's play area is built around a three-story tree house. The Land of the Dragons is home to Dumphrey, a whimsical and friendly beast.

Kids are invited to explore the winding stairways and mysterious towers of the treehouse. The area also includes a children's theater, slides, a rope climb, a ball crawl, and a gentle waterfall. The rides area includes a mini-sized Ferris wheel, flume ride, and a dragon carrousel.

## Bird Gardens

**Bird Gardens** is the oldest area of the park, built in the shadow of the brewery in 1959; the brewery is now closed. The lush foliage includes nearly 2,000 exotic birds and birds of prey, representing 218 species and including one of the largest managed flocks of Caribbean flamingos.

**Feeding Times**
**Alligators.** Morocco. 10:30 A.M. and 2:30 P.M.
**Elephants.** Nairobi. 10:45 and 11:30 A.M.; 1:10, 1:45, 3, and 4:30 P.M.
**Orangutans.** Stanleyville. 1:15 and 2:30 P.M.
**Tigers.** Congo. 1:30 and 3 P.M.
**Tortoises.** Nairobi. 1:15 and 2:30 P.M.
**Warthogs.** Stanleyville. 1 and 2 P.M.

**Busch Gardens Bird Show.** Several performances each day of a show that includes macaws, cockatoos, and birds of prey in free-flight demonstrations.

**Lizard Habitat.** One of the park's newest environments showcases Asian water monitors, crocodile monitors, rhinoceros iguanas, and green iguanas from regions including Indonesia, South America, and the Caribbean.

> **Respect the animals.** Please don't throw anything into the animal preserves. Human food disrupts the animals' natural diets, and plastic objects—like straws or drink lids—could be lethal playthings.

**Hospitality House Stage.** A musical variety show including ragtime jazz piano. Regular stars are **Dr. Dave's Trio.**

**Animals.** Some of the park's most famous species are on display here, at **Flamingo Island, Eagle Canyon,** and the **Koala Display.** Eagles on display alongside the brewery include golden and American bald eagles. The koala habitat also includes Dama wallabies and rose-breasted cockatoos.

The park's Chilean Flamingos ordinarily live in large colonies on brackish lagoons in South America. Their bent bills are fringed at the edges and when held upside down in the water filter out mud and retain shrimp and algae.

**Koala Display.** A series of educational exhibits leads up to the home of the park's koalas, among the most unusual animals at Busch Gardens. You'll glide past the glassed-in cages on a moving sidewalk; at the end, you can also climb up some stairs to a stationary viewing area.

Koalas are marsupials, unique mammals with a pouch that covers the mammary glands on the abdomen. In the Americas, the only current species of marsupial is the opossum.

## Special Programs

Busch Gardens offers a variety of educational programs; check with the park for a schedule. Among the offerings is **Zoo Camp,** five different weeklong summer camp programs for children from kindergarten through ninth grade, aimed at helping develop an understanding of the role zoos play in conservation.

## Eating Your Way Through Busch Gardens Tampa
### Morocco

**Boujad Bakery.** An exotic place to grab breakfast or a sweet at any time of the day. Check out the gigantic blueberry and other types of muffins; also sold are impressive turnovers and pastries for $2 to $3 each.

**Zagora Cafe.** An exotic outdoor bazaar setting for unexotic burgers ($5.50), onion rings, and turkey sandwich platters ($6.25). Breakfast is served until 11 A.M.

### Congo

**Vivi Storehouse.** Near the Python coaster, this restaurant is open in season only from 11:45 A.M. to 4 P.M. Offerings include sandwich platters for about $5.59, chicken fajitas, and other specialties.

## Crown Colony

**Crown Colony House.** A lovely 240-seat restaurant with spectacular views of the Serengeti Plain from its glass-walled Veldt Room. Another interesting location is the Library, stocked with antique books and a collection of photographs from Colonial days in Africa. A piano player entertains during meals.

Featured is Crown Colony's Famous Family-Style Chicken Dinner: platters of batter-dipped chicken, cole slaw, soft yeast rolls, dressing, mashed potatoes and gravy, garden vegetables, and cranberry relish. $8.95 per person; diners 12 and under are billed a reasonable $3.95. The same platter can be ordered with batter-fried fish instead of chicken. Other offerings include a broiled Florida grouper sandwich for $7.95 or a chicken breast filet for $6.95. Children's meals include drumstick platters or spaghetti and meatballs for approximately $4.

There are only 12 tables next to the windows in the Veldt Room, and they go fast. No reservations are accepted. The least crowded times are before noon, and from 4 to 5:30 P.M.; each day a throng heads for the restaurant about 12:15 P.M. when the midday ice show lets out.

**Anheuser-Busch Hospitality Center.** Pizza, sandwiches, and free samples of beer and snacks made by Anheuser-Busch companies.

## Timbuktu

**Das Festhaus.** The ceiling is an attractive blue-and-white striped tent. In the center of the large 1,200-seat hall is an elevated bandstand, home of the **Bavarian Colony Band and Dancers** who present the **German Show.** The show harks back to the early German settlers in Africa who made their home in Timbuktu. Also seen on the stage is the **Festival of Nations Show,** which features music and performances from around the world.

Offerings include the Alpine Platter (corned beef, potato salad, cabbage or sauerkraut, and drink), the German Sampler Platter (two sausages and side orders), or a turkey sandwich, each for about $6. There is also a spaghetti platter for $4.95, canneloni for $5.49, and a Safari kids spaghetti meal for $2.99. A range of Anheuser-Busch beers is offered.

**Oasis.** Fruit juices and churros.

## Stanleyville

**Stanleyville Smokehouse.** Slow-smoked chicken, beef brisket, and pork ribs, served with french fries and cole slaw. Prices range from $5 to $7.95; a good deal is the $7.95 combo platter. Grab a bunch of napkins and prepare for a tasty mess.

**Bazaar Cafe.** Barbecue beef sandwich platters at $5 and salads for $2.

## Bird Gardens

**Hospitality House.** Pepperoni and Chef's Combo pizzas, at $3 to $4 per slice. Tampa sandwiches—salami, turkey, cheese, and salad on a roll—sell for about $5.50.

## Adventure Island

Although the tidal wave and rafting expeditions at Busch Gardens are guaranteed to dampen your hairdo, if you want to get really wet, you may want to head around the corner to Adventure Island.

The 22-acre water park, also owned by Busch Entertainment Corp., offers giant speed slides, body flumes, diving platforms, inner tube slides, a wave pool, water games, a white sand beach, and volleyball courts.

The newest slide is **Aruba Tuba**, a "tubular" slide that twists in and around and below Calypso Coaster; the ride can be enjoyed by solo riders or two at a time.

**Calypso Coaster** is a spiraling snake-like ride down an open flume in an inner tube or raft for two; **Rambling Bayou** is a slow float along a rambling river around bends, under bridges, and

| ADVENTURE ISLAND 1996 Ticket Prices (Tax included) Prices are subject to change | |
| --- | --- |
| Adult | $22.21 |
| Child (3 to 9) | $20.09 |
| **Busch Gardens Tampa/Adventure Island Combo** | |
| Adult | $37.30 |
| Child | $31.75 |
| **Parking** | $2.00 |
| **Season Pass** | $63.85 |
| **Surf 'n Safari (Annual pass to Adventure Island and Busch Gardens Tampa)** | $111.75 |

through a man-made rain forest; the **Caribbean Corkscrew** takes riders from a four-story tower down a fully enclosed, twisting translucent tube; **Water Moccasin** is a triple-tube water slide which cascades riders downward through a spiral before dumping them in a pool; **Tampa Typhoon** is a free-fall body slide which drops from a height of 76 feet before it levels out in a slick trough; and **Gulf Scream** is a speed slide in which riders can go as fast as 25 mph down a 210-foot fiberglass slide.

**Everglides** takes riders down a steep 72-foot double slide on water sleds which hydroplane up to 100 feet over a splash pool; a lift system carries the sleds back to the top of the slide platform. **Runaway Rapids** is a 34-foot-high artificial mountain featuring five separate curving and twisting water flumes as long as 300 feet.

**Paradise Lagoon** is a 9,000-square-foot swimming pool fed by waterfalls; built into the surrounding cliffs are 20-foot-high diving platforms, a cable drop, a cannonball slide, and tube slides. Stretching overhead across the pool is a hand-over-hand rope walk. The **Endless Surf** is a 17,000-square-foot pool that mechanically produces three- to five-foot waves for body and rubber raft surfing.

**Fabian's Funport** is a children's play area designed for the youngest visitors, featuring a scaled-down wave pool and water play toys.

The **Spike Zone** is a 12-court volleyball area set up for friendly or professional competitive events.

Adventure Island is open from the end of March daily until after Labor Day, and weekends into October. Call (813) 987-5660 for schedules.

# BUSCH GARDENS

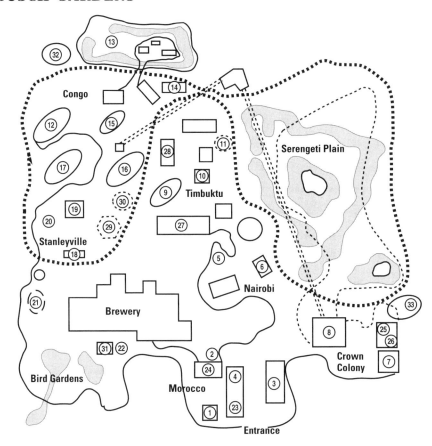

1. Marrakesh Theater
2. Sultan's Tent
3. Moroccan Palace Theater
4. Rabat Label Store
5. Myombe Reserve: The Great Ape Domain
6. Train Station
7. Questor
8. Skyride and Monorail Station
9. The Scorpion
10. Carousel Caravan
11. The Phoenix
12. The Python
13. The Congo River Rapids
14. Congo Train Station
15. Claw Island
16. Stanleyville Falls Log Flume
17. Tanganyika Tidal Wave
18. Stanleyville Station
19. Stanleyville Theater
20. Zambezi Theater
21. Land of the Dragons Children's Play Area
22. Hospitality House Stage
23. Boujad Bakery
24. Zangora Cafe
25. Crown Colony Restaurant
26. Anheuser Busch Hospitality Center
27. Festhaus
28. Oasis
29. Stanleyville Smokehouse
30. Bazaar Cafe
31. Hospitality House
32. Kumba
32. Montu

## Discount Coupons

Look to your left, look to your right. One of you three people on vacation in Florida is paying the regular price for attractions, hotels, meals, and shopping. One of the three is paying above regular price. And one pays only discount prices.

Which one would you rather be?

I'm happy to present a special section of discount coupons from Orlando and the surrounding area. A careful reader of this book could save several hundred dollars or more on a trip to Central Florida using just a few of the coupons.

The presence of a coupon in this section does not in any way affect the author's opinions expressed in this book.

Let us know how you are received when you use them, and give us your opinions of these merchants—and others—in Central Florida.

**THE #1 MOVIE STUDIO AND THEME PARK IN THE WORLD!**

## $2.50 Off
Valid for up to 6 people

**Thrill to over 40 of the most spectacular rides, shows, and attractions only at Universal Studios Florida—The only place on earth you can Ride the Movies©.**

FL97-78

Present this coupon at any Universal Studios Florida admission window to receive your discount. Discount valid for up to six people toward the purchase of a one-day adult or child studio pass through December 31, 1997. This coupon has no cash value. Not valid with any other specials or discounts. Offer subject to change without notice. Parking fee not included. Coupon must be presented at time of transaction.

©1996 Universal Studios Florida. All Rights Reserved.

For more information call: (407) 363-8000.
Entrances: Turkey Lake Road (Exit 29, 1-4) and Kirkman Road (S.R. 435, Exit 30B, 1-4).
Expires 12/31/97

FL97-78

## NEW! KEY WEST AT SEA WORLD℠

Limit six guests per certificate. Not valid with other discounts or on purchase of multi-park/multi-visit passes or tickets. Present certificate at Front Gate before bill is totaled. Redeemable only at time of ticket purchase. Photocopies not accepted. Operating hours and general admission price subject to change without notice. Certificate has no cash value.
Valid through 12/30/97 only.

**Orlando, Florida**
**Let The Adventure Begin.**

- - - - - - - - - - - - - - - - - - - - - - - - - - - - - - - - - - - - - - - - - -

## Aloha POLYNESIAN LUAU

Limit six guests per certificate. Reservations required. Inquire at Information Center or call (407) 351-3600. Offer not valid with other discounts. Present certificate before bill is totaled. Redeemable only at time of luau attendance. Luau separate from park admission. Park admission not required. Photocopies not accepted. Seating begins at 6:30 p.m. Operating hours and prices subject to change without notice.
Valid through 12/30/97 only

**Sea World®**
**Orlando, Florida**
**Let the Adventure Begin.**

# $3 Off Admission
## to Busch Gardens, Tampa Bay

Present coupon at Front Gate before bill is totalled. Not valid with any other discounts or special offers. Limit 6 guests per coupon. Photocopies not accepted.

Operating hours and general admission prices subject to change without notice.

**Busch Gardens Tampa, FL 33674, (813) 987-5082**
Expires 12/31/97

FL97-21

**PLU #3071C/3072A**

---

# $3 Off Admission
# to Adventure Island

Present coupon at Front Gate before bill is totalled. Not valid with any other discounts or special offers. Limit 6 guests per coupon. Photocopies not accepted. Operating hours and general admission prices subject to change without notice.

**Adventure Island Tampa, FL 33674, (813) 987-5660**
Expires 10/26/97

FL97-22

**PLU #3071C/3072A**

---

# Hey, check this out!

Econoguide Readers receive **10% off regular room rates** at over 1,400 Super 8 Motels. Present the following I.D. number when making reservations to obtain discount.

For toll-free nationwide reservations call **1-800-800-8000**

I.D. Number
8800-166137
Offer expires
Dec. 31, 1997.

FL97-01

Please present this coupon at check-in to receive discounts. This offer is not valid in conjunction with any other discount. If guaranteed reservation is made and subsequent neither used nor cancelled, the traveler will be billed for one night's room charges plus tax.

## Super 8 Motel Handling Instructions

Please send a copy of the coupons received to:
Super 8 Motels, Inc.
Marketing Department
1910 8th Ave. N.E.
Aberdeen, SD 57401

# Green Meadows Petting Farm

## $2 Off Each Person up to 6 Persons

2-Hour Guided Tour of Farm Animals. More than 300 farm animals. Pony rides for the children. Tractor-drawn hay rides. Everyone milks a cow. Continuous tours between 9:30 a.m. and 4 p.m. Open until 5:30 p.m.

**5 miles south of Hwy. 192 on Poinciana Blvd., Kissimmee, FL 34742**
**(407) 846-0770**
Expires 12/31/97

FL97-32

---

# $3.00 Off
## Admission to Splendid China

Splendid China is a Chinese-themed attraction featuring more than 60 incredibly detailed exhibits of China's most renowned landmarks. Live entertainment, Chinese artisans, shopping, and authentic Chinese cuisine. Present this coupon prior to entering the park and receive $3.00 off the regular daily adult or children's admission price.

This coupon has no cash value and is not valid with any other discount offer. Coupon not valid if duplicated. Limit six (6) persons per coupon.

**Splendid China (407) 396-7111 or Toll Free (800) 244-6226**
Expires 12/31/97

FL97-33A

**189028/189036**

---

# 15% Off
## Dining at Splendid China

Present this coupon before ordering at any Splendid China restaurant for 15% off your total!

Located 12 miles southwest of Orlando on Highway 192 in Kissimmee, FL, only two miles west of Walt Disney World's main entrance road.

Food discount does not apply to alcoholic beverages. This coupon has no cash value and is not valid with any other discount offer. Gratuity not included. Coupon not valid if duplicated.

**For information call (407) 396-7111 or Toll Free (800) 244-6226**
Expires 12/31/97

FL97-33B

**189028/189036**

# Passage to India Restaurant
## 50% Off

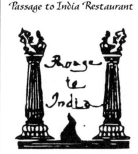

*Passage to India Restaurant*

*Dinner Entrees Only. Buy One Menu-Priced Dinner and Get the Second Menu-Priced Dinner at Half Price!*

Not valid with any other offer, or thali.
Coupon must be presented to server when ordering.

**5532 International Drive, Orlando, FL, (407) 351-3456**
Expires 12/31/97

FL97-08

---

# 25% Off Each Admission
## Limit 6 persons per coupon

**Flying Tigers**
**WARBIRD AIR MUSEUM**

A flying and working museum specializing in the display and restoration of World War II aircraft. Tour with knowledgeable guides. Experience "hands-on" displays.

Open daily 9 a.m. to 5:30 p.m., Sunday 9 a.m. to 5 p.m.
Admission: Adults, $6 plus tax. Children under 12 and adults over 60, $5 plus tax.

**231 N. Hoagland Blvd. (Just off Hwy 192), Kissimmee, FL 34741, (407) 933-1942**
Expires 12/31/97

FL97-09

---

# New Punjab Restaurant
## Rated ★★★★ by *The Ledger*
*"An Exceptional Treat" — Scott Joseph, Food Critic, Orlando Sentinel*

## 10% Off Dinner Only
With this coupon. Please present before ordering. Not valid with any other offers.
**Lunch & Dinner: Tues.–Sat. 11:30 a.m.–11 p.m. Sun. & Mon. 5 p.m.–11 p.m.**

**7451 International Drive, Orlando (behind Dunkin' Donuts); 3404 W. Vine St. (Hwy 192), Kissimmee**
**Reservations: Orlando (407) 352-7887; Kissimmee (407) 931-2449**
Expires 12/31/97

FL97-11

---

# Dinner for Two
## Chicken & Steak $16.95
## Chicken, Steak & Shrimp $18.95

**OSAKA**
**JAPANESE STEAK HOUSE**

Dinner includes: Soup, salad, fried rice & Japanese vegetable.
Dinner prepared at your table.
Open for Lunch Sun.–Fri. 11:30 a.m.–2:30 p.m.
Open for Dinner 7 days a week 5 p.m.–10 p.m.
Must present coupon when ordering. Good for up to 10 people.

**3155 W. Vine St., Dyer Square Shopping Center (next to Kash-N-Karry),**
**Kissimmee, FL, 34741, (407) 847-8822**
Expires 12/31/97

FL97-13

econoguide '97

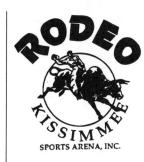
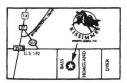

## Visit the Wizard
## at the Mystery Fun House
## Where You Become Part of the Fun

# 50% Off

*one admission with purchase of second admission*
*on a Mystery Fun House attraction ticket*

Just minutes from Walt Disney World and Sea World
in Florida Center.

**Across from Universal Studios,**
**Mystery Fun House, 5767 Major Blvd., Orlando, FL, 32819, (407) 351-3355**
**Open daily 10 a.m.–9 p.m.**
Not good in conjunction with any other discount. Expires 12/31/97
FL97-18 **COUPON ID #160**

---

## Introductory Offer

# $1 Off

## Starbase Omega
## *"The Ultimate Lazer Game"*

(Not good in conjunction with any other discount.)

Just minutes from Walt Disney World and Sea World in
Florida Center. Open daily 10 a.m.–9 p.m.

Located at Mystery Fun House

**5767 Major Blvd., Orlando, FL 32819**
**(407) 351-3355**
Expires 12/31/97

FL97-19

**COUPON ID #160**

---

# World's Greatest
# Horses & Riders!

## $5 Off the Show Voted #1 in Orlando
## Two Years in a Row!

Present this coupon at the Arabian Nights ticket booth and
receive $5 off each admission. Not valid with any other
coupons, discounts, or special events.

**Reservations: 407-239-9221 or 1-800-553-6116**
**6225 W. Bronson Hwy, Kissimmee, FL 34747**
Expires 12/31/97

FL97-23

# Free 18 Holes of Golf
## With Purchase of 18 Holes at Regular Price.
Limit one free 18-hole game per coupon

**Kissimmee, FL, 4777 W. Irlo Bronson Hwy.**
**(407) 396-6900**
Expires 12/31/97

FL97-20A

---

# Free 18 Holes of Golf
## With Purchase of 18 Holes at Regular Price.
Limit one free 18-hole game per coupon

**Orlando, FL, 6312 International Drive**
**(407) 352-0042**
Expires 12/31/97

FL97-20B

---

# Free 18 Holes of Golf
## With Purchase of 18 Holes at Regular Price.
Limit one free 18-hole game per coupon

**Altamonte Springs, FL, 531 W. State Road 436**
**(407) 682-4077**
Expires 12/31/97

FL97-20C

---

# Free 18 Holes of Golf
## With Purchase of 18 Holes at Regular Price.
Limit one free 18-hole game per coupon

**2100 S. Atlantic Ave.**
**Daytona Beach Shores, FL**
Expires 12/31/97

FL97-20D

---

# Free 18 Holes of Golf
## With Purchase of 18 Holes at Regular Price.
Limit one free 18-hole game per coupon

**Clearwater, FL**
**20060 US 19 North**
Expires 12/31/97

FL97-20E

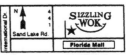

# Miniature Golf
# Buy One Get One Free

Coupon cannot be used with other coupons or discounts.
Located across from the 192 Flea Market.

Hole-N-One prizes given out daily.

Open 9:00 a.m. to 11:00 p.m.

**Pirates Island, 4330 W. Highway 192, Kissimmee, FL 34746, (407) 396-4660**
Expires 12/31/97

FL97-39

---

# Miniature Golf
# Buy One Get One Free

Coupon cannot be used with other coupons or discounts.
Located next to Old Town, behind Red Lobster.

Hole-N-One prizes given out daily.

Open 9:00 a.m. to Midnight

**Pirates Cove, 2845 Fla. Plaza Blvd., Kissimmee, FL 34746, (407) 396-7484**
Expires 12/31/97

FL97-40

---

# Save up to $24

- *Two-hour Dinner & Show*
- *Four-Course Chicken & Ribs Dinner*
  - *Specialty Acts*
  - *Patriotic Finale*

Valid only at Wild Bill's box office.
Show coupon at door.
$4 off per person, up to six people.
Not valid with any other offer.

**5260 U.S. 192 (East of I-4), Kissimmee, 351-5151 or 800-883-8181**
Expires 12/31/97

FL97-42

ECONOGUIDE

econoguide '97

# 50% Off Deluxe Rack Rates
### Based on availability.

Just off International Drive. Walk to Wet 'n Wild, Factory Outlet Mall, and International Drive. Free roundtrip shuttle bus to major area attractions.

**7050 Kirkman Road, Orlando, FL 32819**
**407-351-2000 or 1-800-327-3808**
Expires 12/31/97

FL97-63

---

# 50% Off Deluxe Rack Rates
### Based on availability

Just off International Drive. Minutes from Magic Kingdom, Epcot Center, Universal Studios, and other major attractions.

## Econo Lodge

**5859 American Way, Orlando, FL 32819**
**1-800-327-0750 or 407-345-8880**
Expires 12/31/97

FL97-64

---

### *$19.95 single, extra person $2*
(1/4–2/6, 4/21–6/11, 9/1–12/22)

### *$29.95, 2 persons, extra person $2*
(2/7–4/20, 6/12–8/31)

## Flamingo Inn
*Better Quality than Franchise*

**New Motel**

• Minutes from attractions • Pool, remote TV with HBO • Free refrigerator and microwave in every room • Free Morning Coffee • Extra long double beds or king size beds • Smoking or non-smoking rooms • Car rental available Rates subject to change during Holiday Periods.

Approved

**801 E. Vine St. (Hwy. 192), Kissimmee, FL 34744**
**Telephone: (407) 846-1935, Reservations: (800) 780-7617, FAX: (407) 846-7225**
Expires 12/31/97

FL97-65

---

# Black Angus Restaurant & Lounge
## All-You-Can-Eat Breakfast

Buffet Senior Citizen $3.75; Adult $4.59; Children $2.99. Buy 1 dinner, get second of equal or lesser value at ½ price. Steak or seafood dinner for $7.99. No coupon valid with $7.99 special. Best breakfast in town, three eggs, three pancakes for $1.99. Texas size drinks. 7 a.m.–11:30 p.m.

Not valid with other discounts or specials. Prices subject to change.

**2001 W. Hwy. 192 next to Holiday Inn, Kissimmee, (407) 846-7117**
Expires 12/31/97

FL97-66

# Quick-Find Index to Attractions
(See also the detailed Contents)